Criticism of Theology

On Marxism and Theology III

D1522130

Historical Materialism Book Series

More than ten years after the collapse of the Berlin Wall and the disappearance of Marxism as a (supposed) state ideology, a need for a serious and long-term Marxist book publishing program has arisen. Subjected to the whims of fashion, most contemporary publishers have abandoned any of the systematic production of Marxist theoretical work that they may have indulged in during the 1970s and early 1980s. The Historical Materialism book series addresses this great gap with original monographs, translated texts, and reprints of "classics."

Editorial board: Paul Blackledge, Leeds; Sebastian Budgen, London; Jim Kincaid, Leeds; Stathis Kouvelakis, Paris; Marcel van der Linden, Amsterdam; China Miéville, London; Paul Reynolds, Lancashire.

Haymarket Books is proud to be working with Brill Academic Publishers (www.brill.nl) and the journal *Historical Materialism* to republish the Historical Materialism book series in paperback editions. Current series titles include:

Alasdair MacIntyre's Engagement with Marxism: Selected Writings 1953–1974, edited by Paul Blackledge and Neil Davidson

Althusser: The Detour of Theory, Gregory Elliott

Between Equal Rights: A Marxist Theory of International Law, China Miéville

The Capitalist Cycle, Pavel V. Maksakovsky, translated with introduction and commentary by Richard B. Day

The Clash of Globalisations: Neo-Liberalism, the Third Way, and Anti-Globalisation, Ray Kiely

Critical Companion to Contemporary Marxism, edited by Jacques Bidet and Stathis Kouvelakis

Criticism of Heaven: On Marxism and Theology, Roland Boer

Criticism of Religion: On Marxism and Theology II, Roland Boer

Exploring Marx's Capital: Philosophical, Economic, and Political Dimensions, Jacques Bidet, translated by David Fernbach

Following Marx: Method, Critique, and Crisis, Michael Lebowitz

The German Revolution: 1917–1923, Pierre Broué

Globalisation: A Systematic Marxian Account, Tony Smith

The Gramscian Moment: Philosophy, Hegemony and Marxism, Peter D. Thomas

Impersonal Power: History and Theory of the Bourgeois State, Heide Gerstenberger, translated by David Fernbach

Lenin Rediscovered: What Is to Be Done? in Context, Lars T. Lih

Making History: Agency, Structure, and Change in Social Theory, Alex Callinicos

Marxism and Ecological Economics: Toward a Red and Green Political Economy, Paul Burkett

A Marxist Philosophy of Language, Jean-Jacques Lecercle, translated by Gregory Elliott

Politics and Philosophy: Niccolò Machiavelli and Louis Althusser's Aleatory Materialism, Mikko Lahtinen, translated by Gareth Griffiths and Kristina Köhli

The Theory of Revolution in the Young Marx, Michael Löwy

Utopia Ltd.: Ideologies of Social Dreaming in England 1870–1900, Matthew Beaumont

Western Marxism and the Soviet Union: A Survey of Critical Theories and Debates Since 1917, Marcel van der Linden

Witnesses to Permanent Revolution: The Documentary Record, edited by Richard B. Day and Daniel Gaido

Criticism of Theology

On Marxism and Theology III

Roland Boer

Haymarket Books
Chicago, IL

First published in 2011 by Brill Academic Publishers, The Netherlands
© 2011 Koninklijke Brill NV, Leiden, The Netherlands

Published in paperback in 2012 by
Haymarket Books
P.O. Box 180165
Chicago, IL 60618
773-583-7884
www.haymarketbooks.org

ISBN: 978-1-60846-197-4

Trade distribution:
In the US, Consortium Book Sales, www.cbsd.com
In Canada, Publishers Group Canada, www.pgcbooks.ca
In the UK, Turnaround Publisher Services, www.turnaround-psl.com
In Australia, Palgrave Macmillan, www.palgravemacmillan.com.au
In all other countries, Publishers Group Worldwide, www.pgw.com

Cover image of *Still Life with Letters: The Spectrum of Refugees*, 1919,
by Ivan Puni. Cover design by Ragina Johnson.

This book was published with the generous support of Lannan Foundation
and the Wallace Global Fund.

Printed in Canada.

10 9 8 7 6 5 4 3 2 1

Library of Congress Cataloging-in-Publication data is available.

Contents

Preface

A third book already that offers an intimate commentary on leading Marxists who have engaged with theology and religion! Sometimes I have the odd feeling that this is a never-ending project, a continuous book that keeps on being written. It has certainly grown in the writing, but any reader brave enough to have ploughed through at least parts of the two earlier volumes, *Criticism of Heaven* and *Criticism of Religion*, will probably be pleased to know that I do have an end in mind. This is the last volume to deal with the various Marxists who have devoted some serious and significant energy to the question of religion. Two other volumes follow this, one dealing with Marx and Engels themselves and a final one in which I develop my own position in response to all that has gone before.

In this book, you will meet more-or-lesser known works by an assortment of Marxists who have made contributions that are worth reconsidering – Max Horkheimer, E.P. Thompson, G.E.M. de Ste. Croix, Michael Löwy, Roland Barthes, Gilles Deleuze and Félix Guattari, and Antonio Negri. Where possible, I have worked with both the available translations and texts in the original German and French. I write 'where possible', since I am not able to read the original texts of the Italian who turns up in the last chapter, Antonio Negri. Other than that, the task has been relatively easy, since the translations are in reasonably good order. Two deserve some extra comment. The translated texts by Horkheimer are piecemeal. The English text *Dawn and Decline* includes selections from both the early *Dämmerung* and the later *Notizen, 1950–1969*. Many of the original notes and aphorisms have not made it into the English version. Further, in a trap for the unwary, the English collection *Critique of Instrumental Reason* does not match the German text with the same title, *Zur Kritik der instrumentellen Vernunft*. That German text has appeared as *Eclipse of Reason* in English, while what is called *Critique of Instrumental Reason* actually contains essays scattered through Horkheimer's *Gesammelte Schriften*.

Fortunately, those collected works are available in full in what one has come to expect from organised German publishing.

The situation with Roland Barthes's translated texts follows the more typical pattern of publications and translations of French works. To begin with, the French *Œuvres complètes*, appeared first in three volumes, but were then found to be not-so-complete, so a new five-volume edition was published with the same title. I have made extensive use of that longer and more complete edition. Barthes was an essayist first and so, after his death, one collection after another has appeared in French and then in English, often with a reshuffling of the French collections. In the work that interests me most, *Mythologies*, which was published during his lifetime (1957), the English translation included only half of the original text. But then, many of the chapters left out of that first translation appeared in a second collection, *The Eiffel Tower and Other Mythologies*. One opens that book only to find that it includes yet more essays not in Barthes's original French book on mythologies. Confusing? It is when you need to hunt down the essays in question, as well as the good number of texts that have not made the occasionally treacherous passage from French to English.

A few words of thanks are needed. I have benefitted enormously from the comments made at various points by Jan Rehmann, David Roberts, Carsten Pallesen, Mads Peter Karlsen and Ward Blanton. The precise, direct and enthusiastic support of Sebastian Budgen for the project has been inestimable. And Peter Thomas, an Australian in Amsterdam, has become a close colleague, especially after I spent a month living in a small apartment above Peter and Sara Farris in 2007. Above all, I would like to thank Christina, who has discussed more items from these chapters than I care to remember. Two writers living and working in the same place, each bringing the other up to date on the latest stage of their writing, the difficult point that taxes us, and sharing the joys of breakthroughs – it seems to work and for that I am thankful.

On the T99 train,
Somewhere between Shanghai and Hong Kong, China,
June 2009

Introduction

My gathering of Marxists over the last century or so who are interested in religion is becoming a crowd. Initially, in *Criticism of Heaven*, there were only eight; with *Criticism of Religion*, the number grew to seventeen. And, now, I have another seven who join the throng. Marx and Engels, the guests of honour, are yet to arrive. Soon, this motley collective will need to move into larger accommodation, or add a few tents to the camp. Perhaps it is a commune, with caravans, huts, tents and, for those accustomed to more refined quarters (mostly the French), an old if somewhat rundown mansion. In the third wave of arrivals, the well-dressed and somewhat busy Max Horkheimer arrives by train, late as usual, hurrying, a copy of the Hebrew Bible clutched under an arm and a satchel, overflowing with copies of the *Zeitschrift für Sozialforschung*, hanging from a shoulder. Close behind and from across the English Channel comes Edward Palmer Thompson, topped with a mop of white hair. He has by now eased off from his involvement with the Campaign for Nuclear Disarmament and so has some time for our gathering. He pulls out of his canvas backpack tattered copies of *The Making of the English Working Class*, *Witness Against the Beast* and the collection of poems known as *Infant and Emperor*. The first two books everyone knows very well, but a few eyebrows rise with the appearance of the third, for the poems offer contemporary political readings of the Christmas-story. The next to join our growing crowd is Geoffrey Ernest Maurice de Ste. Croix. With he and Thompson side by side, one soon notices the contrast: beside Thompson's slender figure and white mane, Ste. Croix has the faded body of a powerful athlete and a massive bald pate. Both are, of course, Marxists, and both are historians, one of seventeenth and eighteenth century England and the other of ancient Greece. Ste. Croix has with him his thick tome, *The Class Struggle in the Ancient Greek World*, along with a collection of essays on the New Testament and early Christian martyrdom that would eventually become *Christian Persecution, Martyrdom, and Orthodoxy*. Michael Löwy soon joins the group, although he has had a long trip from Paris. The urbane and precise Löwy carries in his neat leather briefcase his *The War of Gods*, a text on Latin American liberation-theology, and his earlier work, *Redemption and Utopia*, as well as sundry essays on Max Weber. Equally sophisticated and far more French is Roland Barthes, who pauses at the sight of the crowd, waves warmly to one or two of those who have been there for a while and then reaches into his pocket for a cigarette. After cupping his hands around the end of the smoke and concentrating for a moment on the flame of the lighter, Barthes produces an early work, *Mythologies*, although he has with him the French edition since it is almost double the length of the English translation. I notice that pages of the long essay at its close, 'Myth Today', have the darkened corners from the finger oil of many readings. Immediately, an unkempt pair follows after Barthes: Gilles Deleuze and Félix Guattari. Gilles has run out of cigarettes on the long walk from the railway station, so he asks Roland if he has one. Barthes knocks one out of his pack of du Maurier; Gilles seizes it and the proffered lighter with relish … and a slight cough. But Félix is the one who carries the key text, *A Thousand Plateaus*. Gilles wonders why the books on Spinoza do not join the pile, but Félix points out that Gilles does not mention Marx in them very often. Lastly, the distinctive grinning face of Antonio Negri arrives. He smiles, groans at the embraces of greeting, mutters about creaking bones and ageing muscles and happily proffers his recently translated work, *The Labor of Job*.

This ongoing little story of a growing gathering of Marxists has another agenda apart from introducing the main figures of this book. If you have had the opportunity to ponder even for a moment the two books that precede this one, you may wonder what the difference is between the titles – *Criticism of Heaven, Criticism of Religion* and *Criticism of Theology*. Am I making fine distinctions between heaven, religion and theology with each book? Not really, for I follow the poetic parallelism (a feature of biblical poetry)[1] that is found in Marx's famous statement:

> Thus the criticism of heaven turns into the criticism of earth, the *criticism of religion* into the *criticism of law* and the *criticism of theology* into the *criticism of politics.*[2]

Under these three heads, I have invited and gathered a range of variegated Marxists who deal precisely with these overlapping topics of heaven, religion and theology. The way they have come together has been a little serendipitous, following my own interests, wayward reading habits, and, in the process, discovering often lesser-read works by them on religion. Yet there has been one consistent criterion: to qualify for consideration, the author must operate within a Marxist framework (although I interpret that reasonably broadly) and deal with theology and religion. The catch was that, the more I read, the more Marxists I found who deal substantively with theology and religion. The work grew in the writing, so that now I have a collection of another seven for a third volume. I can promise any persistent reader that the collection is now complete, apart from Marx and Engels themselves and my own response and contribution.

Let me say a few words concerning the method of reading I have developed for dealing with this motley crew of Marxists. My approach may be summed up by the phrase 'critical commentary'. The term and the approach come from the venerable and somewhat neglected tradition of biblical commentary, itself two-millennia old. Although it has fallen into disuse, except by that relatively small group known as biblical scholars, I have developed it in my own way over the last few books of this series. Such a critical commentary has five distinct features: it is intimate, immanent, comparative, historical and constructive.

To begin with, the approach is *intimate*. By that I mean a careful and patient reading that refuses to rush over texts. Commentary of this type pays attention to the various twists, contradictions, problems and insights of a text. And

---

[1] Poetic parallelism, a defining feature of biblical Hebrew poetry, is a process of saying the same thing in strikingly different ways.
[2] Marx 1975a, p. 176; Marx 1974b, p. 379.

it does so by working with the texts in their original languages as far as possible. In the process of such commentary, the commentator comes to know the text very closely. The approach is also *immanent*, which means I seek to draw the terms of analysis and critique from the text and thinker in question, applying their own approach to their texts. Further, it is *comparative*. The approach compares the arguments and positions concerning theology in light of the others. In order to avoid overlap with the immanent part of the analysis, this comparative moment is a second step. My approach is also historical, or rather, *genealogical*: the search for and exploration of the various historical paths a tradition of thought has taken. In this case, I refer to the tradition of engagements between theology and historical materialism. I hope that critical work like mine may establish that such a tradition exists, or at least change the shape it once had. Finally, my approach is *constructive*: I seek to build a coherent body of thought in response to the various contributors to this tradition and thereby renew the debate concerning religion within Marxism, if not among theologians interested in Marxism. Not merely the focus of the fifth book in the series, my readings of each critic in the other four volumes, including this one, also search – patiently and carefully – for insights, ideas and categories that may become part of this last volume.

For this book, I have before me three philosophers (Horkheimer, Deleuze, Negri), two historians (Thompson and Ste. Croix), a radical psychoanalyst (Guattari), a social theorist (Löwy) and a literary and cultural critic (Barthes) who happen to have joined one another for the time of this book. As is my wont, I provide a brief synopsis of the arguments of each so that the reader seeking a specific topic rather than taking on the book as whole may slip into one chapter or the other.

The book opens with Max Horkheimer, whose ongoing relative neglect is to the impoverishment of criticism. On the matter of the theology, Horkheimer rehearses a theme throughout his work that strengthens in his later years: an authentic Christianity or Judaism owes its allegiance to and longs for a 'totally other' and not any temporal power such as the state. Indeed, in the name of this other – understood in either ontological or temporal terms – Christians would do well to remember the trenchant criticisms of vested power and wealth and Jews would do equally well to remember the basic impulse of not being conformed to this world. In short, such a religious standpoint is one of persistent and incorruptible resistance to the world in every fibre of one's being. The problem is that religions like Judaism and Christianity have betrayed that resistance in the name of the totally other and made deals with the world – with the state, with wealth, with influence and with the economic systems of the day. This betrayal shows up, for example, in the way Christianity has often become an established religion, in the establishment of a Jewish state and in liberal theology. I must admit that I am not taken with this grand opposition, which trades on the distinction between authentic and inauthentic, the latter functioning as a betrayal of the former. Far more interesting are the moments when Horkheimer sets his dialectical skills to work on this opposition. When this happens, I find him arguing that the 'betrayal' was often a necessary process for the survival of the religion in question, for any religion that followed the precepts of Jesus as recorded in the Gospels would soon have been ground into the dust. This dialectical approach is what I would like to draw from Horkheimer and use further.

E.P. Thompson is my subject in the second chapter. Thompson shifts in his treatments of English Christianity in the seventeenth and eighteenth centuries from a comprehensive condemnation of methodism as 'psychic terror' to an appreciation of the radical possibilities of Christianity in fringe-churches like the Muggletonians. In particular, Thompson finds this radical theological position with William Blake, who was a member of one or two of those groups. The key doctrine for such groups was justification by faith, drawn straight out of Paul's letters in the New Testament and read in terms of a radical antinomianism that covered both spiritual and temporal law. For Blake, at least according to Thompson, this doctrine provided the theological validation of his Jacobin politics. Even more, Thompson comes to argue that this doctrine, read in a radical direction, was a prime source for Blake's political radicalism. In this light, a closer look at Thompson's treatment of methodism finds that in between the lines of Thompson's condemnation – in terms of a moral machinery for ensuring a complaint labour-force in an industrialising England and a political conservatism that supported the status quo – a long list of methodist radicals turns up. Thompson tries to dismiss such figures as aberrations, but his text does reveal a political tension at the heart of methodism between reaction and radicalism. This tension interests me immensely, for it meshes in with Horkheimer's dialectical approach to resistance and betrayal. The chapter closes with a commentary on Thompson's little known poems for Christmas called *Infant and Emperor*, for here we find re-readings of the infancy-narratives of Jesus with a distinct political and even eschatological bent.

Less subtle than Horkheimer or Thompson is G.E.M. de Ste. Croix, who had quite a lot to say about early Christianity, both in the New Testament and in the years following. I divide the chapter into two phases, theology and history. Ste. Croix argues that he is a historian and not a theologian, but that belies the attention he gives to theological matters. So we find him arguing that Jesus may have strongly attacked the presuppositions and acts of the Roman and Jewish propertied classes, but that the early Church soon threw a thick blanket over those sayings and with impressive speed accommodated itself to the ruling classes. So, early Christianity supported the assumptions of the ruling classes concerning property, slaves and women with but few exceptions (although I explore those exceptions in some detail). I argue that this is a problematic argument, since it follows the narrative of a fleeting authenticity followed by a comprehensive betrayal, a narrative that reminds one of some of Horkheimer's arguments. I also register problems with Ste. Croix's tendency to argue that religion was a primary cause for the ills of the early Church and indeed the Roman Empire. A major reason for such an argument is that Ste. Croix sought to excise the legacy of his youthful encounter with Christianity in the form of his mother's commitment to the British Israelites. Ste. Croix would dearly have liked to see Christianity, after it became the religion of empire, as the prime cause of the persecution of heretics, pagans and factions. But this approach sits ill with the overall Marxist framework of his reconstruction. As for the historian in Ste. Croix, I trace his proposals concerning class, the collapse of the Roman Empire, the distinction between *chora* and *polis* (countryside and city) and his critique of the tendency to see trade as the major producer of surplus in the ancient world. While I have a few small criticisms of his reconstruction of class and class-conflict, the other three proposals are extremely persuasive. More problematic is his stern refusal to deal with both mode of production and, surprisingly given the central role of the 'propertied classes', property itself.

In the fourth chapter, I engage with Michael Löwy, particularly on the topics of elective affinity and Latin-American liberation-theology. While the notion of elective affinity shows promise, I also find it lacks clarity. Developed from alchemy, emergent chemistry, literature (Goethe) and then social theory (Weber), elective affinity in Löwy's hands describes the way two discrete and relatively equal entities may come into touch with one another and merge. My interest is in the way Löwy deploys this idea in the connections between Marxism and religion. Now, the reason why he makes use of elective affinity in such a case is clear – to negate the oft-repeated argument that Marxism is merely a secularised version of Jewish and/or Christian eschatology – but the approach also has its problems. It assumes two reasonably equal political movements, bodies of thought, worldviews, and perhaps economic assumptions, but elective affinity cannot, at least in the form put forward by Löwy, deal with unequal partners, prior histories of influence, connection and disconnection. Löwy also leaves undeveloped the dialectical side of elective as well as its erotic dimensions. The other part of the chapter on Löwy comes to close quarters with his treatment of Latin-American liberation-theology, especially in his *The War of Gods*. While the book is an excellent introduction to liberation-theology for those on the Left who may be suspicious of radical religious movements, I find that Löwy skims over some crucial features of the phenomenon. This situation gives me the opportunity to offer my own assessment, through a critique of Löwy, of liberation-theology and I do so through three steps: a close consideration of the tradition of Roman-Catholic social teaching which is so important for liberation-theology and strangely neglected by Löwy; the ontological reserve characteristic of liberation-theology, in which too-close an identification with any political movement, including Marxism, is justified on the basis of allegiance to God (the connection with Horkheimer should be obvious here); and the multiplicity of liberation-theologies – black, feminist and queer – of which Latin-American liberation is but one form and thereby neither unique nor original.

In the fifth chapter, I switch direction slightly to focus on a text that nearly everyone has read, but has done so a little too quickly – Roland Barthes's 'Myth Today' from his *Mythologies*. Other works, of course, come into this discussion, but my agenda is to read this text carefully and in the same way that Barthes reads other texts, that is, looking for various hints and suggestions that open up other possibilities. So, in the first part of my chapter, I trace Barthes's argument quite closely, distinguishing between his careful, dispassionate and technical description of myth in terms of a basic semiological schema and his passionate condemnation of myth. The former attempts to be a universal description of the workings of myth; the latter is a critique of the mythologies of the French bourgeoisie. Barthes also tries to find modes of resistance to such a dominating collection, but his search ends up being forlorn and futile. At this point, I turn and reread Barthes, tracing hints that the myths with which he deals are not so uniform or so suffocatingly dominant. Picking up the passing suggestion that the best option may be to turn myth against itself, I explore what myth conceals (its process of distortion), how it produces resistance and seeks to close it down, how it preserves such resistance, leaving open the possibility that resistance may twist out from under the hand of oppression and gain a voice of its own once again. At this moment, I bring in some of Barthes's own myths, especially the utopian one of an imaginary Japan in *Empire of Signs*. Here is an alternative myth of resistance that emerges precisely when it seems as though the semiological foothold for myth has been eliminated.

The major contribution of Deleuze and Guattari, the concern of Chapter Six, is to show that resistance is multiple rather than singular. From *A Thousand Plateaus*, I focus on two plateaux, '587 B.C.–A.D. 70: On Several Regimes of Signs' and '1227: Treatise on Nomadology: – The War Machine', for the reason that here both Marx and the Bible turn up (for the same reason, I do not deal with Deleuze's engagements with Spinoza, since Marx is far from the scene in these texts). My reading of Deleuze and Guattari has three lines: one is to trace the way their initial argument that the eternal state must deal with external opposition eventually comes to the admission that such resistances are as much internal as external. Indeed, they are constitutive of that state, which soon becomes the despotic state of the signifying régime. Another line is to connect the four régimes of signs – pre-signifying (the segmented tribe), signifying (the despotic state), counter-signifying (the numbered nomadic war-band) and post-signifying (the scapegoat wilderness-community) – with Marxist discussions of the Asiatic mode of production and tribal society. Deleuze and Guattari opt for the régimes of signs precisely to avoid connecting them too closely with any one people, language, society or indeed economy; yet the bulk of their examples do come from the ancient world. The third line relates these régimes to Marxist biblical scholarship and to the Bible itself, especially the texts to which Deleuze and Guattari refer, namely the scapegoat-ritual in Leviticus 16 and the advice given to Moses by his father-in-law, Jethro, in Exodus 18 to provide judges and number his people. However, a closer look at the biblical material shows how the patterns of opposition are actually internal to one another. Moses is simultaneously the despot of the signifying régime (Leviticus 16), leader of a numbered war-band (Exodus 18), and the leader of a scapegoat-community in the wilderness (Leviticus 16 again). But then, to their credit, Deleuze and Guattari admit that that these régimes are not only multiple, but also fluid and overlapping.

Finally, it is Antonio Negri's turn in Chapter Seven. My concern is a recently translated book, *The Labor of Job*, written during the time when Negri fled into exile in France in 1984. It is nothing less than a commentary on the Book of Job in which Negri seeks to process the spectacular defeats of the far Left in Italy in the 1970s and 1980s. I trace five elements of Negri's commentary: radical homiletics; philosophical commentary; *kairós* and *ákairos*; measure and immeasure; and then my translation of those two terms into the biblical patterns of chaos and order. As for radical homiletics, I argue that Negri offers a reading that comes close to the theological tradition of homiletics – bringing the text into the present in order to find within it possibilities for today. The philosophical commentary links Negri with a potted tradition of philosophical readers of the Bible (not biblical critics or theologians), who have their own sets of questions to put to the text. Negri has, of course, been careful to consult at least some biblical critics, but he also moves beyond them. Neither a historical-critical fragmentation of the biblical text, nor a claim to literary coherence, Negri offers, instead, a reading that seeks philosophical coherence. It may described as a form of textual reasoning. This type of commentary leads us to two of his great themes, the oppositions of measure and immeasure and of *kairós* and *ákairos*. Or, rather, I argue for the second opposition, reading against and beneath Negri to set *ákairos* against Negri's favoured *kairós*, the untimely against the timely, the out-of-place against the well-placed. In searching for the political and economic ramifications of the opposition, I end up favouring *ákairos*. However, it also turns out that both terms, in their basic senses, designate what is measured and unmeasured. All of which brings me to investigate the other opposition of measure and immeasure, through which Negri passes the topics of value, labour, pain, ontology, time, power, evil, theodicy, creation and cosmogony. However, I am interested in the way measure and immeasure gain complexity through the text of Job as both positive and negative features. Initially, measure is negative and immeasure comes through as positive, blasting the myriad means of measure (doctrines of retribution and so on) out of the water. But, then, immeasure takes on a negative hue and a renewed measure appears on the scene. At this point, I translate the two terms into the biblical and mythical categories of chaos and order, or, rather, chaos and creation as the process of order. Negri's desire is to follow Job, challenge God, bring God to account, and take on the creative task along with all human beings. He wishes to appropriate that immense creative labour for human beings, to whom it rightly belongs. However, I wish to tarry with the immeasurable, for it is the zone of political chaos against imposed order, or what – given the overlap of meaning with *ákairos* – may be called the akairological. This sense appears both sharply and unwittingly in Negri's reading of the final section of Job, the famous voice from the whirlwind. In the midst of what is a brilliant interpretation – Job's triumph is that he actually forces God to appear and answer – I espy an *aporia* on Negri's part. He cannot quite decide on how to read a vital text, where Job either submits to God or resists God. This uncertainty and openness is a signal of the akairological and immeasurable chaos I seek.

The conclusion deals less with the various criticisms I gather through the book and more with what may be retrieved and re-used. Here, I draw out the question of myth, especially from my treatments of Barthes and Deleuze and Guattari. The apparently unrelated matter of economics follows, where Ste. Croix and Deleuze and Guattari appear. In this case, I develop some of their suggestions for reconstructing the economies of the ancient Near East and biblical societies: the value of spatial analysis, the emphasis on minimal trade, and the need to consider multiple patterns of internal oppositions within such an economic system. However, the major topic is how one understands the endlessly repeated patterns of reaction and revolution within a religion like Christianity. Each of the critics with whom I deal offers a different perspective on this matter, and so I seek to integrate those perspectives and offer a proposal as to why this pattern is so characteristic of Christianity.

Chapter One

The Superstitions of Max Horkheimer

> I mourn the loss of the superstitious belief
> [*Aberglauben*] in a Beyond.[1]

Any reader of Max Horkheimer's multitude of essays
and apothegms soon detects a persistent substrate
of theology, perhaps summed up best in this comment: 'What is needed, further, is a knowledge of the
theological tradition, for our knowledge of the inex-
tricable meshing of human freedom and it condition-
ings...have their historical roots in that tradition'.[2]
Horkheimer may never have had the inclination or
the time – in the midst of his often onerous duties of
directing the Institute for Critical Theory – to write a
book on theology or the Bible like Theodor Adorno,
Ernst Bloch, Karl Kautsky, Lucien Goldmann,
Michael Löwy, Alain Badiou, Slavoj Žižek, Giorgio
Agamben or Terry Eagleton, but theology is a persistent theme throughout his work. Often, it prefers
to stay in the shadows, peering out every now and
then to alert us to its presence. At other times, theology comes into the open, perfectly happy to enter
into debate over matters as diverse as early Church
councils, neo-Thomism, the council of Trent, Luther,

---

[1] Horkheimer 1978, p. 223; Horkheimer 1991a, p. 393.
[2] Horkheimer 1996, p. 7; Horkheimer 1985e, p. 59.

Calvin and liberal theology.[3] In the midst of these forays, I am most interested in his observations concerning opposition and accommodation, resistance and compromise within religion.[4]

It is precisely this double theme – between resistance and compromise – that beats most strongly throughout Horkheimer's reflections on theology. It will reappear in my treatments of E.P. Thompson, G.E.M. de Ste. Croix and Michael Löwy in the next few chapters; their emphases and subject-matter are quite distinct but this basic tension runs throughout their various texts. However, I have begun this book with Horkheimer, since – in the end, at least – he offers one of the most subtle dialectical analyses of that tension. Around it, I have organised a number of other categories concerning religion in Horkheimer's work. So, under the banner of resistance, we find the 'longing for the totally other [*die Sehnsucht nach dem ganz Anderen*]'[5] beyond all temporal arrangements of power (state, economics, church, synagogue, and so on), continual observations on the character and politics of the 'founder' of Christianity, the nature of freedom and the individual and then atheism. Each of these points gathers around the argument that any religion worth its salt – although Horkheimer's prime foci are Christianity and Judaism – will resist any push to be conformed to this world and this age.

Never far away is the other side of the tension, that of betrayal and compromise. Here, we find constant observations on the way theology has all too often entered into dirty little relationships with the state, betraying itself when the longing for the other becomes a longing for the state, when the object of religious commitment and devotion becomes synonymous with the state. A distinctive feature of that analysis is Horkheimer's criticism of the Zionist expectation that all Jews would, from 1948, identify themselves with the state

---

[3] The persistence of these reflections belies the reconstruction – as found in Brittain 2005 and Hughes 2003 – of a late Horkheimer who became disillusioned with Marxism and other dogmatisms, turning to a non-dogmatic form of theology. In this respect, I follow Shaw 1985, who sees a persistence of religious concerns in Horkheimer's work.

[4] I must acknowledge the influence on this chapter of Michael Ott's careful studies of Horkheimer's critical theory of religion. See Ott 2001, 2006, 2007. Some useful elements may also be found in Brittain 2005; Hughes 2003; Kim 1996; Shaw 1985. Of far less use is Gur-Ze'ev 1998, who argues that Horkheimer borrowed heavily from Walter Benjamin.

[5] This is the title of Horkheimer's interview with Helmut Gumnior in 1970. See Horkheimer 1985q.

of Israel (he is not one of them). Under the label of compromise, we also come across deep suspicions of liberal-Christian theology as well as complex deliberations over the question of evil.

So this double theme of resistance and compromise forms, in all its various dimensions, the axis of my analysis. I explore and question Horkheimer's arguments, all the while seeking what might be useful and what may be taken further. However, two preliminary matters must be dealt with before I can delve into Horkheimer's reflections on religion: the connections with Adorno and Horkheimer's own religious sensitivities. Apart from their habits of railway-travel, patterns of work, or, indeed, the way Gretel Adorno recorded the conversations that led to *Dialectic of Enlightenment*,[6] the pressing question is whether it is possible to distinguish their respective thoughts, attributing some to Horkheimer and some to Adorno. The catch with trying to determine which idea belongs to whom is that, for friends who talk with one another over decades, ideas become shared, cross over from one to the other, are transformed and take on new shape. For example, I could argue that Horkheimer's criticisms of the liberal theology championed by Paul Tillich and John A.T. Robinson were taken over by Adorno, for they appear in the latter's *Jargon of Authenticity*. Or did such criticisms pass the other way, from Adorno to Horkheimer? Or did they arise late one night over many drinks and cigars, not merely in long-ranging conversations between the two of them, but occasionally with Tillich himself? It is impossible to tell, especially in light of the way ideas form and transform, so I will adopt the only viable position: where the same idea appears either in a joint work or in individual works, I assume it is a shared idea; where an idea appears only in a work exclusively

---

[6] See, however, the careful attempt to distinguish the respective contributions by Horkheimer and Adorno to *Dialectic of Enlightenment* by Noerr 2002. Legend has it that Horkheimer was habitually late and so Adorno, as he spent time on railway-platforms waiting for Horkheimer to arrive, would jot thoughts, aphorisms and longer comments in his notebook. This growing collection eventually became *Minima Moralia*. One might speculate that the length of individual pieces – some run onto ten pages or more – directly correlates with the time spent at the railway-station. As far as the Institute for Critical Theory is concerned, Horkheimer once quipped that he managed while Adorno wrote, although Adorno was the keener of the two to insist that much of their work was really collaborative work. See further, Noerr 2002, pp. 219–20.

by Horkheimer (even if he may have come up with the idea in discussion with Adorno), I restrict myself to assigning it to him.[7]

As for the matter of Horkheimer's own religious perspective, by 1965 he could write: 'In Judaism, the religion I myself profess [*zu dem ich mich bekenne*]'.[8] Precisely what 'profess' or 'confess' means here is uncertain, since he maintained a critical-Marxist perspective on religion until his death in 1973. Yet again, on his tombstone in the Jewish Cemetery in Bern, Switzerland, appear the words from Psalm 91: 'Denn du Ewiger bist meine Zuversicht' ('Because you, eternal one, are my confidence'). It all seems straightforward: we might conclude that Horkheimer had recovered his Jewish faith, especially if we keep in mind that *Zuversicht* also means trust or faith. But it is far less straightforward than it seems, for this text cannot be found in Psalm 91 as is. The closest is 'Denn der Herr ist deine Zuversicht' from Verse 9 ('Because the Lord is your confidence'), a text that Horkheimer quoted from the Psalms and commented upon in 1968.[9] His parents may have been happy with a direct quotation from the same psalm on their grave,[10] but not Horkheimer. We might attribute the difference between Horkheimer's gravestone and the Psalm itself to an accidental looseness, but that merely makes it even more symptomatic of Horkheimer's ambiguity concerning any religious commitment. Let me line up the three versions (now including the Hebrew) to see what has changed:

Hebrew: Because you, O Lord, are my refuge.

German 'translation': Because the Lord is your confidence.

Gravestone: Because you, eternal one, are my confidence.

---

[7] Since I have dealt with Adorno at some length in an earlier study, I do not discuss his work here except where it involves joint work. See Boer 2007a, pp. 391–445.

[8] Horkheimer 1996, p. 150; Horkheimer 1985i, p. 272. So also, 'Jewish thinking, as it is my tradition...' (Horkheimer 2006, p. 116; Horkheimer 1985o, p. 208). See further, Horkheimer 1985q, p. 387.

[9] Horkheimer 2006; Horkheimer 1985o. The Bible was by no means foreign to Horkheimer, as the regular invocations of and comments upon biblical texts show. For instance, see Horkheimer 1978, pp. 42, 67, 83–4; Horkheimer 1987c, pp. 351, 381–2, 405–6; Horkheimer 1996, 35; Horkheimer 1985h, p. 174; Horkheimer 1996, pp. 52–3; Horkheimer 1985k, pp. 198–9. See also Horkheimer 1991a, pp. 243–4; Horkheimer 1988l, pp. 399–400, 404.

[10] 'Who lives in the shadow of the Most High is in the safety of the shadow of the Almighty' – Psalm 91:1 (Horkheimer 2006, p. 116; Horkheimer 1985o, p. 208). Even here, there is looseness in quotation, for in the text of the Psalm itself provided on the previous page, Horkheimer has 'You who sit under the shelter of the Most High and remain under the shadow of the Almighty'.

Note what has changed: in one respect, the gravestone comes closer to the Hebrew, using 'you' and 'my', but, in another crucial respect, the gravestone departs from both Hebrew and the German 'translation' – 'the Lord', *der Herr* has been removed. In its place comes 'eternal one [*Ewiger*]'. In whom does Horkheimer have confidence as he lies beneath the stone? It is not specified; the Jewish predilection for avoiding even the mention of a euphemism for God (here *der Herr* or, in Hebrew, *adonai*) become an extraordinarily useful ruse. Horkheimer has left the question concerning who or what provides confidence and trust – *Zuversicht* – undefined. This last indication, from his grave, leaves the question open.

Religion as resistance

As I mentioned above, the underlying pattern to which Horkheimer returns again and again is that a Christianity or a Judaism honest with itself stands in opposition to the ways of the world. Conversely, when either expression of faith makes some deal with the world, or manifests itself in a way that justifies the status quo, then it speaks a lie, for it has betrayed its initial and authentic impulse. At times, Horkheimer assumes this position largely as I have stated it, but there are moments when he offers a more dialectical reading in which the two sides are entwined like strands in a rope. To my mind, this dialectical approach is more insightful, so I watch carefully for its appearance. Yet, too often, Horkheimer wavers between such a dialectical take and a stark opposition between authentic resistance and craven betrayal, a distinction between honesty and lie. When he slides towards this simple contrast, he opens himself to a range of problems which I will explore in some detail.

Longing for the totally other

Let us take one side of the contrast – that of a resistant and defiant religion – in order to see what Horkheimer does with it. Every now and then, a phrase or a sentence leaps forth to give voice to this protesting role of religion. Religion was once, he writes, 'the longing for the other compared to which this world showed itself as the evil it was'.[11] What is this 'other' for which

---

[11] Horkheimer 1978, pp. 184–5; Horkheimer 1991a, p. 330. See also Horkheimer 1985q, p. 389. Similarly, in 'Theism and Atheism', Horkheimer writes of the 'longing

we long? Although he does use the terminology of God or the 'Eternal', he asserts repeatedly that we have no knowledge of God and cannot prove God's existence. He is comfortable with such a widely abused name only when it means utter opposition to conformism with anything constructed by human beings. And that 'indwelling protest against things as they are' is actually aimed at something beyond the status quo or indeed nature – 'a just, right order'.[12] The key, then, is that religion, at least in its original and authentic mode, protests against all that is in the name of something better, namely a just society. For Horkheimer, religion is not to be conformed to this world; it resists such conformity in the name of another, higher and more just order which finds that the present always falls short.[13]

Already, we come to the question concerning the origins of this theory of religion. Horkheimer is not one to cite many sources, so any suggestions must rely on hints and some educated sleuthing. Observations that critical theory – Horkheimer's conscious designation of his own and the Institute's research-programme – regarded the social role of religion as the 'projection of earthly conditions into a beyond'[14] suggest Ludwig Feuerbach. As is reasonably well-known, Feuerbach argued that religion – his concern was almost exclusively Christianity – is a projection of all that is best in us into the heavens. Human love, hope, strength, knowledge, justice and aspirations become hypostatised in a figure we call 'God', who then appears as a real figure who is far more powerful than us, so much so that we perceive God to be the source of all these attributes. Not so, argued, Feuerbach, for we have neglected our role in producing and projecting God in the first place, for only then will we be able to reintegrate these features within ourselves and achieve our highest

---

for something other than this world, the standing-apart from existing conditions' (Horkheimer 1996, p. 50; Horkheimer 1985h, p. 186). See also Horkheimer 2006, pp. 116–17; Horkheimer 1985o, pp. 208–9; Horkheimer 1988l, pp. 510–11, 517; Horkheimer 1973, p. xxvi; Horkheimer 1985s, p. 431. Alternatively, it is a 'homesickness [Heimweh] that cannot refrain from the thought of paradise' (Horkheimer 2006, p. 117; Horkheimer 1985o, p. 209).

[12] Horkheimer 1978, p. 185; Horkheimer 1991a, p. 330.

[13] In this way I read the argument – made by Brittain 2005 – that Horkheimer's notion of 'God' designates a negative notion of truth.

[14] Horkheimer 1978, p. 184; Horkheimer 1991a, p. 329. Note also: 'Religion indeed derives its whole content through the psychic elaboration of earthly data, but in the process it acquires its own specific form, which in turn influences the psychic apparatus and destiny of men and is a reality within social evolution as a whole' (Horkheimer 1982, p. 58; Horkheimer 1988d, pp. 347–8).

aspirations.[15] Feuerbach's argument is in the end a theological one, for he sought to perfect each doctrine of Christianity by showing what he felt was its truth. Or, as Feuerbach puts it, theology is really anthropology: 'the divine being is nothing else than the human being, or, rather, the human nature purified, freed from the limits of the individual man, made objective – i.e., contemplated and revered as another, a distinct being'.[16]

However, Horkheimer does not rest with Feuerbach. Following both Marx's fourth thesis on Feuerbach[17] as well as the famous sentences concerning religion in Marx's 'Introduction' to his *Contribution to the Critique of Hegel's Philosophy of Law*,[18] Horkheimer points out that religion is both a sign of alienation and protest against it. So we find that religion is produced by the needs and trials of existence, like hunger and thirst; even more, it is 'aroused' by the 'worse order'[19] that prevails all around us. Yet religion is at the same time a protest against injustice, against things as they are, for they are not as they should be. Compare Marx: '*Religious* suffering is, at one and the same time, the *expression* of real suffering and a *protest* against real suffering'. Even more, religion 'is the sigh of the oppressed creature, the heart of a heartless world, and the soul of soulless conditions'.[20] Like so many afterwards, Horkheimer seems to adopt these statements in a slightly more positive way than Marx's

---

[15] Feuerbach 1989; Feuerbach 1924. See the detailed discussion of Feuerbach in Boer forthcoming.

[16] Feuerbach 1989, p. 14; Feuerbach 1924, p. 18. See also Feuerbach 1989, pp. 98 and 140; Feuerbach 1924, pp. 121–2 and 140.

[17] 'Feuerbach starts out from the fact of religious self-estrangement [*der religiösen Selbstentfremdung*], of the duplication of the world into a religious world and a secular one. His work consists in resolving the religious world into its secular basis. But that the secular basis lifts off from itself and establishes itself as an independent realm in the clouds can only be explained by the inner strife and intrinsic contradictoriness of this secular basis. The latter must, therefore, itself be both understood in its contradiction and revolutionised in practice. Thus, for instance, once the earthly family is discovered to be the secret of the holy family, the former must then itself be destroyed in theory and in practice' (Marx 1976c, p. 4; Marx 1973, p. 6).

[18] Marx 1975a, pp. 175–6; Marx 1974b, pp. 378–9.

[19] Horkheimer 1978, p. 185; Horkheimer 1991a, p. 330. On the needs of a person that constitute the truth of religion, see Horkheimer 1978, p. 177; Horkheimer 1991a, pp. 319–20. So also, 'Isn't religion always needed because the earth remains a place of horror even if society were as it ought to be?' (Horkheimer 1978, p. 181; Horkheimer 1991a, p. 325)'.

[20] Marx 1975a, p. 175; Marx 1974b, p. 378. See the detailed discussion in Boer forthcoming.

text suggests. 'Slightly' – because Horkheimer is wary about taking them too far, as we shall see soon enough.

The founder

To use terms such as 'longing for the other' can only get us so far, for they eventually beg for some content. Eventually, Horkheimer invokes specifically Jewish and Christian items such as God, the prophets and Jesus Christ. Horkheimer does not need some new spin on the question of God, taking the central doctrines of creation and God's omnipotence to argue that allegiance to God means that no power, being, man or God can stand in the way of this higher allegiance. Even more – and here he becomes quite Protestant – human beings cannot influence God although they so often try to do so, through institution, rite, covenant, or any work or deed.[21] As soon as someone, some political group or state claims that this omnipotence actually sanctions their own position, opinion or power, we know that the radical opposition required of the doctrine has been compromised.

As far as the 'experience of the prophets' is concerned, Horkheimer gives most of his attention to the 'dangerous doctrine'[22] and 'inflammatory speeches'[23] of the founder [*Stifter*] of Christianity, the prophet come lately who was murdered for his uncompromising attitude of mind, resistance to power and disdain for his own life.[24] When Horkheimer looks back at Jesus of Nazareth – the 'Nazarene' as he tends to call him – and the early Christians, he does so with a mix of admiration, wonderment and perplexity – admiration for the revolutionary opposition to power, wealth and privilege; wonderment at how people can be so committed that nothing can stand in the way of their cause; and perplexity at the way in which that early impulse has been so comprehensively overturned.

I will come back to the last of these responses below in my discussions of both compromise and dialectics. However, in regard to admiration and wonderment, Horkheimer finds the sayings and acts of Jesus clear and unambigu-

---

[21] See Horkheimer 1996, p. 149; Horkheimer 1985i, p. 272.
[22] Horkheimer 1978, p. 222; Horkheimer 1991a, p. 394.
[23] Horkheimer 1996, p. 49; Horkheimer 1985h, p. 185. See also Horkheimer 1991a, pp. 292–3; Horkheimer 1985n, p. 297.
[24] Horkheimer 1996, pp. 35–6; Horkheimer 1985h, pp. 174–5.

ous. Indeed, he hopes that even with the bowdlerised Christianity he sees everywhere around him, some – whether believers or not – might be found to offer resistance like the Nazarene.[25] The founder's position was inescapably insurrectionist and his early followers understood him in exactly this way: 'he thought little of prevailing rules and customs; he acted contrary to accepted ways; he was much closer to the heretic than the orthodox'.[26] Such an implacable position is, for Horkheimer, comparable to the Resistance during the Second World-War, the moment that informs so much of his work.[27] An extraordinarily dangerous undertaking, with treacherous death crouching in every doorway and at every corner, one joined the Resistance realising full well the consequences. We might compare it today with the 'suicide-bombers' unleashed by militant Islamist groups in their struggle with US-imperialism – except that the 'bombs' for Jesus and the early Christians were words and acts that challenged the power of imperial Rome. Surely compromise was and is the easier option, preserving one's life for a better day.

The reason why Jesus and the early Christians kept true to the cause and faced an almost certain death may be found, argues Horkheimer, in the certainty of heaven, which really means absolute justice guaranteed by the divinity, a place where the last would be first and all suppression and persecution would come to an end. And it was not that heaven was a distant and barely imaginable place; it was all too near and one entered it through the doorway of death, a brief passage that could be hastened by a cross, wild beasts of the arena and flames of the stake. Since all of us, especially the lowest and the poor in spirit, are made in God's image, such a death was a way to be near God and become more like God. Above all, each martyr's death – on the stake, cross, or gallows, or in the arena and the gas-chambers – was 'a symbol

---

[25] Horkheimer 1996, p. 49; Horkheimer 1985h, p. 185. See Horkheimer 1988f, where he praises the Roman-Catholic theologian, Theodor Haecker, who remained in Germany and opposed Hitler for theological reasons. Horkheimer cannot bring himself to agree with Haecker's theological arguments for God's existence or his theodicy, but he admires his 'longing for universal justice' (p. 91), even if it was for many of the wrong reasons. See the discussion in Ott 2001, pp. 69–77.
[26] Horkheimer 1996, p. 156; Horkheimer 1985i, p. 277. See also Horkheimer's comments on Christianity coming into the world as a scandal to the prevailing norms and customs in Horkheimer 1982, p. 283; Horkheimer 1988j, p. 430.
[27] 'When the stakes were still smouldering, it was different. Resistance addressed itself to the reign of terror. Refusal then, like the refusal to give the Hitler salute in the Third Reich, was a signal for everyone who wanted something better' (Horkheimer 1978, p. 223; Horkheimer 1991a, p. 397).

of Christianity',[28] for each one followed in the steps of that first martyr, the Nazarene. Heaven – the place where the founder had so recently gone and where he awaited to welcome newcomers with salve for their wounds and to administer stern punishment for their torturers – gave concrete reality to justice, hope and love. Although Horkheimer elsewhere admits that he mourns the loss of a 'superstitious belief in the Beyond'[29] and that he sees little gain in liberal theology's retreat to myth and symbol,[30] 'heaven' is, for Horkheimer, a primary marker of the love, hope and justice of an uncorrupted totally other.

Is there any value in this interpretation of a radical Jesus and an oppositional early Church? It is, of course, hardly new, being a persistent way in which Christ has been appropriated within and without Christianity since its earliest moments – a minority tradition, to be sure, but remarkably enduring. Martyrs would go to the arena to face beast, sword and flame in defiance of repression; the desert fathers and mothers would retreat into the desert in poverty, penitence and resistance to the increasing compromise of the Church with the state; Lollards, Taborites and Bohemian Brethren in the middle ages would form communes – in the tradition of Christian communism – and, at times, take up armed resistance; Thomas Müntzer and the peasants would wage a revolutionary war in sixteenth-century Germany in the name of Christ and the kingdom, as did the Anabaptists in the Münster Revolution in the same period; and political and liberation-theologians in our own day would follow in the same tradition, espousing a deeply political Christ and preferential option for the poor as central to the Christian message.[31] Even mainstream biblical scholars today argue for a more or less political and radical Jesus, whether implicitly or explicitly insurrectionist, pacifist, or non-conformist.[32] However, Horkheimer also stands in a Marxist tradition that goes back to Engels's argument for the revolutionary nature of early Christianity.[33] As for Horkheimer's own take on this tradition, he is not so interested in the apoc-

---

[28] Horkheimer 1996, p. 35; Horkheimer 1985h, p. 174.
[29] Horkheimer 1978, p. 223; Horkheimer 1991a, p. 393.
[30] Horkheimer 1996, pp. 154–5; Horkheimer 1985i, pp. 276–7.
[31] See Horkheimer's own effort to identify the theological elements of freedom-movements, as well as those theological traditions that suppressed freedom in Horkheimer 1993, pp. 49–110; Horkheimer 1988e.
[32] As a small sample of such scholarship, see Crossan 1993; Crossan 1995; Horsley 1992; Horsley 2002; Horsley 2008a; West 1995. For liberation-theologians, see my discussion of Michael Löwy in Chapter Four.
[33] Engels 1990b; Engels 1972. See the detailed discussion in Chapter Ten of Boer forthcoming.

alyptic Christ who mistakenly expected the end of the world within a few years, nor does he play up the political nature of Jesus's resistance in his own time (Roman Empire and Jewish religious system), preferring to let such politics mutter and rumble just behind the text.

But what of Horkheimer's explanation for this implacable resistance to power, even to the point of death? Is it enough to argue that the nearness of heaven, anticipated in the hope of God's justice, drove them to risk death? At one level, Horkheimer's proposal answers a curious absence I will explore in Ste. Croix's treatment of the same material (see Chapter Three). Despite his detailed knowledge of the sources concerning the early martyrs and despite the conclusive evidence that a good number of early Christians were voluntary martyrs, the only explanation Ste. Croix finds viable is that they were pathologically disturbed believers who welcomed death – anyone who would do so must be utterly deranged. What Ste. Croix misses in all of this is the motif of the imitation of Christ – those who were hung, burnt, beheaded and mauled to death did so in the belief that they were emulating their founder and that like him they would soon ascend to heaven. For Ste. Croix – a former believer in a rather sectarian and extreme form of Christianity – this is simply nonsense. By contrast, Horkheimer allows room for the powerful motivational force of such beliefs. Yet it is not quite enough to leave the reasons in that, rather idealist, shape. What is missing is an assessment of why these beliefs had traction, particularly in light of Horkheimer's observations elsewhere that nature, need, and social and economic conditions provide ample nourishment for religious beliefs. Relatively short and painful lives (life-expectancy for peasants was barely 30), systemic colonial oppression, brutal crushing of revolts, mass-enslavements and inordinate taxes, as well as the cultural denigration of the colonised peoples – all of these were more than enough to give urgent credence to belief in a heaven in which all such earthly trials would be overturned and the colonial oppressors brought to justice. More than one person would find it enough of a reason to fight and die.

With all this talk of the founder of Christianity, Horkheimer brushes up against an issue that threatens to undo his careful delineation of a persistent and admirable oppositional figure. I speak of the criticism of the personality-cult that Horkheimer and Adorno explore in *Dialectic of Enlightenment*.[34]

---

[34] Horkheimer and Adorno 2002, pp. 145–7; Horkheimer and Adorno 1987, pp. 206–9. See Boer 2007a, pp. 433–5.

In a few perceptive comments that draw upon Adorno's elaboration of the ban on images in the second commandment of the Decalogue, Horkheimer and Adorno outline the way Christology has constructed the framework for the personality-cult in political movements ever since. Their argument is not that the divination of this human being is one that would be emulated time and again throughout the two millennia to follow, for that is by no means an uncommon motif across many cultures and historical moments. Rather, what is distinct about Christian theology (in its combination of biblical narrative and Greek philosophy) is that Christ is God who has become a human being and then returns to heaven to be one with God the Father. This theological schema sets up the possibility for the personality-cult, for any charismatic leader may thereby become a son of God, catching the ride, as it were, as Christ touches on earth and sets off for heaven and divine status. The implication of such an argument, at least for my point here, is that Christianity itself faces the perpetual problem of the personality-cult – not merely in terms of pope, reformer, founder of a new church, or even major theologian, but especially in terms of Christ himself. Further, the answer is not to be found in emphasising the humanity of Jesus, whether as teacher, healer, or resolute resistance-fighter, for Christology lays a dialectical trap for the unwary who make use of such an answer: Christology's deep logic is that the more one emphasises the humanity of Jesus with all his earthly limits (and, I would suggest, his failings), the more one brings forth his divinity – and vice versa.[35]

So where does this leave Horkheimer's calling upon the founder of Christianity as a model not only for Christians but also for all who seek to break out of the mechanised and monotonous life of routine capitalism? Does his quiet stress on the earthly Jesus unwittingly push his various comments towards the divinity of Christ and thereby a full-blown personality-cult? A reader who pays careful attention to the moments when Jesus does turn up will see that Horkheimer is exceedingly cautious: he prefers to write of the 'founder [*Stifter*]' or the 'Nazarene' rather than 'Christ', the 'anointed' one (the Greek translation of 'meshiach' or 'messiah'). And he does not speak of

---

[35] One who falls into such a snare is the late Eagleton, especially with his return to many of his theological positions of some three or more decades ago when he was an active member of the Catholic Left and an amateur theologian. See Eagleton 2001; Eagleton 2003b; Eagleton 2003c; Eagleton 2003a; Eagleton 2007; Eagleton 2009. For a critical assessment, see Boer 2005a; Boer 2007a, pp. 321–4.

'Jesus', which is theological code for the human, earthly Christ. Further, when the founder does appear it is nearly always in a collective context. He is one of a number, found among followers, or perhaps witnesses or martyrs of the early Church, or indeed the prophets of the Hebrew Bible. I get the distinct sense that Horkheimer wants to put as much distance as possible between this founder of a militant collective on the one side and a philosophically inspired Christology on the other, with its speculation over the divine and human natures of Christ, his role in the three persons of the Trinity, and concern over the economy of salvation, in which Christ comes to earth, suffers and dies and then becomes the means for salvation for all who believe. None of that elaborate gobbledegook, suggests Horkheimer; the model this founder offers is a modest one, a simple and persistent resistance to conformity with stultifying systems of economics and society.

On freedom and the individual

The basic items of Horkheimer's position on religion are by now clear – a position of implacable resistance to conformity with this world and all its routine brutality in the name of a totally other beyond all that is of this world. But, now, we come across a couple of contentious items where Horkheimer risks his hand. These are his dual themes of freedom and the individual, which are riveted to one another in his analysis. The question of the individual, whether in ancient Greece or the Enlightenment, is, of course, of major concern to Horkheimer,[36] but I am interested in how he relates these wider concerns to religion. In his own time, he tracked with dread, dismay and resignation the increasing mechanisation of everyday-life – with examples from crossing the street, driving a car, passports and the treatment of animals – and the closely associated spread of instrumental reason.[37]

---

[36] For example, see Horkheimer 2004, pp. 87–109; Horkheimer 1991b, pp. 136–64; Horkheimer 1982, pp. 77–97; Horkheimer 1988d, pp. 367–87; Horkheimer 1988k, pp. 128–9, 137–8, 141–2.

[37] 'I know of no era in which productive forces, technology, commerce, and the scientific and political situation developed more quickly and in a more wrenching way than the last hundred years' (Horkheimer 1996, p. 138; Horkheimer 1985i, p. 263). See also Horkheimer 1978, p. 147; Horkheimer 1991a, p. 252; Horkheimer 1982, pp. 258–60; Horkheimer 1988i, pp. 337–9; Horkheimer 2004, pp. 63–86; Horkheimer 1991b, pp. 105–35. This perspective leads Shaw 1985 to argue for an abiding pessimism in Horkheimer's work. Granted, although realism is probably a better term, but Shaw

Horkheimer also espies the individual losing his or her freedom beneath an all-pervasive emphasis on collectivity, whether at the level of the clique, the professional caste, party or nation. In this context, characterised by the vivid memory of fascism, the continuing project of the Soviet Union, the newer ones of China and myriad other Communist states, as well as the mass-politics of capitalist nation-states, Horkheimer seeks to recover an authentic form of individual resistance against such collective conformity, even though he is all too aware that assertions of individual freedom have an inbuilt tendency to lead to the surrender of freedom. In one sense, Horkheimer wishes to recover the radical assertion of individual powers that had challenged the stifling conformity of the unified Christianity of medieval Europe, although he is fully aware of how that assertion was part of the bourgeois revolution.[38]

We do not have to wait long to find the implications for religion. One argument proposed by Horkheimer is that some strains of Christianity – especially in Protestantism – have tended to urge individuals to keep their religion private and acquiesce to the state.[39] Another argument is that even the Church may become a stifling collective with an ever-present tendency to authoritarianism. Against this oppressive collective, Horkheimer asserts that a decisive feature of Christianity is the way it links 'the individual soul' with a 'determinate individual ego',[40] which then leads to the position that freedom of the individual is 'the freedom without which Christianity is inconceivable'.[41] And that freedom manifests itself as 'interior independence of this world,'[42] a resolute stand by the individual against all that would press him or her into the mould of the world. All of Horkheimer's comments on the oppositional role of Christianity, the longing for the other which sets genuine Christians at odds with the world and even the muted model of the founder, threaten to be sucked into this focus on the interiority of the individual. Or as Horkheimer puts it, 'a society that is automatizing itself integrates the individuals as autonomous subjects and makes the collective, the nation first of all, into an

---

makes a facetious connection with chiliasm and messianism, which then gives him (shaky) ground to offer a scathing critique of Horkheimer.

[38] Horkheimer 1993, p. 365; Horkheimer 1987b, p. 239.

[39] Horkheimer 1993, pp. 275–8; Horkheimer 1988g, pp. 248–52.

[40] Horkheimer 1996, p. 155; Horkheimer 1985i, p. 276. See also Horkheimer 1978, p. 233; Horkheimer 1991a, p. 414; Horkheimer 1988l, p. 392.

[41] Horkheimer 1996, p. 158; Horkheimer 1985i, p. 279.

[42] Horkheimer 1996, p. 149; Horkheimer 1985i, p. 272.

idol'.[43] Against this situation, non-conformity through obedience to 'an other than the status quo'[44] becomes a task of the individual Christian – especially when that 'Someone Other' to whom Christians owe their allegiance is an omnipotent God who is well beyond any earthly power and who is in no way subject to any human efforts to bend that God's will.

I must admit to finding this argument about the nature of Christianity quite problematic, but will give my reasons in a moment. Before doing so, let me trace Horkheimer's troubled argument as to why this freedom is under threat.[45] It goes as follows: the possibility of freedom for a Christian or Jewish believer depends on the crucial influences of one's upbringing, especially one's relation with parents. If this complex process is full of warmth, the imbibing of commitment to a God who is above the allegiances of this world and a sense that one should love one's neighbour as oneself in the name of this God, then human freedom has a good chance of flowering. However, since this familial bond has been challenged, changed and often broken by modern developments, the child's upbringing increasingly involves coldness, impersonality and a sense of separateness from people. The result is no longer allegiance to a beyond, to a totally other, but to one's own agenda. Everyone else becomes a mere instrument for one's advancement and, before we know it, the individual is no longer opposed to the world but very much part of it.

A number of threads weave through this argument, such as Horkheimer's interest in child-psychology, nostalgia for what has been lost[46] and the linking of individual freedom with love for neighbours, but I am interested in a basic tension that runs throughout. In short, there are two contrasting categories of individual and of collective that emerge from Horkheimer's texts. The first type of individual is one who grows up to exercise neighbourly love while the second is self-serving, treats others as instruments for self-advancement and is, in part, due to the privatisation of religion under bourgeois pressure.[47] Further, one collective, that of the family and the community of

---

[43] Horkheimer 1978, p. 233; Horkheimer 1991a, p. 415.
[44] Horkheimer 1996, p. 149; Horkheimer 1985i, p. 272; translation modified.
[45] See the crucial pages 150–2 in Horkheimer 1996; Horkheimer 1985i, pp. 272–5. See also Horkheimer 1985q, pp. 399–401.
[46] See his defence of this resort to what is past as a critical tool in Horkheimer 1996, pp. 137–8; Horkheimer 1985i, pp. 263–4.
[47] See also Horkheimer 1993, pp. 211–12; Horkheimer 1988c, pp. 319–20. This second and less appealing individual reappears as the new focus of prayer, especially when

individuals exercising neighbourly love, is clearly desirable, while the oppressive and authoritarian collective is far less pleasant. If we look more closely at Horkheimer's argument, it turns out that the first type of individual actually comes out of a desirable collective – a loving family and community – to which that individual then contributes as a member. Indeed, it seems as though this collectively-produced individual is under threat from two angles, from the instrumental individual (whom he or she threatens to become) and from the authoritarian collective. As if there were not enough tensions – between the two types of individual and two kinds of collective – yet another shows its face, this time between the undesirable individual and equally unlikeable collective, for they jostle with each other for dominance. The only way out of this final bind is with a dialectical argument, yet it is one that Horkheimer, curiously, does not produce: both the self-serving individual and oppressive collective are two sides of the same process, since that collective is characterised by the instrumental relations of individual against individual, each vying for their own advantage.[48] But, to make that point, we need a dialectical theory of capitalism in which the apparent striving of private individuals against one another is actually a collective feature of capitalism itself. Even though Horkheimer does not produce that final step of the argument, his main point remains, namely, that the system we have now is one that has lost the deep grounding of non-conformity within religion's allegiance to one beyond this world.

This argument – at least those elements put forward by Horkheimer – is problematic on a number of counts. To begin with, to state that Christianity concerns the individual, especially in terms of election and life of the soul in the world beyond, is, at best, a caricature. It does not help matters when Horkheimer compares Christianity with Judaism's collective focus on the Messiah and the future, for this is a facetious contrast that is no truer the more

---

prayer becomes less a collective concern and more the means for expressing the wishes for individual bourgeois advancement; see Horkheimer 1978, p. 206; Horkheimer 1991a, pp. 368–9. See the detailed investigation of positive and negative approaches to human nature (with a helping from theological traditions) in Horkheimer 1993, pp. 49–110; Horkheimer 1988e.

[48] Horkheimer does offer the glimmer of a different dialectical argument but does not take it very far. Observing that the pervasiveness of collectives has the advantage of washing away egoism and self-love, he wonders whether it will lead to a new and higher perception of the ego or the loss of the individual entirely. See Horkheimer 1996, p. 158; Horkheimer 1985i, p. 279.

often it is repeated. All I need do in response is point to Christian theology's concern with creation, the natural world, history (often called salvation-history), the nature of the Church as a collective, and the concern with the end of history as the Eschaton. To be fair to Horkheimer, he wants to enlist what he perceives to be the individualistic nature of Christianity in his effort to recover the oppositional nature of the individual, but it is not an angle with much mileage.

Further, out of all Horkheimer's observations concerning religion, these on freedom and the individual seem most dated. It feels like I am reading something from a vastly different era, for, in our own context, the problem is certainly not rapidly-spreading collective blocs but the inability to think in terms of collectives at all. The individual would seem to reign supreme in a world now saturated with capitalism and the ideologeme (or ideological building block) of individual rights and choices, no matter how empty they may be in reality. Of course, as I indicated above, we face a deep paradox at this point. The continued assertion of the individual, rights, freedom of choice and freedom of expression rings empty in a world in which everyone operates in the same fashion – the dialectical logic of capitalist conformity and its associated ideology of liberalism.

Finally, Horkheimer's championing of the Enlightenment-agenda, at least on the question of individual freedom, is increasingly problematic. This grasping of Enlightenment-values would become a wholesale effort to recuperate the need for reasoned communication in the work of Jürgen Habermas.[49] Horkheimer is, of course, very conscious that the ideology of the modern individual is part and parcel of bourgeois ideology, but he tends to identity such an individual with the self-centred and instrumental figure I identified earlier. Perhaps the best way to view Horkheimer's effort to recover the resisting individual is that he sought to develop the positive side of the Enlightenment, to push that element of the dialectic beyond its tangle with myth and barbarism that he and Adorno explored with such devastating effect in *Dialectic of Enlightenment*. One signal of that project of recovery is Horkheimer's effort to negate the regressive effect of religion by enlisting it on the side of his project. So he can write that Roman-Catholic and evangelical (Lutheran) utterances

---

[49] Habermas 1987; Habermas 1981.

on the question of freedom are 'in substantial agreement with the Enlightenment, Voltaire, and above all, Emmanuel Kant'.[50]

Can anything be retrieved from this argument concerning individual
freedom? Perhaps there is one element, although it is a dialectical one. Let
us go back to the two types of collectives and individuals. Implicit within
Horkheimer's argument is the suggestion that the individual who is given to
non-conformity with this world in the name of allegiance to one who is beyond
it – an individual who thereby lives in terms of the ideal of neighbourly love –
comes out of a collective environment characterised by precisely these features of everyday life. In other words, this collective and this individual are
inseparable; one leads into the other and then back again. The crucial point
is that, even with Horkheimer's extreme valorisation of individual resistance,
he does not fall into the trap of arguing for the primacy of the individual, from
which we must then try to understand how collectives work (as conglomera-
tions of individuals). Instead, Horkheimer's narrative of the individual works
in a dialectical between the two.[51]

Atheism and resistance

I am far more enthused by Horkheimer's deliberations concerning atheism.[52]
At times, his observations on Christianity lack the dialectical finesse one
would expect, but not on this topic. If we grant Horkheimer's premise that
a Christianity or Judaism true to itself is given to resist any shape human
society might take, or any political form we might encounter, then what
happens with atheism? He cannot argue that atheism operates in terms of a
longing for a totally other, especially not in terms of allegiance to an other in
whose name people will refuse to bow to temporal power. But what he does
argue is that, when atheism takes its stand against a religion that has made its
deal with the devil and identified itself with the powers of this world, then
atheism too becomes a form of resistance: 'Atheism was once a sign of inner
independence and incredible courage, and it continues to be one in authori-

---

[50] Horkheimer 1996, p. 136; Horkheimer 1985i, p. 262.
[51] See especially, Horkheimer 1993, pp. 244–56; Horkheimer 1988a, pp. 196–211.
[52] What follows in this section is a close engagement with Horkheimer's essay,
'Theism and Atheism' in Horkheimer 1996, pp. 34–50; Horkheimer 1985h. See also
Horkheimer 1989b; Bracht et al. 1989.

tarian and semi-authoritarian countries where it is regarded as a symptom of the hated liberal spirit'[53] – a description that echoes Horkheimer's depiction of religion as inner resistance. In other words, the underlying impulse of opposition is the key: any political or social structure in which power settles into a comfortable pattern of oppression must be opposed. If religion does so in the name of another allegiance, then well and good; if atheism does so because its adherents find the massive cathedrals, prayers for rulers and identification with a national cause unacceptable, then atheism joins the ranks of resistance.

Atheism is, however, a mode of resistance come lately. Horkheimer traces the way modern atheism took its time to capture the imagination and grip both those wielding power and the masses.[54] For all its efforts to postulate Nature as an alternative to God, the metaphysical atheism of the Enlightenment did not have the ability to provide images and narratives to live by, nor indeed the institutional strength to become a serious threat to Christianity until the twentieth century. Only with the massive changes of that century, with its world-wars, unimaginable population-growth, explosions in scientific knowledge and national awakenings – comparable to the decline of antiquity or the middle ages – did atheism find the historical narrative and institutional power it so desperately sought. But, as soon as it did so, it began to give up its oppositional stance: like Christianity had done so many centuries earlier, atheism became an ideology, a feature of state-power and a social mechanism. Characteristic for his time, Horkheimer cites both the fascist and Stalinist eras as dual manifestations of such institutionalised atheism. In the same way that Christianity betrayed itself by dealing with tyrants and oligarchs, so also did atheism become a state-ideology. However, in its authentic moment, atheism is one with religion in terms of a resolute resistance to any mode of authoritarian power.

This alluring argument has a number of unexpected ramifications. To begin with, it shifts the line between religion and atheism to one between oppressive power and resistance to that power. On the central question of non-conformism (a defining feature of authentic Christianity), both religion and atheism may find common ground. As Horkheimer puts it,

[53] Horkheimer 1996, p. 49; Horkheimer 1985h, p. 185.
[54] See Horkheimer 1996, pp. 41–5; Horkheimer 1985h, pp. 178–82.

> The idea of a better world has not only been given shape in theological treatises, but often just as well in the so-called 'nihilistic' works – the critique of political economy, the theory of Marx and Engels, psychoanalysis – works which have been blacklisted, whether in the East or in the West, and provoked the wrath of the mighty as the inflammatory speeches of Christ did among his contemporaries.[55]

Yet this common ground of atheism and religion may also take a wrong turn. Both may have been responsible for a decent amount of good, but they also bear the responsibility of more than enough evil. So when atheism becomes the official dogma of a state – Horkheimer has in the mind the way it became so in some Communist states (in a profound misreading of Marx and Engels) – then atheism, too, must be resisted. The problem is that 'it is enormously difficult to avoid making a new religion of its very absence'[56] – atheism in its turn becomes a new ideology of repression. All of this means that we need to read the situation carefully: when a religion becomes the ideology of a power-structure, as we find in medieval states or in the long years of absolute monarchy in Europe, and when it actively sets out to pursue, round up, condemn, expel and execute those who do not toe the line, then atheism becomes an oppositional stand, along with those religions which have been proscribed. But, if atheism succeeds in ousting all religion and becomes, in its own turn, the dominant ideology of a repressive state-apparatus, then religion itself becomes a position of opposition to such a situation.

Now we face the perennial question as to whether atheism is a religious position characterised by the denial of God. Marx took this position in his response to Bruno Bauer, pointing out that atheism is 'the last stage of *theism*, the *negative* recognition of God'.[57] Horkheimer tracks a different course, arguing that even though irreligion falls all too often into a new form of religion, there is 'no logically compelling reason for replacing the toppled absolute by

---

[55] Horkheimer 1996, pp. 48–9; Horkheimer 1985h, p. 185. Further, 'Those who professed themselves to be atheists at a time when religion was still in power tended to identify themselves more deeply with the theistic commandment to love one's neighbour and indeed all created things than most adherents and fellow-travellers of the various denominations' (Horkheimer 1996, pp. 49–50; Horkheimer 1985h, pp. 185–6).

[56] Horkheimer 1978, p. 65; Horkheimer 1987c, p. 379.

[57] Marx and Engels 1975, p. 110; Marx and Engels 1972, p. 116. See also Engels 1995, p. 173; Engels 1973d, p. 186.

some other absolute, the toppled gods by others, devotion by denial'.[58] The upshot is that Horkheimer becomes a champion of a position he admits is extraordinarily difficult to put into practice – a situation of tolerance in which absolutes have no place.

He is astute enough to avoid arguing in favour of a secular state, since such a state is fraught with problems. I think here of the secular state Marx describes in 'On the Jewish Question':[59] basing his analysis on the USA, he points out that in such a state, religion leaves public life to become a private affair. This state does not exercise freedom from religion but freedom of religion. Religious tolerance means that I allow you to carry on your own rituals and modes of worship while I carry on mine, but we will not let them interfere with our public life as citizens of the state. Marx, obviously, finds this situation problematic, since it breaks human beings up into discrete zones of private and public life – in terms of work, business, family, religion, and so on. In other words, the secular state is no solution, especially if we keep in mind Marx's point that such a state arose in an effort to overcome the contradictions of the Christian state. The catch is that those contradictions are by no means resolved; they shift ground and show up as contradictions at another level. We can see those contradictions at various levels, such as the way the USA has a legal separation of Church and state but, in everyday-life, they are wrapped in a tight embrace, or the way Turkey has a form of established religion for the very purpose of keeping watch on that religion (Sunni Islam) so that it does not make any statements or any moves that interfere with the secular nature of the state.[60]

Horkheimer's suggestion that irreligion need not lead to another absolute – and, particularly, the implication that the best outcome is one in which there are no absolutes, for they slip far too easily into brutal intolerance – runs up against his consistent characterisation of an oppositional Christianity defined by allegiance to another. Does not such an authentic Christianity operate precisely in terms of an absolute? Two answers are possible, one supplied by Horkheimer himself and one that needs to be supplied. For Horkheimer, this absolute is fine as long as it does not identify itself with a temporal form. It

---

[58] Horkheimer 1978, p. 66; Horkheimer 1987c, p. 379.
[59] Marx 1975b; Marx 1974a.
[60] See further Boer 2007b.

is, if you like, permanently suspended above the dirty deals of human power, constantly finding them inadequate. The religious absolute is religious only if it does not become absolute power, an absolute state. This argument leads us to the next point: an absolute, as Alain Badiou has argued,[61] need not be singular. In the same way that universals and truths may be plural, so also may absolutes be plural. Indeed, to identify the universal truth of the absolute with the One is precisely the travesty and betrayal Horkheimer seeks to block. So, I would suggest that an argument for the multiplicity of absolutes – in religious terms, it may be Christian, Jewish, Muslim, Buddhist or whatever shape religion may take – is one that places a stern 'no through road' sign before any effort by an absolute to become singular and thereby exclusive, intolerant and oppressive.

Arguably, the most significant ramification of Horkheimer's argument is that theism and atheism – as he tends to call the pair – may form what I have elsewhere called a politics of alliance.[62] While Horkheimer directs his comments at the historical alliance between atheism and the Left (at least from the time following Marx and Engels), my argument is directed at both the secular Left and the religious Left. Both may indeed find common ground in the struggle against forms of coercion and tyranny – as we find in the common struggle of some of the Christian churches and the Communist Party in South Africa during the apartheid-era, or as we find today in the links between Christian, Muslim and left groups in the Palestinian resistance against Israeli state-oppression.[63]

Honest religion

A longing for the other, fidelity to the words and acts of the founder, a problematic emphasis on individual freedom and an interpretation of atheism as resistance to authoritarian oppression – these are the features of what has turned out to be a multi-faceted effort by Horkheimer to find what is valuable in religion, especially Christianity. However, let me close this treatment of religion as resistance with a couple of Horkheimer's stark sentences

---

[61] Badiou 2006a; Badiou 1988.
[62] Boer 2007b, pp. 33–49.
[63] See also Horkheimer's comments on the common ground of Marxism and Christianity in Horkheimer 1985n, p. 299; Horkheimer 1985p, pp. 312–13.

which express the core of what he seeks in religion (and indeed atheism) in the 'good sense':

> To sustain, not to let reality stifle, the impulse for change [*Impuls, daß es anders warden soll*], the desire that the spell be broken, that things take the right turn. We have religion where life down to its every gesture is marked by this resolve.[64]

In these sentences, Horkheimer employs a terminology of stifling and spells for the threats to honest religion, which is, at heart, an impulse for change. But, in an age that has become weary of change, in which politicians within capitalist parliamentary democracy routinely offer 'change' in a way that guarantees more of the same, what type of change does Horkheimer seek? It is, of course, more specific than empty promises (which he will connect with religion in the bad sense), for such an impulse to change is focused on the monotony of mechanised and instrumentalised life under capitalism. To resist this life with all of its habitual brutality and systematised oppression is what constitutes religion 'honest with itself'. The second sentence suggests what such a resolute opposition really means: every gesture of everyday life, no matter how trivial or ordinary, should embody this resistance. It is a life lived at an odd angle to the world, implicitly and explicitly opposing all that it stands for. In Horkheimer's eyes, that constitutes religion – the same may be said for an oppositional atheism.

Religion betrayed

Horkheimer knows well enough that the history of Christianity (and indeed Judaism) is piled high with the corpses of those killed in its name and that the courts of Judgement-Day will be overloaded with the millions of cases

---

[64] Horkheimer 1978, p. 163; Horkheimer 1991a, p. 288. See also: 'To be conscious of the untold, horrible physical and psychological pain, and particularly physical torture which is suffered at every moment in penitentiaries, hospitals, slaughterhouses, behind walls and in full view of the world over, to see all this means to live with open eyes. Without such awareness, every decision is blind, every sure step a misstep, every happiness untrue. But happiness and truth, like truth and grief, are one. This is what Christianity means where it is not betrayed by its mindless adherents' (Horkheimer 1978, p. 222; Horkheimer 1991a, p. 395). Even more, 'The truth of Christianity is to break out of the circle' (Horkheimer 1988k, p. 117). See further Horkheimer 1988l, p. 544.

to be heard. So how does he make sense of the fact that Christianity has rarely if ever lived up to the principles of its founder, to the authentic religious impulse of resistance to domination? The answer is deceptively simple: when Christianity becomes an ideology and practice of brutal oppression, it has betrayed itself. Now, this is by no means a new position, for we find it with the various oppositional groups that keep cropping up throughout the history of Christianity, especially the groups that emerged from the radical Reformation. I will have more to say about them later, since I want to let Horkheimer speak first.

The manner in which the betrayal takes place may vary, but the underlying pattern is the same. It may be when Christianity ceases to oppose the state in the name of a higher allegiance and becomes united with the state, when the state itself merges with God and one is expected and compelled to serve that theocracy. It may be when religion becomes the justification for bourgeois capitalism, in which religion is no longer the protest against misery and despair but their justification.[65] It may be the cynical claim by ruling classes to the moral high ground in order to justify murder and villainy, a claim to which those who are ruled seem all too ready to affirm, serving the divine state with passion and vigour.[66] It may be due to the fact that so-called 'Christians' are not genuine; gathering under the flag of Christianity is merely a convenience so that they may pursue aims that are by no means Christian. It may be when religion becomes privatised, relegated to the inner sanctum of the individual and thereby of no relevance to public life. It may be due to self-interest, when so-called Christians turn the other way when faced with suffering – since to do something about such misery would bring them discomfort and harm. It may be the moment religion becomes an instrument of bourgeois competition, a justification for one's own self-advancement at the expense of others (the bad form of individualism I noted above).[67] It may happen due to wilful blindness on the part of those who should know better, especially scientists, poets and philosophers whose own principles should lead them to oppose such a situation but who deliberately forget their principles. It may be when the command to love both one's neighbour and one's enemy fades away and

---

[65] Horkheimer 1978, pp. 88, 90–1; Horkheimer 1987c, pp. 412, 414–15.
[66] Horkheimer 1978, pp. 88–9; Horkheimer 1987c, pp. 412–13.
[67] Horkheimer 1993, pp. 211–12; Horkheimer 1988c, pp. 319–20.

hatred takes its place. It may be when the Christian church has actively sought to soften and even dispense with the words of its founder (here, as we shall see, Horkheimer comes close to Ste. Croix). It may happen because of sheer hypocrisy, worshipping one who sacrificed himself for humanity and yet torturing others in his name. In each case, the result is the same: the 'compromise between the implementation of religion and its inexpedient abolition' which becomes the reconciliation with 'God via the all-encompassing lie'.[68]

Now, all of these arguments may well have a grain of truth in them, but they tend to miss the dialectical complexity that we have come to expect from Horkheimer. Thankfully, there is one exception, which happens to be his most powerful argument: this betrayal and accommodation by Christianity was a necessary and lamentable evil for the sake of survival.[69] Had Christians really lived up to the ideals and example of their first teacher, they would have 'perished like fools'[70] and the movement would have come to grief as quickly as it arose. Christ did not lay the groundwork or structure for a workable religion, for what he espoused was not the stuff of an organised global movement. That task fell to his more worldly followers, who saw well enough that any chance of success lay in making a deal with this world. Betrayal was bred of the need for survival, even if that betrayal meant war, empire and persecution of dissidents – who were uncannily like Christ. Without that betrayal, we would not have had the cathedrals, the great achievements of art and science, the strides forward in philosophy, the extraordinary creations of literature, the gains of human rights or, at an everyday level of lived space, the village-church without which Europe's countryside is inconceivable. Obviously, these achievements drip with the blood of those who died due to that betrayal, but without it Christianity would not be around today.

The argument I have just traced raises a question that will undergird the discussion which follows: does Horkheimer end up arguing for the necessary negative of Christianity's betrayal of itself? I get the sense that he would prefer it if Christianity had not made this bloody compromise, that it had held true to its initial impulse of opposition and change. However, given the short

---

[68] Horkheimer 1978, p. 91; Horkheimer 1987c, p. 414. See also Horkheimer 1982, pp. 129–30; Horkheimer 1988b, pp. 326–7; Horkheimer 1985n, pp. 297–8; Horkheimer 1988k, pp. 129–30.
[69] See especially Horkheimer 1996, pp. 34–40; Horkheimer 1985h, pp. 173–8.
[70] Horkheimer 1996, p. 36; Horkheimer 1985h, p. 175.

life-spans of movements driven by such an impulse, without compromise the outcome may well have been the end of the impulse itself.

The state

One of Horkheimer's main themes concerning the modern world is, as we saw earlier, the increasing pace of automation and the associated routinisation of all facets of human life, but, when it comes to religion, a prominent feature is the role of the state – that collective gone bad. His experiences were not the best: he had fled the Nazis in the early 1930s, resettling the Institute for Critical Theory at Columbia University in New York; he had witnessed from afar what was taking place under Stalin in the Soviet Union; he and especially his colleague, Adorno, were not enthused at all by the vigorous capitalism in the United States. With these tendencies all around, it should not be surprising that Horkheimer would scan history for similar tendencies – and he found them with both Christianity and Judaism.

As for Christianity, Constantine the Great – son of a Christian mother and who himself converted at least in 312 CE (if not earlier) before the famous battle of the Milvian Bridge in which he gained control of the Roman Empire – is the main culprit. By 313, Constantine and Licinius (then emperor in the east) issued the Edict of Milan, which legalised Christianity, and Constantine set about an aggressive programme of building churches (in the main centres of Jerusalem, Constantinople, Rome and elsewhere in the empire), paying for a whole new class of state-bureaucrats, the priests, calling church-councils (especially the first ecumenical council in Nicaea in 325 CE) for the sake of Christian doctrinal unity, and ensuring favourable treatment for Christianity. Even though it was not until 380 CE that Theodosius I proclaimed Christianity the sole religion of the Empire, the deal had been done and the Christian church had moved from a marginal religion under pressure of state-censure to become extraordinarily powerful, wealthy and used to employing strong-arm tactics against opponents, as we will see in my discussion of Ste. Croix.

For some, this epochal shift was the sign of Christianity's success. The Eastern Orthodox and oriental Orthodox churches made Constantine a saint, and ideologues such as Eusebius of Caesaria, the first church-historian, opined in 320 CE that a unified Christian empire was God's will. For others, it was the great moment of betrayal. Radical Reformers in the sixteenth century, who suffered persecution at the hands of both the Roman-Catholics and the

Protestants, saw Constantine's conversion and adoption of Christianity as the religion of empire as the moment when Christianity sold out and betrayed that for which Jesus and the early Christians had stood. Horkheimer agrees wholeheartedly: this was when Christianity became rather embarrassed at what Jesus had said and done. And so it developed 'a secret and indomitable hatred for that attitude of mind for which its founder had earlier been put to death'.[71]

The consequences for theology and practice were momentous: evil and hell became necessary categories for those who did not conform; orthopraxis combined with orthodoxy to define who submitted to the will of the Church and who broke ranks; prayer slid from intercession for rain, the crops, the ruler or the people to the furtherance of one's own (later bourgeois) goals;[72] theology began its delicate task of reconciling the clear demands found in the Gospels with the requirements of power. On this last item, Horkheimer and Ste. Croix would have had much to discuss over a long night, many empty beer-bottles and an overflowing ashtray – Horkheimer with the theoretical depth and Ste. Croix with his inexhaustible references.

Yet the theme that keeps recurring in Horkheimer's observations concerning this complex betrayal is the way the longing for the other becomes identical with longing for the mother-country. At this point, Horkheimer's invocation on the ban on idolatry from the second and third commandments in Exodus 20 and Deuteronomy 5 has some weight: 'critical theory...rests on the thought that the Absolute – that is God – cannot be made into an object [*nicht zum Objekt gemacht werden kann*]'.[73] Adorno would make this ban on idolatry into the *Bilderverbot*, a persistent leitmotiv of his thought; even though the theme is more muted in Horkheimer's writings, it still has significant critical bite. Identification of the state, the mother-country, with the Absolute is the worst form of idolatry. And, like all idols, it demands sacrifice in blood, justifies wars of aggression and brutal suppression. Horkheimer compares this compromise to a skyscraper in which the 'basement is a slaughterhouse, its

---

[71] Horkheimer 1996, p. 35; Horkheimer 1985h, p. 173. See also Horkheimer 1991a, pp. 340–1.

[72] Horkheimer 1978, p. 206; Horkheimer 1991a, pp. 368–9.

[73] Horkheimer 1985s, p. 431. See also Ott 2007, pp. 176–7; Ott 2001, pp. 28–9.

roof a cathedral, but from the windows of the upper floors, it affords a really beautiful view of the starry heavens'.[74]

This elision of the totally other and the state may have first happened under the Emperor Constantine, but Horkheimer pinpoints this elision as a growing feature of Christianity in more recent centuries. People, he notes, have become far more willing to sacrifice themselves in wars for the 'defence' of their own country rather than for the sake of love for the enemy; 'faith in God has now become faith in one's own people'.[75] Less than a decade ago, I would have been able to observe that this situation may have applied in the earlier twentieth century, but, with the explosion of economic and cultural globalisation in the latter decades of that century, such identification with one's God and country had begun to look quaint. But how matters have changed in the space of a few years; against a perceived 'threat' from Islam, those self-same countries of Western Europe have resurrected this old alliance between God and state, between Western Europe and Christianity. One by one, leaders and citizens of countries such as Denmark, the Netherlands and England have asserted that they are inconceivable without Christianity – and this from people who only know what a church-building looks like from the outside. Once again, sacrifices are made to preserve a 'Christian country' under the threat from the infidel hordes. Doors are closed and a past golden age is constructed in order to be preserved, replete with Christian moral codes, civil liberties, freedom of the press, and so-called equal rights, applicable of course only to those who happen to be a citizen of such a country.

On the Jewish state

Horkheimer reserves most of his observations for Christianity, especially in the astonishing survey of Christian history in the essay, 'Theism and Atheism'.[76] Yet, as one who admitted that Judaism was the religion he knew all too well, on this matter of identification with the state he voices profound reservations concerning the state of Israel. Horkheimer's position on Zionism and the Jewish state comes out of a long, sustained and detailed examination

---

[74] Horkheimer 1978, p. 67; Horkheimer 1987c, p. 380.
[75] Horkheimer 1996, p. 40; Horkheimer 1985h, p. 177. See also Horkheimer 1987a, p. 268; Horkheimer 1988l, pp. 326, 398–9, 410–11, 498.
[76] Horkheimer 1996, pp. 34–40; Horkheimer 1985h, pp. 173–8.

of Judaism, anti-Semitism, Jewish immigration and the diaspora.[77] He is no Zionist, by any stretch of the imagination, describing Zionism as a result of despair and finding the establishment of the state of Israel in his own time a deep betrayal of Judaism itself, a moment when the language of the prophets, Hebrew, has become a language of success. In contrast to the hope that lay with the anticipation of the Messiah – a hope that a mother held for the time of her daughter or son, a hope expressed in the saying, 'Next year in Jerusalem', a hope for justice at the end of the world – the establishment of the state of Israel was precisely that event which undermined such a hope. At that moment, some began to say that the hope had been realised and that the promise had been fulfilled, that God's will could be found in this new state, and that the messianic era had begun without a Messiah; in short: 'Jewry is now to see the goal in the state of Israel'.[78] It was nothing less than the same act Christianity had performed so many times already – the identification of a distinct and very human political formation with the divine will. Horkheimer's comment on Judaism applies just as much to both: 'How profound a resignation in the very triumph of its temporal success'.[79]

Although Horkheimer distinguishes – quite problematically – between Judaism's collective hope for a future Messiah and Christianity's focus on the individual soul's passage to heaven, he does identify the nature of the 'longing for the other' in Judaism as formally similar to Christianity. That longing brings with it the concern for justice and love for enemies in the name of what is beyond this world and this age; in fact, the necessarily delayed messianic hope is the reason why Judaism espouses these ideals and will not be conformed to this world. The state of Israel is a profound betrayal of what Horkheimer holds dear in Judaism.

The ramifications of this compromise with the ways of the world show up in a number of passing observations that feel as though they were written yesterday. So, we find that the cry, in the mouths of Jewish capitalists, of 'anti-Semitism' at the slightest criticism of Judaism or the state of Israel is really a

---

[77] Horkheimer 1987d; Horkheimer 1987e; Horkheimer 1988h; Horkheimer 1985b; Horkheimer 1985c; Horkheimer 1985a, pp. 263–4, 294–5; Horkheimer 1985d, pp. 303–5; Horkheimer 1988k, p. 139; Horkheimer 1988l, pp. 314–15, 331–2, 340–1, 370, 388–91, 404, 408–11, 413, 418, 452, 480–1, 513, 527, 533–4. See also Horkheimer and Adorno 2002, pp. 137–72; Horkheimer and Adorno 1987, pp. 197–238; Horkheimer and Adorno 1985.

[78] Horkheimer 1978, p. 207; Horkheimer 1991a, p. 369.

[79] Ibid. See also Horkheimer 1985q, p. 398.

screen for a perceived threat to bourgeois values and goods, for bourgeois
Jews are no different from bourgeois Christians, willing to sacrifice everything – their own superstitions and the lives of others – before they will
sacrifice their own capital.[80] As another example, Horkheimer offers a critical assessment of the long desire by German Jews to be recognised as one
group among others in the German state.[81] This was not a new issue, as the
debates between Marx and Bruno Bauer in the 1840s show all too well.[82] But
Horkheimer is less than impressed by the extra degree of nationalistic zeal
exhibited by assimilated Jews and by the shift from the hope for justice to
the desire to become a religion like any other. He would rather they hold
onto what made Jews, especially orthodox Jews, stand at an odd angle to the
world, or even better the 'critico-negative [kritisch-negativen]'[83] spirit of a long
line of Jewish thinkers and activists. The problem with the identification of
Jews with the German state is that it made those Jews no different from the
Christians who saw in Germany the saviour of the world. And there is no difference between this identification and that with the state of Israel – different
state, same problematic compromise.

One of the most significant examples of the betrayal of the resistance
and perseverance at the core of Judaism was the trial of Adolf Eichmann.[84]
Horkheimer writes after Eichmann's covert and illegal capture in Argentina
on 11 May 1960 and the beginning of his trial in 1961 (Eichmann was then
hanged in 1962). Horkheimer argues that Israel has no jurisdiction outside the
state that it established, rightly or wrongly, for the role of the law is to punish
crimes committed within one's borders for the sake of deterrence. To abduct
someone illegally from another state and then put him on trial for acts not
committed within Israel goes against any sense of law – it is, he writes, simply 'bad metaphysics'.[85] Indeed, the only competent act for the Israeli court,
which refused to rule on precisely the matter of its own jurisdiction, would

---

[80] Horkheimer 1978, pp. 42–3; Horkheimer 1987c, p. 351.
[81] Horkheimer 1996, pp. 101–18; Horkheimer 1985g.
[82] Marx 1975b; Marx 1974a; Bauer 1843c; Bauer 1978; Bauer 1843b.
[83] Horkheimer 1996, p. 109; Horkheimer 1985g, p. 166.
[84] Horkheimer 1996, pp. 119–23; Horkheimer 1985f. Repeated in Horkheimer 1978, pp. 193–6; Horkheimer 1991a, pp. 347–50. See also Horkheimer 1991a, p. 364.
[85] Horkheimer 1996, p. 119; Horkheimer 1985f, p. 156. The macabre paradox of Eichmann is that he worked closely for a time in 1937–9 with Zionists to enable Jews to immigrate to Palestine in order to form a Jewish state, but the British were not in favour of such a state.

be to declare itself incompetent. On all counts, argues Horkheimer, the trial is a sham: it is ludicrous to see it as deterrence; it is poor education for Israeli youth concerning the Third Reich and the persecution of Jews; the use of a criminal trial for political purposes will undermine its value and makes Israel no better than totalitarian states; everyone will see through the show-trial; there is nothing unique about mass-murder in history; the idea that Eichmann would atone for all the Jewish deaths makes a mockery of those deaths; and, above all, it is a travesty of the value of those who have suffered and died. In short, the trial is yet another example of the betrayal of Judaism.

So what role should the persecution of Jews, and in particular the genocide at the hands of the Nazis, play in the annals of justice? Rather than becoming an ideological backing for oppression of others in the name of 'survival' of the Jewish state, Horkheimer argues instead that people 'should become sensitive not to injustice against the Jews but to injustice as such, not to persecution of the Jews but to any and all persecution, and that something in them should rebel when any individual is not treated as a rational being'.[86]

Now, although his arguments still have an edge today, Horkheimer is by no means unique in this position, for he taps into a long tradition that has gained increasing viability in the face of Israeli atrocities in Palestinian territories, namely the value of diasporic Judaism over against Zionism.[87] Although Horkheimer feels that the diaspora had become at the time of writing (1961–2) the backwoods rather than the centre of Judaism,[88] we have witnessed since then a significant revival of the value of diaspora. Rather than diasporic communities throughout the world looking to Israel as their guiding light, giving voice to a nationalism that differs in no way from any other nationalism, routinely defending, in ever more desperate ways, the latest brutality of that state in the name of 'survival', calling up the Holocaust yet again in order to justify whatever Israel does, proponents of diasporic Judaism argue that the greatest achievements of Judaism – in philosophy, art, music, politics, and economics – took place precisely because the Jews who made them were diasporic Jews. The names of Moses Maimonides, Sigmund Freud, Karl Marx, Ernst

---

[86] Horkheimer 1996, p. 118; Horkheimer 1985g, p. 174.
[87] Among a vast amount of literature on this topic, see Boyarin and Boyarin 1995; Docker 2001; Sand 2009; Badiou 2006b, especially the essay, 'Israel: The Country in the World Where There Are the Fewest Jews'.
[88] Horkheimer 1978, p. 221; Horkheimer 1991a, p. 392.

Bloch, Walter Benjamin, Georg Lukács, Hanna Arendt, Theodor Adorno, and Horkheimer himself are names that come from such a diaspora. The key to this argument is that the permanent suspension, or rather potentiality, of the hope for justice in the messianic age is precisely what produces the value of Judaism. To say that the hope has arrived, that the future is here, destroys that suspended moment of creativity and hope. Horkheimer could not agree more.

Liberal theology

Given what we have seen from Horkheimer thus far, his thoughts on the state and on Zionism should have come as no surprise. But the next topic – liberal theology – is far less expected,[89] at least if one has not read Adorno in one of his lesser studied works (*The Jargon of Authenticity*).[90] For Adorno, the problem with liberal theology is that it has taken half a step towards the treacherous terrain of secularised theology, which he saw perniciously at work in Martin Heidegger, with its covert transferral of the powers of God to the thinker or the state. Horkheimer shares the suspicion of liberal theology, but for somewhat different reasons. Like the secularisation of theology,[91] liberal theology is another version of accommodation to the world: in arguing that the unpalatable stories of the Bible were really myths and legends or that the key motifs of death and resurrection, oppression and deliverance, sin and forgiveness, were symbols and principles of existential life, liberal theology gave up the valuable oppositional stance of such stories and themes. It agrees with the world – yes, these are just myths of another, non-scientific, age, but you need not worry about them since they are really fables, tales and symbols of our walk through life. Such a move – 'an escape route which the

---

[89] Horkheimer 1978, pp. 219–20, 222–3; Horkheimer 1991a, pp. 389–90, 392–3; Horkheimer 1996, pp. 46–7; Horkheimer 1985h, pp. 183–4; Horkheimer 1996, pp. 154–6; Horkheimer 1985i, pp. 276–7; Horkheimer 1985r; Horkheimer 1985q, pp. 392–3.

[90] Adorno 1973; Adorno 2003a; see Boer 2007a, pp. 422–30.

[91] For this reason, I disagree with Ott's argument that Horkheimer sought a secularisation of the protesting impulse of Judaism and Christianity via the determinate negation of critical theory (Ott 2001, pp. 8, 31, 66–7, 81–102; Ott 2007, pp. 167–70, 186). Although there are elements in Horkheimer's thought that justify such an argument, it runs into the problem that such secularisation was a version of the compromise with the world that Horkheimer criticises again and again.

despairing take without admitting their despair to themselves'[92] – gave up far too much that was vital about Christianity or indeed Judaism. It spells nothing less than the end of religion.[93]

Horkheimer names two liberal theologians, one a populariser and one more profound. The former is John A.T. Robinson, who wrote a brief, very personal account of the need to shake up theology and the Church in *Honest to God*.[94] A former New-Testament lecturer and Cambridge-don, Robinson's little book caused a howl of controversy, largely because he made available to a wide public in England what had gone on in biblical and theological scholarship for some time (the usual distance and time-lag applying in the relation between theology and the wider Church). Here, we find an array of German liberal theologians – Rudolf Bultmann and his demythologisation of the New Testament, Dietrich Bonhoeffer's ethical authenticity, and Paul Tillich's symbolic Christianity – presented in an accessible form.

More substantial is Horkheimer's reference to the 'unforgettable' Paul Tillich,[95] a long-time friend, collaborator and colleague whom Horkheimer appreciated deeply but with whom he also disagreed.[96] Tillich, an opponent of Hitler and a Christian socialist, shared much political ground with Horkheimer and yet, on the matter of reinterpreting the key-themes of Christianity as symbols, in terms of deeper significance, meanings, values and existence, Horkheimer felt that Tillich had given up precisely the most non-conformist elements of theology. A symbol, after all, must point to something concrete to have any sense; the abstract categories to which Tillich sought to redirect these symbols were as empty as symbols without any reference-point at all. By

---

[92] Horkheimer 1996, p. 155; Horkheimer 1985i, p. 276.
[93] Horkheimer 1985q, p. 392.
[94] Robinson 1963. See also Bracht, et al. 1989, pp. 155–6, 162.
[95] Horkheimer 2006, p. 119; Horkheimer 1985o, p. 211. See also Horkheimer 1985m; Horkheimer 1985j; Horkheimer 1985l; Horkheimer 1989a; Horkheimer 1988l, pp. 338, 352; Horkheimer 1995; Tillich and Tillich 1996; Horkheimer 1996a; Horkheimer 1996c; Horkheimer 1996b; Tillich 1996b; Horkheimer 1996d; Tillich 1996a; Horkheimer 1996e; Horkheimer 1996f; Horkheimer 1996h; Horkheimer 1996g.
[96] A detailed study still needs to be made of the complex relations between Tillich, Horkheimer and Adorno. Tillich, who moved from Germany to Union Theological Seminary in New York before the War, was the habilitation-supervisor for Adorno's book on Kierkegaard, invited Adorno to give a lecture on Kierkegaard at Union, and maintained close contact with both Horkheimer and Adorno when they moved back to Germany. See the roundtable-discussion that includes Tillich and a number of other theologians in Adorno, et al. 1987. See also Tillich 1951–63; Tillich 1952.

reinterpreting theology – no matter how creatively – in light of contemporary philosophy, which really meant existentialism, Tillich had granted too much ground to the world he sought to oppose.

What, then, is the answer, at least for Horkheimer? It is not to be found in a resolute orthodoxy and piety that denies the changing world and holds obstinately onto beliefs – although, at times, it seems as though Horkheimer does suggest as much with his longing for superstitious beliefs. On this point, he agrees with Tillich: profound changes in knowledge, science and politics demand creative responses from theologians. It is just that Tillich has not offered a reply that enables theology to remain at odds with the world. Tradi-tional thought must forever find new forms of expression in the terms of the age while simultaneously contradicting it. Now, all this is very well, and most theologians would agree to some extent. The catch is that Horkheimer does not give us much in the way of content. Is paradise to remain a garden lost and hoped for? Is the Eschaton a time when the physical messiah is sent from God, when justice will be handed out at a divine tribunal? Does Christ really ascend and return through the clouds, leading an invincible force of angels in the last days?

While I can see the value of Horkheimer's criticism, especially in the inabil-ity of liberal theology to distinguish itself at times from secular philosophy, I am not sure he has treated myth and symbol as well as he might. He is, of course, beholden to the deep suspicion of myth that characterised Adorno and Benjamin, especially in light of the extensive mythologising of blood, soil and the Aryan heritage under Hitler and his cronies. And Horkheimer and Adorno did argue in *Dialectic of Enlightenment* that myth was both the first solidifying step in the oppressive organisation of society and the signal of a barbarism that kept turning up as the dialectical obverse of enlightenment from the Greeks onward. But all that is to lock myth into a function that is far too restrictive. For, as Ernst Bloch argued for his whole life, albeit at times too enthusiastically, myth also gives voice within the midst of oppressive nar-ratives to a spirit of rebellion and utopia that simply will not go away. Or, as I have argued recently, in its very cunning, myth may also offer distinct possibilities for the Left that it ignores at its peril.[97] It is not so much a case of giving ground as of enabling alternative voices of chaos and insurrection to

---

[97] Boer 2009b.

come forth, precisely because the myths of repression have preserved those voices, so much so that they puncture the myths of the Right, those of order and sobriety. But this is a different argument to the liberal theologians, who wanted to give up the myths of the Bible and reinterpret them in line with the language and aspirations of 'modern man'. I would rather retain them (like Horkheimer), call them myths (unlike Horkheimer) and let them speak their word of non-conformism and rebellion.

Religion in the bad sense, or, the dialectic of evil

When I set out to wrap up the earlier section on Horkheimer's positive appreciation of religion, I made use of one of his aphoristic pronouncements. Religion in the 'good sense', he wrote, is an unbending pursuit of change, one that saturates the smallest acts of everyday life. However, when it comes to religion in the 'bad sense', matters become a little more complex. It is as though Horkheimer has realised he is actually dealing with the question of evil; that awareness makes him pause before the temptation of clear state-ments. So, we find him exploring various ways in which one actually speaks of religion in the 'bad sense'. The first of these follows on from the earlier comment on honest religion. By contrast, religion in the 'bad sense', he writes, is the impulse for change found in honest religion,

> ...but in its perverted form, as affirmation, prophecy, that gilds reality in the very act of castigating it. It is the lie that some earthly or heavenly future gives evil, suffering, horror, a meaning. The lie does not need the cross, it already lives in the ontological concept of transcendence.[98]

Perversion is the nature of religion that has betrayed its initial impulse to change for the better and that has compromised its stance against the ways of the world. We need to be careful, paying close attention to what Horkheimer is arguing: this dishonest religion does not necessarily have an existence on its own; it is a distortion, a perversion of religion as it should be. It seems to offer the prospect of change – like an adept politician – but, in doing so, actually affirms the status quo. It tells us we have not achieved the world we seek but then implicitly lets us know that the world we have is actually

---

[98] Horkheimer 1978, p. 163; Horkheimer 1991a, p. 288.

better than we think – we have, in other words, already arrived. How does such a religion do so? It admits that suffering exists but, instead of pointing out (like Marx) that religion is a protest against that suffering, it tries to give that suffering meaning with reference to an idealised future. Your suffering has a purpose, it says, perhaps as a trial put in your way by God, or perhaps to remind you of your sinful state, or even as deserved punishment for a wrong from which you must now repent.[99] All we need do is to refer to some transcendence, whether ontological or temporal, and it all makes sense.

As an example of this process of subtle perversion, let me take a biblical text that comes very close to Horkheimer's own position: 'Be not conformed to this age' (Romans 12: 2). One interpretation takes this verse as a slogan for resistance to the ways of the world at every level, whether theologically, politically or personally, especially in the insignificant acts of everyday-life. It was obviously one of the key texts used by non-conformist sects and churches in countries where an established church ruled the roost and punished those who would not conform. Yet another interpretation is possible as well, one found too often for comfort among conservative Christians: being not con-formed now means that one should be opposed to the evil ideology of 'secularism', evolutionary theory, gay rights, abortion – in short, any manifestation of a pagan world that is the work of the devil. But this approach gives the impression of non-conformity while upholding a revised form of Christendom. The state should support religion, but only a conservative form that aligns precisely with the form of evangelical (in the English sense) Christianity espoused by its adherents. And it should come as no surprise that one way of the world is affirmed with vigour – capitalist economics and social relations. Here, we find an apparent impulse to non-conformity that gilds reality in the act of denouncing it.

Back to Horkheimer: take care and note what has happened with the text quoted above. Religion in the 'bad sense' does not have an existence of its own; it is a perversion of what is authentic. Now, this argument is consistent with the general position that such religion is a betrayal and compromise,

---

[99] As Matt Chrulew, a PhD student of mine, points out, this is a deeply Nietzschean theme. By leading the weak to interpret their pain as punishment, the ascetic ideal of Christianity provides a psychological theodicy, giving suffering meaning. See Nietzsche 1994 pp. 109–11, 127–8.

but it does mean that bad religion is parasitic on the good. Barely hidden beneath such an argument is a long tradition of reflection on the problem of evil. Let me put it this way: theology has usually been faced with four possibilities concerning evil: it is a positive entity, sometimes personified as the devil, but that position raises the conundrum as to how one accounts for the origin of such an entity (hence, the myths of Satan's beginning as an angel and his subsequent fall from heaven); as omnipotent creator of all that is, God is the source of both good and evil (a position one does find in the Bible but which has been ruled out as far too dangerous in most theological thought); a created being, having been given free choice, brings about evil by exercising that choice (whether Satan himself or human beings); or evil is a negation and distortion of the good. These positions often overlap one another, but what Horkheimer has done, at least on this occasion, is take the last option – religion in the 'bad sense' is a negation, a perversion of good religion.

Also worth noting is that Horkheimer invokes the dialectic when it comes to the question of evil. Often the dialectic seems but a distant memory, even in the text quoted above: honest religion is one of resistance to a corrupt world, while dishonest religion betrays that impulse to resistance and makes its compromise with the tyrants of this world. Honest religion seeks to break the spell that justifies oppressive reality, while perverted religion invokes that spell ever more strongly. The religion worth attention needs no elaborate spin that tries to give suffering meaning, for that religion is honest. The contrast could not be stronger: resistance and betrayal, good and bad, honesty and lying, reality and a spell. But, then, in the midst of this intractable opposition, we come across a more dialectical way of dealing with the question of religion. Horkheimer writes that religion in the 'bad sense' is, in fact, the same impulse as religion in the 'good sense', except that religion appears in a perverted (I would suggest inverted) form; bad religion also criticises reality and urges change, but it presents such a message in a way that actually 'gilds reality', affirms it while criticising, reassures while castigating.

The question of evil brings out the best in Horkheimer. Evil does not want to leave him alone, partly because he had lived through some of the most barbaric and brutal moments of the twentieth century. And so, Horkheimer keeps returning to evil to see if he can make sense of it yet again. The dialectical entwinement of good and bad religion is but one instance; another appears in a very different dialectical reading that might be called a dialectic of exacerbation. In brief, the more good seems to gain ground, the stronger does evil reassert itself. Let us see how Horkheimer sets up this dialectic before offering some criticism.

In a brief reflection called 'Evil in History',[100] Horkheimer begins with Kant's observation that human beings have the dubious distinction of laying claim to a unique form of radical evil: among all living beings, humans know what is good yet do what is bad.[101] For Horkheimer, the question becomes one of knowledge and progress. If the formula holds, then the greater the knowledge of good, the more does evil increase; the more we progress, the greater do we regress. All of which leads to the paradox that the burgeoning of knowledge (of what is good) does not actually make us better and more able – it simply makes us worse. Horkheimer is keen to assert that this is not merely a mathematical formula, an inverse ratio of good and evil, for it is a 'real historical process'.[102] He brings forth some well-known examples of rationalisation and mechanisation – telescopes and microscopes, tapes and radios – in order to show how technological progress and the advance of scientific knowledge do not merely refine the methods of violence, but actually constitute a profound regression to barbarity. We could add any number of examples, such as nuclear physics, computerisation, and the internet, only to show that there is a barbaric swerve built into their very invention. Superhuman achievements produce superhuman evil. And, just in case we feel Horkheimer has slipped out of the realm of religion, the closing sentence reminds us of the difference between honest and dishonest religion: 'The evil person has forgotten what longing is', for he 'only knows its opposite, assent to what is'.[103]

Anyone with a passing knowledge of the joint work with Adorno, *Dialectic of Enlightenment*, will recognise in these comments the pattern of their treatments of myth, morality, culture-industry and anti-Semitism. Here, we find the argument that at any moment of enlightenment – beginning with the ancient Greeks – a moment of barbarism is not far behind.[104] In fact, they are two sides of the same coin: the more one pushes the side of enlightenment to

---

[100] Horkheimer 1978, p. 162; Horkheimer 1991a, pp. 287–8.
[101] See the excellent collection on Kant and radical evil in Copjec (ed.) 1996.
[102] Horkheimer 1978, p. 162; Horkheimer 1991a, p. 288.
[103] Ibid.
[104] See also Horkheimer 1978, pp. 144–5, 180–1, 200–2; Horkheimer 1991a, pp. 246, 324–5, 357–9.

its dialectical extreme, the more do the various manifestations of barbarism show up. But what this brief comment on 'evil in history' reveals is that the dialectic of enlightenment may also appear in a dialectic of evil. I am not arguing that the dialectic of evil is the *fons et origo* of the dialectic of enlightenment, or any other comparable dialectic, since I have argued elsewhere that any claim to the superiority of theology for historical or ontological reasons must be subjected to a rigorous process of relativising in which theology becomes merely one mode of thinking about such matters.[105] In light of Horkheimer's comments, we can see the likeness to Paul's reflections on good, evil, sin, law and grace in Romans 7. As Paul writes in Verse 19, 'I do not do the good I want, but the evil I do not want is what I do'. However, at the moment Horkheimer and Paul touch one another, they move apart. Paul argues that the knowledge of evil comes from the law, which raises his awareness of evil but does not offer a way out, not because the law is itself problematic (after all, it is supposed to come from God), but because he can do no good on his own initiative; for that he must rely entirely on God through Christ.

This dialectic of exacerbation is but the second manifestation of the dialectic of evil in Horkheimer's thought. The third really constitutes an admission that the question cannot be resolved, for, in a comment called 'Difficulties with Evil',[106] Horkheimer rolls out a series of contradictory ways of dealing with evil. He finds that the positive presence of evil generates an absurdity, for one cannot actually profess evil through speech in any meaningful fashion. But, then, is evil, in a conventional theological opposition, merely an absence of the good? Not quite, for there is what may be called an opacity in every belief, a moment that manifests itself as idolatry. It may also be, he argues elsewhere, a form of temptation: faced with the impotence and powerlessness of the good and unable to love the good for these reasons, the temptation to sup with the devil is far too great.[107] So, now, Horkheimer begins to undo his earlier statement that the positivity of evil is absurd, for it turns out that whenever we engage in the tricky business of honest speech – aware of its vanity without giving up on naïveté, of its impotence while believing in the need for truth – we cannot avoid realising that evil is necessary. But, then, what does that

---

[105] See Boer 2009a, pp. 205–52.
[106] Horkheimer 1978, p. 115; Horkheimer 1991a, pp. 190–1.
[107] Horkheimer 1978, p. 146; Horkheimer 1991a, p. 248.

mean? Is evil good? Does it serve the good in a metaphorical sense? Or does it become the necessary opposite to good, as in gnostic dualism, from which salvation must free us? In sum, evil may be presence, absence, opacity, temptation, necessity, or good (as either serving the good or a dualistic opposite).

Horkheimer does not, in the end, opt for any one formulation, since he sees problems in each one and is ready to allow objections to each and every take on evil. I would suggest that the problem of evil pushes Horkheimer to resort not only to a conventional dialectic with its opposite poles, but to explore a plural dialectic in which a number of possibilities vie with one another. But that opens up quite a different approach to his contrast between good and bad religion, between resistance and betrayal.

Conclusion: modalities of the dialectic of religion

On a number of occasions now, I have espied a more desirable dialectical approach to theology in Horkheimer's texts and sunk into those sections with some pleasure. But, by and large, I have traced a great dividing range: on one, well-watered, side is religion as resistance to the ways of the world, usually due to a longing for another order of justice and love for one's enemy; on the other, much drier side (in the rain-shadow), religion becomes betrayal and compromise, in which the desire for the other becomes identical with desire for the formation of power, usually in the state, or perhaps it gives up what is distinctive about religion and seeks to express itself in the terms of that world (as in liberal theology). The problem with this approach, which is quite pervasive in Horkheimer's thought, is that it trades on a well-worn but problematic position: one identifies the authentic core of a religion like Judaism or Christianity and from there it becomes possible to discern its distortions and abuses. The problem is not merely who decides what is authentic and for what reason, but also the very notion of what is authentic in the first place. Christianity is overflowing with examples of the search for an original core that does away with all the accretions of time, examples that are guilty of both falling into the pattern they decry and of constructing some pristine core than never existed.

So what are the other possibilities? One is a grudging admission that compromise was and is necessary for survival, without giving up on the idea of what is authentic. We found this above in the treatment of the state, in which Christianity's sidling up to Constantine enabled his lavish support and thereby the 'success' of Christianity. Any movement that had stuck with the teachings and examples of Christ would have run into the mud soon enough, as the sad litany of rebellious movements has shown all too well. The achievements of Christian societies and cultures would simply not have been possible, even if they are spattered with blood and gore. Horkheimer makes a comparable move when he considers the survival of Judaism, which is the result of the much-derided obstinacy of Jews. Without that hard-headedness which kept them apart from European society through the long centuries of the middle ages, diasporic Judaism would not have stood a chance.[108]

Yet a dialectic of survival, however realistic, is at best a bitter dialectic. It evinces a sad realisation of what is perhaps necessary without giving up on the pattern of authenticity and betrayal. Little better is what may be called a prophetic dialectic – in which the prognostications of someone with whom one disagrees turn out to be correct. Here, I think of Horkheimer's reflections on Theodor Herzl, widely acknowledged as a key figure in the founding of Zionism. Herzl argued that there was no place for Jews in Europe, that the path to pluralistic toleration would turn out to be a dead end, and that the only option for the Jews was a state in which they would find protection from the persecution they had suffered for so long. And, so, Herzl argued for a different type of assimilation, one that drew on the growth of patriotism, the development of nation-states and the patterns of European colonialism. Despite Horkheimer's profound criticisms of Zionism, he admits that the 'saddest aspect of contemporary history, saddest for the Jews as well as for Europe, is that Zionism has proved a true prophet [*daß der Zionismus recht behielt*]'.[109]

Is there something less depressing than Horkheimer's assessment? I would suggest that the first glimmers appear in his comments on the deep pragmatism and the creative tension of religion, as well as his argument that the time of compromise nurtured the seeds of rebellion. As for pragmatism, on one of the few occasions Horkheimer writes of religions such as Buddhism or Islam, he notes both the synthetic, artificial nature of all religions and the credit that must be given to believers for realising that they are indeed manipulatory

---

[108] Horkheimer 1978, p. 119; Horkheimer 1991a, p. 195.
[109] Horkheimer 1996, p. 110; Horkheimer 1985g, p. 167.

concoctions.[110] One gets the sense that Horkheimer admires the way people can both realise that religions are artificial and still believe – much like the way believers continue to pray even though they know very well that prayer is impotent, or the way lovers continue to love in full knowledge of the social and psychological conditions of love, or the way one can set aside scepticism while being cognisant of the reasons for such doubts.[111] Further, Horkheimer does broach in passing the suggestion – so dear to Ernst Bloch – that the negative side of religion, its inveterate tendency to compromise with power, actually helped to nurture its 'indwelling protest [*innewohnenden Widerspruch*]'.[112] We can detect a sense of the necessity of this compromise, a sense that goes beyond the need for survival: the ability to survive and even flourish through compromise sustains the perpetual need for renewal until at last it can take new forms in both the theism and atheism of the Enlightenment.

Further, on the matter of creative tension he writes: 'That the prevailing, worse order aroused it [a just, right order] and justified it, yet simultaneously denied its fulfilment, gave it its productive forces, and it is this force which has run down in the West'.[113] There is obviously the negative last clause of this sentence, in which the creative tension of a suspended and permanently hoped-for just order that generates all manner of possibilities has begun to run out of steam. Yet the very idea of a justified yet denied, hoped-for yet unfulfilled, promised yet constantly out-of-reach other world is at least a more positive dialectic. More importantly, it also brings us within range of what is the most profound assessment of religion in Horkheimer's texts – the suggestion that the opposition between authentic and inauthentic religion, between resistance and compromise, is inherent within Christianity and, indeed, Judaism.

At least two perceptive moments appear when the full dialectic is on display, the first in a brief exegesis of Psalm 91 and the other concerning theology itself. In his comments on the Psalm (as noted above, an altered version of the ninth verse appears on his gravestone), Horkheimer points out that the name of God has been used to justify all manner of bloodthirsty injustices including the Crusades and the Inquisition. Yet, on this occasion, he does not suggest

[110] Horkheimer 1978, p. 123; Horkheimer 1991a, pp. 203–4.
[111] Horkheimer 1978, p. 206; Horkheimer 1991a, pp. 368–9.
[112] Horkheimer 1978, p. 185; Horkheimer 1991a, p. 330.
[113] Ibid.

that such moments are distortions, offering a counterpoise of resistance and love for neighbour; instead, the position of rebellion emerges from those more vicious manifestations: 'its own love for the truth, its contempt for manipulation by unscrupulous cliques, finally even that faith *owes itself to that which it denounces* [*sich verdanken, den er denunziert*]'.[114] Here, we have a full dialectic, for if compromise is a betrayal of authentic religion, then that authentic form owes itself to and is a response to those oppressive forms. Horkheimer goes on in the same vein: 'Still through bitter disdain, with which *it disavows its own manifestation* [*mit dem er die Erfüllung leugnet*], it unconsciously recognises a homesickness that cannot refrain from the thought of paradise'.[115] All that is negative about religion is not a foreign body; it comes from within, is its own manifestation. And precisely because of that manifestation from within do we find the bitter disdain which is at the same time recognition of homesickness, a longing for the other. Horkheimer moves on to explore how refuge (in the psalm) assumes danger, shelter must be shelter from ruin and disaster, but what we have here is a deeply dialectical sense of the ambivalence of Judaism and Christianity. They may run in one or other direction, but they cannot be separated from one another in terms of truth and its distortion.

For the second instance of this dialectic, we need to return to theology itself. A little earlier, I noted an insight concerning the birth of theology: Horkheimer points out that theology arose as a compromise between the demands of the Gospels and power.[116] It is not that theology betrayed itself once the Church found itself inside the halls of power, but that theology was born of this compromise. I cannot emphasise this insight enough, for it goes beyond arguments such as those of Ste. Croix and often Horkheimer himself and it links up with the perceptive late years of E.P. Thompson.[117] For Horkheimer – at least at this moment – theology is an enormously ingenious and acute – if somewhat compromised – discipline, for it realised that for the Church to survive the words of Christ and the right of the stronger had to be brought together, that the laws of heaven and the laws of earth should not remain at implacable odds with one another. Theology worked overtime to carve out space for Christianity in a corrupt and sinful world, seeking a way for people of all classes to find their

---

[114] Horkheimer 2006, p. 117; Horkheimer 1985o, pp. 208–9; emphasis added.
[115] Horkheimer 2006, p. 117; Horkheimer 1985o, p. 209; emphasis added.
[116] Horkheimer 1996, p. 36; Horkheimer 1985h, pp. 174–5.
[117] See Chapters Two and Three.

place in the new order. And the results, as Horkheimer is perfectly willing to admit, are some of the great achievements of human culture – architecture, art, complex systems of thought such as the artful patchwork of scholasticism with its complete worldview that gave people for centuries a sense of their place in the universe, or the breakthrough of the Reformation which fed into a stream that led to human rights, civil liberty, reason and the importance of the individual.[118] But each achievement is mired in the misery of the masses and intolerance to those who differed, born of that compromise which lies at the heart of Christian theology.

Let us take this insight into theology's inherent tension a little further. Horkheimer presents that tension as a devious and (grudgingly) brilliant effort at *Realpolitik*, but there are also matters of form and content that broadcast such a tension at all levels. In its effort to apply systematic categories, derived in part from Greek philosophy, to the narratives of that new genre, the Gospel, theology enacted a compromise in form and content. In form, there is the tension between story and system, between variant narratives and coherent doctrine, while, in content, there was the obvious tension between outright resistance, especially by Christ, and the statements found elsewhere that one should obey the rulers of this world (Romans 13: 1–2), comply with the powers, principalities and magistrates (Titus 3: 1), submit to kings and governors (1 Peter 2: 13), and offer prayers and intercessions for all in authority (1 Timothy 2: 1–2). Or, as Horkheimer observes, the utterances of the biblical prophets stand side by side with what he calls 'biblical patriotism', embodied above all in the stories of Joshua's campaigns to conquer the land of Canaan.[119]

I would go one step further and argue that, while theology shows up all the tensions of its first emergence between the non-conformity of the early-Christian movement and the conformity that came with the first taste of power, it actually embodies a tension in content that was bequeathed to it from the texts that were so important to the early Christians – the sacred texts that eventually became the Bible. However, even this last observation has its own dialectical turn: Christian theology did not inherit a ready-made set of sacred texts, nicely copied and bound in the newly invented codices; rather, it played an active part in deciding which texts would be included and which excluded

---

[118] Horkheimer 1996, p. 37; Horkheimer 1985h, p. 175.
[119] Horkheimer 1996, p. 115; Horkheimer 1985g, p. 171.

in the variant canons. Here, we must keep in mind a number of features of this messy period: the Christian canon was not finalised until the fourth century CE, after Christianity became a world-power and as a result of imperial pressure for unity and conformity; theology was, as always, a jungle with myriad paths (Arianism, Nestorianism, mono/miaphysitism and so on); communities that followed these variant-positions favoured different texts; and the canon was never finalised as one canon, for multiple canons have always existed. Horkheimer has happened upon far more concerning theology than he may well have realised, for it is a compromise at all levels.

What can be done with this inherent contradiction at the heart of Christianity? We may take it as is and admit that the Christian, and indeed the Jewish, tradition is far too complex to develop any sense of what is best within it, for as soon as one does so, another contrary position will emerge from within the sacred texts themselves. That leaves us without any political options in a 'broad church' which includes a full range of political and theological positions. Such an approach is fine (to some extent) if one's primary purpose and commitment is to preserve an institution like the Church or the Synagogue. But neither I nor Horkheimer are impressed with such an approach. Another possibility would be to argue that this contradictory situation has much to do with the deeply conflictual context in which the Bible and the early Christians first arose – a situation fraught with imperial repression, constant insurrections, systemic brutality, and the clash of modes of production. This is a necessary step and one that I have argued in detail elsewhere: the differing positions and internal contradictions of the New Testament, especially the thought of Paul, are signals of the effort to mediate and resolve ideologically a tension-ridden political and socio-economic situation in which the Romans viciously imposed a slave-based social formation over an older formation in Palestine and the ancient Near East.[120] Yet another approach is to dig into Althusser's idea of ideological state-apparatuses and argue that a movement and institution like Christianity or Judaism – part of the apparatus of religion – is one riven with vital ideological conflicts.[121]

---

[120] Boer 2009c. See also the fuller discussion in the conclusion to this book. This older social formation I have named the 'sacred economy'. See Boer 2007c.

[121] Althusser 1971, pp. 127–86; see Boer 2007a, pp. 107–62.

On this occasion, I would like to suggest yet another option, namely to take sides. Given that Christianity is split by all manner of tensions, due to the nature of this multifarious institution and to its origins in a social and economic context in profound transition, then the next step is to decide for those elements within it that push not for compromise, abuse and room for the odd tyrant, despot or even oppressive collective, but for resistance, insurrection, and non-conformity. By now, we have come back to the beginning, except that we do so after an entirely new way of reading the deep rhythm of Horkheimer's take on religion.

Chapter Two

The Dissent of E.P. Thompson

This gave a particular moral resonance to their protest, whether voiced in Owenite or biblical language.[1]

My concern is a central insight of Edward Palmer Thompson: his slow (re-)discovery of a political tension between reaction and revolution at the heart of Christian theology. Those accustomed to the other Thompson may find this point a little strange. After all, is he not the great proponent of 'social history' from the bottom up,[2] the political activist (especially with the Campaign for Nuclear Disarmament) who was also a scholar, the one who recovered the history of a distinctly British radical tradition,[3] and a great story-teller?[4]

---

[1] Thompson 1966, p. 295.

[2] An approach first presented with *The Making of the English Working Class*, a work that fundamentally changed the way history was written. This is a history from the side of the losers, the silenced, from those who left few records barring the ones of their opponents – the labourers, peasants, the poor without work, the barely literate or illiterate and their clubs, friendly or benefit-societies, illegal trade-unions, occasional insurrections, religious groups and sects who met in any number of homes or taverns.

[3] Although it borders every now and then on English exceptionalism. See, for example, 'It was perhaps a unique formation, this British working class of 1832' (Thompson 1966, p. 830), and his essay 'The Peculiarities of the English' (Thompson 1978, pp. 245–301).

[4] The best storytellers are those who can tell a tale that changes the dominant story itself. Friedrich Engels was one of these: I am not the first to see Thompson's *The Making of the English Working Class* as an updated and extended version of Engels's *The Condition of the Working-Class in England* (Engels 1975f; Engels 1974), but I am struck by the way that they share a deep affinity in their storytelling ability. Michel

Of course, he is all of these things, but I am interested in the role of theology in Thompson's work. He really cannot escape religion, since it is a major factor in his favoured historical period – British history in the late eighteenth and early nineteenth centuries.[5] As a historian, he is interested in religion because so often at crucial moments 'religion *mattered*'.[6] What we find is that the tension I have named – between the revolutionary and reactionary tendencies of Christian theology – is the key to his extended treatments of the various streams of English dissent. Out of this mix, Thompson devotes most of his energy to the mild and compromised dissent of methodism and then, in his last work, the more radical dissenting groups embodied particularly in William Blake. However, there is a difference between these two foci: in his study of methodism Thompson stumbles across the insight into the political ambivalence of Christian theology despite himself; indeed, he is not fully aware that he has made a discovery at all. By contrast, when we come to William Blake in *Witness Against the Beast*, the tension between reaction and revolution has become the organising principle of the whole book. Or, rather, in the comments on methodism in *The Making of the English Working Class*, Thompson emphasises the reactionary side of Christianity, while, in his Blake-study, the radical and revolutionary side comes to the fore.

Foucault was another. Indeed, Foucault's great skill was to tell a different narrative of how we got here and where we are going. In order to generate a different future, he rewrote the past. China Miéville is another. This member of the International Socialist Tendency has been busy reshaping fantasy-fiction – with a good dose of horror- and science-fiction – into a distinctly political genre. In the world of Bas-Lag, with a surfeit of imaginative reconstruction, oppression and revolution are but a breath away. See Miéville 1998, 2000, 2002, 2004b, 2005. Thompson is one of these, and you get the sense very early on that he loves to tell a good, long story well into the night.

[5] The debate and secondary literature on Thompson, especially *The Making of the English Working Class*, is vast. It is not my place here to examine his treatments of experience, the consciousness of agents, class, the mistrust of theory, the charge of 'culturalism', the heated debates with Perry Anderson, and what has been called 'pointillism' (building up a coherent picture from disparate materials). On these matters see, for instance, Blackledge 2006, pp. 169–78; McLennan 1981, pp. 113–28; Kaye 1984, pp. 182–5, 188, 201–2. As far as Thompson's dealings with religion are concerned, many simply skip by the question as quickly as possible – for example, Dworkin 1997; Palmer 1994. I have, however, benefitted from the excellent study on Thompson and methodism by Hempton and Walsh 2002 as well as the survey by Kaye 1984, pp. 167–220, who gives some much needed attention to Thompson's treatment of methodism. See also the useful works by Dreyer 1986, Jaffe 1989, Currie and Hartwell 1965, pp. 640–1, Gilbert 1979, Heathorn 1998, Griswold 1987, and Taylor 1995.

[6] Thompson 1978, p. 268.

However, I will not say more about that tension here since this chapter is, at least in its first half, an exercise in detective-work. So, like an amateur sleuth, I follow a series of hints that lead me on. Focussing on *The Making of the English Working Class*, I begin with Thompson's own condemnation of methodism as psychic terror and political reaction. The problem is that, throughout his analysis, more and more political radicals turn up in the chapels and Bible-classes – a long string of methodists end up as Luddites, organisers of the Peterloo protest, among the Chartists and so on. Thompson is too good a historian not to deal with these matters, so I seize on a number of contradictions and passing hints in Thompson's account which suggest far more than he is willing to recognise at this stage (in 1966) of his work.

Once I have uncovered what runs beneath this intriguing treatment of methodism, I move to a close analysis of the book on William Blake – the engraver, autodidact, poet, artist, dissenting Christian and political radical for whom Thompson always had a soft spot.[7] The reason: within the beliefs, social structure and politics of radical dissent the 'dormant seeds of political Radicalism' lay, 'ready to germinate whenever planted in a beneficial and hopeful social context'.[8] Indeed, Thompson wishes at times that the evangelical revival which swept through England in the late eighteenth century had originated not with the methodists but with one of these groups where an underground tradition of political radicalism was ready to spring forth. So, in the second major section of this chapter, I offer an intimate commentary on Thompson's study of Blake, for the specific purpose of discerning what Thompson's take on theology is by this late stage in his life.

The main texts I consider are those I have mentioned: *The Making of the English Working Class* and *Witness Against the Beast: William Blake and the Moral Law*.[9] There is, however, one further text. It is difficult to find, held only in rare book-collections in but a few libraries. Yet, in Thompson's *Infant and Emperor: Poems for Christmas*,[10] we come across some rather good poetry that evokes a distinctly apocalyptic feel. The poems were written in response to global political events and Thompson's involvement in the nuclear-disarmament

---

[7] We find favourable references to Blake already in *The Making of the English Working Class* – see Thompson 1966, pp. 41, 50–2, 57, 94, 97, 175, 374, 446, 832.

[8] Thompson 1966, p. 36; see further pp. 97–8, 148–9, 427–8.

[9] Thompson 1966; Thompson 1993b. See also Thompson 1976b.

[10] Thompson 1983.

campaign. But the most surprising feature of them is that Thompson gives voice to his own political radicalism through poems that recast nothing less than the birth- and infancy-narratives concerning Jesus. A commentary on these poems forms the third and final section of this chapter.

Corrupt parsons and the impetuous Irish

I begin, then, with the passionate criticism of methodism, although I do so by means of small detour – a comparison (and thereby a foil for the treatment of methodism) with Thompson's relatively superficial treatments of the established Church of England and the Irish-Catholic labourers who arrived en masse in England. Too much in the pockets of 'Old Corruption', the established Church is, with the rarest exceptions,[11] full of absentee-parsons, plural livings,[12] desperate defenders of the corrupt status quo as well as the new factory-system,[13] propagators of the theory that poverty encourages people to work and not waste idle hours in drunkenness.[14] It is for these reasons that the Church is subject to the hatred of the starving rural communities[15] as well as the radical press and its cartoonists. Having long ago abandoned the close connections between religious life, rites of passage, and popular customs and calendars, and having done its dirty little deal with the gentry whereby parsons were often magistrates and the gentry's sons took up rural parsonages, the Church had clearly sided with the vested interests of wealth and privilege.[16] Nothing sums up the Church of England better than the image of the local parson at Middleton, who, during a mob-rampage through the village in search of Painites and Reformers in April 1794, 'stood

---

[11] I could find only two exceptions in a book of over 800 pages. The first is Thomas Walker, a churchman, Manchester-reformer and agitator for the repeal of the Test and Corporation Acts (Thompson 1966, p. 52). The second is the curate of the isolated Cragg Dale, who spoke out against child-labour in the mills and found himself the target of persecution by the mill-owners (Thompson 1966, p. 347).

[12] E.g. Thompson 1966, p. 222.

[13] E.g. Thompson 1966, p. 346.

[14] Thompson 1966, p. 277.

[15] E.g. Thompson 1966, p. 233.

[16] Thompson 1993a, pp. 50–1.

on a hillock pointing out fugitives to the ruffians: "There goes one.... That's a Jacobin; that's another"'.[17]

The other caricature is the Irish Catholics. Arriving in waves throughout the period of his study, the Irish men are pictured as hard-working labourers engaged in the purely physical and unskilled tasks at the bottom of industrial society – such as working the docks on the Thames or as coal-heavers – that the English working-class men could no longer do, weakened as they were by the factory-system. That the Irish, already accustomed to less-than-subsistence living conditions, would accept work for much less pay than the English made them a boon for employers. But the Irish also brought their hatred of British colonial rule and a republican spirit. The recent history of some of the most brutal counter-revolutionary repression by English colonial forces in Ireland did nothing to make the Irish feel favourable towards the English. With the white terror that followed the crushing of the United Irishmen's rebellion of 1798 and the subsequent Act of Union in 1800, the British Empire perfected its much-hated techniques of cruel repression that it was happy to exercise wherever and whenever it felt the need.

The Irish also brought their priests. Integrated with the peasants and working poor as no other clergy, not least because they shared their lives of poverty with them, only the priest had the authority and reverence that allowed him into the back-streets of Irish quarters where no other man of authority dared to go. Trusted, not bound to employers or magistrates or the ruling class, sharing the national aspirations of the Irish, travelling often between Ireland and England, the priest provided a living, daily connection for a population up-rooted from their old way of life. Two passages paint a vivid picture of the priesthood:

> When the Irish poor came to England, the priesthood used every means –
> devoted ministration (with a knowledge of the mind of their parishioners
> which no English clergy could equal), psychological terror, financial aid and
> financial extortion, pressure on relatives, comfort in distress – to maintain

---

[17] Thompson 1966, p. 116 Comparable is the story from 1743 of the vicar of Walsall leading a mob he had roused (not an uncommon pastime among the clergy) to the house where the Wesleyan preacher John Nelson was holding a service: 'At the door of the house...it was the parson who cried out to the mob, "Pull down the house! Pull down the house!"' (Thompson 1966, p. 69). See also Thompson 1966, pp. 37, 69, 222, 233, 351, 562, 571.

their hold on their flock; and they trusted to the only form of evangelism likely to succeed in Protestant England: the birth-rate.[18]

...[T]he most enduring cultural tradition which the Irish peasantry brought – to the third and fourth generation – into England was that of a semi-feudal nationalist Church. In the most squalid cellars there might still be found some of the hocus-pocus of Romanism, the candlesticks, the crucifix, and the 'showy-coloured prints of saints and martyrs' alongside the print of O'Connell, the 'Liberator'.[19]

Thompson was known for urging us to be aware of the messiness and complexity of history, but the Irish and their Catholicism come through as a little too one-dimensional.[20] This picture is not that far from some of the colonial administrators in Ireland with their dismissal of the backward and superstitious Irish. So also with the Irish labourers: here, Thompson's reliance on accounts from the time affects his own judgement – the Irish are driven by personal rather than economic incentives, are generous but quarrelsome, hard workers but impulsive, moral but clannish, given readily to trade-unions and 'combinations', with none of the frugal discipline, nor indeed the forethought and application that puritanism and methodism supplied. In short, they are pre-Industrial Revolution labourers, alternating between immense energy and 'boisterous relaxation'.[21] Even when he comes to the natural connections between Irish-nationalist opposition to the British ruling class and the various currents of radicalism and agitation in the period 1790 to 1850, Thompson falls back into caricature: here we find 'the confluence of sophisticated political Radicalism with a more primitive and excitable revolutionism'.[22] To be sure, he does point out that for all their identification with their parishioners, there were no clergy who became working-class leaders, for the Roman-Catholic

---

[18] Thompson 1966, p. 438.

[19] Thompson 1966, p. 439.

[20] There is but one moment where he does show some complexity, namely with the changing patterns of Irish immigration. Thus, among the earlier Irish immigrants there were a good number of radical, 'Jacobinical' dissenters from Ulster. Only later, when the post-rebellion suppression found its stride, when the potato-crops failed yet again in 1821–2 and when peasant freeholders were evicted between 1828 and 1830, were the Irish immigrants predominantly Roman-Catholic. But these moments are far too rare in his treatment of the Irish Catholics in the early nineteenth century.

[21] Thompson 1966, p. 432.

[22] Thompson 1966, p. 443.

Church was keen to avoid drawing too much attention to its growing presence. Even here, I wonder whether his judgement is sure, for was it not the
Irish situation and independence from England that was the primary political
concern? The Church's support of the compromising O'Connell is less a sign
of its political weakness[23] than its primary agenda.

The 'psychic terror' of methodism

These treatments of the established Church and Irish Catholicism are rather
one-dimensional. By comparison, the various streams of dissent come in for
intense scrutiny. The reason for such an extended treatment is obvious: for
good or ill, dissent played a large hand in the English political radicalism
that helped shape the English working class – for good in the case of radical
dissent, for ill in the case of the methodists. Thompson is less interested in
the older forms, the non-conformist groups that had become staid such as the
presbyterians, baptists, congregationalists and independents. By contrast, he
is fascinated, drawn and often repelled, by those that the 'uneducated' and
poor took up with gusto – groups like the Muggletonians and the methodists. Thompson may have been drawn by the former, but he was repelled in
no uncertain terms by the latter.

For Thompson, methodism was nothing better than a curse for the working poor. As a religious movement with its own theology and organisational
practice, methodism was, he argues, simply too conservative to make any
contribution to the development of a distinct working-class consciousness.
Thompson makes three specific points against methodism. It is a form of 'religious terrorism'[24] that visited 'psychological atrocities'[25] and deformities upon
the working poor (especially the children), all in the name of moral rescue.
Further, he argues that methodism provided the crucial 'inner compulsion'
that ensured the fundamental shift in work-rhythms needed for the workers
of new mills and factories. Sobriety, discipline, foresight and subdued application to the repetitive tasks at hand all constituted a massive shift from the
rural patterns of intense work and festivals tied so closely to the seasons. It

---

[23] Thompson 1966, p. 442.
[24] Thompson 1966, p. 378.
[25] Thompson 1966, p. 377.

was the methodists who provided the workers with the inner drive – for religious and personal reasons – to make such a fundamental shift in the patterns of work. Finally, the Toryism of its cranky founder, John Wesley, ensured that there would be a consistent strain that supported the divinely ordained rulers. Any alternative position was swiftly cut down or expelled by the Wesleys (both John and Charles). Let me say a little more concerning each of these features of methodism in Thompson's analysis.

Religious terrorism

As for psychological atrocities, high on the list are the need for repentance, conversion from sin, recourse to the emotions and sexual repression. Concerning conversion, Thompson's main point is that it marks 'the psychic ordeal in which the character-structure of the rebellious pre-industrial labourer or artisan was violently recast into that of the submissive industrial worker'.[26] Conversion, however, was not some careful and rational consideration of the pros and cons and then a decision for Christ. It was an emotionally charged affair, touching the soul with cries, shouts, temporary paralysis, sobs of relief and so on. I must admit that I too find such things uncomfortable. If I happen, for my sins, to be in the company of charismatics, with their hands in the air, closed eyes, speaking in 'tongues' and loud halleluiahs, then I find all this exhibitionism a bit much. Our modern-day charismatics are really the current versions of methodist revivalism, and even that was but one moment in a much longer history of revivalism. Yet, for all my discomfort, it does not mean I share his condemnation. He finds these emotional outbursts nothing less than signs of psychological disturbance. In the violent upheaval of conversion, the emotional energies of the working poor were redirected to the 'psychic trap' of the box-like methodist chapel stuck in the midst of industrial districts.

A rather grim picture, is it not? Thompson goes further to argue that methodists were not happy with a once-off conversion, for people readily went back to their former ways of life once the emotional charge of the revival rally was over. In response, the methodists argued that conversion was not simply a case of giving up one's former life of sin and becoming a new person in the

---

[26] Thompson 1966, pp. 367–8.

Lord. Rather, the trick in this case was to introduce the category of 'back-sliding'. Salvation and grace were always provisional, dependent on the continuation of one's new life. In particular (and in order to avoid salvation through works), converts were expected to offer their services to the Church (Sunday-school teacher, flower-arranger, cleaner and what have you), to feed themselves spiritually through Bible-reading, prayer and attendance at worship, and, most importantly, exhibit a life of virtue, of sober and frugal labour. Should one spend a night on the town only to wake with a massive hangover, not attend worship as often as before, ease off at work or stop playing the organ on Sunday, then one faced the dreadful path of backsliding to one's old life. Needless to say, confession and forgiveness were needed all over again, subject to honest examination of one's soul. All of which ensured a continual surveillance of one's moral life to ensure that the new life came out on top and the old life did not reclaim you.

This pattern led to the characteristic tension in methodism between moments of emotional release, usually during the Sunday worship-service, and the calm, disciplined life of week-day labour in factory or mill. A somewhat obvious analysis would suggest that such release was a necessary safety-valve in the context of dehumanising and soul-destroying factory-work (much like Alexis de Tocqueville argued for the success of Christianity in the new cut-throat commercial world of the United States at about the same time),[27] that it was no different from the weekend-drunkeness and carousing with which working people relieve the sheer drudgery of week-day work, that it was a survival mechanism, or even that it was the new shape of festival-licence and release that had characterised pre-industrial work. By contrast, Thompson takes a pop-psychological approach. These intermittent outbursts are 'a ritualised form of psychic masturbation', 'Sabbath orgasms', the redirection of otherwise dangerous and revolutionary currents, indeed 'a central disorganisation of the human personality'.[28]

I cannot help thinking that apart from Thompson's sheer dislike of this 'enthusiasm' (in the original sense of being filled with the 'spirit') he simply cannot come to terms with the sense and feeling of conversion. Whatever the real outcome may be, it does feel like one's life has changed for good, that

---

[27] Tocqueville 2003.
[28] Thompson 1966, pp. 368 and 369.

there is a massive turn-around and that nothing will be the same afterwards. This absence in his analysis is even stranger if we think of the experience of political conversion to which Marxism itself is not immune: any militant, political movement, especially with the rich history and depth of Marxism, also has its converts, people who have come to a blinding realisation that Marxism is on the right track and that they wish to devote the rest of their lives to the Cause. Now, Thompson is correct in pointing out that religious conversion is often a redirection of other, more social and political energies. There is a distinct family-resemblance between religious and political conversion. After all, the original Greek term from the New Testament, *metanoia*, means taking on a wholly new mind or perspective [*noia*] that is both 'after' the former one and 'among' (both are senses of *meta*) a collective of those who are like-minded. *Metanoia* is, therefore, a fundamental change of mind, whether political or religious.

Thompson does not argue this, however. He wants to pile up as many indicators of methodism's psychic terror as he can, the last of which is sexual perversion. The question left begging is precisely what the methodists were masturbating – psychically – over. Here he draws on the symbolism of the hymns and finds a feminised Christ endowed with a bleeding vagina.

> 'Tis there I would always abide,
> And never a moment depart,
> Conceal'd in the cleft of Thy side,
> Eternally held in thy heart.[29]

Or, to be more precise, the hole in Christ's side is a result of the soldier's spear (performed, we are told in John 19: 34, to see whether Christ was dead – he was, apparently, since blood and water flowed out). Not quite as explicit in expressing their wishes as their one-time brethren, the Moravians, the Wesleyans yearned often enough to rest in Christ's open side. Add to all of this a potent cocktail of maternal imagery (Christ who loves his children and the desire to return to the womb), self-mortification (through personal discipline to tame the desires of the flesh), sado-masochism (the glorification of Christ's death and the wish to take up his cross), the cult of death (the fear

---

[29] Thompson 1966, p. 372.

of hell and the yearning to get to heaven) and the systematic physical and psychological abuse of children as corrupt and evil natural-born sinners.[30]

It is no surprise that Thompson finds all of this 'perplexing and unpleasant',[31] so much so that it 'is difficult to conceive of a more essential disorganisation of human life'.[32] Now, on one level, I want ask what is wrong with masturbation? Perhaps Thompson would prefer an actual physical masturbation took place? But does not all masturbation deal with the realm of fantasy, some more vivid and 'extreme', some less so? At another level, as I suggested earlier, the methodist emotionalism on a Sunday was but another form of the release, one that the grog-shop supplied before one was converted. At yet another level, Thompson shows that he is merely a prude, finding this entire sexual emotionalism a little too lacking in decorum.

But is it just the methodists who are guilty of such onanism? In a brief footnote, Thompson admits that 'this obsession' – that concerning the essential dirtiness and evil of the penis and the resultant unproductive impulses – 'came to permeate English culture – especially working class culture'.[33] Now, one could argue that Thompson attributes this pervasive 'obsession' to the methodists, that they were the ones who bequeathed to us this abiding gift. But he actually opens up another argument entirely: the methodists did not merely tap into, but they actually gave the clearest expression to this deeper tendency in English culture. This is the culture of smutty jokes, the pornographic magazine hidden in the garden-shed, the dirty story told to one's juvenile mates in a quiet corner. Beneath this superficial culture of niceness and politeness, one can hardly expect anything other than a seething mass of unrealised and repressed desires.

Moral machinery

The second major feature supplied by methodism was, according to Thompson, a compliant and disciplined industrial labour-force – what he

---

[30] We may also add to this general condemnation the ban in the early years of the nineteenth century – in the hands of the pedestrian and conservative successor to Wesley, Jabez Bunting – on children and indeed adults learning to write in the Sunday-schools. Reading was fine, for one needed it to read the Bible, but writing was a secular business and profanation of the Sabbath.

[31] Thompson 1966, p. 370.

[32] Thompson 1966, p. 372.

[33] Thompson 1966, p. 370.

calls a 'methodised' moral machinery. That machinery included submission, the infamous methodical ordering of one's life, discipline, frugality, diligence and 'moral opacity',[34] all of which suited the (often methodist) mill-owners, manufacturers and foremen very well indeed. Nothing makes a factory-owner happier than quiescent and obedient workers. To methodism's eternal shame, argues Thompson, it did not oppose industrialisation and the factory-system in any way. In short, in addition to Weber's Calvinists and Tawney's puritans,[35] Thompson wishes to add the methodists as crucial players in the transition to fully-fledged capitalism. But with this crucial difference: Weber and Tawney focused largely on the effects of Calvinism and puritanism on a growing middle class, with its combination of acquisitiveness, individualism, self-discipline and freedom. Thompson wants something more, and it is provided by Eric Fromm's idea of inner compulsion.[36] It is not enough to impose such work-disciplines upon people, for they will resist them. The key, then, is to get the labourer to appropriate these values as his or her own; in short, to turn workers into their own slave-drivers. This is precisely what methodism, as a religious movement of and largely by the working poor, succeeded in doing – to bring about, through inner conviction, a fundamental shift in work-patterns from pre-industrial to industrial labour, from bouts of intense work and celebrated leisure (including the Bacchanalian festivities with their excesses of eating, drinking, sex, dancing, riotous village-'sports' and general carousing)[37] to the week-in week-out regular rhythms of factory-work or the out-work of weavers and so on. It was no less than the mediation of the coercions of industrial labour, with its focus on discipline and order.

Political reaction

As far as the conservative strain is concerned, Thompson is not so dismayed by an unequivocal identification with the ruling class, but rather by methodism's equivocation. Falling 'ambiguously between Dissent and the Establishment',[38] the Wesleyans pledged support for authorities who regarded them with dis-

---

[34] Thompson 1966, p. 355.
[35] Weber 1992; Tawney 1962.
[36] Fromm 2001.
[37] Thompson 1966, pp. 408–10.
[38] Thompson 1966, p. 350.

dain. The state's enemies were their enemies, and they opposed anything that would unsettle or overthrow the status quo. Yet those same authorities did not return the favour, keeping the methodists outside the gates of power. This ambiguity goes back to the founding of methodism, for John Wesley had really hoped to transform the Church of England and only reluctantly realised he would need to move outside the circle of those who rejected his proposed revival of the Church itself. Thompson does grudgingly admit what may well be the best explanation, namely, that, as methodism grew rapidly among the emerging industrial working class, it did not wish to upset the government or established Church any more than need be. The latter could have made things extraordinarily difficult, or at least far more difficult than they were. Yet Thompson cannot forgive the methodists for the long campaign to remove any seditious tint from their ranks. Through the hierarchy's mistrust of the poor taking governance into their own hands, by clamping down hard on outbreaks of more radical streaks and by exercising a hard discipline, the methodist church became, if anything, more conservative. All the same, the very fact that this process was necessary and that it happened brings me back to my initial point: within methodism there was a more radical, even revolutionary streak. The leaders knew it and worked as hard as they could to negate that tendency in whatever way they could.

In Thompson's analysis, the methodists do not come off very well. He agrees wholeheartedly with the assessment of W.E.H. Lecky: 'A more appalling system of religious terrorism, one more fitted to unhinge a tottering intellect and to darken and embitter a sensitive nature, has seldom existed'.[39] Politically, intellectually and emotionally, he finds the whole exercise distasteful and excessive. His reasons are mixed: a dislike for emotionalism and religious fervour (the methodists were simply too enthusiastic), a stronger dislike for political conservatism and the way the methodists played a crucial role in producing, by means of an 'inner compulsion', a labour-force suited to the new industrial rhythms. He is also keen to counter the common position that methodism was the champion of the workers and provided the ideological core of the trade-union movement (he stresses that working-class political organisation was due to its own initiative rather than some paternalistic

---

[39] Quoted from W.E.H. Lecky, *History of England in the Eighteenth Century*. 1891 edn. 3 vols. Volume 3, pp. 77–8, in Thompson 1966, p. 374.

imposition from above).[40] The pages on methodism express the hidden wish that it had never afflicted the rising working class in England and set that class back so much. Indeed, the methodists are tellingly omitted from the list of other dissenting groups such as presbyterians, baptists, congregationalists, quakers and independents, since these groups at least held on to a 'slumbering Radicalism' – embodied clearly in Bunyan's *Pilgrim's Progress* – even when they retreated to the 'kingdom within' when it became apparent that Christ was not about to return and sweep away their persecutors.[41]

Radicals in the ranks

In all of this, it seems to me that Thompson has, for a moment or two, lost his characteristic stress on the complexity and messiness of history.[42] Methodism was a curse on the poor, pure and simple. But, at this point, he faces a problem: how to account for the long string of methodist radicals, whether Luddites, Chartists or one of the many other radical movements? Thompson is too good a historian not to notice these things, but what intrigues me is the way he accounts for them.

First, let me provide a list of all those radical methodists mentioned in Thompson's text. There is 'Bro. M.', who was charged with attending a political meeting rather than a Bible-class in Halifax, and who was, we presume, deprived of his membership. Or the unnamed correspondent from Newcastle,

---

[40] On this point, he stresses again and again how the increasing organisation and discipline of working-class movements, such as the friendly societies and trade-unions, as well as the great orderly protests such as Peterloo, were purely working-class initiatives, that sobriety and discipline were as much radical virtues as methodist (Thompson 1966, pp. 740–2). Even more, he argues that properly working-class culture (over against the tendency for methodism to become the faith of tradesmen and privileged groups of workers) came to reject methodism, or any sort of religion, in many areas by the 1840s (Thompson 1966, pp. 427–8).

[41] Thompson 1966, pp. 29–34.

[42] With two exceptions: the methodist suspicion of poetry, biblical criticism, philosophy and political theory (intellectual enquiry) is countered by the encouragement of interest in sciences such as botany, biology, geology, chemistry, mathematics and applied sciences (useful knowledge). So we get the wonderful image of 'that peculiar phenomenon of early Victorian culture, the nonconformist parson with his hand on the Old Testament and his eye on a microscope' (Thompson 1966, p. 739; see also Thompson 1978, pp. 270–1). The other is the way the methodist 'heresy' of female local preachers, along with the experience of methodist classes, combined with the larger presence of women in factory-labour to give impetus to the participation of women in political-reform movements (Thompson 1966, p. 415).

who speaks of a 'small number of our leaders' who are 'the most determined friends' of the radicals, along with the 'misguided sisterhood' who made their colours.[43] The list goes on: the many local preachers who were 'expelled or "struck off the plan" for political as for religious "backslidings"';[44] the political statements of the ministers of the independent methodists who broke from the methodist connexion when radical lay preachers were expelled in 1819;[45] the use of prophetic biblical texts (Ezekiel 21: 25–8) by the Lancashire conspirators in 1801;[46] the various methodist Jacobins, Luddites, trade-unionists and demonstrators at Peterloo;[47] the Chartist hymns and chapels that derived from the (primitive) methodists, including leaders and lay preachers like Ben Rushton (who was also a Plug Rioter) and William Thornton, or John Skevington from Loughborough, who was both stocking-weaver and local preacher with the primitive methodists;[48] the methodists who took part in the Pentridge uprising of 1817, one of them a local preacher;[49] the deep involvement of Samuel Bamford in the Peterloo demonstration of 1819;[50] the 'Tolpuddle Martyr', George Loveless;[51] the methodist chapel at Ripponlea loaned for a meeting organised by an activist for the ten-hour day;[52] the common cause between chapel and pub during strikes;[53] the old methodist lay preacher at Hebden Bridge who fumed and preached against the evils of the factory-system;[54] the kick-start given women's emancipation through the Wesleyan 'heresy' of women lay preachers and class-leaders that was then enhanced by the greater participation of women in the spinning-mills;[55] the influence of Wesleyanism on the power that the famous oaths of the Luddites and trade-unions had upon its members;[56] the singing of a methodist hymn by the Luddites executed at York

---

[43] Thompson 1966, p. 253.
[44] Thompson 1966, p. 352.
[45] Thompson 1966, p. 393.
[46] Thompson 1966, p. 392.
[47] Thompson 1966, p. 391.
[48] Thompson 1966, pp. 294, 398–9. On the connections between Chartism and radical Christianity see Yeo 1981.
[49] Thompson 1966, p. 394.
[50] Thompson 1966, pp. 394, 680–2.
[51] Thompson 1966, p. 394.
[52] Thompson 1966, p. 346.
[53] Thompson 1966, p. 393.
[54] Thompson 1966, p. 346.
[55] Thompson 1966, p. 415.
[56] Thompson 1966, p. 513.

in 1813, the fact that a number of them were methodists and the demand by the crowds to have burial services for the executed men in the chapels, so much so that the 'fervour of the Old Testament had become assimilated to a class solidarity';[57] the methodist influence in moulding the legend of the 'free-born Englishman' along with the vaguer comment that religious movements number among the 'strongly-based' and 'self-conscious working-class institutions';[58] the 'softer and more humanised' version of methodism that Thompson finds among the weavers at the turn of the nineteenth century;[59] among these same weavers he points out that 'there are two deeply transforming experiences – those of Methodism and of political radicalism';[60] the breakdown of the old and quite despicable English system of deference to the 'higher orders' in which methodism also (although with the qualifier 'despite itself') had a hand;[61] the propensity of the working class to form clubs wherever and whenever they could is also a legacy, in part at least, of methodist influence;[62] the primitive-methodist camp-meetings – large open-air revival-meetings – feed into the growth of organised protests for reform, along with army-veterans, trade-unions and friendly societies;[63] the 'Political Protestants', an organisation that sprang up in the formerly passive Newcastle after the Peterloo massacre and led a mass-protest on 'Radical Monday' (11 October 1819) that included pitmen and sailors and which marked the emergence of Newcastle as a major centre for radical reform.[64] Finally, there was the mix of Christian (or, more specifically, methodist and Moravian) themes with Owenite socialism. Thus, Christian charity and the imagery of 'brotherhood' came together with the common use of Isaiah 61: 6 as a preface to many Owenite societies and stores: 'They helped everyone his neighbour; and every one said to his brother, be of good courage'.

Such lists are always a little tedious and I hardly expect the reader to have gone through this one in detail. But I have provided it to show how persistent

---

[57] This insistence by the crowds flew in the face of the methodist ministers who refused to do the burial-services; see Thompson 1966, pp. 585–7.

[58] Thompson 1966, p. 194.

[59] Thompson 1966, p. 276.

[60] Thompson 1966, p. 294.

[61] Thompson 1966, p. 672.

[62] Thompson 1966, p. 673.

[63] Thompson 1966, p. 680.

[64] Thompson 1966, pp. 690–1.

this other side of methodism is in Thompson's own account, so much so that a good number of methodists took up political radicalism with gusto. Even more, I would like to argue that, even within Thompson's own account, there appears a political tension within methodism.

Now, Thompson can hardly ignore this tension, so let us see what he makes of it. As the following quotations show, he actually sides with the methodist establishment (although he by no means condones it). I begin with Thompson's own assessment:

> But in the years 1790 to 1830 it would be as ridiculous to describe the participation of rebellious Methodist lay preachers and others in extreme Radical agitations as a 'Methodist contribution' to the working-class movement, as it would be to describe the practice of free love among extreme Antinomians as a 'Puritan contribution' towards sexual liberation.[65]

In other words, methodist radicals were exceptions in what was otherwise a reactionary movement. Contrast this statement from Thompson with a quotation from a letter from the congregation in Newcastle to Jabez Bunting, the successor of John Wesley:

> I am glad to say, several members have quitted their classes (for they have adopted almost the whole Methodist economy, the terms 'Class Leaders', 'District Meetings' etc., etc., being perfectly current among them). If men are to be drilled at Missionary and Bible meetings to face a multitude with recollection, and acquire facilities of address, and then begin to employ the mighty moral weapon thus gained to the endangering of the very existence of the Government of the country, *we* may certainly begin to tremble...[66]

This was in 1819, just after the massacre at the working-class rally known as 'Peterloo'. There is more suggested by this text than a few exceptions to dominant methodist politics (or lack thereof): the letter gives voice to an inherent tendency within methodism. Yet, rather than trace the way these members moved easily from missionary and Bible-meetings, using their new skills of public address and organisation, into radical movements and asking why such a shift was possible and happened with startling regularity,

---

[65] Thompson 1966, p. 394.
[66] Thompson 1966, p. 353.

Thompson actually sides with the methodist ruling élite. If they say – as they often did – that this was an aberration of the true gospel of methodism, then Thompson all too quickly agrees. Thus, for Thompson, the methodist Committee of Privileges expresses the correct view of methodism on political radicalism. Coming out with a statement following the Peterloo massacre, it condemned the 'wild and delusive political theories' that 'introduce universal discontent, insubordination, and anarchy'.[67]

Despite his many observations concerning methodist radicals, Thompson would like to think that methodism and radicalism were at opposite poles. If one of the former drifted over to the latter, then Thompson has all manner of ingenious solutions at hand: the radical was a renegade from true methodism; it was nothing more than a 'libertarian antithesis' in which the older patterns of working-class opposition reasserted themselves against the grain;[68] it was the working poor who broke away from the conservative methodist Establishment with their lay preachers to form groups like the primitive methodists or Bible Christians and eventually to feed into the trade-unions and political radicalism.[69] Indeed, he goes so far as to argue that the reactionary Jabez Bunting of the Methodist Connexion and radical Ben Rushton, the primitive-methodist lay preacher, Chartist leader and Plug Rioter, were not from the same movement at all.[70] It is almost as though his argument for an essentially conservative methodism as a curse to the poor dies that old death of a thousand qualifications. I think I have said enough to show that Thompson's own contradictory account suggests that the two are more entwined that he cares to admit.

The ambivalence of the methodists

It seems to me that Thompson's solution – methodist radicals were an aberration from methodism's true nature – is by no means adequate. The oft-remarked comment that no religious movement is monolithic needs to be reasserted here. Methodism is no exception, for as Hempton and Walsh

---

[67] Ibid.
[68] Thompson 1966, p. 391.
[69] Thompson 1966, pp. 396–7.
[70] Thompson 1966, p. 400.

emphasise, the movement oscillated between revivalism and radicalism,[71] or, as I would put it, the debates and breakaways all signal a struggle between the more radical potential of methodism and the wish by leaders such as John Wesley and Jabez Bunting to block the radical implications of their message.[72]

What are we to make of all this? Thompson takes a distinct position against the 'psychic terror' of methodism, then notes a persistent tendency of methodists towards radicalism, but then again sides with the methodist establishment in condemning it as an aberration. However, if we sift through the evidence with a little more patience and care, a slightly different reason for what is really an ambivalence within methodism begins to emerge. We come across a few passing references in Thompson's own text that suggest something else: an awareness of a deeper tension at the heart of methodism. And that is a distinct ambivalence between a strong reactionary identification with the ruling class *and* an insurrectionary tendency. What I find exceedingly curious is that, in Thompson's treatment of methodism, he recognises this tension only to close it down. It turns up well into his discussion of methodism and then only as a lead-in to disparage Wesley's theological opportunism. Here, in a comparison with Lutheranism, is the key passage:

> Methodism dropped all doctrinal and social barriers and opened its doors
> wide to the working class. And this reminds us that Lutheranism was also
> a religion of the poor; and that, as Munzer [sic] proclaimed and as Luther
> learned to his cost, spiritual egalitarianism had a tendency to break its banks
> and flow into temporal channels, bringing thereby *a perpetual tension* into
> Lutheran creeds which Methodism also reproduced.[73]

In comparison to Thompson's hero, William Blake, as well as the radical dissent for which he stands, the methodists sought to curtail and dampen this egalitarian, rebellious and antinomian element of the doctrine of grace.

---

[71] Hempton and Walsh 2002. See further Hempton 1984 and Hempton 2006. Hempton sets out emphasise the complexity of methodism in contrast to scholars like Thompson.

[72] The ultimate source for Wesley's thought comes not in systematic theological reflection but in his sermons. See especially Volumes 5, 6 and 7 of the *Collected Works* (Wesley 1979). The sermons may also be found at <http://gbgm-umc.org/umhistory/wesley/sermons/> (accessed 15 February 2008).

[73] Thompson 1966, p. 363; emphasis added.

Further, in breaking with the Reformation-doctrine concerning election –
something that both Luther and especially Calvin made central to the new
system – Wesley gave voice to a deep egalitarianism. Salvation was available
for all, no matter what station in life. All it needed was an acknowledgement
of and repentance from sin (for it too is universal), a conversion of the heart
and any man or woman could be washed clean by the blood of the Lamb
and be the recipient of God's grace. I must admit that, while Thompson recognises this democratic side of Wesley's theology, he does so in a handful of
sentences and then passes on.[74] In fact, Thompson is keen to criticise such a
break with Reformed doctrine as the sign of 'promiscuous opportunism', a
doctrinal 'mule' that chose the worst and threw out the best of puritanism.[75]
When Thompson does write of the democratic tendencies in methodism, such
as the secessionist Methodist New Connexion led by Alexander Kilham after
Wesley's death in 1797, they are the result of 'alien tendencies',[76] coming from
older dissenters who joined the methodists. Or when he tries to account for
methodism's wide appeal among the working poor, all he can come up with
is indoctrination from childhood through the Sunday-schools.[77] Or, when he
speaks of the community-sense of the methodists, the sense of belonging that
the chapels provided for the weary and uprooted working poor,[78] he does not
connect this feature with the egalitarian gospel the Wesleyans preached. Yet,
he cannot escape it so easily, for this doctrinal egalitarianism was the secret
to methodism's appeal to swathes of the English proletariat. Even more, it is
equally no surprise that one after another, methodists are found in the radical
organisations, movements, protests and insurrections that Thompson traces
in such detail. For it is a small step between a universal, egalitarian and demo-

---

[74] Thompson 1966, pp. 42–3, 363.

[75] Thompson 1966, p. 363. This assessment is in some tension with his earlier comments concerning John's Wesley's genius in combining the right amounts of discipline
and democracy, as well as emotionalism and doctrine (Thompson 1966, p. 38).

[76] Thompson 1966, p. 44.

[77] I agree that Sunday-schools are a curse, but the argument for indoctrination really
does not wash. Indoctrination by a small movement requires a much more intense
programme than Sunday-school. It is far more successful through a whole society,
within which the shared cultural values of at least a class if not a society as a whole
become 'common sense'. In fact, the belief that children were little moral reprobates
who were born sinners is no different from a society in which it seemed perfectly
normal to beat children and send them to the factories.

[78] Thompson 1966, pp. 379–80.

cratic doctrine and the republican and Jacobin elements of English radical movements.

Let us see how far our exercise in detective work has come. Moving on from Thompson's condemnation of methodism on the counts of psychology, industrial work-rhythms and political reaction, I tracked the way a rather large number of methodist radicals emerged between the lines in his text. At one level, the tensions in Thompson's own analysis manifest the tensions within the methodist movement itself: he realises the methodists were important for large swathes of English working poor, wishes to debunk the common argument that methodism provided the roots of the trade-union movement, finds the graphic focus on the cleansing blood of the Lamb of God abhorrent and indeed pathological, and yet notes again and again the presence of methodists among the radicals that interest him so much. Despite Thompson's efforts to dismiss such a tendency as an aberration, or perhaps due to external influences, I also found a few passing moments where he acknowledges a more basic political tension within methodism – although he does slip by it as quickly as he mentions it.[79] All the same, there is the glimmer of an insight which he would not let pass, for Thompson has stumbled on an insurrectionist element at the heart of Christian theology. In order to see what that insight might be, we need to turn his last book from 1993, *Witness Against the Beast*, a work where Thompson finally comes to terms with the barely acknowledged tension within methodism.

William Blake and the politics of radical dissent

If methodism is a blight on England's political history, then, for Thompson, radical dissent is where the revolutionary possibilities of Christian theology may be found. One person really stands for radical dissent in Thompson's

---

[79] I am no defender of methodism, or of any other shape the Christian church wants to take. By contrast, there are plenty of apologetic texts on methodism. Should one wish to consult them, see Thorsen 2005, Wood 2007, Dreyer 1999 and Tomkins 2003. On a refreshingly critical note, see Kent 2002. All the same, it seems to me that Wesley was an heir of the Reformation. For methodism was, in many respects, a very belated and very English Reformation. Henry VIII and the established Church really do not count as a reforming moment, not least because it did not touch and shake up the poorest of English society. That Wesley and the methodists did, if somewhat despite themselves.

work, a person whose judgement Thompson trusts and whom he cites approvingly – William Blake. He trusts Blake's judgement on methodism, Thomas Paine, corruption of the ruling class, exploitation of workers and the alienating nature of industrial labour.[80] Within in his own pantheon, he places Blake beside Marx.[81]

Antinomianism, or, justification by faith

The unique move of the Blake book is that Thompson does not seek the reasons for Blake's radicalism purely in social and economic conditions, or in the specific formation of British politics at the turn of the nineteenth century. It is due just as much, he argues, to Blake's distinct theological system, especially his antinomianism.[82] On that doctrine everything turns. The trick is that antinomianism is not merely a theological position, for it also has political and economic ramifications. In other words, Blake's theological system is fully integrated with Blake's Jacobin politics. In this light, I would suggest that this last book is Thompson's most Marxist book of all, for he is not out

---

[80] Thompson 1966, pp. 41, 50–2, 57, 94, 97, 175, 374, 446, 832. As one example of Blake's assessment of methodism approvingly cited by Thompson: 'It was in 1818 that he emerged from his densely-allegorical prophetic books into a last phase of gnomic clarity in *The Everlasting Gospel*. Here he reasserted the values, the almost-Antinomian affirmation of the joy of sexuality, and the affirmation of innocence, which were present in his earlier songs. Almost every line may be seen as a declaration of "mental war" against Methodism and Evangelicalism. Their "Vision of Christ" was his vision's "greatest Enemy". Above all, Blake drew his bow at the teaching of humility and submission. It was this nay-saying humility which "does the Sun & Moon blot out", "Distorts the Heavens from Pole to Pole", "Rooting over with thorns & stems / The buried Soul & all its Gems"' (Thompson 1966, p. 374).

[81] Thompson 1978, p. 316. Another member of this pantheon is the subject of one of his first works, *William Morris: Romantic to Revolutionary* (Thompson 1976a). However, the only comment on religion in this lengthy work is that Morris was deeply interested and was often engaged in preserving medieval churches.

[82] My interest is not in whether Thomson's reading of Blake is 'correct', firstly because such a singular reading is impossible (interpretation characteristically comes up with multiple positions), and, secondly, because such a task would be another study entirely. In this section, I focus on what Thompson sees in Blake, not on Blake himself. Those interested in various positions on Blake may consult the major studies of the last century by Wilson 1927; Bronowski 1943; Erdman 1977; Hill 1972; Mee 1992; Bentley 2001; Makdisi 2003; and Rix 2007. There are, of course, many, many others. All of Blake works may be found in Blake 1997. I have gained much by consulting especially Fine 1994, who argues that Thompson attempts but also fails in some ways to follow Blake's effort to think of 'contrary states', particularly with respect to politics, law and love. See also Butler 1995; Kenny 2000; Lamont 2006; Lynd 1997, pp. 111–21; Smith 1994.

to find some reductionist argument to explain Blake; instead, antinomianism is a multi-faceted position.[83]

What is so engaging about the loving treatment of Blake – and he is nothing less than an 'original yet authentic voice of a long popular tradition' of radical dissent[84] – is the way Thompson hits gold on his first strike. And this from someone who admits that theology does not always make sense to him. At the beginning of *Witness Against the Beast*, he states that antinomianism is the key to Blake's religious commitment and political radicalism.[85] That key lies with 'the doctrine of justification by faith, in its antinomian inflexion', which 'was one of the *most radical and potentially subversive* of the vectors which carried the ideas of seventeenth-century Levellers and Ranters through to the next century'.[86] Absolutely! Even more, the focus of his Blake study – his last book, published posthumously – is not on Blake's Jacobin politics per se, but on his own rather unique take on Christian theology.[87]

There is a crucial page in the Blake book that I wish to exegete in some detail before considering Blake and dissent more generally. Here is Thompson:

> for much of the eighteenth century, the doctrine of justification by faith was –
> and was seen to be – the more 'dangerous' heresy [than the doctrine of
> works]. And this was because it could – although it need not – challenge very
> radically the authority of the ruling ideology and the cultural hegemony of
> Church, Schools, Law and even of 'common-sense' Morality. In its essence
> it was exactly that: *anti*-hegemonic. It displaced the authority of institutions

---

[83] On the multifarious and contradictory political nature of dissenters like the Muggletonians and Thompson's engagement with them see especially Fine 1994.

[84] Thompson 1966, p. 52. I use the term 'radical dissent' to make a rough distinction between the various small groups (sometimes called 'sects') such as the Muggletonians from the milder and more 'respectable' dissenters such as presbyterians, congregationalists, baptists and so on. See the discussion in Thompson 1966, pp. 26–8. Unfortunately, the review of *Witness Against the Beast* by Bridget and Christopher Hill is rather lame and a little too adoring (Hill and Hill 1994).

[85] Thompson 1993b, p. xvii.

[86] Thompson 1993b, p. 5. The meanings of both antinomianism and justification by faith will unfold as my discussion proceeds.

[87] When I first read *Witness Against the Beast* some ten years ago, I thought it interesting if a little quaint. After all, the doctrine of justification by faith was a little too close to the Calvinist heritage I had inherited from my Dutch parents and from which I was still fleeing. However, when I read the book again recently, I realised that this is very much *my* book: a well-known Marxist tries his hand at understanding the nature of a distinct theological doctrine and then traces the way one of the great radical figures of English history dug out its radical political potential.

and of received worldly wisdom with that of the individual's inner light – faith, conscience, personal understanding of the scriptures or (for Blake) 'the Poetic genius' – and allowed to the individual a stubborn scepticism in the face of the established culture, a fortitude in the face of its seductions or persecutions sufficient to support Christian in the face of the State or of polite learning. This fortitude need not necessarily be accompanied by evangelistic zeal or affirmative social action; it might equally well be defensive, and protect the quietism of a private faith, or the introverted spiritual pride of a petty sect. But it could also nourish (and protect) a more active faith which rested upon a confidence in spiritual 'freedom', liberated from the 'bondage' of Morality and Legality.[88]

Justification – rendering justice – has a number of functions in this crucial slab of text. It provides an anti-hegemonic ideology, foregrounds the individual's 'inner light' and is the source of stubborn scepticism, fortitude, support, protection and nourishment. On one count, I can agree with Thompson: a theological doctrine like this is not merely a language or code for political opposition. In other words, he does not argue that the truth of justification lies elsewhere, that it is an outer garb for a more basic political resistance. His point is that justification by faith was itself the challenge to the ruling ideology. It is, in a classic Gramscian sense, an anti-hegemonic position, an alternative hegemony of those opposed to the dominant one.

On another count, I am not in agreement. Thompson slips from a collective political emphasis to an individual one: the 'radically and potentially subversive' doctrine that was a challenge to the ruling ideology and culture becomes all too quickly an individual affair of private faith and personal understanding of the Bible. By the end of this quotation, we have the distinct image of an individual resisting through his or her private faith the institutions of the established culture and the state. Thompson has succumbed here to the privatisation of faith that is all too characteristic of our own notions of religious belief and practice. To be sure, the trends were well in place during the time Blake was writing, especially with the idea of the inner light and Protestant emphasis on each person reading the Bible for him or herself. But I would have expected Thompson to challenge such a privatisation of faith rather than

---

[88] Thompson 1993b, pp. 5–6.

buy into it. Surely the nature of an anti-hegemonic stance is a collective one, a position that unites those in opposition to the dominant culture and ruling ideology? His opening suggests as much. One of the (not wholly conscious) reasons for such a slippage is that Thompson sets out to emphasise the individual genius and agency of Blake himself. Indeed, at this level, there is a tension that runs throughout the Blake book, between the collective context of Blake's thought – whether the obscure dissenting traditions that fed Blake's antinomianism or the immediate context of his involvement in, and then break from, the Swedenborgian New Jerusalem Church – and his unique, creative agency, his 'system' by which he reshaped all that he received and gave it a new and forceful expression.

However, Thompson has hit upon something that is vitally important, namely the close connection between Blake's theological position and his radical politics. Let me put it this way: what Blake does is realise the inescapably political and social radicalism of justification by faith. But whence does this doctrine of justification by faith (through grace) derive? It comes from none other than the letters of Paul in the New Testament. These texts, especially Romans and Galatians, throw out sentences such as: 'a man is not justified [*diakaioutai*] by works of the law but through faith in Jesus Christ' (Galatians 2: 16); 'For we hold that a man is justified [*dikaiousthai*] by faith apart from works of the law' (Romans 3: 28); 'you are not under law but under grace [*charin*]' (Romans 6: 14). The Greek verb in question, *diakaioō*, is usually translated in light of its heavy theological baggage as 'justify' or 'make right (with God)'. However, its basic sense is to show justice, or to do justice to someone. The point in these texts, then, is that God renders justice not through the law but through 'grace' – by means of a favour or as goodwill. Once you have the rendering of justice outside any legal framework, you challenge the basic nature of that law. Needless to say, this can be a profoundly unsettling political move.

These texts were, of course, the great slogans of the Reformers, Luther and Calvin. They equated salvation by works with the Roman-Catholic Church, with its penances and indulgences and endless tasks to assure salvation. By contrast, no one can be made righteous on his or her own – 'since all have sinned and fall short of the glory of God, they are justified by his grace as a gift' (Romans 3: 23–4) – and so salvation must rely completely on God's gift, or *charis*, grace. These texts were also at the centre of the challenges, internal ruptures and schisms of dissent in eighteenth- and early nineteenth-century England. In fact, these texts from Paul were also the slogans of the various dissenting groups on which Thompson focuses, groups for whom justification by faith gave the very 'justification' for their break with and separation from the dominant religious culture.

Justification by faith may run in a number of directions, such as Calvinist predestination (since we are completely reliant on God's grace we are also reliant on God's decisions as to who will be saved and who damned), the methodist tendency to Arminianism (God's grace is available to all but we can accept or reject it), licence (if we are of the Elect then nothing we do will change that), puritanism (in response to grace we need to live lives acceptable to God), quietism (it is all up to God), activism (showing the fruits of grace) and political radicalism (grace is, after all, the theological version of the revolution).[89] All these possibilities show up either in Paul's own letters, since he was not always clear – in fact he is often contradictory – about the consequences of his 'discovery', or in the groups to whom he addresses his letters. As some of the classic studies of the Corinthian and Galatian correspondence have argued, Paul seems to be putting out fires for which he himself was initially responsible.[90] While the Galatians erred on the side of sticking with the law, the Corinthians pursued Paul's arguments far further than he was willing to countenance. They pushed Christian freedom from the law into all manner of directions such a freedom in regard to sex, worship, Roman law and so on. Underlying it all is a distinct antinomian tendency. Once this became clear to Paul, especially through those who took up justification by faith with gusto, he realised with some shock what he had let loose. So he tried to rein it in, setting boundaries on what 'freedom' meant – not to insult or injure one's 'brethren', not to dispense with the law entirely, for it is good,

---

[89] Thompson's list is little more restricted: he lists Calvinist predestination, the protestant mainline-effort to compromise between grace and works (a little too much Church of England here), and a radical opposition between grace and works that ends up in antinomianism (Thompson 1993b, pp. 12–14).

[90] See Longenecker 1990; Martyn 2004; Matera 2007; Martin 1999; Thistleton 2000; Keener 2005; Fitzmyer 2008. For the sake of argument, I assume with the bulk of studies of Paul that his references to opponents and opposing positions actually reflect real opponents. It would be far more interesting (but a different study) to explore the possibility that Paul manufactures these opponents in a deft piece of rhetorical shadow-boxing. By doing so, he brings his readers onside by arraying himself against a range of imaginary opponents.

arguing that there is another law, the law of Christ, banning the sexual licence that some saw in the idea, limiting the freedom that women were taking in some of the churches and so on. The same person who wrote 'not under the law, but under grace' also wrote, 'Let every person be subject to the governing authorities' (Romans 13: 1). Paul, along with those who took up his radical ideas such as Luther and Calvin and Wesley, found they were pulled in a direction that was far too uncomfortable, far too unsettling, so they wanted to tie it down again, to re-attach the leash and haul it in. Not so Blake, who was prepared to throw away the leash and see where justification by faith took him – right into what the British like to call 'Jacobinical' politics, into radical and revolutionary directions that showed up in an overthrow of privilege and inherited rights, in republicanism and democracy, in the utopian possibilities of a new heaven and new earth.

Muggletonian Marxists

But let us return to see what Thompson makes of Blake and of dissent more generally. *Witness Against the Beast* has two parts: the first traces the dissenting traditions that influenced Blake, especially the Muggletonians; the second considers what Blake did with these traditions. It is, in many respects, a curious book, part historical enquiry, part theology and part literary criticism (especially when Thompson delves into Blake's poems to offer his own detailed readings).

Thompson is, above all, a historian and his passion is for the political (and, where connected, the theological) currents that run just out of reach, not merely of mainstream-culture but even of the conventional modes of historical enquiry. More often than not, he comments on the absence of material concerning groups such as the Luddites, expresses the wish that someone, somewhere had coughed up a few details (apart from the difficult terrain of police spies). So also with the antinomian traditions of which Blake was deeply involved, whether the Muggletonians who may well have influenced Blake, or the Swedenborgian New Jerusalem Church, of which William and Catherine Blake were founding members. Both groups were part of the mix of radical eighteenth-century dissent which included such colourful groups as the Moravians, Irregular Methodists, Seekers, Universalists, Quakers, Fifth Monarchy Men, Philadelphians, French Camisards, Sandemanians, Hutchinsonians, Sabbatarians, Seventh-Day Men, Thraskites, Adamists, Brownists,

Tryonists (vegetarians), Salmonists, Heavenly-Father-Men, Children of the New Birth, Sweet Singers of Israel, or prophets such as Richard Brothers, Laurence Clarkson, William Erbery, William Huntingdon, Elhanan Winchester, John Robins, Thomas Tany, Tobias Crisp, Richard Coppin, Jane Lead, and, last but not least, John Reeve and Ludowick Muggleton, the founders of the Muggletonians who called themselves God's 'Messenger' and his 'mouth' respectively. Before them lie the Ranters, Diggers, Behmenists (followers of Jacob Boehme from Bohemia, 1575–1624), hermeticists and heresiarchs of the late sixteenth and early seventeenth centuries. Out of this bewildering mix (which is remarkably reminiscent of the various sects on the Left), Thompson wants a *tradition* and he finds it in the continuity from the ranters through the quakers, adding some Behmenist and Philadelphian leaven, but ultimately focussed on the Muggletonians. And it is not merely a written tradition (the favoured haunts of scholars), but that embodied in the continual movements, as followers shifted from one group to another, between the 'little churches and sects'[91] scattered throughout London.

These Muggletonians – originating in 1652 with the prophetic words of John Reeve and his cousin Ludowick Muggleton and then running on for more than three centuries with perhaps a maximum membership of 500, with their meetings in rooms in pubs, the absence of formal worship (including prayer) apart from reading, discussion and singing 'divine songs' (not hymns), evangelising purely through the publication of the writings by the prophets (which were therefore maintained in print), and a tradition of protective secrecy – provide the crucial link, the passage from these various dissenting streams to Blake himself. Or they almost do so. For all his delving into Muggletonian texts and traces, for all his effort to secure the Muggletonian archive bequeathed to him by the 'last Muggletonian',[92] for all his efforts to establish that Blake's mother, Catherine Hermitage/Harmitage, may have come from a Muggletonian family (a George Hermitage is the author of two divine songs), Thompson is reduced to possibilities. 'We could suppose', he writes, that Blake had contact with the Muggletonians, or even entertain the

---

[91] Thompson 1993b, p. 52.
[92] Thompson 1993b, pp. 115–19.

'pleasant fiction' that Blake's mother, Catherine, crooned Muggletonian songs to the baby William.[93]

In contrast to the baleful influence of the methodists, with their emotionalism, religious fervour and political conservatism, the Muggletonians and groups like them tended to exercise their intellectual faculties rather than wild emotions, to meet in convivial places such as upper rooms in pubs, smoking, drinking beer, reading, discussing and singing a few 'divine songs' set to popular tunes. They really constitute the image of a revolutionary cell with a religious flavour, a microcosm of a communitarian new society that was not all that strange for radical dissenters.[94] Above all, Thompson is enamoured because of their consistently anti-hegemonic stance against privilege, vested interest and polite learning. They saw and therefore resisted the fact that the apparently classical and genteel culture of England acted as a smokescreen for the violence and exploitation of capitalism.

Thompson would dearly love to have found that Blake was *directly* influenced, indeed to uncover a dusty and tangible piece of evidence that Blake had been a member of the Muggletonian sect. But he cannot, so he has to content himself with tracing the way some ideas of Blake fit closely with the Muggletonians and with arguing that they are a vital conduit for that tradition which fed Blake. In the end it is a mixed conclusion: Blake was not a card-carrying member and yet he was deeply influenced; in short, Blake was (in terms of the intangible fit of ideas) and was not (tangibly having been a member or at least a close friend or even a neighbour of a Muggletonian) influenced. In the end, he settles for the position that it must have been some such group. It is just that the records of the Muggletonians have (somewhat fortuitously or even miraculously) survived, showing in great detail what groups like this believed.

What is the result of this spadework? For all his unique originality, Blake did not create his ideas *ex nihilo*; they come from a tradition. The specifically Muggletonian themes that turn up in Blake are, in brief: their antinomianism, Reason as the Satanic principle and the fruit of the tree of knowledge of good

---

[93] Thompson 1993b, pp. 103–5, 120–1.

[94] See also his discussion of the communitarian thread connected with the quakers, camisards and Moravians, as well as Robert Owen's secularised form of the shaker communities in North America in Thompson 1966, pp. 47–8.

and evil, the Fall as the copulation between Eve and the serpent, and God as fully in Christ, even through his death and resurrection.[95]

Radical dissent

But what interests me most is the way Thompson brings out the political resonance of that tradition:

> What must, however, be insisted upon is the ubiquity and centrality of antinomian tenets to Blake's thinking, to his writing and to his painting. Throughout his work there will be found this radical disassociation and opposition between the Moral Law and the gospel of Christ which is known – as often in the antinomian tradition – as 'the Everlasting Gospel'.[96]

More than other critics who have noticed the antinomian tendencies in Blake's thought, Thompson argues for its 'structural centrality'[97] right through from his revolutionary enthusiasm to his more quietist phase.

However, at the same time that he makes the point (quite strongly) that the antinomian push of the doctrine of justification by faith is central for Blake, Thompson equivocates. On the one hand, the antinomian emphasis on the evil of the moral law (as part of Satan's Kingdom) and the 'everlasting Gospel' of grace is the cornerstone of the cultural and political oppositional stance of someone like Blake; on the other hand, it is an ideological complement, a buttress for such a political position. We need to be careful here. While the first position is relatively clear, the second changes shape at different points

---

[95] See the discussion in Thompson 1993b, pp. 91–101. A more detailed list includes the following: the idea of three ages with the unique designation in terms of water (the Law and Old Testament), blood (Christ and the New Testament) and spirit (the Commission of and writings by Reeve and Muggleton); the active principle of God who works on a pre-existing inactive matter, from which arises evil and the Devil – not by God but through God's permission; the manifestation of God through the contraries of nature, matter and reason; the Fall as the copulation of Eve with the Serpent/Devil in the form of an angel of light, from which diabolic seed enters into the human race to do battle with the divine seed that comes from Adam (the doctrine of the Two Seeds); the redemption through Christ being enabled by God who enters Mary's womb and is conceived as Jesus, thereby undoing the diabolic seed; the consequent radical monotheism in which God was in Christ and therefore not in heaven, so much so that for a time God was indeed dead until the resurrection; and the awakening of the soul as if from a seed at the Second Coming (Thompson 1993b, pp. 70–8, 83–4).
[96] Thompson 1993b, pp. 18–19.
[97] Thompson 1993b, p. 20.

in his discussion. At times, he argues that the theological ideas of the dissenting sects provided 'an uncrackable doctrinal defence',[98] an outer shell that resisted the polite culture of learned England (itself a veneer for some of the most brutal of colonial acts). Good historical materialist that he is, Thompson presents the theological element as an ideological feature of the radical politics of Blake and his fellow radicals. So we find a persuasive argument concerning the independent and oppositional class-nature of the various artisans, tradesmen and shopkeepers. Eschewing the later and anachronistic term 'petite bourgeoisie' with its conservative ring, Thompson argues that these artisans and tradesmen found themselves excluded from the circles of power and high culture that marked the 'gentry'. Language, dress, classical training and referencing, the polite learning of established academia – all of these signalled the sharp difference between the ruling class and the independence of artisans and tradesmen. Located in this fiercely independent group, Blake also shared the deep ideological attachment to dissenting sects. And that provided the ideological opposition, their anti-hegemonic stance (borrowing here from Gramsci), as well as the justification and confidence of their opposition to the moral law and serpent reasoning of Satan's Kingdom. In short, groups like the Muggletonians provide the language of opposition, a set of beliefs that made sense of that anti-hegemony.[99]

At other times, Thompson takes a slightly different line. Here, it is a case of confluence or conjunction, more specifically with Blake. Thompson argues that Blake's earlier antinomian theological views met with his emerging radical political positions: it was a confluence that Blake worked together in his own way. Revolutionary thought came to Blake through the Enlightenment-inspired, ultra-radical and atheistic work of the French revolutionary C.F. Volney (through the poem 'The Human Abstract') and English expatriate Thomas Paine (through the poem 'London'). Indeed, the second half of the Blake book attempts to follow the conjunction of these two streams and how a 'Blakean mutation'[100] arose when antinomianism and Jacobin thought met. All of which was mediated by William and Catherine Blake's enthusiasm for and then disillusionment with the Swedenborgian New Jerusalem Church.[101]

---

[98] Thompson 1993b, p. 112.
[99] Se especially Thompson 1993b, pp. 108–14.
[100] Thompson 1993b, p. 128.
[101] Thompson 1993b, pp. 129–73.

I have nothing against the argument that Blake's antinomianism had to nego-
tiate these newer currents, but it seems to me (and it is fact my argument here)
that, rather than some effort at compromise, Blake was able to see that they
gave expression to a distinct direction of antinomianism itself. In other words,
there is an intrinsically radical political element of antinomian thought and
practice that drew Blake to such radicalism.

More often than not, Thompson pushes further to argue that the theology
of the dissenters was much more central. It lay at the heart of their worldview,
but above all it was the motivating force of their opposition. This is particularly true of *The Making of the English Working Class*, where he argues that,
within dissent, for all its schisms and mutations, the 'dormant seeds of political Radicalism' lay, 'ready to germinate whenever planted in a beneficial and
hopeful social context'.[102] The most noted example is the firebrand Tom Paine,
author of the radical and atheistic *Rights of Man*, who came from a quaker
background. It was a small step from anti-state church (and indeed anti-state)
to anti-Christian and revolutionary. As for the Blake book, the use of the term
'antinomian' enables Thompson to make this connection, for antinomianism
is both a distinct theological direction in which the doctrine of justification
by faith may go *and* it is a distinct political position that challenges the rule
of law (in the hands of the propertied ruling class), an economic system of
exploitation and the assumptions of privilege. I would like to push Thompson
even further on this matter: it is not merely the case that the antinomian logic
of such a doctrine of grace acts as an ideological girder for radical politics,
nor even that it is one possible direction in which such a logic may go; rather,
what Thompson does through his explorations of Blake is show that such a
doctrine is inescapably and radically political. This is what the likes of Paul
and Calvin and Wesley saw all too well, only to recoup the rule of law in
order to close down the politics of grace. Blake's genius, then, is that he took
the deep antinomian logic of grace all the way. This, it seems to me, is what
emerges between the lines of Thompson's text, rather than some effort by
Blake to marry the antinomianism of grace and radical politics.

In this light, it comes as no surprise that Thompson consistently notes the
involvement of dissenters with the political radicals, especially in *The Making of the English Working Class*. For instance, Joseph Gerrald of the London

---

[102] Thompson 1966, p. 36.

Corresponding Society quotes the Bible before the corrupt Scottish judge, Cockburn,[103] the famous oaths of the Luddites and the trade-unions often referred to God and the Bible,[104] and Thomas Evans's agrarian-socialist book is, after all, called *Christian Policy the Salvation of the Empire*.[105] Even more, he notes the enthusiastic response of a baptist chapel-minister to the acquittal of Thomas Hardy, the first and founding secretary of the London Correspond-ing Society,[106] the thundering denunciation of the debilitating effects of indus-trialism in the words of a Sheffield dissenting minister,[107] the radical-Christian protest against the war (with France),[108] and the Bible-text on the banner of the Barnsley radical uprising: 'He that smiteth a man so that he die, shall surely be put to death'.[109] The same author who often talks of the anti-religious strain of radical politics can also point out that many of the protests against exploita-tion might be expressed in Owenite or biblical language, and that those 'who were sent to gaol might know their Bible better than those on the Bench'.[110]

None of these are exceptions, I would suggest, especially if we take the argument of the Blake book into account. They are what we would expect, for each of them glimpsed Blake's insight into the radical implications of such a strange theological position as justification by faith through grace. The Mug-gletonians and groups like them, but above all William Blake, realised the full theological and political possibilities of the doctrine of grace and that was nothing less than a persistent opposition to the moral law, to 'Satan's king-dom', understood in both theological and political senses.

Poetry and apocalyptic

Apart from the obvious point that religion is integral to Thompson's remak-ing of his favoured period, I have been tracking a curious shift in judgement from mild dissenters like the methodists to the more radical groups such as the Muggletonians. The former do not fare well in his analysis, while if

---

103 Thompson 1966, p. 128.
104 Thompson 1966, pp. 510–13.
105 Thompson 1966, pp. 162, 614.
106 Thompson 1966, p. 136.
107 Thompson 1966, pp. 470–1.
108 Thompson 1966, p. 471.
109 Thompson 1966, p. 707.
110 Thompson 1966, p. 831.

he had been around at the time, I can well imagine him being part of the Muggletonians, or at least chatting, plotting and spending a good deal of time with them. Perhaps his responses to the following two assessments sum up his vastly different take on each group. The first, which I quoted earlier, is taken from W.E.H. Lecky in 1891: 'A more appalling system of religious terrorism, one more fitted to unhinge a tottering intellect and to darken and embitter a sensitive nature, has seldom existed'.[111] In this case, Thompson agrees wholeheartedly. And yet, when it comes to a very similar assessment of the Muggletonians, Thompson is dismissive: 'Donald Davie, who has cast a casual and partial eye upon the "antinomian and heretical sects" which "*effectively* influenced Blake" has concluded that "as specifically *religious* insights, their ideas are beneath contempt"'.[112] I can well imagine that he would agree with Davie had he said this about the methodists. But no, instead he comes to the defence of the Muggletonians. Although he does mention that the Muggletonian doctrines provide a 'silly enough picture',[113] partly to avoid his comrades on the Left thinking that he had become some-what unhinged, more often than not, he comes to their defence. In the end, it really boils down to this: 'I like these Muggletonians...'[114]

There is one further reason as to why he likes them and with that I close this study. It concerns millenarianism or chiliasm, the fervent anticipation of the end of history and the coming of the Lord with his chariots and his horse-men. The problem is that his assessment of chiliasm shifts tellingly from one side to the other: while the methodists exhibit an inauthentic millenarianism, the radical dissenters tap into an authentic version. As far as the method-ists are concerned, Thompson argues that the millenarian impulse was the result of counterrevolution, especially during the Napoleonic Wars between

---

[111] From Lecky's *History of England in the Eighteenth Century*. 1891 edn. 3 vols. Vol-ume 3, pp. 77–8, in Thompson 1966, p. 374.

[112] Quoted from Donald Davie, *A Gathered Church* (1978), p. 52, in Thompson 1993b, p. 108.

[113] Thompson 1993b, p. 85.

[114] Thompson 1993b, p. 90. See also: 'I want to put in a word here for the Muggle-tonians, who have had a bad historical press...' (Thompson 1993b, p. 78). More extensively: 'I will suggest that – a few peripheral doctrines apart – Muggletonians beliefs were logical, powerful in their symbolic operation and have only held to be "ridiculous" because the Muggletonians were losers and because their faith was pro-fessed by "poor enthusiasts" and not by scholars, bishops or successful evangelists' (Thompson 1993b, p. 79).

England and France. When the revolutionary hopes of social change have been disappointed, when the police and spies and army move in to capture, imprison and execute the leaders, then where do those radical energies and hopes go? They may go underground, to be nurtured until another time (the work of the radical dissenters), or they may find expression in fervid outbursts of religious revival. This second form of chiliasm becomes a desperate and dismal creature, especially when it becomes one of the reasons (in Thompson's opinion) for the success of his loathed methodists. With their emotional meetings, damnation of sin, calls for conversion and millenarian imagery, the Wesleyans were able to give an outlet to these frustrated hopes of the poor. Thompson even hints that the methodists preyed on the dashed hopes of social change. All of the outward manifestations of the methodist meetings – groaning, crying out, fainting, shouting, weeping, paroxysms and even mass-hysteria – become signs of the psychic process of counterrevolution, the 'chiliasm of despair'[115] and not revolution itself. And so, he designates it an inauthentic millenarianism in contrast to the Jacobin agitations of the late eighteenth century.

But, when he comes to radical dissenters like Blake, he changes his tune. Now, he resists dismissing millenarianism as the raving of lunatics (a dismissal one hears all too often today in 'learned' circles). So we find him countering the caricature of chiliasm as the terrain of disturbed individuals, suffering from paranoia and megalomania, by arguing that it is a language, an imagery of the poor and oppressed. Or, rather, while there may indeed be the occasional deranged individual (or methodist), the biblical imagery of the Whore of Babylon, the Beast and the New Jerusalem has consistently provided the language of opposition by minority-groups.[116]

It takes little guesswork to notice that such language is drawn directly from the Bible. Before I proceed, some terminological clarity is needed. I prefer to use the more technical term, apocalyptic, rather than millenarian and chiliastic. The word 'apocalyptic' functions as a noun and an adjective and refers either to an apocalyptic genre of literature (which contains apocalyptic themes), to an apocalyptic worldview, or to an apocalyptic movement. As a

---

[115] Thompson 1966, p. 388. See also Jaffe 1989 for a treatment of the 'chiliasm of despair' in light of subsequent debates.
[116] Thompson 1966, pp. 48–50.

genre, it is well known from the Bible where there are two works that belong to the apocalyptic genre: Daniel and Revelation (also known by its Greek title, the 'Apocalypse').[117] The original Greek word, *apokaluptō*, means the revelation of a truth, but since that truth refers (in the biblical books) to knowledge about the end of the world, the term apocalyptic came to refer to the end times. Apocalyptic also refers to a particular *worldview* in which the world was full of signs of the end and in which one waited impatiently for the final cataclysm. By contrast, an apocalyptic movement (also designated as apocalypticism) is one which anticipates and tries to predict when the end time will come, often under the guidance of leader. Such movements have come and gone throughout history, but, in Christian circles, they have often arisen during times of social unrest and economic crisis. We may picture it this way: an apocalyptic movement operates with an apocalyptic worldview, all the while reading and attempting to interpret apocalyptic literature. However, an apocalyptic worldview and apocalyptic literature are not restricted to such movements, for anyone may read such literature or take on such a worldview. In what follows, I use the term 'apocalyptic' in these three senses, designating variously and at times interchangeably a genre of literature, a worldview and a movement.

In light of this distinction, Thompson is interested in the second and third features, although he is also vitally interested in apocalyptic literature, as we will see soon enough. The movements are, of course, his favoured sectarian dissenters, as well as the whirlwind-followings of various prophets, while the worldview was both informed by the Bible and expressed their deep opposition to the corrupt status quo. For those who flocked to hear and follow Mother Jane Wardley (the Shakers) or Richard Brothers in 1793–4 and 'Zion' Ward in 1829–36,[118] their worldview was steeped in the Bible and the traditions of radicalism. It was a time 'when men's psychic world was filled with violent images from hell-fire and Revelation, and their real world filled with poverty and oppression'.[119] But they were also those who flocked to Robert

[117] Outside the canon, there are far more, such as the *Apocalypse of Adam and Eve* or the writings from Qumran (Dead Sea Scrolls).

[118] Not, however, Joanna Southcott of the early years of the nineteenth century. The reason: she too arrives in a time of political reaction and reveals the truth of the methodist appeal, for large numbers of methodists followed her for a time.

[119] Thompson 1966, p. 801.

Owen's version of communism in the early nineteenth century that Engels was to praise so much. This is the apocalyptic worldview Thompson finds in William Blake, a man who was ensconced within apocalyptic and sectarian movements. The fact that an apocalyptic worldview 'touched Blake with its breath',[120] that it runs deeply throughout his poetry and painting, that Blake cannot be understood without its imagery is enough for Thompson to give it some space.

What are we to make of this sharp difference between condemnation and approval on the very same topic of apocalyptic? Rather than a clear case of misguided dislike of the methodists and zeal for Blake, I would suggest that Thompson has discovered the political ambivalence at the heart of apocalyptic literature and worldviews and even apocalyptic movements. It is what that great champion of apocalyptic Ernst Bloch calls the 'discernment of myths',[121] for apocalyptic deals in the language and imagery of myth. Thompson's criterion is the same as Bloch's: how is that apocalyptic imagery used on a political level? In Thompson's judgement, the methodists used it for reactionary and escapist reasons, while radical dissenters like Blake found a more politically revolutionary use. But I would go further than Thompson on two counts. First, since a good deal of apocalyptic frenzy today emanates from the vast numbers of fundamentalist Christians in the United States,[122] and since this is by no means the preserve of those excluded from power and oppressed, we need to cast a very sceptical eye over this type of apocalyptic worldview. It becomes a means for the powerful (religious and political) Right to assert its historical 'mission', as well as express the fear that their own political might is crumbling.[123] Second, it is not merely a matter of the use to which apocalyptic imagery is put, for it also bears within itself the political ambivalence I have been tracing. In other words, apocalyptic is part of that tension between reaction and revolution I have identified as the key to the methodists and radical dissent. It may go one way or another, or, as is more often the case, it reproduces that political ambivalence within the groups that appropriate it.

---

[120] Thompson 1966, p. 50.

[121] Bloch 1972, pp. 34–58; 1970, pp. 41–58.

[122] As one example among many, see the 'Rapture Index' at <http://www.raptureready.com/rap2.html>. Everything from a Democratic victory through to possible failure of the war in Iraq sends the index climbing.

[123] See Runions 2004a, 2004b.

Thus, the imagery of the Beast and the Whore become potent polemic against a corrupt state of oppression (in the hands of a Blake or a Daniel), but the anticipation of the Last Judgement can also become a justification for the self-righteous agenda of reaction (as has so often been the case for the Church). This means that I find Thompson's argument that the methodist's millenarian tendencies were a result of counterrevolution less than persuasive; rather, that counterrevolutionary direction comes out of apocalyptic.

The apocalyptic Blake also runs in Thompson's veins in other ways. I think of the approving nods towards such a Blake at the end of *Witness Against the Beast*. Thus, with his affirmations of 'Thou Shalt Love' and 'Thou Shalt Forgive', Blake provides 'a plank in the floor upon which the future must walk'.[124] But the two items I wish to pick up here are Thompson's anti-nuclear campaigning and his poetry, the one clearly a movement with its literature and worldview, the other more strictly a genre. The former is far better known, while the latter is a little harder to find. And both make extensive use of what can only be called apocalyptic themes.

Anti-nuclear

The story of Thompson's involvement in the disarmament-movement has been told often enough. Beginning spasmodically in the 1950s, it became almost a full-time pursuit in the 1970s and 80s, especially during the time of Margaret Thatcher and Ronald Reagan. Both the Campaign for Nuclear Disarmament and END (the European Nuclear Disarmament movement) – vast popular movements with connections across Europe, both East and West – demanded so much in terms of travel, meetings, talks and popular publications, that he put his other writing on hold.[125] Rather tellingly, *Witness Against the Beast* was much delayed as a consequence, and the planned book on romanticism never eventuated (what we have is a collection of odd pieces edited by Dorothy Thompson).[126] In a sense, we might see the Blake book as a belated justification of his disarmament-work.

But is the nuclear-disarmament movement an apocalyptic movement and are the writings Thompson produced during this time apocalyptic literature?

---

[124] Thompson 1993b, p. 228.
[125] See further Bess 1993.
[126] Thompson 1997.

Here are some of the titles he produced at the time: *Beyond the Cold War: A New Approach to the Arms Race and Nuclear Annihilation;*[127] *Star Wars: Self-Destruct Incorporated;*[128] *Exterminism and Cold War;*[129] *The Heavy Dancers;*[130] *Zero Option;*[131] *Protest and Survive;*[132] *Prospectus for a Habitable Planet.*[133] I would add to these doomsday-scenarios the chilling conclusion to *The Sykaos Papers.*[134] In this rambling and too-clever attempt at science-fiction, the best part is the heroine's final account of the nuclear Armageddon from her vantage-point of the moon. In one sense, the novel – with its alien visitor trying to make sense of Earth – all leads to this final cataclysm. Further, this struggle for disarmament was both a distinct movement based on a feared end of the world and it made use of the full range of apocalyptic language within a distinct literary genre – two of the elements of apocalyptic I indicated earlier. And it was a struggle that informed the actions and writings of E.P. Thompson for some two decades.

Now, we can frown and say that Thompson was getting carried away, that the world did not end and that all this was mere fantasy. Or we can point out that the fear of nuclear annihilation, or for that matter, global warming and environmental destruction, are displaced fears and anticipations of the end of capitalism. But I remember at the time, when I became deeply aware of the threat of an all-out nuclear war in the 1980s, that these prospects were real. Human beings had the capacity, for the first time in that species' history, to make a swift end to it all. Some human beings, animals and plants would probably have survived, but not in any way that was known at the time (perhaps there is some truth in that anticipation of the end of capitalism). Of course, the Cold War came to a swift end; there were revolutions all across Eastern Europe; Communism 'lost' and the capitalist West 'won'. Since then it has been plain sailing…

There is, however, a distinct difference in the way the anti-nuclear movement used apocalyptic themes. It was not that they welcomed such a

---

[127] Thompson 1982a.
[128] Thompson and Thompson 1985.
[129] Thompson 1982b.
[130] Thompson 1985.
[131] Thompson 1982c.
[132] Thompson and Smith 1980.
[133] Thompson and Smith 1987.
[134] Thompson 1988.

cataclysm, calling on the Russian and US-leaders to press their fatal buttons. They used the threat of a nuclear conflagration to bring an end to the arms-race, to bring a groundswell of opposition to the policy-makers and warmongers. In other words, they sought to avert Armageddon and bring about what Thompson will call in his poetry a 'soft apocalypse'. But is this not a call to repentance in its own way? It reminds me of the little fable of Jonah in the Bible. Jonah is called by God to pronounce doom on Nineveh, which he does after some fishy persuasion. But the people of Nineveh repent, go around in sackcloth and ashes and God spares them. All to Jonah's profound chagrin, for he had wanted their end. This is not a call to repentance so that one may be among the Elect at the Last Judgement; it is a call that seeks to avert that judgement and take a radically different path.

Political Christmas

I did promise a second element in the apocalyptic appropriation of Blake by Thompson, and it comprises are the little-known poems gathered under the title *Infant and Emperor: Poems for Christmas*.[135] Written at various moments over the three decades onwards from 1950 and finally gathered together in the early 1980s, they put various moments of the infancy-stories of Jesus in touch with political events – such as the Suez invasion and the Hungarian uprising in 1956, the atrocities of the Korean War in 1951, or the activities of the Campaign for Nuclear Disarmament. Or, rather, these events were the initial reasons for writing some of the poems in the first place. Three things fascinate me about this collection. First, when faced with events of global significance, Thompson resorts to biblical language and themes, melding apocalyptic literature and Christmas. Second, he recovers the revolutionary side of Christianity that I have stressed so much. Third and somewhat paradoxically, he can do so because he does not buy into the belief-structure; he takes it as fable. Let me take each in turn.

---

[135] Thompson 1983. Along with his re-conception of revolution as peaceful, these poems added fuel to those who accused him of 'socialist humanism' and 'utopian socialism'; see Bess 1993, p. 23. There is very little critical literature on these poems, partly because they are largely ignored. Bidney 2004–5 offers a study of the influence of Blake on Thompson's poems and mentions one in this collection, 'Lullaby'. Taylor 2001 is unexciting, writing in a theological journal, and Hamilton 2008 frustratingly does not mention the Christmas-poems in his study of Thompson's poetry.

Myriad-images meet in these poems, but the major ones focus on apocalyptic images and the dual interplay between Herod and the child of the poor. As for apocalyptic imagery, we find 'fabulous holy armies',[136] Herod assuming 'his hour',[137] Leviathan, the Beast, the inherited kingdom, the perpetual threat of 'Horsemen and Eagles, Emperor, Wolf and bull',[138] and the massacre of the innocents. But there are also two poems that are more explicitly apocalyptic – 'Scenario for the Flight into Egypt'[139] and 'Prayer for the Year's Turning'.[140] The first is modernised a little too much, with its 'Heaven's Angel' winging in like a bikie, directions for camera-use (zoom in, fade out, extras, cut, etc.), the 'rival holy armies' using fighter-bombers, snipers and grenades and with marines crawling up beaches and massive civilian casualties. By contrast, 'Prayer for the Year's Turning' is much better, for it weaves together the natural cycles of earth (winter solstice and spring), the hope of Christmas and the very human threat of self-inflicted annihilation. It takes a few stanzas to realise that the various constellations and heavenly bodies – Mars, Trident, Poseidon, Polaris, Vulcan, Hades and the Neutron Way – are a mix of warlike ancient ones and the new hardware of surveillance and nuclear warfare. But the poem itself turns from heaven to earth, calling on people to watch below, to 'search about the planet's floor / For the nativity of hope'. At that moment, the solstice with which the poem begins, the winter-festival of Christmas (at least in the northern hemisphere), becomes the 'arrested solstice' of the 'boreal' Cold War. Just as the earth turns from the midst of winter's Christmas, so also Thompson calls for a 'soft apocalypse of Spring'. It is, of course, the major drive of the anti-nuclear campaign, but with a brilliant inversion: the apocalypse of nuclear destruction must give way before a very different apocalypse that averts the former.

The second group of images clusters around two symbols: Herod and the child as a sign of the poor. Blake, too, peers from behind much of the imagery, with its Leviathan and Beast, the gate of a woman's womb, the seed and a pervasive antinomianism. While Herod becomes the symbol of oppressors

---

[136] Thompson 1983, p. 1.
[137] Thompson 1983, p. 2.
[138] Thompson 1983, p. 10.
[139] Thompson 1983, pp. 15–17.
[140] Thompson 1983, pp. 18–19.

(at one point merging with the Roman Emperor)[141] who march their holy armies through history, the child becomes the symbol of hope for the oppressed 'walking and walking down the centuries' with the 'stubborn stamina of God's forgotten poor'.[142] Thus, in the excellent poem 'Nativity',[143] the Christmas-story becomes an 'arctic legend' in which kings, angels and mysteries are all frozen...except for two who escape: one is the brutal Herod 'on the high horse of power' who continues to send his soldiers and magistrates to attack, arrest and beat the innocent. The other is the child who passes 'though the only gate / No magistrate may guard' and to whom the poor gather in assistance to drive back the guards so that the 'seed' may grow. The oppressor and his armies may still be with us, but so is the collective hope of the poor.

At times, Thompson puzzles over why the birth of a child should bother the Herods of history so much. Is it the assertion of independence from Mary, the deception that hints of love, innocence and peace, as the poem 'Annunciation'[144] suggests? Is it because a sleeping new-born challenges the corruptions of power, drawing upon almost forgotten qualities of human life?

> Frost-bitten mercy, hope pulling off her gloves
> Crusted with ice, benighted company
> Numb from the cold. And even at the inn
> They stir the failing fire, long for release –
> Will no-one bring the kindling of love,
> A sprig of innocence, a twig of peace?[145]

Is it because innocence, hope and love nurtured in a mother's womb or arms are the first stirrings of 'insurgent provinces, revolt within the State'?[146] Is it because the poor will not be put down to remain submissive? They – like the shepherds and wise men who have become beggars in 'Visitor at the Inn'[147] – have a knack of knocking on the window while the 'feast of the banknote' rages on inside.

---

[141] Thompson 1983, p. 10.
[142] Thompson 1983, p. 16.
[143] Thompson 1983, pp. 2–3.
[144] Thompson 1983, p. 1.
[145] Thompson 1983, p. 5.
[146] Thompson 1983, p. 10. See also the 'stirring in the womb' that 'alerts the testy police' (Thompson 1983, p. 13).
[147] Thompson 1983, p. 6.

I have already slipped into my second point – the revolutionary edge of these poems – but it is difficult to separate that element too sharply from the language itself. What Thompson has done, perhaps unintentionally, is give voice to the scandal of these infancy-narratives from the Gospels. Over and against the syrupy celebrations of Christmas everywhere around us, he has pinpointed the political challenge that lies barely concealed in these stories. Perhaps it can be done these days only by one who openly confesses that he is not a believer, that the theological mumbo-jumbo makes little sense to him. There is little piety here, just as it should be, it seems to me (the most obnoxious people I have met are precisely those pious ones with one eye on heaven and the other looking for a moment to do you in). So the 'Holy Roman church' becomes a deluded venture – 'cross-natured Christendom' that built a 'world of faith' out of Mary's 'faithlessness'.[148] He is all too aware that the Church has had a very cosy relationship with the Herods of this world, blessing and praying for and with them.[149] In an excellent section of 'Lamentation in Rama', he has heaven become an informer: 'The gracious powers above / Keep watch on the little streets?'.[150]

This down-to-earth scepticism comes not a moment too soon, for at times Thompson risks getting a little too sentimental about innocent babies as symbols of love and hope during millennial crises. He is much more forceful when he reminds us that much of what the Church has made of Christmas is pious clap-trap. For example, when he takes head-on the myth of the birth of the son of God in 'The Infant',[151] he suggests 'some seraph goofed' and accidentally teleported 'Him' as a puny baby, a 'helpless sod' full of wind and unable to save himself. Or, in Mary's 'Lullaby', she calls Jesus 'Master Egotrip', 'Mister Big' and 'prince of Pandemonium':

> Windy boring preacher
> Wrapped in a shawl –
> Stop bawling your commandments
> Shut up and rest,

---

[148] Thompson 1983, p. 1.
[149] See 'The Massacre of the Innocents', which really bears the spirit of Marx's own satire against the seamless connection between corrupt power and religion (Thompson 1983, pp. 11–12).
[150] Thompson 1983, p. 13.
[151] Thompson 1983, p. 7.

And sleep full of the sermon
Of your saviour's breast.[152]

Much of it is excellent poetry and far better than his novel, *The Sykaos Papers*.
Yet the question remains as to how Thompson manages to give the Christmas
stories a radical political edge. The paradox is that, whereas Thompson
probably thought he was undermining the stories themselves, he has in fact
brought out their radical tendencies. I have already mentioned one reason,
namely that he does not believe all the high claims made by the Church
and can thereby dispense with the theological twaddle. Another is that he
is far more interested in the human and earthy elements of the stories. Less
interested in angels 'coming to' (Luke 1: 28) virgins, or a pious Joseph trying to do the right thing by God, shepherds directed by a singing choir of
angels to visit the baby (the voices they heard was only the wind), or pagan
magi following a star, or even the claim that this is the birth of the son of
God, Thompson focuses on what is all too human in the stories – illicit sex,
discomforts and pains of pregnancy, mothers who take no bullshit, the ever-
present police, magistrates, armies and tyrants.

Yet, there is a far more important reason why Thompson touched on the
radicalism of stories of infant and emperor: they are nothing less than fables:

Nothing will alter because a child is born.
That was a fable.[153]

The 'fable' in question is both Mary's made-up story to cover up an 'illicit'
pregnancy – about a divine child announced by some angel known as
Gabriel – and the birth-narratives as a whole (they appear only in Matthew
and Luke in rather different forms). They are indeed fables; no serious biblical
scholar takes them as anything else. I would go one step further and suggest that they are necessary fables. Any political movement needs its fables,
or political myths as I prefer to call them.[154] In drawing upon this stock of
images, symbols and stories in order to bring out their radical possibilities,
Thompson has managed these stories in the form of political myth. The rea-

---

[152] Thompson 1983, p. 9.
[153] Thompson 1983, p. 1.
[154] Boer 2009b.

son: 'It was the other part that the poor understood – Herod, the Roman magistrates, the cross'.[155]

Conclusion

There is no need to reproduce my argument here – that Thompson's assessment of the methodists and radical dissenters turns on a political ambivalence in the heart of Christianity between reaction and revolution – save to make the following points.

Firstly, there is a deep political ambivalence or tension within Christianity. It may go one way or the other, towards reaction or revolution. If various pieces of the Christian Church have all too often carried on a dirty little relationship with the odd Roman Emperor from the time of Constantine onwards, or with the lords and kings of the middle ages, or indeed the political right wing in our own day (and here there is little difference between conservative popes or evangelical-Protestant Christians), then other elements have tapped into a deep revolutionary current, such as Gerrard Winstanley and the Diggers in seventeenth century England, or Thomas Müntzer and the Peasants' Revolt in sixteenth-century Germany, or the guerrilla-priests of liberation-theology like Camillo Torres in the twentieth century. In fact, this ambivalence may also be found in the Bible, where the murmuring and rebellious Israelites in the myth of the wilderness-wanderings challenge Moses time and time again, or some of the prophets call for an end to exploitation, or the rebel Jesus who is put to death by the Romans as an agitator, or the perpetual theme of revolutionary chaos that threatens the order the ruling class desperately tries to assert, or indeed that curious message of grace in the letters of Paul, something that erupts unexpectedly and undeservedly into the everyday run of life and changes all the coordinates of our existence. My point here is not that one take on the Bible or Christianity is closer to the truth and another a misinterpretation; rather, both are perfectly valid: the Bible may very well be read as a friend of the rich and powerful, but it may equally well be an inspiration for revolutionary groups seeking to overthrow their rich and powerful oppressors. Ernst Bloch's two comments on the Bible sum it up rather well: while it is

---

[155] Thompson 1983, p. 1.

'often a scandal to the poor and not always a folly to the rich', it is also 'the church's bad conscience'.[156]

Secondly, the argument that Thompson's has (re-)discovered a deep tension with Christian thought does not entail a reversion to some form of idealism, arguing that an idea has had profound historical effect. Rather, as I have already pointed out in the chapter on Horkheimer, the reason why the doctrine of grace has had such an effect is due to its own origins. It was forged in an ambivalent political and socio-economic situation: the Palestine in which Christianity arose was torn by one anti-imperial struggle after another. In a situation in which the dilemma of resistance or accommodation shaped the focus of different politico-religious groups (Sadducees, Pharisees, Essenes and Zealots), a new group would have to take a position. Instead, the belief-structure of Christianity embodies such tensions within itself, leaving them unresolved. It is no wonder that the various elements of English dissent struggled with the same issues in a different time that seemed to have many of the same features.

In light of all this, what are we to make of Thompson's appropriation of a Blakean radical apocalyptic in his own political activism and in his poetry? It seems to me that here we find the embodiment of my argument. Quite simply, in his anti-nuclear activism, but especially in his poetry, Thompson has realised the radical side of the political ambivalence of Christianity.

---

[156] Bloch 1972, pp. 25 and 21; Bloch 1968, pp. 53 and 41.

Chapter Three

The Zeal of G.E.M. de Ste. Croix

> Wild beasts are not more hostile to mankind
> than are *most* Christians [*plerique Christianorum*]
> in their deadly hatred of one another.[1]

G.E.M. de Ste. Croix belongs to a rare breed of classics-scholars who have offered Marxist readings of ancient history.[2] However, I would like to claim Ste. Croix for another intermittent tradition, namely, materialist readings of the Bible. More specifically, it was the New Testament and early Christianity that continually drew his attention. Anyone who has read the anchor-like tome known as *The Class Struggle in the Ancient Greek World* will be struck by how often Ste. Croix refers to Christianity (whether in his own day or at its earliest moments), the Church, and the Bible. These references take the form of continual asides (often bracketed), as well as whole sections given over to women, property, slavery, Jesus of Nazareth, martyrdom, persecution, and the workings of church-councils.

---

[1] Ammianus, quoted on a number of occasions: Ste. Croix 1981, p. 451; Ste. Croix 2006, pp. 222 and 260.

[2] See also Rose 1992, and Arthur and Konstan 1984, who provide a full bibliography up to the early 1980s. The whole notion of classics, defined in the traditional sense as dealing with ancient Greece, Rome, and perhaps ancient India, needs a strong challenge. Not only does it perpetuate the Enlightenment-classicist narrative whereby the 'West' may trace its origins from ancient Greece and Rome, but it also neglects the large number of other ancient cultures which have remained the domains of anthropologists, historians and so on.

Apart from offering a critical commentary on Ste. Croix's treatments of early Christianity and the Bible, I am also keenly interested in usable insights he may have to offer. These insights, which should not be left to that eccentric corner of scholarship known as 'classics', emerge as much from my criticisms of Ste. Croix as for the points I can draw directly from his work. In order to dig out these insights, I have organised this close encounter with Ste. Croix in terms of the following topics. I begin with his zesty, politely belligerent and engaged style. Somewhat idiosyncratic, it soon makes one forget the forbidding number of pages in his great works. The style leads me into his complex encounters with theology, which he always opposes to history. Needless to say, theology usually comes off worse for the encounter, for Ste. Croix was a trenchant anti-clerical campaigner. However, in the meantime, Ste. Croix makes some valuable points towards a materialist reading of the Bible, especially the insight concerning the tension between *chora* and *polis* in the New Testament. The complexity of his engagement with theology has to take account of his biography, not least of which is his conservative Christian upbringing at the hands of a mother, who was a British Israelite.

On the other side of that great opposition between theology and history lies Ste. Croix's avowed profession as a historian. Although I am fascinated by the way he makes the familiar territory of the ancient Greek and Roman worlds come alive, my interest here is with the contributions to ancient economic history. Much remains to be done on this score, especially in relation to the ancient Near-Eastern context of the Bible. Ste. Croix must be a major figure in any reconstruction, and that for the following reasons: he highlights the crucial roles of class-conflict; provides an extraordinarily useful correction to dominant assumptions concerning trade and commerce; and he shows that such reconstructions are inevitably politically engaged. If you are so engaged, then it pays to be explicit about it.

The texts in question are relatively few, although they are dense enough. I have already mentioned the book on class-struggle.[3] Less useful for me is the other work published in his lifetime, *The Origins of the Peloponnesian War*,[4] as well as the posthumous collection on Athenian democracy.[5] However,

---

[3] Ste. Croix 1981.
[4] Ste. Croix 1972.
[5] Ste. Croix 2004.

towards the end of his life Ste. Croix devoted his attention to biblical matters, planning two volumes, *Early Christian Attitudes to Women, Sex and Marriage*, and *Essays in Early Christian History*. With his memory and eyesight failing, the various essays never quite gelled, so he planned to condense them into one volume, *Radical Conclusions*. In the end, out of the mass of his papers what did appear was the posthumously edited collection entitled *Christian Persecution, Martyrdom, and Orthodoxy*.[6] Along with the class-struggle book, this posthumous work is my major concern.

The politics of style

Ste. Croix's sentences are a pleasure to read. Engaged and punchy, they invite you into a conversation where his positions, political passions, likes and dislikes are never far away. The initial impression of a book like *Class Struggle* is daunting. There are 742 large, densely printed pages weighed down with an extraordinary mountain of evidence; it is more than a decent read and can easily double as a significant addition to a body-builder's collection of weights. However, the bulk soon becomes a blessing when you start reading; at the mid-point, you begin wishing for more.

The sentences seem to be an intrinsic part of this solid, powerful man with a massive bald pate. Often long, full of colons, semi-colons, dashes, parentheses, snatches of Greek and Latin, acronymic references and elaborate subordinate clauses, they never draw attention to themselves as in some way pretentious. Soon enough, I wanted to find out what comes next, anticipating the next insight that might jump out in the next paragraph or page. For me, at least, it was like seeing a familiar story retold in a way that illuminated many of its cul-de-sacs and opaque corners. Having studied classics and then early church-history for many years, the general contours of the narrative are still imprinted on my mind. But Ste. Croix recasts it in a way that makes an awful lot of sense.

Yet Ste. Croix's sentence production is also idiosyncratic. I do not mean the cultivated eccentricity of English academia, especially of the stuffy and parochially arrogant air of Oxford or Cambridge. Rather, it is mark of someone keen to assert the presence of an odd one out – a Marxist among

---

[6] Ste. Croix 2006.

conservative classicists. The maze of in-text abbreviated references to primary and secondary literature must have taken some insistence for the publisher to accept. Really a complex series of bracketed acronyms, this code takes some cracking, at least if one wants to check all of them, but the enticing style does not encourage you to do so unless there is some need to chase up a crucial reference. Apparently, Ste. Croix had an even greater struggle to get the press (Duckworth) to keep the point after 'Ste.' – in that he obviously won out as well. The text itself is peppered with brief notes that really act like feature boxes (where will I put this one on that curious plural of *demokratiae* in pope Hippolytus's commentary on the book of Daniel?),[7] comments such as those on his favourite van Gogh painting, *De Aardappeleters* (it adorned the original cover of the book), comparisons with contemporary politics, jibes at self-serving and obnoxious ruling classes,[8] the Church, Christianity, and on and on.

Writing and life seem to merge with Ste. Croix: Macau-born (1910), school leaver at 15, articled clerk and then solicitor (1926–40), air-force pilot, given to vigorous marches through the country, tennis-player with some ability, so much so that he competed at Wimbledon in 1929 and defeated Fred Perry, who dominated world-tennis in the 1930s and was the last great English male player, and then finally classics-scholar from the age of 40. For me at least, the puzzle is his name: how can it be that someone with a name like Geoffrey Ernest Maurice de Ste. Croix was an Englishman, or at least, if he was such, then he must have come from the old aristocracy. Not so, it seems, since he was of Huguenot extraction, his ancestors having fled to England during the persecution of Protestants in France some centuries earlier.

Inviting, idiosyncratic, and also engaged: this is probably the most appealing element of Ste. Croix's style. His Marxism is never merely a tool for historical analysis, for, on every page, his commitment to the Marxist political and economic programme shows through. It might involve showing up the late Athenian Isocrates's despicable defence of property and privilege, or the spirited defence of Greek democracy as a genuine avenue for the poor and the artisans to have a say in politics and the law, or the way the Romans sought to ensure that those born to rule did so without too much interruption

---

[7] Ste. Croix 1981, p. 315.
[8] Among the best of these is his ironic use of the quaintly British 'cultured gentleman' (see Ste. Croix 1981, p. 13 and many more).

from the annoying masses, or the profound dislike of Christianity and the Church. Often, the political comments turn up in parentheses, as, for example, with the discussion of slavery as a result of an accident of Fortune in which the good and wise man is never 'really' a slave and that the bad man is in bondage to his lusts. Ste. Croix writes parenthetically, '(I fancy that such austere philosophical notions are of greater assistance in the endurance of liberty, riches and peace, than of slavery, poverty and war)'.[9] These moments appear on nearly every page. The underlying cause for Ste. Croix is that of the masses who were continually ground into the dust, as well as the uncovering of the mechanisms by which the 'propertied classes', as he calls them, ensured that they remained propertied. More often than not, Christianity was far too comfortable with the propertied classes, supporting them where possible, deriving benefits for itself, with little care for the large numbers of poor in its own ranks. When it comes to the crunch, Ste. Croix finds that the Church would always side with the fat cats. Far too much was at stake for it to do otherwise.

As inevitably happens, I have already passed from the form of Ste. Croix's sentences to their content. The life-long engagement with theology is a major feature of that content; its great opposite is history. Or, at least for Ste. Croix, they are opposites. When he deals with the Bible, theology or the Church, he is keen to point out that he engages with this material not as a theologian, but as a historian. 'Theologian' means an inevitable obfuscation, a religious commitment that clouds analysis of a biblical text or a historical situation. 'Historian' means none of these things: rather, it designates a clear analysis of the data and a search for factual truth. The opposition is sharpest when Ste. Croix deals with biblical texts, persecutions in the early Church, martyrdom, ecumenical councils, and practices concerning women, slavery and property. It is hardly necessary to point out that the opposition is a troubled one, so what follows may be read in part as an effort to problematise that opposition, for Ste. Croix is as much a theologian as a historian.

---

[9] Ste. Croix 1981, pp. 418–19.

Theology...

For some curious reason, Ste. Croix never explains precisely what he means by 'theologian' and 'historian', probably because the distinction seems obvious – or at least he assumes so. In this pair, Ste. Croix presents himself as the humble and hard-nosed historian, concerned purely with historical reconstruction on the basis of available evidence. What about theologians? The assumption is that they approach the material from a position of religious commitment and that, for this reason, they read it in a way that is favourable to that commitment. The rough edges are carefully smoothed down, the harsh facts avoided or dismissed. In short, their faith leads them to misread the texts. None of this is spelled out in so much detail, but it underlies the opposition.

As I pointed out above, the opposition turns up only when Ste. Croix discusses matters concerning Bible and Church.[10] Obviously, he has little need of it in his treatments of democracy in Athens and elsewhere, or the oppositions to the propertied classes in Greece and especially Rome, or in his search for the motor of history in the Greek world. It also offers another reason for his wariness of New-Testament criticism, since much biblical criticism is still driven by religious commitment in one shape or another. More importantly, it marks a struggle over the appropriate hermeneutic framework one brings to these texts. Although he occasionally slips up, Ste. Croix is not so silly as to take an empiricist line, arguing that his only concern is the facts and that any theoretical framework obscures those facts with some anachronistic system arbitrarily imposed on the texts. Instead, his position is that 'theology' is less fruitful than the Marxist framework he adopts.

So, what happens when we put theology on the chair under the single globe and ask it a few more probing questions? It is easy enough to point out that theology is not a monolithic entity (neither is Marxism for that matter), so there is little point in pursuing that angle. More interesting is the question whether all biblical critics or historians of the Church are theologians, or that they come to the material with theological assumptions. Biblical criticism has fought a long and difficult battle for well over a century to distinguish itself

---

[10] As but one example among many, see Ste. Croix 2006, p. 285.

from theology.[11] Part of this struggle was an institutional one: biblical criticism in (especially European) universities had to show that it was a 'scientific' discipline. In order to do so it followed two paths. First, biblical criticism claimed to be scientific in the desire to distinguish itself from systematic theology. Most biblical critics still react strongly to the common assumption found outside the discipline that their own discipline is really part of theology. Second, biblical criticism dropped the faith presupposition, as well as any notion that divine causality plays a role in biblical interpretation. And what came in its place? It was a resolutely historical focus, deliberately named *historical-criticism*, which developed its own sub-disciplines (source, form and redaction criticisms) in order to undertake a dual task – the search for the history of the literature of the Bible and for the history behind it. Those who are still beholden to this position often describe themselves as historians, much like Ste. Croix, albeit without the Marxist framework (although there are a good number of Marxist biblical critics as well).

Ste. Croix would have pointed out that all this is really a subterfuge and that many critics may attempt do their scholarly work in such a fashion, but that they actually still hold to some religious faith, attend worship on a Saturday or Sunday, and vainly try to keep these two parts of their lives separate. And he would be perfectly correct. Indeed, it is one reason why the former dominance of historical-criticism within biblical studies has been slowly crumbling in the last three or four decades (other reasons include the limits and staleness of such a method). Paradoxically, one outcome of this hegemonic challenge has been the resurgence of Marxist interpretations of the Bible.

Further, there is the logical question whether theology (as a distinct discipline from biblical criticism) necessarily entails religious faith. It does, if we take Anselm's description of theology as faith seeking understanding, *fidens quaerens intellectum*, but I would argue that there is no logical necessity for it to do so. Rather than seeing belief in a god as the over-arching and defining feature of theology, it is but one contingent element in a much wider collection of items that make up theology. Theology may be understood as a distinct language; as a collection of topics such as creation, history, anthropology,

---

[11] Since I cannot assume that all the readers of this book have a working knowledge of biblical criticism, every now and then I cover some basics of that discipline in order to set the scene.

ethics, human relations, collectives, and the nature of belief; and also as a system of ever-changing thought with its own history of problems, questions and debates. In this respect, it is no different from, to cull a few examples from a rather long list, philosophy, theoretical mathematics, and literary criticism. In other words, it is perfectly possible for someone to be an atheist and practise theology.[12]

All of which means that it is a little facetious on Ste. Croix's part to use 'theology' as a blanket term to describe all that he abhors as dubious scholarship on the Bible and early Christianity. What he really means are apologists for Christianity and, on that score, I wholeheartedly agree with him. There are more than enough efforts to detoxify the Bible and make it better for you. Ste. Croix's ire was always fanned by such efforts to render palatable toxic biblical texts.

We cannot avoid Ste. Croix's own background here, for the denigration of theology is also a signal of the rejection of that background. Ste. Croix's mother was a British Israelite, one of those quaint Christian groups that only the English can produce. Appearing first in the millenarian turmoil of the English Revolution, the British Israelites hold, among other beliefs, that the British are genetic descendants of the lost ten tribes of Israel (only Judah and Benjamin stayed in Palestine), that biblical characters such as Jeremiah, Joseph of Arimathea and Paul spent time in Britain, and that the royal family is descended from King David. With the spread of the British Empire, this amorphous collection of beliefs too crossed the seas and germinated above all in the American colonies. (In Australia, they are now known as Christian Israelites and form their own small church.) Rather than form a distinct group under a notable leader, the British Israelites originally tended to remain part of their own churches. So Ste. Croix would have experienced some unique and convoluted modes of biblical interpretation in his youth. It would be too easy to point out that Ste. Croix was rejecting a distorted form of Christianity and its modes of biblical interpretation. I would rather take a different line: the interpretive modes of the British Israelites (and other similar groups) show up the truth of mainstream-apologetics for the Bible. The content of the arguments may differ, but the form is the same: engage in what interpretive con-

---

[12] See the more extensive discussion of this issue in the conclusion to Boer forthcoming.

tortions are necessary to render the Bible palatable. In particular, Ste. Croix found highly problematic the efforts to make the bloodthirsty, genocidal God of the Hebrew Bible into a God of love. Or, according to Ste. Croix, Yahweh, the God of the Hebrew Bible was 'a cruel and vicious creature, guilty of innumerable acts and commands which no one today, whether Christian, Jew, agnostic or atheist, would regard with anything but detestation'.[13] Further, in his last years, Ste. Croix spoke of the freedom in which he could, 'After almost a whole long lifetime of false politeness towards the deity whom I was brought up to worship and adore,... speak and write exactly as I please about the ancient genocidal monster represented by his worshippers as glorifying in the mysterious name of Yahweh'.[14]

Yet this should not be taken as the sole cause of Ste. Croix's suspicion of the Bible and Christianity; at most, it is one element that plays a role in his dealings with the Bible and early Christianity. So it is extremely unfortunate that the editors of the collected essays, *Christian Persecution, Martyrdom and Orthodoxy*, take this approach. In an extraordinary moment, the pious Joseph Streeter dismisses Ste. Croix's Marxism in a sentence or two and then suggests that most of the blame should be laid at the feet of his widowed British-Israelite mother.[15] The argument offered here is that Ste. Croix's extreme, unreasonable and even fundamentalist rejection of the Bible and Christianity should be seen as a reaction to his mother's equally fundamentalist Christianity. A common assumption underlies this argument: it is either all or nothing; the strength of one's former commitment determines the strength of one's rejection.[16] This assumption is a neat way of sidestepping the challenge to Streeter's own beliefs, which he wears openly in a multitude of notes and corrections to Ste. Croix's texts. In other words, such an argument is a way to

---

[13] Quoted in Streeter 2006, pp. 10–11.

[14] Quoted in Whitby 2006, p. 326.

[15] Streeter 2006, pp. 9–10. The footnotes and comments by the editors of the collection *Christian Persecution, Martyrdom, and Orthodoxy* are astonishing. In an extraordinary case of editorial overkill, they coddle Ste. Croix, quietly hide his Marxism in the backroom, disagree with him and correct some of his points. And the references are some of the most parochial I have seen, restricted by and large to Oxford and Cambridge presses in a way that can only be read as an archaic reassertion of long-lost imperial dominance.

[16] This position was first championed in a systematic fashion by Barr 1977, 1984, and has become orthodoxy since. Of course, as an ordained minister of the Church of Scotland, Barr's own position was suitably mainstream.

ensure a suitably mainstream-Christianity does not need to face the criticisms Ste. Croix develops. It also falls foul of the problems of mono-causality, which I do not need to rehearse here. It is obvious that Ste. Croix's background may have been *one* element in his total approach to Christianity (as I have already argued), but the tradition of Marxist critique of religion is surely another, along with the need to face up squarely to the many problematic texts of the Bible.

Chora *versus* polis

I turn now to the specific issues in Ste. Croix's engagement with what he calls 'theology' (although it is as much New-Testament criticism as theology): Jesus, women, slavery, property, persecution and martyrdom. On the first four, he has a strong point to make concerning the rapid loss by early Christianity of its founder's radical position. He also begins to uncover some important political contradictions within Christianity, but then he does not really take them far enough. As for the last two items – persecution and martyrdom – here, the argument shifts to highlight both the cruelty and intolerance of early Christianity and, curiously, to insist that religion was the primary cause of these less than endearing features. I take each topic in turn.

A significant and, from what I can tell, original feature of Ste. Croix's analysis of the figure of Jesus is the distinction between *chora* and *polis*. It is really a form of spatial analysis, albeit linked in with Ste. Croix's wider Marxist programme. Some basic definitions first: *chora* refers to the countryside, the vast stretches of territory with peasant-farming, village-communes, as well as wilder areas at the limits of human presence; *polis* designates, as the name suggests, the town or city.[17] However, the terms may leak at the edges, for sometimes a village may be called in the literature a *polis*, while at other times the land surrounding and under control of the town may be called *chora* as a synonym for *agroi*, the fields. The latter point is particularly true of the early Greek city-states, which needed those farms to keep everyone fed.

Yet, if we move a few centuries later to Palestine, after the invasions of Alexander in Asia and Egypt, when the Romans ran it as a colonial province,

---

[17] Ste. Croix 1981, p. 9, suggests that, in light of the notorious difficulty in defining a *polis*, the best definition is that a *polis* was one if recognised as such.

when Greek culture was dominant and when the Gospels were written, the opposition between *chora* and *polis* takes on a somewhat different and technical sense.[18] In this case, the *polis* clearly designates a Hellenistic city with varying levels of autonomy, either one established after the invasions of Alexander the Great, perhaps by the Ptolemies or Seleucids (who struggled for possession of Palestine) or an existing city that had become Hellenised. To be 'Hellenised' had architectural, cultural and colonial senses. Architecturally, a Hellenistic city was felt to need an amphitheatre, gymnasium, public buildings, market place and fountains of water; culturally, it meant that the language of governance, law courts, and intellectual matters was Greek; in the colonial sense, a *polis* signalled the presence of a Greek colony in a land that was anything but Greek.

By contrast, *chora* is all the territory outside the colonial city. There the language is the one spoken by the locals (in Palestine, it was Aramaic), the dominant life of peasants and agriculture continues as it had done before the *poleis* arrived, and there was relatively little interaction between the two except for the extraction – often by force – of a very thin margin of surplus-produce to feed the cities, as well as forced labour for city projects. From the perspective of those in the *polis*, they inhabited islands of civilisation in a sea of barbarians; from the side of the *chora*, the *poleis* were alien and brutal tribute-gathering parasites. In short, the exploiting ruling class of Palestine belonged to the *polis*; those upon whose backs they lived were in the *chora*. Ste. Croix is keen to point out that ethnic and linguistic differences in the colonised East should not obscure the basic class-difference between the propertied classes of the *polis* and the non-propertied classes of the *chora*.[19] However, here there is a twist: the distinction itself reflects the perspective of Greek and then Roman colonial presence, for no literature exists that gives voice to those colonised. In order to gain that perspective, we need to read against the grain.

In this context, Ste. Croix places Jesus of Nazareth. He is clearly of the *chora* and avoids the *poleis* until the fateful entry into Jerusalem. Palestine at the

---

[18] There is a shift in the relationship between *chora* and *polis* between the Greek and Roman periods: during the period of the kings who succeeded Alexander, the *chora* was administered directly by the royal bureaucracy; under the Romans much of the *chora*, especially the agricultural areas with their *komai*, villages, came under the administration of the *polis*.

[19] Ste. Croix 1981, pp. 16–17.

time was a client kingdom (directly under Herod Antipas) of the Romans, passing from the Greek rule of the Seleucids to Roman rule, but the sharp distinction between *chora* and *polis* was entrenched. I do not need to go through Ste. Croix's exhaustive analysis of the terms used in the Gospels,[20] since he makes it perfectly clear that Jesus did not bother with the *poleis*. If he came close, it was merely in the fields surrounding a *polis*. One telling point is worth noting: close by Nazareth were Sepphoris, which was six kilometres away, and Tiberias, which was on the shore of Lake Galilee at almost the point closest to Nazareth. Both were Jewish in population and religion but Greek in their administrative structures. Not once in the gospels does Jesus enter them. Quite clearly, as far as the gospels are concerned, Jesus lives, wanders and teaches exclusively among the people of the *chora*.[21]

This spatial feature of the Gospel narratives explains for Ste. Croix the oppositional nature of the words attributed to Jesus. Perhaps the best way to describe his position is that Jesus was an implicit rather than a militant revolutionary. His eschatological message that the 'Kingdom of God' was at hand – literally God's imminent arrival – had profound implications for his approach to property and wealth (and thereby the propertied classes). Quite simply, the possession of property was regarded as an evil and as a massive hindrance to joining this Kingdom of God. Jesus valorises simplicity over luxury and forgoes the influence and power that comes with wealth. In short, everything about him stands against the deep values of the Hellenistic propertied classes, almost uniquely in the literature of the ancient world. Ste. Croix never tires of pointing out that Christianity was no different from its Greco-Roman environment in regard to property, *except for Jesus*.[22] Over against the valorisation of property and the denigration of its lack that he finds everywhere in the Christian literature, Jesus – at least in the Gospels – stood against such an ideological system. Here is Ste. Croix: 'I am tempted to say that in this respect the opinions of Jesus were nearer to those of Bertholt Brecht than to those held by some of the Fathers of the Church and by some Christians today'.[23] Jesus speaks on behalf of those exploited by the colonial, Hellenistic *polis*.

---

[20] Ste. Croix 1981, pp. 427–30; Ste. Croix 2006, pp. 330–6.
[21] Following a path distinct from Ste. Croix but coming to similar conclusions are the excellent studies by Horsley 1996; Horsley 2007; Horsley 2008b.
[22] Ste. Croix 1981, pp. 425–41.
[23] Ste. Croix 1981, p. 433.

The Zeal of G.E.M. de Ste. Croix • 115

What can be said of this analysis? It is a mixture of new and old, of sheer insights and of some quite conventional positions in the never-ending search for the historical Jesus. One insight comes from the crucial role of *chora* and *polis*, an analysis that shows not merely how the figure of Jesus may be placed spatially within the gospel narratives or indeed first-century Palestine, but also how he fits in with an over-riding feature of the Greco-Roman world. Another insight is drawn from his wider analysis of Greco-Roman moral and class-codes. Focusing on some key stories and sayings in the gospels – the camel through the eye of the needle, the rich ruler who must sell all he has, Jesus's quotation from Isaiah 61, the parable of Lazarus, the Beatitudes and the Magnificat – Ste. Croix directs us to the Greek terms. For example, *ptōchos* is far stronger than the usual translation of 'poor': it means those who are filthy, destitute, down-and-out – it is a term used for beggars. It appears again and again in these passages, carrying both moral and class-connotations. In the same way that *kakos* and *agathos*, as well as a host of related terms,[24] have moral and class-meanings – bad vs. good, poor vs. wealthy, ignoble vs. noble, cowardly vs. brave, ill-born vs. well-born, ugly vs. beautiful, dregs vs. pillars of society – so also does a term like *ptōchos*. The same applies to *tapeinoi* in the Magnificat: he has 'exalted those of low degree [*tapeinoi*]' (Luke 1: 52). By contrast, in Greek literature, the word is used pejoratively to designate those who are mean, poor, and base. Time and again the gospel sayings reverse Hellenistic class- and moral values: the despised are actually those who are of value, while the propertied classes are absolute scum. Ste. Croix could not agree more.

The unfortunate fact about these insights is that New-Testament critics have not taken notice of Ste. Croix. Much of this has to do with the woeful parochialism of that discipline (although it is by no means alone in that respect). Biblical critics have dipped into classical studies every now and then, but it is still not as regular as it should be, especially given the fact that the time periods overlap. Of all the New-Testament critics that I have been able to consult, I found only a couple of references to Ste. Croix, and they were not to the

---

[24] Ste. Croix 2006, pp. 338–9, provides a host of related terms: *hoi tas ousias echontes, plousioi, pacheis, eudaimones, gnōrimoi, eugeneis, dunatoi, dunatōtatoi, kaloi kagathoi, chrēstoi, esthloi, aristoi, beltistoi, dexiōtatoi, charientes, epieikeis* – all for the 'good' propertied classes; for the 'bad' unpropertied classes we have *hoi penētes, aporoi, ptōchoi, hoi polloi, to plēthos, ho ochlos, ho dēmos, hoi dēmotikoi, mochthēroi, ponēroi, deiloi, to kakiston.*

class-struggle book or his article 'Early Christian Attitudes to Property and Slavery' (in which the same material may be found) from 1975.[25]

At the same time, Ste. Croix's depiction of a reasonably radical Jesus is by no means new. As a small sample among many, we find him in the mildly oppositional Mediterranean peasant identified by John Dominic Crossan;[26] or the figure – identified by Richard Horsley – who was part of a larger pattern of village-based opposition to imperial power that involved peasant-slowdowns, sabotage, counter-terrorism, revolts, and the message of an alternative community which was addressed to debt-ridden, hungry, and poverty-stricken peasants in their own disintegrating communities;[27] or the one of the liberation-theologians who preaches the preferential option for the poor;[28] or the rebellious figure that Terry Eagleton has championed of late in his return to his theological roots among the Catholic Left,[29] or, to go back a century or so, Kautsky's argument that Gospels actually try to conceal the fact that Jesus was indeed a rebel.[30] Ste. Croix also opts for a rather conventional theological tradition that saw Jesus as a non-militant messiah. The argument goes as follows: Jewish expectations pointed towards a war-like messiah who would vanquish all one's foes and instigate the glorious rule of God's people; but Jesus negates that tradition and comes as a more low-key messianic figure, using the word rather than the sword and being mistaken and executed by the Romans as a run-of-the-mill rebel (of which there were a good number). Out of the four examples I gave above, all but Kautsky assume this non-violent tradition – so also does Ste. Croix.

Ste. Croix shares another assumption with many, but not all, New-Testament critics. It is the question as to whether the documents we have contain accurate information about a person who existed at that time and who engaged in these activities. Or do we merely have representations of Jesus, without any verifiable historical information? Ste. Croix desperately wants the material to be historically reliable, at least for the points he makes concerning Jesus and his place. At the same time, he is rather anxious precisely on this

---

[25] The essay is reprinted in Ste. Croix 2006, pp. 328–71.
[26] Crossan 1993, 1995.
[27] Horsley 2008b.
[28] Gutiérrez 2001; Gutiérrez 1983; Segundo 1976; Segundo 1985.
[29] Eagleton 2007.
[30] Kautsky 2007, pp. 305–12.

matter. While he says it matters little to him whether the Gospels accurately identify what Jesus was doing when, or, indeed, while he admits that the Gospels are woefully unreliable on historical matters, he also asserts more than once that they give 'a true picture of the general locus of the activity of Jesus'.[31] More tellingly, his assertion of reliability is stated as an item of belief: 'if we can trust the only information about Jesus which we have, that of the Gospels (as I believe in this respect we can)'.[32] Yet this assertion is placed in parentheses – a feature that manifests all too clearly Ste. Croix's creeping uncertainty concerning the reliability of the Gospel narratives. As Ste. Croix was fully aware, the mountains of research on the Gospels and the figure of Jesus argue about this matter incessantly, especially because there is very little material available apart from the New Testament. Here, a minimalist position is the most appropriate one, since none of the information can be regarded as trustworthy for historical reconstructions. Even the extra-biblical material is open to question,[33] but what that material does not show is an oppositional Jesus. So we are left with the fact that all we have in the Gospels is a story or four about Jesus, representations with their own appropriate emphases and colours. Ste. Croix could perfectly well have argued that these *representations* place Jesus in the *chora* and not the *polis*. From there, one would need to ask precisely why this was a feature of these legendary tales. But Ste. Croix does not do so, preferring to base his argument on unstable ground.

Finally, there is a curious feature of Ste. Croix's spatial analysis. Early in his book on class-struggle, even before the discussion of Marx, we find a detailed introduction to the distinction between *chora* and *polis*,[34] arguing that it is a crucial feature that unlocks much of the mystery of the Greek world. There is much potential here, as Henri Lefebvre and David Harvey have shown in other contexts,[35] for a developed spatial analysis as part of a larger treatment in terms of class and economics. Yet, for some strange reason, this spatial analysis slips out of the picture, lurking in the background for much of the book until we come to the discussion of Jesus, where it steps back into view.

---

[31] Ste. Croix 1981, p. 430; Ste. Croix 2006, p. 337.

[32] Ste. Croix 1981, p. 427.

[33] Tacitus, *Annals* 44, and a brief reference in Suetonius. The references by Josephus in *Antiquities* are generally agreed to be Christian insertions.

[34] Ste. Croix 1981, pp. 9–19.

[35] Lefebvre 1991; Harvey 1999, pp. 373–445.

Indeed, after the introduction of the distinction, the only other place the terms appear is in the treatment of Jesus.[36] I am not quite sure why this happens, apart from observing that it seems to have been developed originally as part of his analysis of the New Testament and then not taken further.[37] If so, it is a pity, since it has extraordinary potential and should be part of any Marxist reconstructions of the ancient world.

From chora to polis: property, slavery and women

Now Ste. Croix stands where many have stood before him: if Jesus – at least as far the representations of him in the Gospels are concerned – expresses opposition to the features of a colonising Hellenistic culture and thereby the Roman imperial presence, then how did Christianity end up with a diametrically opposed stance? What happened to bring about the change?

Here, Ste. Croix's spatial analysis, which had gone underground for some 400 long pages, re-emerges and provides an incisive insight: between Jesus and the early Church, Christianity undertook a remarkable shift from *chora* to *polis*. That move entailed a shift in language (Aramaic to Greek), culture and, above all, class. Christianity took the huge stride from an ideology of the exploited classes to that of the propertied classes and eventually to an ideology of the state. Already by the time of Paul, barely a few decades after Jesus, we can see the change underway.

Yet space is actually a sign or indeed a dimension of class-struggle. Jesus was implacably hostile to the propertied classes, but, in order to survive, the early Christians needed to adapt to those classes or be crushed underfoot. Or, as Ste. Croix puts it, 'Unless Christianity was to become involved in a fatal conflict with the all-powerful propertied classes, it had to play down those ideas of Jesus which were hostile to the ownership of any large quantity of property; or, better still, it could explain them away'.[38] It is a class-generated shift, moving away from the identification with the exploited to the exploiters.

---

[36] Ste. Croix 1981, pp. 9–19 and 427–30.

[37] The seamless connection between the general introduction of the distinction and its specific use in the case of Jesus shows up quite clearly in his essay, 'Early Christian Attitudes to Property and Slavery' (Ste. Croix 2006, pp. 328–71), which was written while he was compiling *Class Struggle*. In this light, *Class Struggle* gives the impression of introducing a massive number of insertions into that earlier essay.

[38] Ste. Croix 1981, pp. 426–7.

Ste. Croix traces the way such a shift took place in terms of property, slavery and women. I take each one in turn.

With a mix of disgust and some amusement, Ste. Croix traces the way Paul and then a string of church-'fathers' (Irenaeus, Tertullian, Cyprian, Lactantius, Hilary of Poitiers, Jerome, Augustine, John Cassian, Clement of Alexandria, Paulinus of Nola, Gregory of Nyssa, Gregory of Nazianzus, John Chrysostom, and Theodoret) twist uncomfortable biblical passages away from their plain sense.[39] For example, Jesus's command to the rich man, who asks for the secret of eternal life, to sell all he has and give to poor appears in all three synoptic gospels (Mark 10: 21; Luke 12: 33 and Matthew 19: 21). However, in contrast to the bald command in Mark and Luke, Matthew adds the conditional, 'If you would be perfect'. It is this version that is quoted by all the orthodox interpreters, even when they seem to be quoting one of the other gospels. Obviously, the conditional phrase conveniently waters down the command to sell all he has, making it a 'counsel of perfection', a perfection to which we should strive but probably never attain. Further, the burgeoning use of allegory was very handy for blunting the effect of the sayings in the gospels. Ste. Croix is not quite fair to the complexity of allegory and its attempt to deal with the uncomfortable truth of a web of contradictions in the Bible. Yet he does have a point in arguing that it was also extremely useful when exegeting the passages concerning property and wealth: faced with a troublesome passage, one need only argue that it has a meaning at another, spiritual level. Ste. Croix finds such an approach tiresome, amusing and a little frightening.

Apart from allegory, there are two main problems with the profound switch undertaken by all the orthodox writers: the idea of almsgiving, which Ste. Croix attributes to Christianity's Jewish heritage, and the concept of sufficiency [sufficientia]. Almsgiving is the great relief-valve for wealth and property, for one may feel comfortable with all that luxury as long as some of it (the exact amount being left largely to the individual) is given as alms to the poor. Ste. Croix is less concerned with the growing idea that alms can actually forgive one's sin, or indeed secure salvation, than with the way almsgiving becomes a justification for the status quo. It provides the giver with a sense of moral superiority and makes the recipient feel degraded. Even more, it

---

[39] Ste. Croix 1981, pp. 433–8; Ste. Croix 2006, pp. 355–68.

becomes an argument in favour of wealth: how can there be alms if there are
no wealthy people to give them?

At this point, Ste. Croix's pattern of mixing political arguments of his own
day in with his analysis of the early Church begins to show itself. The attack
on almsgiving is as much a critique of today's apologists for the Church and
of the continuing practices of charity as it is of the early Church. (Ste. Croix
does after all state at the outset of the class-struggle book that he feels his work
has political relevance for today.) The same applies to the idea of sufficiency.
It boils down to the argument that sufficient wealth is harmless; it becomes
dangerous only when there is too much. But there is a catch: who determines
what is sufficient? The key phrase, *non plus quam necesse est* (no more than is
necessary), basically means that apart from the filthy rich everyone feels as
though they do not have enough.

All the same, Ste. Croix is too good a scholar not to note exceptions and
anomalies with his argument. The first of these actually shores up his assessment, so much so that he delights in pointing out that the only ones who
really find wealth a problem are the heretics. Among a number of examples
the best is a text called *De divitiis*, written by Pelagius or one of his disciples.
It clearly identifies wealth as a crucial problem, suggesting it would really be
better to have no possessions at all. As Ste. Croix puts it, this 'seems to me a
far better approximation to the thought of Jesus' than any orthodox piece.[40]

The other exceptions do not fit so easily within his overall argument. Ste.
Croix notes that one or two early theologians – Origen (c. 185–c. 254), Basil
(c. 330–79), and Ambrose (c. 339–97) – had some pangs of conscience; indeed,
they felt distinctly uncomfortable with property and wealth.[41] As for Origen
(who was condemned as a heretic for a time), wealth was decidedly evil.
Priests were to give up all property, the texts condemning wealth were not to
be allegorised and one should not pray for anything as mundane as earthly
benefits. Ste. Croix spends little time with Origen, apparently since he did
not feel sufficiently knowledgeable about the man, but even these points are
enough to suggest that Origen is hardly a 'partial exception'. The same applies
to Basil, who pushed for the complete renunciation of property in line with
the legendary texts in Acts 2: 44–5 and 4: 32–7, where we find that the early

[40] Ste. Croix 1981, p. 437; Ste. Croix 2006, p. 367.
[41] Ste. Croix 2006, pp. 361–3.

Christians had 'all things in common'. Ste. Croix dismisses Basil's approach as a monastic one that was entirely impracticable when applied to the world at large. But is this not the point? It was precisely in the ascetic movement, where we find both hermits and primitive monasteries (after St. Anthony [c. 251–356]), that the condemnation of wealth and property was sustained and propagated in early Christianity. They took the gospel-texts attacking property very seriously indeed. This theme of poverty would, of course, return in the middle ages (see below), but it seems to me that Ste. Croix slips past Origen and Basil too quickly,[42] granting them a few sentences before passing on, somewhat thankfully, to the more contradictory figure of the aristocratic Ambrose. He at least noted that property was not of the order of creation, that property may well be an evil, but then found all manner of ways to locate an antidote for this 'poison', namely almsgiving. Ambrose suits Ste. Croix's argument far better, since here we find that characteristic move of negating the polemic against property in the Gospels.

When we get to slavery,[43] there are only the merest hints of troubled consciences on the part of Christian writers (I will turn to those in a moment). Ste. Croix's ploughs grimly through a rather sorry story in which Christianity not only continued pre-Christian attitudes to slavery, but it actually exacerbated them. Christian writings are uniformly uninspiring on this account. As Ste. Croix puts it, 'I know of no general, outright condemnation of slavery, inspired by a Christian outlook, before the petition of the Mennonites of Germantown in Pennsylvania in 1668'[44] – and they were outside the mainstream. Not even Jesus offers a challenge, unlike his condemnation of property. All the pagan arguments also appear in the Christian sources, minus the ameliorations. For example, the argument (based on Galatians 3: 28 and Colossians 3: 11) that one is 'really' free in Christ, despite one's earthy status, mirrors the pagan argument that a good man (the gender-specific term is deliberate) is 'really' free even if he happens to be a slave. By contrast, the bad man is a

---

[42] In fact, Origen and Basil appear only in the essay 'Early Christian Attitudes to Property and Slavery' (Ste. Croix 2006, p. 361) and not in the parallel passage from *Class Struggle*, which was published a little later (Ste. Croix 1981, p. 435). Or, rather, they are named in *Class Struggle*, but nothing is said about their positions, for Ste. Croix wishes to focus on Ambrose alone. Is it that Origen and Basil constitute a little too much of an exception for Ste. Croix's comfort?
[43] Ste. Croix 1981, pp. 418–25; Ste. Croix 2006, pp. 345–55.
[44] Ste. Croix 1981, p. 423; Ste. Croix 2006, p. 355.

slave to his passions even if he is free. Slaves had harsher punishments in a two-tiered legal system, were not permitted to marry, and were not permitted holy office – just as in the pagan world.

But Ste. Croix's main point is that Christianity enthusiastically accepted slavery as part of the inescapable social and economic horizon and then went the extra mile, so to speak, going beyond anything found in the pagan sources. One means of doing so was to remove the idea of freedom into the spiritual realm: freedom was only 'in Christ' and to be found in heaven after death, which meant that one should not change one's earthly status (there is plenty in Paul's texts on this matter). Another means was to drum into slaves the need for obedience, neatly slipping the master into the role of Christ (Ephesians 6: 5) and even God (in the extra-biblical *Epistle of Barnabas* and *Didache*). After all, as one Christian writer after another was keen to point out, a faithful slave gives glory to God. In order to drive home his point, Ste. Croix compares non-Christian prevarications concerning slavery with Christian attitudes. Aristotle might cite some thinkers in his *Politics* who thought slavery 'contrary to nature', the famed Roman jurors of the third century BCE may have made the same argument, pointing out that slavery was the only part of the *ius gentium* that was not part of the *ius naturale*, and Philo of Alexandria might speak with admiration of the sectarian Essenes and the Therapeutai as not having slaves and denouncing the injustice of slave-owners. No Christian writer comes close.

However, there are a few small anomalies in Ste. Croix's account. One concerns a favourite opponent, Augustine (354–430). Ste. Croix derides Augustine for an ingenious and twisting argument, namely that slavery is evil in principle but that it is a result of the punishment for the Fall. Augustine also had to deal with the story of the liberation of the Israelite slaves from Egypt, negating its effect by referring to the New Testament. Now, Augustine may have been as enthusiastic a proponent of slavery as one is likely to find, but what interests me is the fact that he saw problems with slavery, both in the Bible and theologically. We might not like his solutions, but he was astute enough to see that there was a difficulty. Another anomaly concerns the ascetic Ephraim of Nisibis and Edessa (c. 306–73), who has Mary say, 'Let the man who owns a slave give him his freedom', but Ephraim goes on to state that the slave should then come to serve the Lord. But it is a small slip in a dismal picture. The other anomaly in Ste. Croix's account is that of Pope Gregory the Great (c. 540–604), who stated upon the manumission of two slaves that 'it is right that men whom nature from the beginning produced free and whom the *ius gentium* has subjected to the yoke of slavery should be reinstated by the benefits of manumission in the liberty to which they were born'.[45] Ste. Croix is perfectly right to point out that Gregory did not proceed to widespread manumissions, except for Christian slaves owned by Jews. But that does not take anything away from the fact that Gregory recognised in principle that slavery was wrong. All the same, I must admit that Gregory's voice is really an exception in an overwhelming picture that is by no means pretty.

A very similar story applies to women as it did to slaves.[46] This is one of Ste. Croix's less original discussions, so I will not spend much time with it. His basic argument is that if it was bad in the pagan world for women, it was far worse in Christianity. He draws attention to the 'unhealthy' attitudes to sex and marriage in the letters of Paul and Revelation, where marriage is a second-order status to virginity. He is concerned to show at great length that Christian attitudes to marriage made things worse for women since they were backed up with divine sanction. He makes much of the subjection of women and the required obedience to men in passages such as I Corinthians 11 and Ephesians 5, the fear of menstrual pollution in Leviticus and the blaming of women for the Fall, but I cannot see anything that has not been said before. It seems there is much shadow-boxing with his past in this section, especially when we come across arguments that the plain meaning of the text – believed to be the word of God – has been held for centuries. He does so to counter apologists (the ubiquitous 'theologians') who try to detoxify the Bible for personal reasons or for church-politics – that task is always worth doing. Yet the polemic is wasted and a little too zealous, since most reasonable biblical critics have accepted that the Bible is deeply sexist and oppressive and see little need to defend it on that score.

Nevertheless, there are one or two bright spots in his argument, albeit for different reasons. I begin with the more substantial and problematic one: Ste. Croix's argument that women form a distinct class, based on his assessment of the shortcomings on this question in Marx and Engels.[47] The premise is

---

[45] *Epistle* 6:12, quoted in Ste. Croix 1981, p. 423.
[46] Ste. Croix 1981, pp. 103–11.
[47] Ste. Croix 1981, pp. 99–101.

the conventional Marxist point that class is determined by one's place in the process of production. Thus, since one of the productive roles of women is the bearing and care of children, then women form a distinct class. Further, the inferior place – politically, economically and socially – of women is a direct result of the desire by men to control and possess them and their offspring. Despite Ste. Croix's own sense of originality, this is not a particularly new position.[48] However, even in the way Ste. Croix frames the argument, it is problematic, for it threatens to confuse the question of one's role within the process of production and gender. In response, let me, like Ste. Croix, take a fairly conventional Marxist approach: if men own the means of production and women do not, then they form distinct classes, but only in terms of production itself and not in terms of gender.[49] Two points may be made here. First, it is rarely if ever the case that all men are owners of production and all women are not; usually some men and fewer women are owners, and most women and men are not. Second, gender is by no means the only feature involved in the division of labour, for it has often happened that the division of labour follows the lines of race, the distinction between coloniser and colonised, between body and mind, town and country, and then in the multifarious directions of capitalist industry and finance. In other words, gender is one factor present in the division of labour and thereby class, but it is not exclusive. If we follow Ste. Croix's logic, then we would also have classes in terms of race, colonialism, town and country and so on.

Further, and on a slightly lighter note, Ste. Croix invokes a certain Martinus Rufus, who offers a pagan foil to the Apostle Paul's obsessions. Rufus really upholds an ideal of marriage that a fairly conventional idealist of our own day might hold: human love as the highest form of love, mutual faithfulness (which excludes sex with slave-girls!), and equal education should apply to girls and boys. I assume Ste. Croix would extend that to gay couples. Finally,

---

[48] Among the almost endless literature on this topic, see the excellent representative collection by Hansen and Philipson 1990. See also Reed 1970.

[49] I stay with a conventional Marxist argument, since that is what Ste. Croix seeks to do. However, it would be interesting to pursue the implications of Marx and Engels's half-acknowledged argument in *The German Ideology* that the first division of labour is in terms of gender. They note it, only to say that it is really preliminary, for the first division of labour follows mind and body. This linking of gender and class at such a basic level would be one track to follow in a Marxist-feminist analysis that sought to avoid mono-causal explanations. See further Boer 2003.

we have the reappearance of a favourite parable, that of Lazarus and the rich man in Luke 16: 19–31. Here, Ste. Croix adapts the final statement of Abraham, when the rich man, suffering in hell, begs Abraham to let Lazarus, now safely ensconced in Abraham's bosom, to go and tell his brothers to amend their ways. 'They have Moses and the prophets…', says Abraham, 'If they do not hear Moses and the prophets, neither will they be convinced if some one should rise from the dead' (Luke 16: 29 and 31). Ste. Croix suggests we replace 'Moses and the prophets' with 'the general climate of orthodox opinion in society' and apply it to our own day.

Assessment

Thus far, I have largely restricted myself to critical exposition, but now let me offer a more sustained assessment of Ste. Croix's arguments. I have raised a few questions already, such as Ste. Croix's reliance on the Gospels for historical information, inconsistency in the use of spatial analysis, anomalies in the overall assumptions in the early Church concerning property and slavery and his argument that women form a distinct class from men. But I want to interrogate his analysis more insistently so that it eventually gives up its secrets and assumptions. Ste. Croix's command of his sources is almost intimidating and his accounts of the Christian attitudes to property, slavery and women are quite compelling. However, any sustained assessment of Ste. Croix must begin with his carefully constructed argument that within Christianity there was an extraordinary shift from the attitudes of Jesus – at least as far as Ste. Croix can determine them – to that of the early Church. Why did this shift take place?

In seeking to explain such a transition, Ste. Croix offers two reasons, one much more astute than the other. Less persuasive is his argument that Christianity came to focus on relations between individuals – 'man to man' as he puts it – which soon enough becomes the relationship between an individual and God. This meant that social relations came a distant second. There is nothing particularly new in this argument and it is not all that persuasive. We find it in the position of some Christians today (of both the conservative and liberal variety) although with a positive turn: Christianity is not a religion in the conventional sense but a relationship with God, and all that counts is that relationship. Here, indeed, the ghosts of Ste. Croix's Christian past are close beside him, even to the point of making a plea that those Christians who have moved away from such an individualistic focus and are increasingly concerned (this in the 1970s) with collective matters of class would do well to consider biblical approaches to property, since they may well have a 'powerful influence' on the future of humanity.[50]

When Ste. Croix comes to the overtly Marxist reasons, he is far more persuasive. In this case, it is clearly a matter of class: the need to survive, the desire to persuade the ruling classes that Christianity was not a threat and the increasing numbers of Christians from those propertied and wealthy classes all played a role. In this situation, the early eschatological beliefs of the movement with their hope for justice at the coming of God were bound to fade, especially since Jesus was certainly taking his time to appear in the heavens, flanked by his chariots and horsemen. Above all, the oppositional nature of the culture and politics of the *chora* was never going to make inroads into or persuade the dominant world of the *polis*.

Fall-narratives

This Marxist argument raises a tension that runs through Ste. Croix's account – between morally culpability and inability to see the problem. I will return to this problem in a few moments, but first I would like to deal with another matter that arises from this account, namely the narrative of a fall. Jesus might have challenged assumptions concerning property, giving voice to the values and practices of the *chora* (of which Ste. Croix approves), but then there was a fall from grace when the early Church enthusiastically embraced the *polis*.

This is a problem that bedevils scholars who work on this early-Christian material – both the New Testament and other documents from the first few centuries. I do not mean scholars those who assume Jesus supported private property, or that he was a harmless purveyor of wisdom-sayings, or, indeed, that disciples like Peter were actually small businessmen (Peter ran a fishing business, or so the argument goes). Instead, I am interested in that sizeable portion of biblical scholars who argue, like Ste. Croix, that there is something radical about the records concerning Jesus. Once you grant this position, then you need to account for the way the Church attained such grandeur and

---

wealth within at most three centuries. The *terminus ad quem* for such a shift is the (in)famous conversion of Constantine, conventionally dated to the night before the battle of the Milvian Bridge in 312 CE. The following morning, as his soldiers marched to fight for Constantine's control of the Empire, they had – or so the legend goes – the symbol XP on their shields (the first two Greek letters of the word 'Christ'). What exactly happened has been the topic of interminable debate (his mother's influence, some perceptive political judgement and so on), but the historical effect of that conversion is almost without comparison.

Within the intervening three centuries, something happened to the Christian movement. It is really a question where you draw the line: did the fall from a rebellious, proto-communist movement happen later or earlier? Some, like the anabaptists and indeed Christian anarchists, argue that the fall happened with that imperial conversion in 312 CE. At that moment, the Church sold out to the devil – a wealthy and powerful one at that. Others place it progressively earlier. In the flood of current 'empire-studies', the fall happened somewhere in the second century. Although some note the ambiguities of the Bible,[51] the majority of these studies argue that significant portions of the New Testament take up an anti-imperial position, challenging the propaganda, religion, power and oppression of the Roman Empire.[52] So, if one agrees that the texts of the New Testament were written during the first and early second centuries, the fall must have happened after they were written. Others push the date earlier. It must come, it is argued, after the first Christian communities mentioned in the Acts of the Apostles, where 'all who believed were together and had all things in common'.[53] In order to sustain this argument, one has to make a significant leap of credulity to assume that this account in Acts provides evidence of a real historical practice. But, if you do, then the fall happens after these early communities, perhaps in the later first century. Yet others push the date earlier still, locating it with Paul. A characteristic motif of liberal theology and biblical criticism in the middle of the twentieth century was that the change took place between Jesus and Paul. Jesus may have been the radical, but Paul is the great institutionaliser, the

---

[51] For example, Moore 2006.
[52] As a sample, see Carter 2004, 2006; Elliott 1997, 2000, 2008; Horsley 2002, 2003, 2008.
[53] Acts 2:44. See also Acts 4:32–7.

one who establishes new churches, puts down excesses (either legalism or libertarianism), and commands women and slaves to be subordinate. In other words, the shift is taking place within the New Testament itself. If we add the point that Paul's genuine letters (there are seven of them – Romans, 1 and 2 Corinthians, Galatians, Philippians, 1 Thessalonians and Philemon) are actually the earliest biblical texts in terms of when they were written, then the shift happens very early indeed – some time around the 40s and 50s of the Common Era. This is where we find Ste. Croix, since, along with Plato and Augustine, Paul is one of his great opponents, the same Paul who wrote gems such as 'Let every person be subject to the ruling authorities' (Romans 13:1).

There are at least two problems with opting for such a fall-narrative. The first is that the Gospels were actually written after Paul's letters. So what looks like a chronological change between Paul and Jesus ignores the chronology of when the texts were written. In terms of that textual sequence, Paul first wrote his troubled texts advocating order and subservience, while the texts about Jesus's challenges to wealth, power and privilege came later. One may answer that, even though the Gospels were written after Paul's letters, they provide a reasonably accurate record of what Jesus said and did. Ste. Croix opts for this approach, but it is shaky ground, for there is no way of knowing whether the Gospel texts are reliable or not. Too many searches for the historical Jesus have come up with different reconstructions for one to have any confidence that the historical Jesus may be recovered with any certainty.

So we are left with a situation that troubles Ste. Croix's fall-narrative (as it does many comparable fall-narratives): the record of Jesus's anti-establishment position comes after Paul's more pro-establishment line. Before I draw out the implications of that situation, let me pick up a second criticism of the fall-narrative: it is far too linear. It assumes some more or less pristine moment – at least the early circle around Jesus – that is subsequently lost. The echoes with the loss of paradise in Genesis 2–3, treatments of the nature of early Israel[54] and, indeed, accounts of primitive communism within some Marxist thought are a little too close to such a linear narrative. A far better and more realistic option in light of the biblical material is to identify contradictions that run through all this material: texts that are quite radical appear side

---

[54] Gottwald 1999; Meyers 1988; Yee 2003; Jobling 1991, 1992; Boer 2005.

by side with others that are decidedly reactionary. The problem, at least for Ste. Croix and so many others, is that these contradictions do not fit easily into such a neat fall-narrative.

On contradiction

As a way into those contradictions, I would like to return to the tension I identified a little earlier between moral culpability and inability to see the problem. If we ask why early-Christian authors almost uniformly failed to challenge property, condemn slavery and the treatment of women, then we find Ste. Croix slipping back and forth between two possibilities: they are morally culpable, or they simply could not see that their positions were problematic. Both are contained within Ste. Croix's answer that it was due to class-struggle. Let me take the example of slavery. As Ste. Croix argues in the opening sections of *Class Struggle*, slavery was one part of the unfree labour (which included serfs such as the *coloni*) that was the central means by which surplus was generated for the dominant and propertied classes of the Greco-Roman world. To challenge that, even to push for its abolition, would have destroyed that socio-economic system. A similar point could be made for property or gender: to undermine the system of property and gender-structures would have sent the system into a tailspin. At this point, we can go two ways. One is to argue that the failure of the propertied classes to condemn property, slavery and sexism was a conscious act for which they are culpable, even if it was a matter of self-preservation. They were not going undermine the system that made them who they were. While I have much sympathy with this position, it attributes a self-consciousness that was simply beyond most (apart from those brilliant Roman lawyers and someone like Aristotle or Gregory the Great). It requires that one has sufficient distance to assess whether a system is reprehensible or not and then decide to support it out of cynical self-interest. But there is, to my mind, a better explanation implicit within Ste. Croix's position: slavery was part of the untranscende-able horizon – or preferably mode of production – of the ancient world. Its abolition was simply unimaginable, unless one was able to imagine a very different world. The wobbles and inconsistencies in the thought of some, such as Augustine or Gregory, reinforce such a position. They saw an anomaly, either in practice or in theory or (in the case of Augustine) in the Bible, but then they came up with ingenious 'solutions' to that anomaly.

There is one element to the treatment of slavery, women and property ignored by Ste. Croix, but vital for my argument. When debates on slavery grew in strength in the nineteenth century, they did so on the basis of the Bible (Ste. Croix's treatment stops before this point with the first statement against slavery by Mennonites of Germantown in Pennsylvania in 1668). Many drew upon the traditional arguments from the Bible – the fabled Curse of Canaan/ Ham in Genesis 9: 25–7 and the multiple texts in the New Testament admonishing obedience by slaves – but others now focused on other texts to show that slavery was not a Christian position.[55] Similarly, the arguments over gender that first began in the late nineteenth century with *The Woman's Bible*,[56] abated for a while and then rushed forth from the 1970s onwards, also took place in terms of biblical texts. Those who wanted to recover a more positive role for women in light of the Christian tradition began using other texts in contrast to those texts on which Ste. Croix gleefully focuses (in his condemnation of Christian attitudes to women). So we find Genesis 1: 27, where God creates male and female in his image, or Galatians 3: 28, where there is neither male nor female, or indeed slave nor free, in Christ, or narratives in which women play a larger role, such as Esther, Ruth, Deborah, or the Song of Songs.

I am less interested here in the extensive debates around such moves by second-wave feminist critics and theologians and far more interested in asking how such debates could arise if slavery and sexism were almost universally supported and indeed exacerbated by Christian theologians and exegetes? I would suggest that it could happen because the horizon had changed, or rather, the untranscendeable horizon had slowly but inexorably become passable. It might have been late, for theology is a notoriously conservative beast, but change it did. Now, Ste. Croix is aware of these shifts, at least with regard to feminism, and he does his best to combat such readings, arguing that they involve special pleading and a contortionist's version of biblical exegesis. As far as slavery is concerned, he conveniently stops his narrative of Christian justifications before the great debates of the nineteenth century. Yet he would have known perfectly well that evangelicals like William Wilberforce knew their Bible well enough to make extensive use of it in their long struggle to abolish slavery.

---

[55] See especially Ste. Croix 2006, pp. 259–319. See also Harrill 2006, pp. 165–92.
[56] Stanton 1993.

So the horizon had shifted and it became possible to read the Bible against the tradition on which Ste Croix stakes his condemnations. In case I am misunderstood, let me make it clear that I am not arguing that the Bible itself brought about such changes, nor am I arguing that the Bible merely provided a language for wider social debates and struggles concerning slavery and then women. There is some limited mileage in such positions, but I am after a different point: the Bible is an extraordinarily contradictory collection of texts, as one would expect for a body of literature collected over something like a millennium. For Ste. Croix, this is a more uncomfortable position, given as he is to what might be called mono-interpretations; as far as he is concerned, there is one correct meaning, although it is not such a good one. What these belated debates reveal is a much more fractious and tension-ridden collection of texts that we call the Bible. I grant that the dominant voices assume slavery and the subjection of women, but even within those voices we find nervousness, inconsistency and problems with such positions (as a reference to, among many, Bakhtin or Jameson would show). It is precisely these contradictions that gave someone like Augustine or Gregory a sleepless night or two, and then much later enabled the lengthy struggles within a different social formation concerning slavery and women.

However, it is when we come to property that my argument gets a real head of steam. As Ste. Croix shows in the stories of Jesus, the texts contain clear statements condemning property and wealth. I would add to those the accounts of communism of goods in the Acts of the Apostles (2: 44–5 and 4: 32–5), even though Ste. Croix dismisses the texts from Acts too readily. This is a shame, since as Luxemburg and Kautsky argued in some detail at the beginning of the twentieth century, the theme of Christian communism carried on in the early Church. Despite efforts to blunt the effect of such texts, efforts which Ste. Croix traces brilliantly in terms of the shift from *chora* to *polis*, these texts from Acts would not go away, so much so that before long we find them becoming the bad conscience of the Church.

For instance, they had astounding resonance in the middle ages, however much we may feel that medieval Christianity was rebarbative in its disgust of sexuality and the human body and all its normal liquid and solid functions. At some point in the eleventh century, there was a notable shift from the older theme of *Christus Victor* to the suffering servant. Christ the Victor had done sterling service, convincing one ruler after another from Constantine the Great onwards that the one who had conquered death was also going to be your best bet in warfare. Across Europe, local chieftains and kings decided that *Christus Victor* would give them that upper hand in battle, or at least bring them on par with that dreadful enemy across the river who had happened to become Christian. Missionaries were aware of this spiritual arms-race and deliberately targeted such rulers. And, once the ruler went over, so did the people, more or less. But then, especially in the life of common people, another theme emerged. The powerful Christ who had overcome death to take his seat at the right hand of God had become less appealing. His place was taken by a Christ who had suffered in humility and died, the one who stated to the rich man, 'sell what you have and give to the poor' (Mark 10: 21), who was essentially a beggar and said that it was easier for a camel to go through the eye of a needle than for a rich man to enter heaven. This Christ was also the suffering servant found in the book of Isaiah (ch. 53), who undergoes torment and humiliation for the sake of others. So we find a common pattern between 1000 and 1500 in which the ideal of poverty came to dominate Christian thought. In protest against the world, the obvious wealth and pomp of the Church, and monastic orders that had become lax, people would seek ever more austere forms of self-denial, poverty and communism in living. Others would be inspired, join the original small band and soon enough another order would be established. Then it too would become wealthy through bequests, land would accrue, the wine would flow, aristocratic sons and daughters would join them, and the original impulse would fade. So someone else would recover the ideal of a simple life in poverty and the process would begin again. In the eleventh and twelfth centuries, a string of new orders sprang up, such as the Augustinian canons, the Cistercians, Premonstratensians, Carthusians, Dominicans and especially the Franciscans. Although they interpreted the call to give up private property in different ways, they were all driven by the criticisms of property and the ideal of poverty which they believed came from the mouth of Christ. It may have been in service to the world, or in contemplative cells with a vow of silence, in simple communities where they practised a communism of goods, or in the extreme form of the Franciscans, who initially lived quite literally as mendicant beggars. Of course, all of this could work in a society where such a life was admired and envied, and where people would give to support such movements, since in that way they sought to secure their own salvation.

This struggle in the medieval world throws a spotlight on the fact that the Bible presented people with contradictory messages concerning property and wealth. One could pull out many verses showing the wisdom of hard work, wealth and property, especially from collections of sayings such as those in the book of Proverbs, or one could point to the vast numbers of cattle and tents in Abraham's hands, which were clearly signs of God's blessing. But then there were those troublesome texts in the Gospels and Acts where the very opposite turned up, texts which would always be the bad conscience of the classes who owned the means of production. It is not for nothing that such texts would form the ideological basis of one utopian movement after another which pushed for the abolition of private property and of money.

I have spent some time with this matter since it brings out the fact that the Bible is a very two-faced collection of texts. Although it is more subdued in regard to slavery and women, such contradictions cannot be avoided when it comes to property and wealth. So what does Ste. Croix do with these contradictions? He is actually torn and follows a convoluted path in his interpretation – at least from what we can see in the material available. On the one hand, Ste. Croix would like a unified text with a singular meaning, for this is easier to assess and, as is often the case, attack. And, if there is any anomaly, he has a tendency to explain it away in light of his over-arching position. But, then, another approach shows itself: Ste. Croix is perfectly willing to admit that there is contrary material, especially since he was known for his careful gathering of mountains of evidence. So, on the question of property, Ste. Croix dutifully notes all those texts attacking property in the Gospels. Even more, there are the apocalyptic texts – in the Bible restricted to Daniel and Revelation but much more numerous outside the canon – which Ste. Croix admits are examples of protest or resistance-literature. So, the book of Revelation with its anti-imperial diatribes is 'splendid, blood-curdling stuff'[57] which gives voice in religious terms to implacable resistance to foreign imperialism. Yet, once Ste. Croix admits such tensions in the biblical and extra-biblical material, he follows two overlapping lines of interpretation. One is to propose a linear development in which the initial anti-property and anti-imperial impulse fades and is overtaken by a pro-property and pro-imperial positions,

[57] Ste. Croix 1981, p. 442.

as we saw very well with the way the early Church dealt with the issue of property. The other line is far more fruitful, for Ste. Croix connects such literature with class-struggle. In this case, the literature gives voice to the cries of the oppressed and downtrodden who suffer in impotent frustration and rage. Needless to say, I find this line far more interesting, since it opens up a way of interpreting the contradictory texts in the Bible as well as the literature that follows it. However, that is an issue with which I deal in more detail below.

Religion as primary cause

Before I move on to consider the question of history, one further aspect of Ste. Croix's treatment of Christianity requires some comment – his argument that religion was the primary cause of the occasionally violent struggles that followed the adoption of Christianity as a state-religion. These struggles took various shapes: it may have been the treatment of non-Christians, who were now no longer in the driving seat of empire; it may have been the bitter conflicts between doctrinal positions, whether Orthodox, Nestorian, Pelagian, Arian, Donatist and what have you; it may also have been the deeply bitter personal conflicts which so often overlapped with the doctrinal ones. At this point, we have left the texts of the New Testament well behind and moved into the later centuries of what Ste. Croix calls his 'Greek World' – the modest stretch of time between the sixth century BCE and the seventh century CE, between ancient Greece and Constantinople.

On these struggles, we find Ste. Croix once again slipping between two positions which, at first, appear to work well together. On the one hand, he argues that Christianity effectively diffused open class-warfare by shifting the struggle to questions of doctrinal orthodoxy and heresy; on the other, he puts forward the argument that religion was the prime cause of those struggles. I am not sure these two positions can be held together all that easily. Like the couple who successfully manage to conceal their tensions for a brief visitor, time and a patient investigation reveal the cracks all too quickly.

Let me take a moment to set what is an extraordinary scene. As the Christian Church gained in power and influence, it was riven by one conflict after another. After Constantine had decided to adopt Christianity in the early fourth century, pour funds into building churches and cathedrals, pay for a significant new number of religious public servants as well as all those elaborate vestments, he suddenly realised what he had let himself in for. Here was a group of religious leaders tearing each other to pieces over the smallest doctrinal difference. This would not do, so he called a major ecumenical council – Nicaea in 325 CE – to iron out the problems. He also set a precedent whereby the emperor would call the council, take a significant hand in its proceedings and enforce the positions which thereby became 'orthodox'. Those who were unfortunate enough to lose out, through less than astute politics, lack of numbers, personal animosity or imperial whim, would find themselves branded 'heretics' and relentlessly pursued.

Ste. Croix expends a good deal of energy on some historical points that are extraneous to my concerns: the extent of persecutions of Christians before 312 (less than previously thought); the number of voluntary martyrs (higher than previously thought);[58] the level of imperial 'interference' in defining church-councils like Chalcedon (much more than...). These are interesting enough in themselves and Ste. Croix makes some telling points that have become part of mainstream-positions, especially regarding voluntary martyrs and imperial interference. But there are some aspects of these analyses that draw me much closer to matters of Marxist methods.

To begin with, the debates were certainly not carried out in a calm atmosphere of quiet and rational discussion. For example, at Chalcedon (451 CE), which is the subject of a major essay by Ste. Croix,[59] the lengthy records show that individuals would try to shout down a position and abuse others, while groups would take up chants like football crowds such as 'exo bales', 'chuck 'em out' – repeated over and over. The vehemence of the abuse led the presiding officials to attempt restraint: 'These vulgar outbursts are not becoming to bishops, nor useful to either party'.[60] And, if a position was reached in which a minority was outvoted, that minority would fear for their lives upon returning home for having given up on the 'true faith'. Their parishioners would

---

[58] See Ste. Croix 2006, p. 305. In his discussion of voluntary martyrdom, Ste. Croix assumes it was odd and fanatical – part of the perversity of Christianity. It was, of course, quite central to the tradition, particularly in light of the *imitatio Christi*, of which the highest expression was to die like Christ for the cause. According to Ste. Croix's definition of voluntary martyrdom, where persisting with an act would draw attention to oneself and potentially lead to death, Jesus too was a voluntary martyr and therefore too fanatical for his own good.

[59] Ste. Croix 2006, pp. 259–319.

[60] Ste. Croix 2006, p. 268.

feel they had given in to pressure and would occasionally lynch them. It was so often a life-and-death issue for those involved. This happened to Proterius, the new patriarch of Alexandria, who was appointed to replace the deposed Dioscorus, whose position had been rejected at Chalcedon and who had been relieved of his position. Proterius was mobbed in his church, dragged out, killed, burnt and his ashes scattered – all for taking up a theological position that was not Alexandrian. Juvenal of Jerusalem (bishop from 422 CE) was a little more careful. In order to ensure his safety upon returning home with a bag full of decisions imposed on him by his opponents, he demanded a strong cohort of troops as security. Juvenal had left Jerusalem for the Council of Chalcedon swearing he would not give up his position, but then did an about-face while at Chalcedon. The carrot of making Jerusalem into a patri-archate certainly helped. It took Juvenal two years to reclaim his see as new patriarch against stiff opposition.

What were the issues? Most of them turned on the nature of Christ. A look at any of the statements from these councils from Nicaea onwards will show that the sections on Christ are by far the longest. Of course, each party regarded its own as position as orthodox and that of the others as heretical. One position was Arianism, which argued that Christ was second in status to God the Father, having been created by God and then made into the Son of God. Although condemned at Constantine's council in Nicaea (325 CE), Ari-anism lived on through the support of Constantine's son, Constantius, being overcome only after his death in 361 CE and the Council of Constantinople (381 CE). Another position was the monophysite one of Dioscorus and Euty-ches, which argued that Christ did not have two natures (God and man), but merely one divine nature. Condoned at the second Council of Ephesus (449 CE – often called the 'Robber Council'), it was roundly condemned at Chal-cedon in 451, which set out to overturn the decisions of Ephesus.[61] Another was the opposite, Nestorianism, which held that there were two 'persons' in Christ, rather than one person who was both God and man. Although Nesto-

---

[61] Many of the bishops who had voted in favour of monophysite positions at the second Ephesus council managed a complete about-face at Chalcedon and supported a two-nature Christology. On these matters, Ste. Croix is at his best: 'It looks as though dozens of bishops, on one or another occasion, committed themselves to a theological position which they did not hold and indeed had regarded as heretical immediately before their change of heart: such inconsistency would, surely, be fatal to their chances of eternal life' (Ste. Croix 2006, p. 304).

rius was deposed from his see in Constantinople at the first Council of Ephesus in 431, his beliefs carried on in the Church of the East based in Persia
and extended through missionary work to the Thomas Christians in India.
Yet another position was Pelagianism, which argued that human beings can
take the initial steps to salvation without God's help. The Catholic Church's
theological hit-man, Augustine, took Pelagius on and by 416 CE managed to
have his position condemned at two councils in Africa and to persuade Pope
Innocent I to excommunicate Pelagius.[62]

These struggles, schisms, condemnations and excommunications all seem
to us now to have turned on theological and metaphysical niceties, at far
remove from everyday-life. Some have argued that they were signs of struggle for supremacy between the major centres of Alexandria, Jerusalem, Antioch, Constantinople and Rome. For Ste. Croix, it is a different story: they are
signs of the sheer intolerance of Christianity. No mercy was shown for one's
vanquished opponents and the victors did not hesitate to call in the armed
forces in order to crush their defeated enemies. Ste. Croix's favourite quotation comes from the pagan writer, Ammianus: 'Wild beasts are not more
hostile to mankind than are *most* Christians [*plerique Christianorum*] in their
deadly hatred of one another'.[63]

However, in order to make this argument stick, Ste. Croix relies on what
is at best a shaky argument: religion was the prime cause of such struggles.[64]
Read in a certain way, the evidence does seem to point in that direction, for
the intense debates were over doctrinal matters, and these matters revealed
in stark relief the intolerance of Christians for one another. Ste. Croix has
an obvious reason to make such an argument, for he wants to attribute all
the blame to a Christianity he simply cannot stand. If you attribute these

---

[62] It could be argued that the raging conflicts over the person of Christ were actually
efforts to define the human subject. Is a human being entirely separated from God
(Nestorianism), or perhaps a divine figure on earth (monophysitism), or even divine
but secondary to God (Arianism)? Is a human being capable of any good on his or
her own (Pelagianism)? In the end, the position hammered out a path through these
options. Human beings are distinct, simultaneously separated from God through sin
but also closely connected with God through salvation (orthodoxy). But which human
beings are the subjects of these struggles? Here, class comes into play. If it is only
the propertied classes who classify as human beings, then these doctrines count for
nothing for the vast numbers of exploited. What of the barbarians who increasingly
hammered on the gates of Rome? Are they included too?

[63] Ste. Croix 1981, p. 451; Ste. Croix 2006, pp. 222 and 260.

[64] See especially Ste. Croix 2006, pp. 201–29; Ste. Croix 1981, pp. 447–51.

conflicts to some other cause (politics, say, or economics), then you diminish the corroding effect of Christianity itself. I also suspect that Ste. Croix wants to counter the argument that has been popular ever since Engels's treatment of the sixteenth-century peasant-revolution in Germany: theology provides a language – the only one available at the time – for what are really very different political and economic issues.[65] Engels tries to have it both ways, for he claims Thomas Müntzer, the theologian of the peasant-revolution, as a revolutionary, but then tries to show that the motivation for Müntzer's revolutionary activity was not Christianity or the Bible, but other political and economic factors that were expressed in theological terms. For Ste. Croix, such a position would shunt religion off to the side and render it irrelevant to the main concerns. And, as far as Ste. Croix is concerned, Christianity was certainly not a revolutionary movement, despite what the pagans might have thought.[66]

Nevertheless, this 'religion-first' position it is a strange one to take, especially for one with a strong Marxist agenda. The problem is that it comes uncomfortably close to an idealist position. We see it today with the 'new atheists', who argue in a thoroughly unoriginal manner that religion is the prime cause of war, mayhem, and intolerance, and that it is the major hindrance to just societies,[67] a position that conveniently removes social and economic factors from the equation. Unfortunately, Ste. Croix's approach draws near to such an argument, driven by a desire to show that Christianity is really not so good for one (and to exorcise the ghosts of his past) and that it has real social, political and economic consequences.

Other problems beset the 'religion-first' argument and they are of Ste. Croix's own making. In his long and entertaining essay on the Council of Chalcedon (381 CE), Ste. Croix works carefully through the detailed records to argue that imperial control and direction was a feature from the beginning. Indeed, it was no different from the famous Latrocinium, or 'Robber Council'

---

[65] Engels 1978; Engels 1973a.

[66] It is telling that Ste. Croix does not refer to any of Engels's works on religion, the Bible or Christianity. He does note, without developing the point any further, that the Romans regarded Christianity as anti-social and a potentially criminal conspiracy. The only reason given is that the Christians were too singular and fanatical in their observance and refused to worship the Roman gods on public occasions (Ste. Croix 2006, pp. 109 and 203). Surely there was more at stake than this?

[67] Dawkins 2006; Dennett 2007; Hitchens 2007; Harris 2005; Harris 2006.

at Ephesus in 449 CE,[68] which took a monophysite position and which church-historians (as well as the Western and most Eastern churches) have dismissed as coerced and wayward.[69] For Ste. Croix, the 'Robber Council' is a sure guide to the functioning of all councils, which were under the firm hand of secular, imperial direction. The catch with this argument is that it actually undermines his 'religion-first' position: the more you stress the role of the state, the more you diminish the primary cause of religion – unless you argue that the impe-rial moves were religiously motivated, which Ste. Croix does not do. I can see the motive behind his argument for state-manipulation, since he wants to counter the 'theologians' who hold that Ephesus was strong-armed but that Chalcedon was not, but in doing so he hobbles the primacy of religion.

Not content to don one shackle, Ste. Croix proceeds to put on another, now in terms of his central category of class. Here we find Ste. Croix making a further argument that stands in some tension with his religion-first position, namely, that these doctrinal debates effectively deflected class-conflict. This argument has the potential to be quite insightful. In order to obscure the mas-sive shift of Christianity towards an ideology of the propertied classes, the ten-sions between those classes and the ones who suffered so much at their hands were shunted off into theological struggles. Now, this argument requires some fairly sophisticated moves concerning traces and distortions of class-conflict in terms of ideological struggles. These moves require one to avoid making direct causal connections between class and ideology, an awareness that such deflections manifest themselves in unexpected ways (often in terms of form), and we need to take up some notion of the semi-autonomous nature of the relations and connections between class and ideology.

All of which brings me to some important issues relating to method, which, in light of my comments in the previous paragraph, I would like to frame in terms of the problem of relatedness. Rather than separating the different

---

[68] 'My overall thesis is that the Council of Chalcedon was every bit as much an engine of coercion as the "Robber" Council of Second Ephesus, and that the machinery of compulsion was actually far more powerful at Chalcedon, so much so that actual force did not need to be used, or even visibly threatened, because everyone knew that resistance to the imperial will would result in his ruin' (Ste. Croix 2006, pp. 273–4).

[69] But not all regard the second Council of Ephesus so, for the oriental Orthodox churches – Coptic, Ethiopian and Syrian Orthodox churches, Malankara Orthodox Syrian Church (India, a branch of the Thomas Christians) and the Armenian Church – hold their monophysite position to be valid and reject some of the decisions of Chalcedon.

areas of religion, politics or even class too sharply, we might adopt an Althusserian approach in which each domain is semi-autonomous: economics, social relations (class), politics, culture, education, philosophy, and religion are all semi-autonomous realms. Add to this the fact that the ideological members of the group, in which religion is to be included, are inseparably connected with material institutional structures; this means that ideology takes a very concrete form. Ste. Croix would be willing to go so far, since the Church was very much an institution of state, supported materially and ideologically. Indeed, one of his major pushes is to show how much the secular arm of the state was involved in doctrinal disputes. Yet he does not make the move to relate these theological debates with other semi-autonomous areas such as culture, philosophy, education, or even economics.

I am quite enamoured with such an Althusserian position, but I would like to take it further, stressing, if you like, the 'semi' over against the 'autonomous'. We are far too accustomed to beginning with the autonomous side of the equation and then need to work overtime to establish the connections between them. But what if we began with the assumed connections and overlaps? One benefit would be to recast a common narrative for dealing with premodern and modern societies. The narrative goes as follows: before the differentiation of capitalism, in which each area is distinguished as an autonomous zone, people did not operate with clearly demarcated realms of economics, politics, religion and what have you. Religion was political and social and economic at the same time. However, with the advent of capitalism (sometimes read as the 'modern' period), all of these realms became differentiated from one another. Yet, if we begin with the assumption that such domains are not discrete but entwined with one other, indeed that they form a collective whole, then the issue is not how they relate to one another but how they may be distinguished. If we wish to stay with some version of the narrative of differentiation, then it becomes one of a change in the way the various realms relate to one another in a larger whole. The implications for Ste. Croix's investigations concerning the early Church become obvious: the doctrinal debates that split early Christianity were inescapably and at the same time political, social and economic. One does not need to seek the connections, for they are already there; what one does need to do is explore the nature of those connections. With that we have already broached the matter of economics, so to that topic I finally turn.

...and history

For this final section, I am concerned with economic matters. Here, I let the 'historian' in Ste. Croix speak rather than the 'theologian' he disdains, quizzing him about his assumptions but, above all, picking up some useful items on the way. And the reason I am interested in economics in the ancient world is that a full-scale and adequate economic history remains to be written. By that, I mean an economic history of biblical societies, those that produced both the Hebrew Bible and the New Testament. There are many reasons why such a history does not exist, not least of which is the fact that most energy is still expended on cataloguing the archaeological discoveries of the ancient Near East.[70] In this respect, studies of ancient Greece and Rome are far more advanced; even in Marxist circles there are some notable works that have generated discussion such as those by Moses Finley, Perry Anderson, Hindess and Hirst, Ellen Meiksins Wood[71]...and G.E.M. de Ste. Croix. So let us see what we can find.

Class

Ste. Croix's chosen entry point is class, which he defines as 'the collective social expression of the fact of exploitation'.[72] His search for the motor of history is conventionally Marxist: what we need to identify is the process by which surplus is produced and from that point determine who benefits and who is exploited. Soon enough (after a rather quaint effort to spruce up Marx's qualifications as a classicist), slaves turn up, for they were put to work without any recompense and would thereby generate surplus well beyond their purchase-price and cost of upkeep. This is where it gets interesting. Ste. Croix is fully aware that slaves numbered less than the vast numbers of peasants – relatively free land-holders who cultivated small plots. So, he points out that the ruling classes (what he calls the 'propertied classes' – I will turn

---

[70] Attend any gathering of the International Assyriological Society, or the American School of Oriental Research and you will soon see how much energy is given over to such projects.

[71] Finley 1999; Anderson 1974b; Anderson 1974a; Anderson 1992, pp. 2–18; Hindess and Hirst 1975 (although they do include a theoretical dismissal of the Asiatic mode of production); Wood 1997; Wood and Wood 1978.

[72] Ste. Croix 1981, p. 43.

to that term in a moment) above all lived on the surplus produced by slaves. The reason: the possessors of the largest tracts of land were precisely the ruling classes and the preferred way of working them was through slave-labour. Often, they would not even supervise the slaves themselves, preferring to appoint overseers to do the job. The produce of these large estates enabled the ruling classes to live in wealth, undertake roles of governance, pursue literature and the arts – all tasks that were possible only on the backs of the slaves who worked the estates. The slaves directly supported the existence of an often brutal ruling class who, in turn, had the time and resources to produce the thought and literature of the classical world.

There is, however, a second modification in Ste. Croix's position which becomes necessary in light of the stretch of time covered by his 'Greek world' (sixth century BCE to seventh century CE). In the latter phase of that world, the development of indentured labour, or *coloni*, increased dramatically. Ste. Croix has no hesitation in calling them serfs, for they were legally and economically bound to the ruling classes. The *coloni* are widely regarded as forerunners to the serfs of middle ages, but Ste. Croix's argument for their emergence (initially in Africa) is very persuasive. As the sources for slaves dried up – mostly conquest – and the cost of slaves sky-rocketed as owners were forced to breed them, new sources of producing surplus were required. So, gradually, the free peasants were forced by the propertied class into indentured roles in order to take up the slack. For these reasons, Ste. Croix opts for 'unfree labour' as a term to cover both slaves and *coloni*/serfs, although, given the persistence of the idea of slavery, the Romans viewed the *coloni* as slaves in all but the technical sense.

As Blackledge points out, Ste. Croix's proposal is an innovative defence of the slave-economy in which slavery is the archetypal form of unfree labour.[73] It offers a distinct answer to the objections of Hindess and Hirst to slavery as a distinct mode of production, it works far better than Moses Finley's emphasis on 'status' rather than class, and it goes well beyond Kautsky's argument that slavery developed out of debt-bondage in both ancient Greece and ancient Israel.[74] Ste. Croix's reconstruction has, of course, been challenged, although the most pertinent points concern whether the transition from slavery to serf-

---

[73] Blackledge 2006, p. 105.
[74] Hindess and Hirst 1975, pp. 109–77; Finley 1999; Kautsky 2007; Kautsky 1977.

dom is really part of the same economic system and the matter of agency. I will deal with the first matter in my discussion of mode of production, suffice to indicate here that Ste. Croix's avoidance of any discussion of mode of production leads him to fail to see that the shift in formations of class – from slave to serf – is part of a larger shift in modes of production. In regard to subjective matters of class, Perry Anderson has argued that Ste. Croix downplays the subjective, conscious element of class-consciousness (a feature of E.P. Thompson's approach) and emphasises what is really the contradiction between forces and relations of production.[75] In response, Anderson argues for the weakening of Rome's ideological hold over slaves as they came to form a distinct sense of identity and thereby resistance to the ruling classes. I have gone beyond my remit, so I restrict myself to the observation that any consideration of class in relation to the Bible and early Christianity should obviously include both factors – the objective tensions between forces and relations of production as well as the subjective elements of class-consciousness.

However, Ste. Croix's class-analysis provides the most persuasive explanation I have read of the infamous decline of the Roman Empire, or, more specifically, why it succumbed to invasions on its borders and crumbled. Given the increasingly brutal exploitation of unfree labour in order to support an exploitative and expensive state, the final straw being the creation of a whole new bureaucracy supported by the state in the form of the Christian Church after Constantine's conversion, many of those labourers had little affection for that state and actually welcomed the invaders. Ste. Croix digs up an impressive range of evidence to show continual desertions, indifference of labourers, and actual assistance to invaders – not least of which are the increasingly harsh penalties for doing so. Perhaps it is best expressed in the fable of the donkey, who stands his ground when his master tells him to hurry into the city because the barbarians are coming. Eventually the master asks, 'Why will you not come?' The donkey replies, 'Will they put two packs or one pack on my back?' The master says, 'One I suspect'. 'Well then', says the donkey, 'you put two packs on my back and they will put one on my back; I am not coming with you'.

---

[75] Anderson 1992, pp. 17–18.

Trade and property

All the same, there are three points I would like to raise with this otherwise very usable account. The first concerns trade, or rather the lack thereof. Ste. Croix continues a tradition of opposing the persistent tendency to see trade as the driving force of both the Greek world and the ancient Near East.[76] The assertion of the primacy of trade takes various forms, such as the argument that a city-state like Athens rose to prominence through sea-born trade, or that trade was the primary reason for the conflict between Athens, Corinth and Sparta, or that the mechanisms of expansion and contraction of empires in the ancient Near East were determined by trade, or, indeed, that there was a full-blown international market-economy in the ancient Near East, replete with systems of production, circulation and consumption.[77] Current scholarship, with its near frenzy at the merest sign of a merchant, could do with a detailed reading of Ste. Croix's observations on trade.[78]

To begin with, there is the simple point concerning transport. By land, the transport of goods was prohibitively expensive. For example, in the period of the Roman Emperor Diocletian, it was cheaper to move the same quantity of wheat by ship from one end of the Mediterranean to another, from Syria to Spain, than it was to transport it 120 kilometres (or 75 miles) overland.[79] Was water-borne trade then the preferred method? It may have been cheaper to transport it as such, but Ste. Croix is sceptical that the Greeks or Romans actually used sea-borne trade as a prime generator of surplus.

Ste. Croix distinguishes between three types of trade: imports, exports and commercial exchange. Obviously, they are related, but he makes the distinction to point out that the primary concern of Greek city-states was the first, imports. The driving force was neither commercial exchange for profit, nor was it to think in terms of balance of trade, seeking to export as much as one might import. Rather, the over-riding concern was import: city-states were interested only in what they could get in, not in what they could send out. Is

---

[76] Others opposing this tendency include Finley 1999; Polanyi 1968 and Wood 1997.

[77] For example, McNutt 1999, p. 195; Thompson 2000, p. 233; Warburton 2003.

[78] The following observations are drawn from a paper originally given in 1959 called 'How Far Was Trade a Cause of Early Colonisation?' (Ste. Croix 2004, pp. 349–70). It reads as though it were written yesterday.

[79] Ste. Croix 1981, pp. 11–12.

there a shortage of grain? Let us get hold of some. I hear that so-and-so has brought in some expensive dye from Tyre and Sidon; let me see if I can get some too. And so on. The question then arises as to how one paid for such imports. Athens was fortunate enough to have its silver-mines and could rely in part on tribute from colonies (another element of bringing goods into the city), but if it became necessary to export products, then that was seen as a necessary evil for the sake of ensuring the desired imports. The absence of a sense of profit (the third type of trade) is reflected in the fact that Athens in the fourth century BCE exacted the same duty (2%) on exports as imports. Surely, if one wished to encourage exports, then the tax on exports would be less or none at all? What then of individual merchants? Surely they were interested in profits in order to make a living? Ste. Croix points out that merchants were always peripheral figures as far as the power-structures of city-states were concerned. They were not organised and exercised no political influence on politics. Merchants were useful for ensuring imports, but city-states did not think of them as 'their own' and they did not form a 'mercantile class'.

Even imports were regarded as a necessary evil, for city-states were ideally self-sufficient. The reason for such an ideal lay squarely with land, the major concern of ruling élites of the city-states. Ste. Croix deftly picks up a standard assumption in studies of the ancient world and brings it to a logical conclusion. It is widely agreed that colonisation was primarily due to land and population pressures and not for the purpose of trade on favourable shipping routes. For example, if one were to consider a settlement on the Propontis or Black-Sea coast for the purpose of trade, one would choose the place where the currents naturally lead, namely the north-western coast where Istanbul now stands (originally Byzantium). However, the first settlement was as Chalcedon, on the other side, where it is extremely difficult to land a boat. And yet, the first settlement by Megarian Greeks in about 651 BCE was precisely at Chalcedon, since it had far better arable land. Only seventeen years later did they settle Byzantium as well. If a town did become involved in trade, it was secondary, coming from the bottom up rather than any initial intention. The persistence of land-based wealth is shown by the occasional example even from Roman times: if someone happened to turn a profit from a trading venture or managed to exact tribute from a province as its governor, he would not invest the profit in another venture; he would use it to acquire some land, which was the only secure form of wealth.

To Ste. Croix's points I would add the following: there was an absence of any mechanism for the creation of credit, a crucial element of any trading system, money-lending for business purposes (one usually borrowed for non-productive purposes), as well as any idea that money should be invested in order to generate more money; there was, in fact, no sense of an 'economy' in the way we use the term.[80] The best thing one could do with money is either buy land or bury it so that it would be there in case of need. Indeed, for trade to function as a generator of surplus, we would first need an extensive network of market-relations and then the attendant process of commodification and the crucial metaphorisation and totalisation of the market that is necessary for trade to work in any way as a dominant mechanism of surplus. To sum up this discussion of trade, it is unfortunate that the old warning must be repeated once more: the imposition of categories developed in the analysis of capitalism to the ancient world is fraught with peril, if not a simple category mistake.[81]

A second matter concerns not so much an insight as a gap in Ste. Croix's texts: the unexamined use of the term 'property'. Ste. Croix prefers to use the term 'propertied classes' rather than 'ruling classes'; the term designates those who held property in societies in which wealth and property were the primary markers of power. In great detail, he shows how property-qualifications were always the issue for admittance to the ruling classes and that it was property in land that was valued most highly. But he does not examine what 'property' itself might mean. I find this omission odd, to say the least, especially in a Marxist study. The issue of private property looms large in any study of the ancient world, since, here again, we face the problems associated with importing our – that is, capitalist – assumptions, in this case in relation to private property, into the ancient world.

The way we understand private property ultimately derives from the ancient world, but not in the way we would expect. It was invented by the Roman jurors of the third century BCE, subsequently lost in the middle ages only to be recovered in the 'Papal Revolution' begun under Pope Gregory

---

[80] See Finley 1999, pp. 21, 141–4, 196–8.

[81] This imposition is the unfortunate agenda of most of the essays in the series of volumes published from the International Scholars Conference on Ancient Near Eastern Economies: Hudson and Levine 1996; Hudson and Levine 1999; Hudson and Mieroop 2002; Hudson and Wunsch 2004.

VII (c. 1015–85) when Roman law itself was adapted consistently into what became canon-law and then civil law.[82] More specifically,[83] private property was a unique invention of Roman civil law. And that innovation was the concept of 'absolute property', or what is known as *dominium ex jure Quiritium* – the right of absolute ownership for any Roman citizen.[84] The crucial distinction is between 'possession' and 'property': the former refers to the control of goods, while the latter entails full legal title to those goods. 'Property' thus refers to the unqualified and absolute legal title to something. Unlike mere possession, property is not subject to any qualification or external constraint. Only in this sense can one speak of private property. And, if one has absolute rights to a piece of property, one also has the right to dispose of it.[85] It is this sense of private property that was forgotten during the middle ages only to be rediscovered before it fed into the sense of private property within capitalism.

How did this crucial development come about? It was the product of specialised jurists who were neither practising lawyers nor state-functionaries. They offered opinions only on problems of legal principle when asked to do so, but never made decisions concerning specific court-cases. And their focus was civil law, rather than the treacherous territory of public law (the relations of citizen to state, patron to clients, and patriarch to his familial dependants) or that of criminal law. More specifically, their concern was the law concerning disputes over property, the questions of contract and exchange between Roman citizens, in short, economic transactions such as sale, purchase, hire, lease, inheritance and property in marriage. They were, if you like, legal theorists rather than judges, with no official status and devoted to analytic and theoretical reflection on civil and economic law.

---

[82] Gianaris 1996, p. 20; Miéville 2004a, p. 195. When I mention, in various contexts, the fact that private property has its own history, including a point of origin and then a rocky road from there, an obtuse resistance often sets in. Is not private property universal to human beings? How can it have been invented when it is so obvious?

[83] See Anderson 1974b, pp. 65–7; Jolowicz 1952, pp. 142–3, 426; Linklater 2000, p. 1432.

[84] *Quirites* is the common name used for Roman citizens after the Romans and Sabines were united (*Romani* was reserved for warriors and rulers). Thus, quiritary ownership applies to citizens.

[85] The Roman jurors defined absolute ownership as the right to dispose perfectly of a material thing in so far as it not forbidden by law [*Jus perfecte disponendi de re corporali nisi lege prohibeatur*].

Such theoretical work was the enabled by the extensive development of the slave-mode of production under the Romans and the attendant conquest of the Mediterranean and that work was undertaken by Roman jurors from about 300 BCE. It was, in other words, one of the enormous theoretical achievements enabled by the expansion of the slave-economy in what became the Roman Empire. With such a large number of slaves to be bought and sold, Roman civil law came up with the clear idea of absolute private property over against the patterns of indeterminate and relative possession that preceded it. This means that one must be extremely careful when speaking of private property before this invention and in places not influenced by it. Neither the Greeks, nor Persians, nor Babylonians, nor Sumerians, nor for that matter, the Israelites whenever they first appeared, knew what private property was in the sense that we use it. What we have instead is the far more relative, tied and indeterminate possession: one might have had control over something in one's possession for a while, but it did not mean that it was private property.

I am really filling in a gap in Ste. Croix's analysis, one that probably should not need filling given his thoroughness as a scholar. More puzzling still is the fact that Ste. Croix mentions the famed Roman jurors,[86] so it is a strange omission indeed to speak of 'propertied classes' without some consideration of what 'property' itself actually meant in a legal and economic sense.

Mode of production

The absence of an adequate consideration of private property may be regarded as a sin of omission; not so the question of mode of production, which is the third question I wish to raise. Ste. Croix finds discussions of modes of production tiring and unproductive, too close to a form of Marxist scholasticism. At one level, I want to applaud, since the use of the terminology of mode of production for the ancient world is often too loose and cries out for a more specific reconstruction based on detailed evidence. But then some engagement with the debates is called for, even if it is an engagement with the texts of Marx and Engels. Instead, we find that Ste. Croix dismisses feudalism as a descriptor of his 'Greek world' since it lacks precision (it is more of a social relation than an economic system), rules out any Asiatic

---

[86] Ste. Croix 1981, pp. 328–30.

mode of production for the ancient Near East (on this matter, he suggests that Perry Anderson has said the last word),[87] and even on the matter of slavery he writes, 'I think it would not be technically correct to call the Greek (and Roman) world "a *slave* economy"; but I should not raise any strong objection if anyone else wished to use that expression'.[88]

However, it is not that Ste. Croix dispenses with all of these modes of production in order to come up with a new term; he avoids such discussion altogether. One reason must lie in the stretch of time he covers: the earlier centuries of his Greek world have slavery as the prime form in which surplus was extracted, but then the later period sees the rise of serfs (or *coloni*). Ste. Croix resolutely sticks with class-terms and avoids the larger and more abstract realms of mode of production. If he had engaged with questions of modes of production, he would have had to come face to face with the reality that the slow shift from slaves (especially after the decline of supplies and rising prices) to serfs was actually the sign of a fundamental shift in economic systems. It will not do to argue that slave and serf are different forms of unfree labour, for, if we followed that line, then there are many forms of unfree labour that fit the category. Instead, I prefer a more conventional line: the change of class-relations is actually a signal of changing modes of production.[89]

There is another problem with Ste. Croix's reconstruction, especially if we take the perspective of modes of production. If we grant his assumption that the 'Greek world' extended well into the ancient Near East under Alexander

---

[87] Ste. Croix 1981, p. 544; Anderson 1974a, pp. 462–549. Strangely, Hindess and Hirst's purely theoretical arguments against both the Asiatic mode of production and slavery as a mode of production do not make an appearance. See Hindess and Hirst 1975, pp. 109–220.

[88] Ste. Croix 1981, p. 133.

[89] On this matter, I am on the same wavelength as Chris Wickham, although not with his proposed solution. Concerning the question of the later phase of Ste. Croix's 'Greek world', Wickham has argued that this phase cannot really be described as a 'slave economy' (Wickham 1994, pp. 9–20). Wickham proposes a reversion to a 'tributary' mode of production in this later phase, a system in which the towns exploited the countryside through taxation or tribute (Marx's ancient mode of production). Here is a classic case of disciplinary blinkers, for Wickham draws the idea not from studies of ancient Israel, where the tributary mode has been a staple since the work of Gottwald 1999 (originally published in 1979) but from Samir Amin. For Wickham, the difference with feudalism is that the taxes were controlled by the landlord, whereas, in a tributary mode, the state controlled taxes from both peasants and landlords. Only after this phase did feudalism arise. By contrast, Perry Anderson 1974b has argued that in this period we find the combination of a Germanic mode, the disintegrating slave-economy and the rise of the *coloni* as contributing factors in the development of feudalism.

the Great's conquests (333–23 BCE), Ste. Croix must also deal with this vast and fascinating realm. With the ancient Near East too, he opts for serfdom as the defining class-structure of exploitation.[90] The effect of this argument is strange, for it draws the ancient Near East into Ste. Croix's later Greek world. If we follow this line of argument, then the serf was the prime form of exploitation in the millennia of ancient Near-Eastern economics (at least from c. 3000 BCE) as well as the later stages of the Roman Empire via the *colonus*. What we end up with a vast porridge called serfdom, into which quite distinct economic systems from different historical periods all seem to fit.

While we are in the ancient Near East, another problem emerges with Ste. Croix's treatment: a studied avoidance of the most sustained work on ancient Near-Eastern economics. I speak of the Soviet-era Russian work on the ancient Near East from the 1930s until the 1980s. For some unaccountable reason, Ste. Croix dismisses such work as so much futile huffing and puffing.[91] I can only attribute this dismissal to his insular Englishness, something we also see with his scoffing at a French Marxism heavily influenced by Althusser as 'French phrasemongering', and with his lecturing of his Polish hosts on a lecture-tour as to how much they had misinterpreted Marx.[92]

This is a shame, since, as I have shown elsewhere, the Soviet-era Russian research developed a degree of sophistication that comes only through prolonged research, debate and refinement.[93] It thoroughly explored both the macro-economic issues of modes of production and the intricate details of available texts and archaeological artefacts. And, after having pulled to pieces and then having reassembled the traditional categories of Asiatic, ancient (or slave-based) and feudal modes of production, those involved in the debate went on to offer their own models. Reading through this material gives one the dislocated feel of living in parallel universes. So, while Russian scholarship had briefly flirted with feudalism as a descriptor of ancient Near-Eastern

---

[90] Ste. Croix 1981, pp. 155–8.

[91] Ste. Croix 1981, p. 544. The only Russian scholar to whom Ste. Croix refers and with whom he differs on more than one occasion is Mikhail I. Rostovtzeff. But this hardly counts, since Rostovtzeff, for all his concern with economic and social matters in ancient Greece and Rome, was a champion of the bourgeoisie and a committed anti-communist (he fled Russia in 1918).

[92] Harvey 2000a.

[93] Boer 2008c. As a sample of this scholarship, see D'iakonoff 1969a; D'iakonoff 1969b; D'iakonoff 1974; D'iakonoff 1987; D'iakonoff 1991; D'iakonoff 1999; Dandamaev, et al. 1982; Dandamaev 1984; Dunn 1981.

economics in the 1930s, it settled into the assumption that slavery was the key feature of the ancient Near East for about three decades and then turned (not without a good deal of debate) to a thoroughly reconditioned and re-greased Asiatic mode of production in the 1970s. Meanwhile, Western scholarship had locked onto feudalism as the best descriptor, decided that the Asiatic mode of production was unviable by the 1970s, toyed with slavery, spent some time in a profound *aporia* about ancient Near-Eastern economics, and then, when the Soviet-era came to an end in the late 1980s, decided to apply categories from capitalism into the ancient Near East. This last phase in Western scholarship, which is still with us as I write, should be read as a symptom of the assumed dominance of capitalism: these scholars assume that capitalism is not only universal in our own day, but they also argue that capitalism is universal in a temporal sense, expressing the basic impulse of economic activity all the way back to the first human beings.

In other words, the absence of this level of discussion in Ste. Croix's text leaves a large hole. He operates mostly at an intermediate level, somewhere between the nitty-gritty of everyday-life (although he does dip into matters of food and transport from time to time) and the sweeping abstract level of modes of production. Ste. Croix opts for the middle zone, that of class. The down-side of his decision is that he assumes it is the correct (and thereby only) way to develop a Marxist reading of the Greek world.[94] The up side is that on the specific issue of class Ste. Croix offers one of the best studies of the ancient world and an extraordinarily fruitful way of using Marxism for such a study.

Conclusion: Ste. Croix among Marxists and theologians

As might be expected, there are some extraordinary insights in Ste. Croix's work in relation to the Bible and early Christianity, but also some false paths and holes. I have said enough about those paths, so I would like to make a few comments concerning what can be retrieved and reused in Ste. Croix's work. The first of these is a relatively undeveloped spatial analysis. The brilliant suggestion concerning the role of *chora* and *polis* in relation to the

---

[94] I also suspect it also has much to do with his British context, where class is barely concealed and so obviously part of everyday life.

ancient Greek world and the New Testament remains curiously understated, so any subsequent work will need to bring this feature to the fore and combine it with the work, among others, of Henri Lefebvre and David Harvey.[95] Another promising avenue is more implicit: the need for a sustained analysis on the matter of class in biblical societies – with the detailed attention to sources characteristic of Ste. Croix. The only comparable text is the monumental but flawed work of Norman Gottwald,[96] which remains restricted to the Hebrew Bible. A reconstruction like that of Ste. Croix needs not only to build on Gottwald but to explore the New Testament as well. And that study ought to move beyond class to reconsider matters pertaining to mode of production.

I would like to finish on a different note – Ste. Croix's place among Marxist critics of the Bible. Ste. Croix was always a lone voice, carving a path on his own that still seems to embarrass that close club of British classicists. But he was also a lone voice in relation to other Marxists who worked on the Bible, as well as biblical scholars themselves.[97] It has always puzzled me why he has been so ignored by both groups.

Ste. Croix should really be seen as part of the tradition of materialist readings of Bible, especially the New Testament and early Christianity.[98] Let me spell out what this means. We can discern two lines of such a tradition, even if it is often not filled with many names. The first line stems from Engels and it includes sundry Marxists who have offered interpretations, usually in the form of historical reconstructions of ancient Israel and the early Church. Engels himself was brought up as a devout Calvinist, was able to read the New

---

[95] Lefebvre 1991; Harvey 1999; Harvey 2000b. See Boer 2007a, pp. 163–214; Boer 2003.

[96] Gottwald 1999.

[97] Predictably, Ste. Croix's work has been celebrated by Marxist historians. Perry Anderson calls it 'one of the most strenuously theoretical works of history ever to have been produced in this country' (Anderson 1992, p. 2) and Paul Blackledge suggests it should 'be numbered among the greatest works of twentieth-century Marxist historiography' (Blackledge 2006, p. 104). Neither is skilled in classics or biblical scholarship. In regard to biblical scholars, Ste. Croix appears occasionally in citations and footnotes but I have not been able to find any sustained treatments. Some of those who cite him in passing include Kelley 2006; Castelli 2004; Crossan 1993; Elliott 2008; Heyman 2007; Horrell 2007; Runciman 2004. The exception is Kyrtatas 1987, but this is a classic case of the exception proving the rule, since although Ste. Croix wrote the forward, the book was published by Verso.

[98] For a survey of Hebrew-Bible (Old-Testament) materialist research, see Boer 2007d.

Testament in Greek and encountered first-hand the great upheavals in biblical scholarship in that pressure-cooker of the 1830s and 1840s in Germany.[99] For distinct historical reasons, public debates over democracy, freedom of speech, republicanism, reunification and reason were fought out on the terrain of the Bible. In this situation, works like *Das Leben Jesu* by David Strauss, or Ludwig Feuerbach's *Das Wesen des Christentums*, or Bruno Bauer's radical work on the Hebrew Bible (Old Testament) and New Testament, caused immense public outcry.[100] Engels's troubled and angst-ridden passage from his deep Calvinism to historical materialism did not mean that he left behind his interest in the Bible and Christianity. His works on Bruno Bauer, the Book of Revelation, the peasant-war and (one of his last pieces) on early Christianity began a tradition in which Marxist scholars interested themselves in matters biblical.[101]

Soon enough, Karl Kautsky and Rosa Luxemburg took up the baton. Luxemburg's essay – or rather, political pamphlet – called *Socialism and the Churches* reconstructs an early Christian communism based on key passages in the book of Acts (2: 44–5 and 4: 32–5), criticises the Church of her own day for having betrayed this early communist spirit, traces the way in which that betrayal took place over time, then argues that early Christian communism was really a communism of consumption and that it therefore needs to be completed with one of production, which is, of course, the communism she espouses.[102] An explicit motive for this little known work is to show the workers pouring into the Social-Democratic Party that Christianity, at least in its 'true' form, is not incompatible with socialism. As for Kautsky, his ambitious and unfinished project arose from extensive discussion with the ageing Engels over the question of Christianity and communism. In *Foundations of Christianity*, Kautsky attempted to offer a materialist reconstruction of early Israel and early Christianity for the sake of coming to some understanding of the 'titanic phenomenon' of Christianity.[103] Although he made much of the communism of early Christianity, he also set out to describe both the

---

[99] For a detailed analysis of Engels's biblical temptations and contributions, see the last two chapters of Boer forthcoming.

[100] Strauss 1835; Strauss 1902; Feuerbach 1989; Feuerbach 1924; Bauer 1838; Bauer 1840; Bauer 1841; Bauer 1842b; Bauer 1842a; Bauer 1843a; Bauer 1850–1; Bauer 1852.

[101] Engels 1978; Engels 1989; Engels 1973b; Engels 1990a; Engels 1990b. See also Engels's early notes on Bauer in Engels 1976.

[102] Luxemburg 1970; Luxemburg 1982.

[103] Kautsky 2007; Kautsky 1977.

mechanisms and genesis of the economic systems of ancient Israel (it was a slave-based one) and of Rome (ditto) as the proper historical background for both the Hebrew Bible and the New Testament. This flawed gem of a book turned out to be part of a much larger project that traced pre-Marxist forms of communism and thereby sought to establish a tradition of which Marxism was the crowning moment.[104]

Since this early push, there has been a sporadic interest by Marxist critics in the Bible, although most of it has remained in the territory first staked out by Engels, Luxemburg and Kautsky – the origins of Christianity. And much of it took place in Eastern Europe during the Communist era. This scholarship has a quite independent history and its methodological assumption was similar to that of Engels, Kautsky and Luxemburg: the rise of Christianity was due to economic, ideological and mythological developments at the time. In contrast to Western scholarship, which preferred to identify Christianity as a primary cause (at times revolutionary), this work argued that it was a secondary phenomenon. No surprise here, since any superstructural element like a system of belief and practice would always come second. A useful survey of this Eastern-European research may be found in Kowalinski.[105] He distinguishes between three types of materialist scholars, distinguished according to how they approach the development of early Christianity: some followed a 'historical' approach, while others took a mythological approach, either moderate or more radical. Even these two mythological approaches were also very historically grounded, but took the position that specific ideological and mythological developments and not merely changes in economic structures led to the spread and success of Christianity. As for Kowalinski himself, he accepts the line of Engels and company, arguing that Christianity began as a revolutionary-messianic movement of slaves, freedmen and the poor of Palestine around the turn of our era; in their number, he includes John the Baptist and Jesus. But then he goes on to argue that the second wave of Christianity was dominated by the apostle Paul, a 'middle class' Jew who moderated the new

---

[104] Kautsky 2006; Kautsky 1947b; Kautsky 1947c; Kautsky and Lafargue 1977; Kautsky 1979; Kautsky 1947a.

[105] Kowalinski 1972. Cold-War assumptions die hard, however. Although there has been since 1989 a growing awareness of this work in Western scholarship, it is often still written of as 'unoriginal' or 'ideologically motivated' even today. I have found the similar responses to the long and rich tradition of Soviet-era Russian work on the ancient Near East; see Boer 2008c.

movement, smoothing away its rough and dangerous elements and focusing on the spiritual dimensions of the messiah known as Jesus the Christ. With the apostle Paul as the leading ideologue, spiritual messianism expressed the beliefs of the 'middle class' Jews and proselytes in the fifth decade of our era; they transformed the historical Jesus into a mystical god and the earthly messianic Kingdom into the Kingdom of Heaven.

The other line of materialist analysis of the Bible is populated with biblical scholars who make use of Marxist analysis. Again, I restrict myself to the New Testament and early Christianity. In this case, we need to distinguish between those who follow an explicit Marxist agenda in interpretation and those (a far greater number) who are influenced by various elements of Marxist interpretations of the Bible, although the line between them is at times a little blurred. Those with an explicit agenda go back no earlier than the 1970s, deeply influenced by the creative turmoil of the 1960s. Within the space of a few short years there arose, at least in biblical studies and theology, the contributions of Latin-American liberation-theology, black liberation-theology, a new wave of feminist theology, as well as Marxist analyses of the Bible.

The first explicitly Marxist analysis by a New-Testament critic was Fernando Belo's *A Materialist Reading of the Gospel of Mark*, published in French in 1974.[106] It produced a wave of excitement, generated discussion-groups and even a handbook that attempted to render this formidable book more digestible.[107] Belo's book offers an interpretation of the Gospel of Mark inspired by a Marxist analysis filtered through Roland Barthes's *S/Z*, which Belo appropriates in his own way and links with a materialist reconstruction of the social and economic context.[108] Inevitably, New-Testament interpretation gravitates to the figure of Jesus of Nazareth (Ste. Croix is no exception). In Belo's case, his book marks the recovery in Marxist terms of a long tradition that sees Jesus as a rebel, if not a revolutionary, against the religious and political forces of the time. We can find this position among the revolutionary movements of Thomas Müntzer and the peasant-war in Germany and Gerrard Winstanley and the Levellers in England, but Belo brings Marxism to the forefront of such analyses.

---

[106] Belo 1981; Belo 1975.
[107] Clévenot 1985; Clévenot 1976.
[108] He relies heavily on Dhoquois 1971 for his reconstruction.

From here on, a steady stream of studies focused on the more-or-less revolutionary credentials of Jesus. His death may have created a revolutionary group known as the *ekklesia* that challenged Roman imperial structures. He may be a radical example of non-violent resistance, especially in the context of the violent Jewish revolt of 66–70 CE, to the powers that be, an example whom we should still follow today.[109] He and his followers may have been radical wandering charismatics who addressed socio-economic tensions between rich and poor, city and country, Hellenism and Judaism, and between accommodation and resistance.[110] He may have taken a distinct anti-imperial stance in the midst of peasant slowdowns, sabotage, prophetic and messianic movements, scribal writings, counter-terrorism and revolts.[111] Or Jesus may have broken from the central economic and political institution of the family in order to set up an alternative community, the 'Kingdom of God' which was the beginning of a new space, one in which the modes of family, gender, politics and economics begin to be transformed.[112] A pervading influence on much of this material is that of Latin-American liberation-theology, especially with its dual biblical themes of the Exodus in the Hebrew Bible and the oppositional politics of Jesus.[113] Some of these studies are wise enough to argue that the figure of Jesus is really a literary construct, for the only information we actually have of him is the literature of the New Testament, yet there is a tendency to assume that this literature provides a window – more or less clear – of the actual historical person.

The various studies I have mentioned above make explicit use of Marxist approaches. At this point, we cross a hazy line into what might be called 'closet-Marxism': studies that assume certain positions without ever identifying their Marxist origins. This comment applies particularly to those who make use of postcolonial criticism,[114] which has mutated into what is now a flood of 'empire-studies'. It seems as though the bulk of the Bible has become a collection of anti-imperial documents, if we are to believe the string of titles

---

[109] Myers 1989.
[110] Theissen 1978; Theissen 1987; Theissen 1999.
[111] Horsley 1989; Horsley 1992; Horsley 1995; Horsley 1996; Horsley 2002.
[112] Moxnes 1997; Moxnes 2003.
[113] See my detailed discussion of liberation-theologies in Chapter Four on Michael Löwy.
[114] See Boer 2008b, pp. 23–35.

that have appeared.[115] Most of these would speak of taking a liberationist perspective, largely due to its more acceptable theological pedigree, rather than
a Marxist approach. Of course, many of these positions are indicators of ideological struggles within the various churches and synagogues between progressive and conservative elements. I, for one, would like to see far more of
such studies, but whenever I peruse this material, I always get the sense that
it is still tied to the assumption that the Bible can be good for you if you read
it correctly. What it needs is some decent ideological criticism, particularly in
the traditional sense of demystification.[116]

Of course, the two lines I have traced all too briefly do overlap at many
points.[117] The most notable example is the way Engels's initial suggestion
that early Christianity was a revolutionary movement drawn from the lower
classes of Roman society made its way into New-Testament criticism and
sociological analysis.[118] But where does Ste. Croix fit within all of this? He
largely ignores either tradition and they have returned the cold shoulder. In
some cases he may be excused, since he stands at the beginning of the recent
spate of Marxist analyses of the Bible. He began work on *Class Struggle* when
the excitement of the 60s was still in the air, delivered some of its content
initially as the Gray lectures at Cambridge in 1973 and finally published it in
1981. By comparison, the early Marxist study of the New Testament by Belo
appeared in 1975 and then in translation in 1981. Yet Ste. Croix does not refer
to even this early work, let alone the studies by Engels, Kautsky and Luxemburg. The reasons why Ste. Croix ignores this work are beyond me, as are

---

[115] Bryan 2005; Carter 2001; Carter 2006; Elliott 1994; Elliott 2000; Elliott 2008; Rieger
2007; Sugirtharajah 2005.

[116] More of the exemplary materialist work of Jorunn Økland 2005 is needed in
this context. Making use of Marxist studies of space in conjunction with feminist
and ritual-studies, she argues that, in Paul's Corinthian correspondence, we find
that the 'sanctuary space' of the *ekklesia* begins to shift from gender segregation into
a hierarchical integration in which the male was closer to the godhead. See also
Økland 2008.

[117] In fact, Hochschild 1999 treats it as one multi-faceted tradition of social-historical
exegesis. He begins with Engels and Kautsky and then moves to the more traditional
social historians of the New Testament (such as Gerd Theissen), the Chicago-school,
the Social Gospel and broader socio-scientific interpretations.

[118] See, for instance, Deissman 1929, 1978, and Troeltsch 1992. This position held
sway until the 1960s, when reaction set in and more conservative scholars reclaimed
the older argument that predates Engels: Christianity drew its membership from the
middle and upper strata of Roman society.

those as to why he has been left out in the cold by biblical critics. This study may, I hope, be one step to restoring him – even if he would have come kicking and struggling with his strong athlete's body – into this dual tradition of Marxist biblical studies, for he is both a Marxist historian of the ancient Greek and Roman worlds *and* a formidable New-Testament critic.

Chapter Four

The Alchemy of Michael Löwy

For two decades or more, Michael Löwy has been exploring the 'elective affinity' between Marxism and religion.[1] Such a connection may be found, he argues, in the libertarian thought of certain Jewish intellectuals in Central Europe from the mid-nineteenth century until the 1930s, or in the thought of one of his heroes, Walter Benjamin, or in Latin-American liberation-theology, which first emerged in the 1960s and 1970s.

I am above all interested in the way Löwy handles Latin-American liberation-theology,[2] partly because any study of Marxism and theology cannot shy away from such a topic, partly because it provides another angle on a theme – resistance and accommodation – that has persisted through the preceding chapters, partly due to the way liberation-theology allows me to subject Löwy himself to sustained commentary and critique, and partly because it allows me to offer my own response to liberation-theology, albeit through Löwy. Central to his quite sympathetic engagement with liberation-theology is what may

---

[1] For some strange reason, the question of Marxism and religion is absent in Löwy's early book on the young Marx – precisely where we would expect to find an extended discussion of religion, for Marx deals extensively with theology in his early texts. See Löwy 2005c.

[2] Löwy 1996. A preliminary and much shorter study appeared in French in Löwy 1988a. See also Löwy 1993.

count as his original idea, namely 'elective affinity [*Walverwandschaft*]'. Dragged out of alchemy, Goethe and the back-woods of Weber's *The Protestant Ethic and the Spirit of Capitalism*, Löwy has made it the centrepiece of his analysis of religion and its relation with Marxism.

I have structured the chapter as follows. I begin with a detailed treatment of elective affinity, focusing on the two main statements where Löwy seeks to reclaim this idea for the sociology of religion – one an article in French on Max Weber and another from the first chapter of *Redemption and Utopia*.[3] From there, I launch into a critical commentary of Löwy's engagement with liberation-theology, where I deal with three matters: the nature and influence of Catholic social teaching (and the curious way Löwy sidesteps such teaching in his treatment of liberation-theology); the ontological reserve of liberation-theology in regard to its infamous use of Marxist analysis; and then the question concerning the plurality of liberation-theologies. This last topic is directed squarely at the assumption, shared by Löwy, that liberation-theology is a peculiarly Latin-American product.[4]

Elective affinities

Löwy's is an urbane and heavily Weberian Marxism delivered in a smooth and easy style. Whenever he needs an insight or a new angle on a problem, he dips as much into Weber as into Marx.[5] Indeed, Löwy's more recent thought may be characterised as a wholesale, and often quite productive, effort to blend Marxist and Weberian thought, even if Marx occasionally slips into the background, often playing second fiddle to Weber. However, a quite specific matter has drawn Löwy to Weber: the more Löwy turned to religion in the

---

[3] Löwy 2004; Löwy 1988b, pp. 6–13.

[4] Why not an extended discussion of Löwy's passion for Walter Benjamin? Not only does Benjamin constitute the high point of *Redemption and Utopia*, but he is also the focus of a recent book and article – see Löwy 2005a; Löwy 2009; see also the earlier engagements in Löwy 1985 and Löwy 1989a. The major reason I have not offered a detailed critique is that I have dealt with Benjamin at length elsewhere in the *Criticism of Heaven and Earth* series (Boer 2007a, pp. 57–105) and I see little point in repeating large chunks of that analysis here. Another reason is that I do not share Löwy's assessment of Benjamin as the greatest philosopher of the twentieth century; Löwy's effort to provide a clear and simple commentary on Benjamin jars with the writing of a man who was by no means clear about what he was writing.

[5] See Löwy 1989b.

last couple of decades, the more he found Weber became useful in providing him with a ready quiver of arrows for dealing with his new target.

Emergence

This is where elective affinity appears, for it is, Löwy argues, Weber's own way of dealing with the connections between capitalism and Calvinist Protestantism. For Löwy, elective affinity operates as follows: 'on the basis of certain analogies, certain affinities, certain correspondences, two cultural structures may – under certain historical circumstances – enter in a relationship of attraction, of choice, of mutual selection'.[6] Before I trace the curious path of this concept, it is worth pointing out that Löwy also has a polemical reason for using it: the persistent assumption that Marxism is a secularised form of eschatological, if not apocalyptic theology. This suggestion goes back to Karl Löwith, Nikolai Berdyaev, and more recently Leszek Kolakowski.[7] It has become such a commonplace that, as soon as one raises the question of Marxism and religion in a gathering, at least one person will jump at the bait and insist that Marxism is a form of secularised theology, usually understood in this case as secularised messianism. The argument is obviously one of influence – Jewish and Christian thought came first and so Marxism offers a pale, secularised copy. The narrative is well known: the evils of the present age with its alienation and exploitation (sin) will be overcome by the proletariat as collective redeemer, who will usher in the glories of a new age when sin is overcome, the unjust are punished and the righteous inherit the earth. Most of the time, the argument is used as ammunition in the hands of conservative and liberal critics, but apostate-Marxists like Berdyaev and Kolakowski add to the chorus of voices proclaiming that there is a dreadfully smelly theological corpse under the floorboards.

The idea of elective affinity is, at one level, Löwy's response to this argument. On nearly every occasion, he introduces the idea of elective affinity,

---

[6] Löwy 1996, p. 68. Or as he puts it in *Redemption and Utopia*, 'By "elective affinity" I mean a very special kind of dialectical relationship that develops between two social or cultural configurations, one that cannot be reduced to direct causality or to "influences" in the traditional sense. Starting from a certain structural analogy, the relationship consists of a convergence, a mutual attraction, an active confluence, a combination that can go as far as a fusion' (Löwy 1988b, p. 6). See also Löwy 1980.

[7] Löwith 1949; Berdyaev 1937; Kolakowski 1981, pp. 372–5.

he is keen to point out that it does not designate a one-way process of influence – Jewish or Christian messianism is not the prior and determining set
of ideas to which Marxism is subject. To be sure, there are similarities, but
a far more complex relationship than mere borrowing needs to be proposed
and explored – hence elective affinity. But I have run ahead of myself, for
I have not yet asked from where this concept began its long journey into
Löwy's theoretical armoury. For some strange reason, Löwy prefers to tell the
story of elective affinity in terms of influence – precisely the type of relationship he seeks to avoid in his treatment of the relation between theology and
Marxism.

So we find that elective affinity emerges from the dark mutterings and
speculations of the alchemists. Here, we find figures such as Albertus Magnus, Johannes Barchusen and the Dutchman Hermannus Boerhave bent over
their simmering pots, gaseous tubes and multi-coloured jars. Why does sul-
phur combine so with metal, they pondered? Why do copper and iron meld
together to become brass? And, most famously, what substances will seek out
each other to produce gold? As Löwy notes, they used terms such as *affinitas*,
amor [love], and *attractionis electivae* [elective affinity] to describe this mysterious attraction. What strikes one when reading through such an account is
the fuzzy line that distinguishes alchemy and chemistry, especially by the
eighteenth century when we find a title such as *Elementa Chemiae* (*Principles
of Chemistry* from 1724) by Boerhave, who is called an 'alchemist', and then
De attractionibus electivae (*Concerning Elective Attraction*) from 1775, written by
the Swede Torben Bergman, who was apparently a 'chemist'. Of course, this
is an old point – that alchemy and chemistry become distinguished through
a process of differentiation, with the result that one is seen in hindsight as
an esoteric and magical venture, while the other takes on the mantle of 'science'. Among the likes of Magnus, Barchusen, Boerhave and perhaps even
Bergman, it was not so easy to make such a distinction at all. Eventually, via
a translation of Bergson's book into German as *Walverwandschaft* (1782–90),
we find that this idea from alchemy/chemistry leaps over into another field
entirely – into Goethe's 1809 novel *Die Walverwandschaften*. From here, it
passes through German culture as a term describing a strong bond between
two people, perhaps comparable to the English notion of soul-mate, until
it gets to Löwy's favoured theorist, Max Weber. In Weber's work, 'elective
affinity' most famously appears in *The Protestant Ethic and the Spirit of Capital-*

ism: the two terms of the title relate to one another in a complex pattern of attraction and combination.[8] Weber seems to have made extraordinarily good use of this new theoretical tool,[9] but Löwy is most intrigued by Weber's own usage in the relations between religion and economics.

However, Löwy is not interested exclusively in the end-product of this unusual story, holding up a smooth and shiny method for the sociology of religion. Instead, he tries to retain various features of elective affinity in its path through alchemy-chemistry, romantic literature and sociology. The result is that, when Löwy tries to formulate the main methodological stages of elective affinity, his language swerves towards alchemy and even mysticism. In the murky realms of alchemical thought, four stages were distinguished: initial correspondence, reciprocal attraction, combination and then a new entity as the product of the union.

So, we find that the first stage or level is one of static affinity: two entities might share similar features and be attracted to one another, but their connection remains potential. These elements have a certain homologous[10] likeness to one another ('like draws to like' was the Hippocratic motto favoured by the alchemists); otherwise there would be no basis for their combination. There follows a moment of what is really choice ('election'), for, in alchemy, the elements seem to have a will of their own and choose to combine with other elements with which they have some affinity. In Löwy's method, this means that the two configurations cease to ignore one another and engage, with the

---

[8] Weber 1992.

[9] In *Redemption and Utopia* (pp. 8–9) Löwy mentions only two uses – between different religious forms and between class-interests and individual worldviews – but, in 'Le concept d'affinitié élective chez Max Weber', Löwy lists no less than ten uses of the term: internal uses in the realms of religion, economics and culture; between the formal structures of communal (especially religious) action and the concrete economic forms; between religious ethic and economic ethos; between religious and economic forms; between economic structures and political forms; between social classes and religious orders; between world-views an social classes; between certain lifestyles characteristic of social classes and the religious life. As becomes clear in such a list, most of these examples deal with religion in its relation to economics, class and politics (Löwy 2004).

[10] Löwy likes to invoke Lucien Goldmann's notion of 'structural homology' every now and then – two elements may be attracted to one another due to formal similarities between them. For a more detailed discussion of Goldmann, see Löwy 1997. See Goldmann 1964, pp. 89–102; Goldmann 1959, pp. 97–114; Goldmann 1980, p. 142. Since I have discussed Goldmann in *Criticism of Religion*, I refer the reader to Boer 2009a, pp. 1–30, especially pp. 20–2.

smallest hint of eroticism, in some stimulation and interaction – in Aristotelian terms, the potentiality of affinity begins to become dynamic. Thirdly, we have contact. When the interaction becomes fully dynamic, various stages of union result, ranging from mutually respecting partners to total fusion. Finally, something entirely new may be created in the process (this is where Goethe is dominant). It may be a new idea, a new cultural form, or even a new politics.

Untidy corners and sexy dialectics

I am not sure whether these steps are meant to be sequential or that this impression is the result of the narrative sequence of writing and the need for some sense of causality and effect. The latter is probably to be preferred, but I am interested in another question: is this a workable method? Does it yield anything tangible? In answering those questions, I need to deal with some untidy corners that peek out from smooth surface of Löwy's text.

To begin with, there are a couple of features which do very little work in Löwy's analysis, coasting at the back of the pack and taking it easy. One of these is the emotional and spiritual dimension that we find in Goethe, while another is the erotic dimension with which the medieval alchemists were enraptured. Löwy is content to stay with seductive suggestions, a meeting of the eyes, an 'accidental' touch, but they remain largely secretive. He talks of the possibility of 'active convergence', of 'reciprocal attraction' and 'mutual stimulation', or an '"alloying" of partners' and even a 'chemical wedding' (this last phrase from the alchemist Boerhave). At one level, these phrases read like the conventional narrative of courtship, marriage and then even the child at the end – the 'new figure' created through the 'fusion' of the two individual elements. All very proper, but there is also the hint of an illicit and underlying narrative of sensuality, seduction, arousal and sex. Of course, the erotic dimension was always there with the alchemists, but I wonder what Löwy's method would look like if the sensual, sexual element was brought out in to the open. What would the argument for the erotic affinity of Calvinism and capitalism look like? Was the attraction between libertarian thought and Jewish messianism in the century from 1850 a sensual one too? And does liberation-theology find Marxism sexy? Why do some authors attract us, fire us up and get the juices flowing? And why do others leave us cold and uninterested? I ask these questions not in jest, for erotic pleasure is very much a political issue and not restricted to one's private peccadillo. Indeed, the attraction of political options, whether of the Right or Left or anywhere in between always has a distinct sensual appeal. For all its sobriety, for all its focus on analysis and action, Marxism also has a distinct sexiness, if I may put it that way. And I find that ascetic forms of religion also have – strange as it may seem – their sensual pleasures.

The dialectical side of elective affinity is another feature that Löwy in no way exploits to its full capacity. In *Redemption and Utopia*, he mentions 'a very special kind of dialectical relationship',[11] but that is it. It is difficult to find any reference to the dialectic in his works on Marxism and religion, which is a pity, for there is not a little in the Marxist tradition that would have assisted at this point. The dialectic makes a belated appearance in Löwy's later study on Walter Benjamin, precisely at the moment when Löwy backs off from the idea of fusion and a new figure.[12] However, in Löwy's earlier works, the dialectic is left to its own devices, perhaps on the assumption that it is sufficiently grown up. At least one way it might have been put to work is in developing Althusser's well-known effort to recast the various realms of culture, politics, religion, education, judiciary and economics as semi-autonomous realms which interact with one another.[13] Economics then becomes the ultimately determining instance only in the last resort. Here, it seems to me, elective affinity might provide one way for speaking of the dialectical relations between these semi-autonomous zones.

In fact, a more vigorous dialectic may well provide another angle on Löwy's own narrative of the development of the idea of elective affinity. This story is one of influence and causality – precisely the type of narrative Löwy seeks to forestall with the idea itself. He presents it as story uncovered through some careful sleuthing, one in which alchemy moves unnoticed into chemistry, then literature and finally sociology. But this narrative is at another level

[11] Löwy 1988b, p. 6.
[12] Löwy 2005a, pp. 20 and 28.
[13] Given Althusser's intense bursts of frenetic writing, the various proposals do not always sit together neatly. In *Reading 'Capital'* he speaks of 'instances' and 'practices', mentioning politics, economics and ideology (Althusser and Balibar 1979, pp. 11–69; Althusser, et al. 1996, pp. 1–79). However, in 'Ideology and Ideological State Apparatuses' he distinguishes between the apparatuses of religion, education, family, the law, politics, trade-unions, communications and culture (Althusser 1971, pp. 127–86; Althusser 1995, pp. 269–314).

self-referential, for, between these different realms, I detect a process of elective affinity. Why does the idea move between alchemy and sociology, between chemistry and literature if there is not a prior likeness and mutual attraction? Is the relation between these different uses merely one of influence and progression, or is there a dialectical interaction between them? My questions become even more pertinent if we consider Löwy's favoured use of the idea: it is no accident that that use is in the connection between religion and social forms, for we find this interaction prefigured in the relations between heretical forms of religion and sociology in the history of the term itself.

Other corners that rupture the limpid surface of the text appear in the shape of Löwy's relation to Weber, one an unconscious appropriation of Weber's assumptions and the other an item of friction. As for the appropriation, Löwy seems to have taken on Weber's well-known liking for ideal types, especially in the way Löwy characterises the two entities that engage in elective affinity. They tend to be quite equal and autonomous, coming in pairs and with histories that are not explored in any great detail. So, we find that Jewish messianism is an ideal type, as are Jewish intellectuals of the late nineteenth and early twentieth centuries, as is liberation-theology. So, the prospective partners for elective affinity are invariably two distinct entities which come into contact through a process of mutual choice. In other words, rather than two dumb, lumbering monoliths, agency and conscious decisions to engage are crucial. And what if these monoliths are not so equal, one far more powerful than the other? Would it not dominate the elective affinity to make it far less than elective?

But there is also some friction between Löwy and Weber. Löwy wants to enlist elective affinity in assessing the engagement between two autonomous zones with relatively equal weight – theology and Marxism, or Jewish messianism and libertarian politics. Weber's agenda is a little different. I can illustrate this agenda in the very text Löwy quotes from Weber's *The Protestant Ethic*. We find the following description: 'At the same time we shall as far as possible clarify the manner and the general *direction* in which, by virtue of those relationships [*Walverwandschaften*] *the religious movements have influenced* the development of material culture'.[14] Löwy gaze is fixed on the inadequate translation by Talcott Parsons of *Walverwandschaften* as 'those relationships',

---

[14] Weber 1992, p. 92; also quoted in Löwy 1988b, p. 9.

but he misses the obvious feature of this sentence (second italics): Weber wishes to explore the possible *influence* of religion on material culture, by which he means economics. Now, Weber's agenda is well known, seeking to offer a counter-narrative to the Marxist emphasis on economics. But the point here is that Weber makes use of 'elective affinity' as a way of determining a specific influence – from religion to economics – out of the myriad confusions and interactions that operate between them. This is not quite what Löwy has in mind with his appropriation from Weber.[15]

Weber's take on elective affinity raises another question. Although Löwy is careful to point out that each entity engaged in elective affinity has its own complex history, I wonder whether it entirely excludes prior influence in either direction. For distinct political reasons, Löwy is keen to block the possibility of influence, especially into Marxism from Jewish or Christian thought. But it may well be possible that the reason for a certain attraction between them is due to earlier influence – in either direction. One last rupture: Löwy faces some difficulties in distinguishing elective affinity from other types of relations. So it is, he argues, not like ideological affinity between similar social and cultural movements; nor is it like the vague correlation between two items; nor is it a relation of influence (as we have already seen); nor is it a version of 'expression' in the classic sense that the superstructure expresses what goes on in the base. All the same, it makes one wonder whether 'elective affinity' is not merely another name for engagement, attraction, interaction, appropriation and so on.

So, in light of these questions, is elective affinity a workable method? I suspect it is may be useful when one is considering the meeting of two bodies of thought and action and when that engagement takes place through the conscious choice of the participants of those movements. But, surely, it must include factors such as unequal partners, the possibility of complex patterns of influence that move in either direction, the presence of more than two ideal

---

[15] Löwy prefers not the second sentence of the text he quotes from Weber but the first: 'In view of the tremendous confusion and interdependent influences between the material basis, the forms of social and political organization, and the ideas current in the time of the Reformation, we can only proceed by investigating whether and at what points certain correlations [*Walverwandschaften*] between forms of religious belief and practical ethics can be worked out' (Weber 1992, pp. 91–2; also quoted in Löwy 1988b, p. 9).

types, indeed a move away from ideal types to a sense of permeable borders between them, and prior histories of interaction?

On that last point, I would like to return to Löwy's overwhelming desire to avoid the charge that Marxism is influenced by Jewish of Christian theology. As we saw, elective affinity is an effort to counter this charge and yet deal with the perceived overlaps between Marxism and theology. But there are other ways to deal with this charge. One is well known, running in a consistent stream from Engels to our own day: yes, theology and Marxism do have affinities with one another, but that is not to the detriment of one or the other but to their mutual benefit. Or it would be possible to show that Marx and Engels honed the historical-materialist method in response to theology. As I will show at some length in *Criticism of Earth*, for distinct historical reasons, the situation in the 1820s, 1830s and 1840s in Germany was saturated with theology.[16] In contrast to the atheistic push of French thought in the line of Enlightenment-*philosophes* like Voltaire and in contrast to the Deism characteristic of English thought, Germany took a much more conservative path. Due to the reactionary push towards a Christian state by Friedrich Wilhelm III and his son, Wilhelm IV (who took the Prussian throne in 1840), debate in Germany over matters such a republicanism, democracy, liberalism, the state, reason, and the political subject took place on the terrain of theology, especially the Bible. The great controversies of the day were generated by David Strauss's *Das Leben Jesu*, Bruno Bauer's radical biblical criticism, and Ludwig Feuerbach's challenge to theology.[17] Marx and Engels painstakingly worked out their approach in critical response to the overwhelmingly theological nature of debate. Even more, Marx and Engels struggled with theology on another front, for the French variety of communism, first introduced to Germany by Moses Hess and taken up by Wilhelm Weitling among others, had a strong Christian odour about it – largely due to the way French communists responded to the atheism of liberal radicals.

In the midst of this process, there is a significant feature that Löwy neglects (he will correct this omission later in *The War of Gods*), namely Engels's argu-

---

[16] See Boer forthcoming.
[17] Strauss 1835; Strauss 1836; Strauss 1839; Strauss 1840a; Strauss 1840b; Strauss 1864; Strauss 1902; Strauss 1983; Strauss 1997; Strauss 2000; Bauer 1838; Bauer 1839; Bauer 1840; Bauer 1841; Bauer 1842a; Bauer 1842b; Bauer 1843a; Bauer 1850–1; Bauer 1852; Bauer 1983; Feuerbach 1924; Feuerbach 1989.

ment that earlier revolutionary movements took their inspiration from Christianity. This argument may be understood as one of the ways Engels came to terms with his earlier deep Calvinist commitment, but the result is quite unique. Already from quite early on,[18] Engels noted that various revolutionary movements were inspired by Christianity and had Christian leaders – he mentions Müntzer, Cabet, Weitling and others. This would remain a consistent theme in Engels's thought until his works on the peasant-revolt in sixteenth-century Germany and the revolutionary nature of early Christianity.[19] Engels's great insight was that Christianity, and especially the Bible, are politically ambiguous, with plenty of material on which the ruling classes could draw to make them feel perfectly comfortable, but also a good deal of justifications for overthrowing such rulers.

But what has all this to do with eschatological Christianity and Marxism? To begin with, Marx and Engels set themselves against this strain of communist thought. Its great exponent was Moses Hess, whose *Die Heilige Geschichte der Menschheit* and *Europäische Trierarchie* introduced to Germany a communism with a strongly apocalyptic flavour.[20] Hess's widely read *Europäische Trierarchie* argued that the combination of the young-Hegelian criticism of theology, French socialist politics and English industrial materialism would bring about the rapid and complete collapse of the existing order and usher in a new age. This was precisely the sort of thought Marx and Engels sought to excise from the communist movement, largely due to the overwhelming theological nature of public debate in Germany of the 1830s and 1840s. Further, the only one with any interest in eschatology and apocalyptic was Engels, and he did so in his youth when he fascinated by the biblical book of Revelation.[21] But he uses this biblical text in jest, satire and as a way to express exhilaration

---

[18] Already in 1843 Engels wrote, 'In general, this is a feature of every revolutionary epoch, as was seen in particular in the religious revolution of which the outcome was Christianity: 'blessed are the poor' [Matthew 5: 3], 'the wisdom of this world is foolishness' [1 Corinthians 1: 20], etc.' (Engels 1975d, p. 380; Engels 1985d, pp. 451–2). See also Engels 1975e.

[19] Engels 1978; Engels 1973a; Engels 1989; Engels 1973b; Engels 1990a; Engels 1990b.

[20] Hess 1837, 1961, 2004.

[21] Engels 1975i; Engels 2008c; Engels 1975g; Engels 2008a; Engels 1975b; Engels 1985b; Engels 1975c, pp. 238–40; Engels 1985c, pp. 312–14; Engels 1975j; Engels 2008c; Engels 1975h; Engels 2008b; Engels 1982, p. 13; Engels 1973c, p. 13; Engels 1975a, p. 67; Engels 1985a, p. 99; Marx and Engels 1975, pp. 210–11; Marx and Engels 1972, pp. 222–3.

at a new discovery, never quite taking it seriously. Later, Engels used exactly the same biblical text to extinguish any apocalyptic fervour by arguing that the apocalyptic book of Revelation is merely a historical book that provides a window into early Christianity.[22] So much for Engels, but is there an influence on Marx, especially in light of the long history of Jewish rabbis in his family? Here, we need to go back to his university-days in Berlin and his very close association with Bruno Bauer, who taught him a course on the book of Isaiah.[23] Isaiah is an eschatological prophetic book *par excellence*. But the catch is that Bauer, as a leading figure of the most radical biblical criticism of the time, would be the last one to argue for an eschatological or even apocalyptic interpretation of a book like Isaiah – such an approach was far too traditional. Bauer's only study of the Hebrew Bible (Old Testament), which appeared the year before Bauer taught Marx, makes that perfectly clear.[24]

So we have reached the point where Löwy's methodological motif of 'elective affinity' faces a number of problems: it is not necessarily the best way to answer the criticism of secularised theology; it tends to operate with equally weighted ideal types, thereby excluding the possibility of unequal interaction; it excludes the possibility of mutual influence or even prior influence; and it makes little of the erotic and dialectical potential. Elective affinity may be workable if it included the complexity of some of these factors.

Liberation-theology

Despite the promise that elective affinity may be used in almost as many fields as one might wish to imagine – within and between economic, cultural, religious and political realms – Löwy makes extensive use of it in two areas: Jewish libertarian thought and liberation-thought. Unfortunately, the study of the former is given over largely to expositing the positions of a range of writers such as Martin Buber, Gershom Scholem, Franz Kafka, Walter Benjamin and Ernst Bloch. It is unfortunate, since Löwy's own voice

---

[22] Engels 1990a; Engels 1990b.
[23] There is small note from Marx's Leaving Certificate from the Friedrich Wilhelm University in Berlin that may easily be missed. It reads as follows: 'V. In the summer term 1839; 1. Isaiah with Herr Licentiate Bauer, attended' (*Leaving Certificate from Berlin University* 1975, p. 704).
[24] Bauer 1838.

is largely muted. Of course, that voice is present to some extent in the selection of writers and the choice of what to consider in their work, but the bulk of the book reads like a collection of summaries of other people's opinions to illustrate the main point that some Jewish thinkers of Central Europe combined various strains of radical thought (some Marxist, most not) with a romanticised and recovered Jewish religious tradition. Apart from noting a number of significant problems with Löwy's treatment – a woefully loose use of the term 'messianism',[25] a one-sided tendency to assume that the primary influence on the thought of figures such as Bloch and Benjamin was Jewish 'theology',[26] and a caricature of Christianity as other-worldly in contrast to the this-worldly focus of Judaism[27] – I should also point out that there is little reason to engage extensively with Löwy's expositions of the thought of those I have dealt with elsewhere.[28]

By far the most productive and interesting of Löwy's deployments of elective affinity appears in his sympathetic study of liberation-theology, *The War of Gods*, which won the 'Sergio Buarque de Hollande' prize in 2000. Since the centre of Latin-American liberation-theology is also Löwy's birthplace – Brazil – it should come as no surprise that liberation-theology has been an ongoing fascination for him. I must admit to sharing this fascination, for liberation-theology was, for me, the gate that opened to Marx more than two decades ago. Unlike Löwy, whose passage has been to liberation-theology from Marxism, I moved from theology to Marxism via liberation-theology. So what this work from a Marxist atheist with a distinct 'ethical and political sympathy'[29] for liberation-theology enables me to do is provide my own

---

[25] What is needed here is a modicum of precision: eschatology is a base-term designating anticipation and hope for the future, and may appear as both the expressed content of a text and the worldview in which such texts operate; messianism is a development of and subset of eschatology, for it focuses hope for the future on a mediator (to speak of messianism without a Messiah is really to speak of eschatology); and apocalyptic is yet a further development of eschatology into fevered speculation, often in extremely oppressive circumstances, about the exact timing of an end that is felt to be immanent.

[26] Any detailed consideration of their work reveals the depth of Christian subject-matter. I have argued this in detail elsewhere – see Boer 2007a, pp. 1–105.

[27] Löwy 1988b, p. 17. Here Löwy is misled by Scholem, but Löwy's later work on liberation-theology would have shown him how erroneous such a caricature is.

[28] Boer 2007a.

[29] Löwy 1996, p. 69.

assessment of that theology. Needless to say, that process involves some argument with Löwy.

Löwy's study of liberation-theology has three main prongs. One is to introduce liberation-theology to a readership, largely on the Left, that is less than
familiar with that theology. Another is to urge the Left to reconsider the role
of religion in its struggles, and a third is to explore how Marxism and Christianity might meet with a common political agenda in what I would call a
politics of alliance.[30] The first two aims are much needed and it seems to me
that Löwy does his job with accessible clarity, but it is the third that interests
me most. Let me put it this way: bearing in mind Löwy's fourfold schema
of elective affinity (see above), do Marxism and liberation-theology achieve
some sort of fusion, a 'chemical wedding' if you will, or even produce a new
figure? In other words, does the interaction attain the third and fourth levels
of elective affinity? The short answer is that Löwy thinks so; I am more sceptical. The long answer will take up the rest of this chapter.

Before I proceed, a preliminary observation is needed: this is the question
as to whether an idealist system, of which Christianity is an exemplar, can
have historical force. One of Löwy's opening moves is to suggest that liberation-theology is too limiting a term, so he opts for 'liberationist Christianity'.[31]
At one level, this is an understandable move to make, for Latin-American
liberation-theology is not merely the result of theologians' thoughts on the
matter; it arises from a distinct history and experience of demoralising and
life-threatening, grinding poverty, the formation of the famous 'base communities' (CEBs) and the subsequent conscientisation of priests, bishops and
theologians.[32] The same applies to the other forms of liberation-theology
I consider below. However, Löwy's shift has another implicit agenda, and

---

[30] An early version of what eventually became *The War of Gods* appeared in 1988
in a shorter pamphlet published by the International Institute for Research and
Education (linked to the Fourth International). Called 'Marxisme et théologie de la
libération' (Löwy 1988a), the title is a far clearer statement of the main theme of the
study than the later book.
[31] Löwy 1996, p. 2.
[32] The ecclesial base-communities, or *comunidades ecclesia de base* (CEB) are grass-
roots-gatherings of people for prayer, simple liturgies, Bible-reading and support-
networks, actively fostered by socially engaged priests in Latin America and now
existing around the world in all forms of Christianity. The term conscientisation
(Portuguese *conscientização*) – an educational model that focuses on developing a
critical consciousness of the world and its contradictions – derives from the Brazilian
paedagogue, Paolo Freire. See Freire 1970.

that is to counter the crass materialist argument that thoughts do not a social movement make. Despite Löwy's tendency to focus on the thoughts of the major liberation-theologians (his favoured reference is Gutiérrez), as well as the meetings and statements of bishops' conferences and the Roman-Catholic hierarchy, I can only agree with this move. For, as Althusser showed so well, an ideological state-apparatus like the Church is as much a material institution with its own conflicts and struggles.[33]

Roman-Catholic social teaching

A couple of central features of liberation-theology deeply influence its engagement with Marxism: the tradition of Roman-Catholic social thought, and what may be called the ontological reserve. However, if we go looking for a sustained discussion of Catholic social teaching in Löwy's book, we will be disappointed. Löwy does not deal with Catholic social thought directly; instead, he approaches it at a tangent. I find this a little strange, given the way that teaching is invoked within liberation-theology as a way to trump Marxism.

One of Löwy's tangential paths is to write what he calls a 'missing chapter' in Weber's treatment of capitalism and Christianity.[34] Even here, we find only four pages concerned with Weber; the rest is given over to various figures who have recognised a 'negative affinity' between capitalism and Roman Catholicism. In his characteristic fashion, Löwy glides effortlessly through his topic, slipping by the rough edges that might trouble his search for a consistent argument. But, first, let us see what he does argue. Implicit in Weber's argument that some types of Protestantism – Calvinism and puritanism – have an affinity with capitalism, indeed that they enabled its spread, is the obverse point: the ethos of Roman Catholicism must be opposed to capitalism. Löwy tracks a few references in Weber's works to suggest that Weber did actually feel that Roman Catholicism (although Weber also adds Lutheranism)[35] was not fertile ground for capitalism. The reasons: the ban on usury, the opposition to competition and individual gain at the expense of community, the

---

[33] Althusser 1971, pp. 141–57; Althusser 1995, pp. 269–314. See also Mack 2008, pp. 49–52.
[34] Löwy 1988b, pp. 19–23.
[35] Weber 1923, p. 305.

pursuit of money, and the abstract and impersonal nature of market-forces. Above all, it was Weber's sense of a reified and impersonal logic, embodied in a market that operated according to its own laws, that the Church found so unacceptable.

Less interested in asking whether Weber has missed the mark or not, Löwy prefers to take this retrieved argument as a distinct insight into Roman Catholicism (he quickly drops the Lutheran reference). He tracks a series of observations from both the Church and from thinkers connected to it to show that there continues to be what he calls a 'negative affinity' between capitalism and Roman Catholicism. There is no denying that Löwy has a point, for elements of Roman-Catholic social teaching do tend in this direction – such as the concern with community, the focus on the poor and the rights of workers, but it by no means exhausts that teaching. And Löwy repeats the oft-made observation that Roman Catholicism, especially in its radical wings, has often been a stepping stone to communism. I could add Louis Althusser's comment that Catholic Action was a recruiting ground for the French Communist Party. Indeed, some of the strongest Communist Parties in Western Europe came from countries with dominant Roman-Catholic populations, especially France and Italy – and this despite the strong opposition of the hierarchy to 'atheistic communism'.

Immediately, a first objection leaps out: the greatest success of Communism has been in countries of an Orthodox-Christian background, if not of a non-Christian background entirely, once we include China. Following Löwy's Weberian argument, then there must be an even greater negative affinity between Eastern Orthodoxy (or, indeed, Buddhism and Confucianism) and capitalism than that between Roman Catholicism and capitalism. Conversely, their 'elective affinity' with communism must be all the stronger. Now the objections begin to pile up. Is the Roman-Catholic opposition to capitalism necessarily progressive? To his credit, Löwy does point out that such opposition was and so often is for conservative reasons, but he glides by this issue far too quickly. This evasion is a shame, since the conservative nature of Roman-Catholic opposition to communism demands more attention than Löwy is willing to grant it, for much of the opposition came from a church fighting a desperate rear-guard action against its loss of temporal power and influence. A modicum of historical awareness makes this all too clear, so let us return to the year 1000.

From this year until the turn to the sixteenth century, papal power rose to unheard of heights only to begin a long decline. The rise of that power was due to a new theory of papal power, energetic popes, European politics and changing social landscapes. The motivation and expression of that power was based on a forgery: the *Donation of Constantine*. Although the *Donation* presents itself as a letter written by the (first Christian) Roman Emperor Constantine to Pope Silvester I on March 30, 315, it was actually written after 750. What does the *Donation* claim? Apart from speaking of Constantine's conversion and baptism and claiming to have been placed on the body of St Peter, it offers the pope control over all churches, especially the great centres of Antioch, Alexandria, Jerusalem, and Constantinople; the Lateran palace in Rome and the imperial insignia; and the transfer from emperor to pope of all earthly power in Rome, Italy and the provinces of the West. It may not be a genuine document, but its truth is to lay out the basic ideas of the medieval papacy. Here, we find the pope as universal bishop following in St. Peter's footsteps, teacher and godfather of the emperor, Christ's agent on earth and lord of the West. In short, it gave all power in church and empire to the pope.

Soon, this power was not enough: from Gregory VII (1073–85) on it was asserted that such power came directly from God rather than the first Christian emperor. There is an extraordinary statement from Gregory's letters that expresses as no other document can the assertion of papal power:

The pope can be judged by no one;

The Roman church has never erred and never will err till the end of time;

The Roman church was founded by Christ alone;

The pope alone can depose and restore bishops;

He alone can make new laws, set up new bishoprics, and divide old ones;

He alone can translate bishops;

He alone can call general councils and authorize canon law;

He alone can revise his own judgments;

He alone can use the imperial insignia;

He can depose emperors;

He can absolve subjects from their allegiance;

All princes should kiss his feet;

His legates, even though in inferior orders, have precedence over all bishops;

> An appeal to the papal court inhibits judgments by all inferior courts;
>
> A duly ordained pope is undoubtedly made a saint by the merits of St
> Peter.[36]

A series of energetic popes after Gregory VII, especially Innocent III (1198–1216) and Boniface VIII (1294–1303), put this theory into practice. Through astute diplomacy, they ensured they were indispensable to medieval society at every level, gathering around them multiple allies who extended their rule into all walks of life. The backward nature of Western-European politics, which paled by comparison to the Byzantine Empire in the east and the Muslim world, ensured that the popes were able to climb to the pinnacle of power. Warring princes, constant territorial conflict and the perpetual search for strategic alliances meant that the pope became a useful ally for any prince seeking to gain influence for himself. Within the feudal system, the pope claimed he was the highest feudal lord, at the peak of the pyramid. Since he spoke God's word on earth, all should obey them.

All this power could not be asserted merely on paper; power must be wielded in real terms. The popes did so by developing a highly complex system of benefices and a legal system. To those who came to Rome and kissed the pope's feet, the pope gave an extraordinary range of benefits. It might be the legal claim to land for a monastery, order or bishop, the confirmation of their customs, freedom from jurisdiction by a local lord, or honours such as the use of papal insignia. The popes showered their increasing number of supporters with these material benefits and signs of status. In this way, they ensured an ever greater number of allies. Further, the papacy created the most effective legal system of the middle ages. At its centre was the recovery of absolute private property, which had been forgotten after its invention by the Romans.[37] By adapting Roman law to feudalism, the murky area of property was clarified. The popes of the eleventh to thirteenth centuries developed a system in which everyone sought the opinion of the papal courts. Land-claims were cleared up, due process for every minute aspect of daily life was established, litigants streamed to Rome for decisions, the pope's legal representatives (legates) were everywhere and papal power spread. This achievement

---

[36] Southern 1970, p. 102.
[37] Gianaris 1996, p. 20; Miéville 2006, p. 195.

of the 'lawyer popes' in what has been called the 'papal revolution' was the beginning of the legal system now dominant in the West.[38]

Through the handing out of benefits, an indispensable legal system and astute diplomacy between warring princes, the pope could call on some princes and their armed forces to further his agenda, as well occasionally paying for his own (as done, for example, by the infamous Pope Alexander VI, 1492–1502, of the Borgia family). As Stalin once retorted, many years later, 'How many divisions does the pope have?'. In the years of papal power, the answer was, 'very many'. It also meant that papal power became a victim of its own success. The sheer volume of legal business turned the popes into administrators devoted to keeping the system running. The machinery ground down the possibility of new ideas in theology, politics or ecclesiology. Over the eleventh to thirteenth centuries, new ideas had been encouraged and helped develop papal power, but, by the fourteenth century, new ideas no longer came from within. They came from outside, so much so that the popes began denouncing one heresy after another. Added to this change were the political machinations of the princes and the growth of the towns and a new merchant-class. Whereas earlier princes would hand over heretics in order to keep favour with Rome, by the fourteenth century, such free thinkers were useful allies in their struggles with the pope. Finally, towards the end of that century, feudalism began to crack at the seams. The interests of the towns and commerce heralded the first glimmers of capitalism on the horizon. New forces that fundamentally challenged the power of the Church – merchants, reformers, free thinkers and new political forms – meant that papal power was on the wane.

I have provided this brief historical sketch since it throws into relief one of the main reasons for the opposition to the new economic and social relations of capitalism: they constituted a fundamental threat to the power of the Church, a power that was already on the wane. The threats posed by the merchants in the towns to existing structures of power, their systematic undermining of a feudal system in which the pope was supposed to be the head and the associated flourishing of new ideas regarding citizenship and politics all gave the popes enough reason to condemn these new-fangled ideas and practices. I hardly need to say that the opposition was deeply reactionary.

---

[38] See Berman 1983; Berman 2006.

This anticapitalist strain is but one of the curious tangents to Roman-Catholic social teaching in Löwy's book; another comes with his search for the elective affinities between Christianity and socialism. Now, we need to careful of the way Löwy uses the term 'Christianity', for most of the time it is a placeholder for Roman Catholicism (he thereby acquiesces to the claim by Roman Catholicism to be the 'Catholic', that is universal, church by its use of the shorthand 'Catholic'). In that more limited zone, he espies a number of items shared by Roman Catholicism and socialism: 'trans-individual values' (ethics and world-views beyond the individual); collectivity and communal life over against selfish individualism; a universal or 'Catholic' perspective beyond race, ethnicity and the nation-state; the hope for a better world characterised by justice, peace and freedom; a focus on the poor as victims of injustice; and a critique of capitalism in the name of a higher good.[39]

I have already explored the last item on this list, but even a brief reflection makes it all too clear that they do not apply to Christianity as a whole (the 'wealth-gospel' in which poverty is a punishment for sin is one glaring example), let alone Roman Catholicism as a whole. For example, the focus on the poor was certainly not a characteristic of the early Church, which bent over backwards to ensure that wealth was not a hindrance to enter the Kingdom of Heaven. Those early church-fathers did their level best to ensure that the rich would have a much easier time of it than any camel who should want to make its way through the proverbial eye of the needle (see the discussion of Ste. Croix in Chapter Three). And, today, a good number of conservative Roman-Catholic clergy attack the deep ills of society – promiscuous sex, abortion, and homosexuality – rather than anything that smacks of poverty.

I would suggest that what Löwy actually has in mind in this list of comparisons is Roman-Catholic social teaching – or, at least, some elements of that teaching. So let us see what that teaching actually says. Although the threads may be traced back through the many-coloured traditions of Christianity, Roman-Catholic social thought formally dates from 15 May 1891, when Pope Leo XIII

---

[39] Löwy 1996, p. 69. I have rearranged Löwy's list for reasons that will become obvious. These items of initial attraction change depending on the bodies of thought in question. So with the affinity of Jewish 'messianism' and libertarian thought we find a somewhat different set of connections: the play between restoration and utopia; a focus on earthly redemption; overthrow of the powers of this world; and anarchist tendencies (Löwy 1988b, pp. 16–21).

issued *Rerum Novarum,* subtitled 'On Capital and Labour'. This text numbers among some of the most influential statements from the Vatican. Others were to follow, refining and extending this initial document – *Quadragesimo Anno* (1931), *Mater et Magistra* (1961), *Pacem in Terris* (1963), *Dignitatis Humanae* and *Gaudiem et Spes* (1965 – conciliar documents from the Second Vatican Council), *Populorum Progessio* (1967), *Octogesima Adveniens* (1971), *Laborem Exercens* (1981), *Solicitudo Rei Socialis* (1987), *Centesimus Annus* (1991), *Evangelium Vitae* (1995), and *Deus Caritas Est* (2005).

A brief look at the dates already tells us much, for these documents appeared at times of economic and social unrest, often with connected labour-crises. So the initial *Rerum Novarum* (1891) came as a response to social instability, class-conflict, worker-agitation, and the rising influence of socialism. Forty years later, as the title *Quadragesimo Anno* (1931) indicates, finds us in the midst of the Great Depression. Then, no less than six statements appeared out of the turmoil of the 1960s. Finally, the last four, bar one, were part of the aggressive agenda of John Paul II, weaving in and out of the impact of liberation-theology, the dramatic rolling back of state-socialism in Eastern Europe and the triumphalism of neoliberal capitalism. The last of these, promulgated by Benedict XVI, comes in the wake of the 'war on terror', asserting that Christianity is a religion of love, not hatred and war. It is also worth noting that liberation-theology came out of the same turmoil of the 1960s, in part taking its cue from the rash of statements that signalled a remarkable opening out to the non-Roman-Catholic world.

The main emphasis of these documents may be summarised in seven points: 1) the sanctity of human life and the dignity of the person from the moment of conception until death, which embraces matters such as abortion, warfare and discrimination; 2) an emphasis on the (heterosexual) family and, by extension, the community, both local and global, which entails an opposition to the collectivism of communism and the laissez-faire 'extremes' of capitalism; 3) rights – to life and its necessities, to freedom of religion and to property – and responsibilities – to one another, families and society, especially so that property is not used for evil; 4) preferential option for the poor and vulnerable (an ancient and intermittent tradition that focused on the ideal of poverty, based on the imitation of Christ, in early monasticism and then flowered in the middle ages) with a focus on concern for and solidarity with the poor, which is now extended to unborn children, the disabled, elderly, terminally ill, victims of injustice and oppression; 5) the dignity of work and the rights of workers, especially in terms of the living wage, safe working conditions, trade-unions, but also to work conscientiously and treat employers and fellow workers with respect; 6) solidarity, based on forgiveness and reconciliation, as well as the idea that there is one human family, which implies that we should welcome the stranger in our midst; 7) care for creation, based on the biblical mandate for stewardship of God's creation, with the implication that the goods of the earth are subject to the 'social mortgage' (the mutual responsibility to protect the environment).

All this is quite a mix, although defenders argue that it constitutes an ongoing effort to claim a distinct position that is beholden to no 'secular' political or social movement. It is worth noting that both the conservatives and progressives within the Roman-Catholic Church can claim this social teaching as their basis. Thus, liberation-theologians argue that what they do is nothing new, for the Church has for a good while been proclaiming a preferential option for the poor and justice for the exploited. But so also can the conservatives who have systematically been placed in senior positions in the Roman-Catholic Church where liberation-theology held sway; they too can argue that their focus on abortion and divorce comes straight out of the tradition of Roman-Catholic social teaching – which, of course, it does. It also explains a feature of liberation-theology which puzzles Löwy: the conspiracy of silence concerning sexual ethics, divorce, contraception and abortion.[40] He wonders how a progressive movement like liberation-theology can take, with only the odd exception, such a conservative line which directly affects the lives of millions of poor women. But when you consider the mixed bag of Roman-Catholic social teaching, it makes perfect sense. It seems that Löwy's presentation of an elective affinity between the Church's traditional positions and Marxism is a little one-sided.

Further, one of the features of the first encyclical, *Rerum Novarum* of 1891, is a trenchant opposition to communism. Leo XIII had roundly condemned radical left-wing politics, framing the document as a direct response to the appeal of socialism to the working class. Paragraph 4 could not be clearer:

---

[40] Löwy 1996, p. 53.

To remedy these wrongs the socialists, working on the poor man's envy of the rich, are striving to do away with private property, and contend that individual possessions should become the common property of all, to be administered by the State or by municipal bodies. They hold that by thus transferring property from private individuals to the community, the present mischievous state of things will be set to rights, inasmuch as each citizen will then get his fair share of whatever there is to enjoy. But their contentions are so clearly powerless to end the controversy that were they carried into effect the working man himself would be among the first to suffer. They are, moreover, emphatically unjust, for they would rob the lawful possessor, distort the functions of the State, and create utter confusion in the community.[41]

By the time *Quadragesimo Anno* was in the works, there was some debate over whether Leo XIII had in mind all shades of socialism, or merely the hardline Communist version. So, Pius IX makes it perfectly clear that even the mildest form of socialism, which many at the time saw as coming into what we might call an elective affinity with Roman-Catholic teaching, has no common cause with the Church:

Whether considered as a doctrine, or an historical fact, or a movement, Socialism, if it remains truly Socialism, even after it has yielded to truth and justice on the points which we have mentioned, cannot be reconciled with the teachings of the Catholic church because its concept of society itself is utterly foreign to Christian truth.[42]

For all the critiques of class-conflict, exploitation of workers, the concentration of capital in the hands of a few and the need for workers to organise in trade-unions, Roman-Catholic social thought has remained firmly opposed to any form of socialism, a position reiterated in the document *Libertatis Nuntius*, issued in 1984 by the Vatican's Congregation for the Doctrine of the Faith under the direction of Cardinal Ratzinger (now Pope Benedict XVI). A direct response to liberation-theology's engagement with Marxism (which it caricatured), the document reasserted the need to remain faithful to the tradition of Roman-Catholic teaching and not be waylaid by the temptations

---

[41] Leo XIII 1891.
[42] Pius XI 1931, para. 117.

of Marxist analysis. Like the earlier documents, this one evidences less a much-vaunted distinct tradition – a 'third way' between the two extremes – than the fact that Roman-Catholic social teaching sought to block the appeal of socialism to so many of the working class. We can put it to simple test: which economic system does it categorically oppose and which does it seek to ameliorate? I hardly need to answer the question.

I have pursued this somewhat lengthy excursus in order to situate liberation-theology and its 'elective affinity' with Marxism. Time and again, a Roman-Catholic liberation-theologian points out that all they say comes straight out of the Roman-Catholic tradition; for that reason, the Church should have no objection to this theology. Indeed, in the name of that tradition, these theologians often seek to distance themselves from Marx. Let me take one of the most significant and influential theologians, Jon Sobrino of El Salvador. Across his works, we find Marx rarely, if at all, and then only as a sign of the second phase of liberation after Kant: while Kant called for reasonableness, Marx called for transforming praxis.[43] Instead, Sobrino makes it perfectly clear that he burrows deep into the tradition – both biblical and theological – to develop his theology. Even more explicit is José Miranda, who argues that the Bible offers a critique very similar to, but with greater ontological depth, than Marx's. In its wholesale criticism of objective and disinterested Western science and epistemology, the Bible is actually the source of the 'prophet' Marx's own critiques.[44] Miranda is, in some respects, much more radical than Sobrino, for he ended up leaving the Church in disgust, but their moves are of the same ilk – outflank Marx by showing that either the theological tradition or the Bible was there before him.

One last example: Gustavo Gutiérrez has written what is widely agreed to be the inaugural and benchmark work, *A Theology of Liberation*.[45] What is telling about this book is that although socialism comes in for some mention, either as a challenge to theology, or in terms of Ernst Bloch's influence on Jürgen Moltmann's 'theology of hope', or, indeed, in reporting the statements of various priests in support of socialism in Colombia, Mexico, Argentina, and

---

[43] Sobrino 1978, p. 348; Sobrino 2004b, pp. 10–15. In his other works, Marx does not rate a mention; see Sobrino 2004a; Sobrino 2004c.

[44] Miranda 1974; Miranda 1982.

[45] Gutiérrez 2001. This work is by far the most quoted text in Löwy's *The War of Gods*.

Chile, Gutiérrez is careful to refer extensively to many of the papal encyclicals mentioned above (at least those which were published at the time he wrote).[46] Many of the themes from Roman-Catholic social teaching are found here: creation, solidarity, human fellowship, the critique of capitalist development and its deleterious effects on people, especially in Latin America. Above all, there is the concluding chapter on the preferential option for the poor.[47] Of course, Gutiérrez's text blew through the wary shuffles of Roman-Catholic theology like a gale and the book is justifiably a major text – and a pleasure to read. Yet the treatments of Marxism and socialism in *A Theology of Liberation* were as far as Gutiérrez would go. Later, Marx virtually disappears from his texts until we get the telling work, *We Drink From Our Own Wells*,[48] a title that bears a double sense: it is not merely the spirituality of the poor within Latin America that is 'our own well', but also the tradition of Catholic social thought. Marx is nowhere in sight, while the encyclicals and statements from bishops' conferences are noticeably present.

So the tradition of Roman-Catholic social teaching is one reason why liberation-theologians have kept Marxism at a distance, often due to the need to keep glancing over their shoulders to check whether that hooded figure is not a Vatican agent. I will let Marx have the final word on this social teaching, since what looks like progressive so often turns out to be reactionary:

> The social principles of Christianity have now had eighteen hundred years
> to be developed, and need no further development by Prussian Consistorial
> Counsellors. The social principles of Christianity justified the slavery of
> antiquity, glorifies the serfdom of the Middle Ages and are capable, in case of
> need, of defending the oppression of the proletariat, with somewhat doleful
> grimaces. The social principles of Christianity preach the necessity of a ruling
> and an oppressed class, and for the latter all they have to offer is the pious
> wish that the former may be charitable. The social principles of Christianity
> place the Consistorial Counsellor's compensation for all infamies in heaven,
> and thereby justify the continuation of these infamies on earth. The social
> principles of Christianity declare all the vile acts of the oppressors against the

---

[46] Gutiérrez 2001, pp. 53, 125–8, 201–5. Compare these observations with references to popes and encyclicals on pp. 52, 72–3, 80, 99, 167–71, 190, 242, 246, 249, 253, 256.

[47] See also Gutiérrez 1997.

[48] Gutiérrez 2005. See also Gutiérrez 1983, 1987.

oppressed to be either a just punishment for original sin and other sins, or trials which the Lord, in his infinite wisdom, ordains for the redeemed. The social principles of Christianity preach cowardice, self-contempt, abasement, submissiveness and humbleness, in short, all the qualities of the rabble, and the proletariat, which will not permit itself to be treated as rabble, needs its courage, its self-confidence, its pride and its sense of independence even more than its bread. The social principles of Christianity are sneaking and hypocritical, and the proletariat is revolutionary. So much for the social principles of Christianity.[49]

The ontological reserve

The second feature that thoroughly influences the interaction of liberation-theology with Marxism is what may be called the ontological reserve. This reserve manifests itself in a wariness of Marxist analysis beyond economics and society. At one level, the project of liberation-theology is quite straight-forward: it offers a critical assessment of capitalist economics, often using the tools of Marxist analysis, but the matters of being and salvation are reserved for God alone. Such a bifurcation has obvious implications for Löwy's the-sis of elective affinity, so let me interrogate that ontological reserve more closely.

The scandal of liberation-theology when it first broke on the scene was that it dared to question the dominant economic model of development in Latin America. And it made use of some Marxist categories in order to so, especially the theory of dependency which came into its own in the 1960s and 1970s. Of course, a rather long, winding and well-known narrative leads up to that stage of economic theory and practice. From the beginnings of European presence, various economic realities and models have beset Latin America: plunder and expropriation for European imperial coffers and wars; raw materials of animal, vegetable and mineral varieties for European industry, a process overseen by colonial overlords and a mixture of slaves and indentured labour; indepen-dence and efforts to emulate market-economies like the United States; and then close on the heels of the previous moment comes the theory of develop-ment that still holds sway in some quarters. If only areas of the world like Latin

---

[49] Marx 1976b, p. 231; Marx 1972a, p. 200.

America, or indeed Africa or Asia (at least in the early half of the twentieth century), could emulate the wealthier regions in Europe and North America, they would 'catch up'. All they needed to do was move from resource-based industries to those of manufacture, get their labour-relations 'in order' and tidy up government spending, and the path from underdevelopment to development would begin. The model was England in the eighteenth and nineteenth centuries, which underwent a rapid process of industrialisation and thereby became a global empire. Now 'development' bore many overlapping senses, moving from crude wealth, through well-being to total social process. Through it all ran not merely an evolutionary model with a smooth path up the scale, but also an assumption that what everyone wants is to emulate the overdeveloped centres of capitalism. In Latin America, dependency-theory was tied up closely with the desire for domestically owned industries which would then export manufactured products in order to generate wealth.

Rather than a smooth process to vast social wealth, Latin-American countries found they were staggering from one economic crisis to another. A brief period of boom, often due to the demand for a particular mineral or crop, was followed by hyper-inflation, government-instability, insurgency and military coup. On this matter, liberation-theologians found Marxist analysis very persuasive, for it offered a theory to account for such a pattern. As Gutiérrez points out, the new effort to make sense of this experience was dependency-theory.[50] In light of the fact that poor nations never seemed to be able to get out of the rut and that the game of catch-up always grew more difficult as the gap increased, the argument shifted to stress the structural inequality of capitalist relations between the wealthy North and the poor South. Simply put, global capitalism, especially in the shape of multi- and trans-nationals, needed the poorer nations of the 'Third World' to supply cheap resources and cheap labour. Internal to the countries of Latin America, it became apparent that a small ruling class within these countries had done rather well with these structural inequalities, amassing fortunes and political influence on par with those in other parts of the world.[51]

---

[50] Gutiérrez 2001, pp. 106–10. In his extensive notes, Gutiérrez refers almost exclusively to Spanish and Portuguese texts from Latin America.

[51] Dependency-theory has of course come under strong attack, especially in light of the growth of India and China, among others. And what has replaced it?

Now all this is fairly basic economic theory, but it was quite shock for both the Roman-Catholic hierarchy and ruling classes with whom the Church was indecently intimate from El Salvador to Chile. To have priests, religious and theologians making use of Marxist-inspired analysis was dreadfully subversive. Add to that the continued viability of Marxist insurrectionary groups, inspired by the success of the Cuban Revolution, and it looked like the liberation-theologians were going over to the Marxists – after all, these churchly thinkers were using the same analytical tools as the rebels.

But that is where it stopped.[52] Theologians such as Gustavo Gutiérrez, Leonardo and Clodovis Boff, Rubem Alves, Juan-Luis Segundo and others made use of what are really rather mild forms of Marxist analysis in order to interpret the economic and social situation of Latin America, especially in solidarity with the poor. But they come to an abrupt halt when it comes to the solution. They might use terms such as liberation and revolution, but they understand the terms primarily in a theological sense.[53]

This tendency is what I would like to call the ontological reserve. It shows up at a number of different points, but, before I explore those, it is worth pointing out that liberation-theology has been charged – both by those within the Roman-Catholic Church and by Protestant evangelicals – of belittling the ontological aspect of theology.[54] However, what this accusation assumes is that the primary matter for theology is the individual's relationship with God. As will become clear, no matter how much liberation emphasises the collective, structural and historical nature of sin and salvation, it vigorously invokes the ontological reserve.

The ontological reserve shows up at the heart of theology, namely with the doctrine of salvation. No matter which theological tradition we might consider, salvation involves a profound process of transformation. As Gutiérrez puts it, salvation 'embraces all human reality, transforms it, and leads it to its

---

Nothing less than a revamped theory of development! For an excellent assessment and argument for the continued validity of dependency-theory, see Surin 2009.

[52] See especially Kee 1990, who argues that liberation-theology preserves its own theology as a no-go zone for Marxist analysis.

[53] Obviously, 'liberation' and its attendant 'freedom' are not the preserve of the Left. For the bourgeois revolutions in France, the United States and Mexico – to cull two or three from a very long list – they are bowdlerised liberal slogans that go hand-in-glove with the 'free market'.

[54] Núñez C. and Taylor 1996, pp. 275–6.

fullness in Christ'.[55] The biblical term for transformation is *metanoia*, which is usually rendered 'repentance', a term that has come to have an overwhelmingly individual focus. It is better translated as a fundamental change of heart and mind, a complete about-face since the present reality is not what it should be. Yet, as soon as we begin speaking of salvation, a whole narrative opens up. The reason we require *metanoia* in the first place is due to sin, which designates an impassable abyss between human beings and God, a road that leads directly away from God and a reconciled world. In order to gain salvation we need a radical change in direction and the only way to do so is through God's agency. The narrative widens to include creation, a Fall due to human disobedience, the need for God's intervention, since human beings cannot attain salvation on their own, the pivot of history in Jesus Christ, the beginning of the re-creation of the world, the need for repentance, forgiveness and reconciliation and then the hope and anticipation that history will culminate in God's final act of redemption and completion of the world's re-creation. Quite obviously, it is a whole theory of history.

The liberation-theologians *reintroduced* into this narrative a collective and structural approach to sin and justice. This was by no means new, but it challenged the privatised turn of theology since the Enlightenment. Sin was just as much an issue of social and economic structures, of societies as a whole, indeed of all humanity. In this light, history becomes not merely a matter of God's glorious march at the head of the Church, but the economic and political realities of everyday life. And, if God through Christ was in the business of forgiving sin and offering redemption from it, then that had as much to do with exploitative and oppressive economic systems as it had with the odd individual peccadillo.

The ontological reserve also manifested itself in the resources used by liberation-theologians for their reflection. Marx may be useful for the analysis of the social and economic reality of Latin America, or indeed global capitalism, but it is not Marx and subsequent Marxist thinkers to whom they turn for elaborating a specific theological position. Here, the 'tradition' for Roman-Catholics and the Bible for Protestant liberation-theologians[56] is the primary and, in many cases, the only resort. Sorely wanting is an engagement with

---

[55] Gutiérrez 2001, p. 149.
[56] See, for example, Pixley 1987; Tamez 1993.

those Marxists who have, at times quite extensively, interacted with theology. What bearing does Engels's argument for a revolutionary origin of Christianity have for liberation-theology? Or indeed, where is any consideration of Karl Kautsky's massive project of tracing the forerunners to communism in Christian revolutionary groups? What has happened to Adorno's extraordinary transformation of the ban on images into a negative philosophical motif, or Benjamin's efforts to bring Marxism and theology into dialectical contact and transformation, or Althusser's fecund theory of ideology and ideological state-apparatuses in relation to the Church, or...?[57] It is to Löwy's credit, at least, that he does have a brief discussion of precisely these Marxists. He uses them as an introduction to show that Marxism and theology are not such strange bedfellows after all. But, for some strange reason, when he gets to liberation-theology, Löwy quietly drops by the roadside all these Marxists who have engaged with theology.

One further feature of the ontological reserve presents us with a paradox – the critique of idolatry and its relation with the Marxist criticism of fetishism. The paradox is that, the more liberation-theology stresses this form of the ontological reserve, the closer it comes to the Marxist critiques. On the one hand, the ontological reserve means that one holds off identifying too closely with any particular person or political movement in the name of idolatry. That includes Marxism. To invest all one's desires and hopes for salvation in, for example, the proletariat or a revolutionary leader runs the risk of idolatry. This suspicion of idolatry means that any theological position must hold itself back, always prepared to criticise and oppose where and when such a movement runs into the mud. Liberation-theology reserves that final role for God, who is, of course, above and beyond idolatry, one who – according to the first and second commandments – does not tolerate any other gods or any likeness made.

Yet the more wary liberation-theology is of Marxism in the name of the critique of idolatry, the more liberation-theology comes to a 'quilting point' (to gloss Lacan) with Marxism. And that point of contact is the matter of fetishism. Quite simply, some liberation-theologians seek to develop Marx's critique of

---

[57] These questions are, of course, part of my project *The Criticism of Heaven and Earth*, of which this book is but one volume. The only exception to this long list is Ernst Bloch, but his presence is only as a conversation partner for Jürgen Moltmann's theology of hope. For example, see Gutiérrez 2001, pp. 201–5.

the fetishism of commodities in terms of the theological attack on idolatry. So we find that capitalism itself in all its aspects – labour, commodities, money, value, profit, as well as national security, the state, foreign debt, and military force – is nothing less than a form of idolatry. On a theological register, such idolatry is sin, for it worships some thing other than God – the idols of death and Mammon, those which devour and destroy.[58] What one need do is put aside such idols, smash them and grind them to dust.

This argument is rich with possibilities and pitfalls, but it is the point where Löwy's much-desired linking of arms between Marxism and theology might actually take place.[59] Löwy is certainly enthusiastic concerning the possibilities of a common front here, but I have a number of reservations. To begin with, none of the liberation-theologians I have consulted makes use of the depth of Marx's analysis of fetishism. Where some more sustained discussion appears, it tends to use the famous section in the first volume of *Capital* on the fetishism of commodities, perhaps mining Marx's other comments in the same work, as the basis for a theory of fetishism. Yet this is but one moment when Marx deploys the idea of fetishism, which he found immensely useful in a number of configurations. As I have argued in some detail elsewhere,[60] Marx developed his theory of fetishism from his early studies of ethnology, drawing upon the work of Charles de Brosses, who, in his turn, had developed the theory in response to the new knowledge – in Europe, at least – of very different religions from the Portuguese colonies of Africa.[61] From de Brosses, Marx took and developed not only the theory of fetishism, but also the vital assumption that idolatry must be included within the broader category of fetishism (this move was itself an answer to the effort to distinguish idolatry from fetishism in work earlier than de Brosses).[62] Indeed, like de Brosses, Marx uses biblical examples – Moloch, Baal, Mammon – to depict fetishism. But he also extended and developed the theory, using it against notions of bourgeois

---

[58] See Hinkelammert 1986, pp. 5–42; Sobrino 2004b, pp. 57, 146, 165–7; Sobrino 2004a, pp. 59, 99; Sung 2007; Scott 1994, pp. 75–109; Lischer 1973. It is also worth noting that very similar arguments were made during the Marxist-Christian dialogues of the 1970s in Europe. See Evans 1984; Suda 1978; Thiemann 1985; Boer forthcoming.

[59] Löwy 1996, pp. 6, 35, 56, 77, 125. Hinkelammert provides the most sustained example of such a confluence.

[60] Boer forthcoming.

[61] Brosses 1760. See Marx's notes on de Brosses in Marx 1976a.

[62] Pietz 1985.

superiority over colonial savages to point out that the real barbarians were precisely these pompous bourgeois lovers of gold. From there, he modified the theory of fetishism to account for the alienation of labour, the products of labour, wealth, the role of money, the commodity-form, use-value and exchange-value, and the personification of capitalism – all of which 'stand on their hind legs vis-à-vis the worker and confront him as capital'.[63] Marx never lost sight of the religious sense of fetishism, as his notes on John Lubbock in *The Ethnological Notebooks* make perfectly clear.[64] While commenting critically on Lubbock's assessment, Marx simply assumes through his references to biblical critiques of idolatry that idolatry is in fact a form of fetishism.

That last point leads to the second problem with the engagement by liberation-theologians with fetishism, namely the subsumption of the whole category into that of idolatry. In other words, the possible breakthrough enabled by Marx's inversion is negated, for fetishism becomes an extension of, or perhaps a way to recover, the biblical and theological category of idolatry. Let us be clear: I have nothing against a fruitful engagement between fetishism and idolatry, but it needs to do so in light of Marx's inversion of the relation between the two. Third, this subsuming of fetishism is closely related to another tendency, which is to argue that fetishism functions perfectly well as a way of describing our sinful state now in terms of commodity, money and capital fetishism, but in order to dig us out of the ditch we need some of the standard theological categories, such as death, resurrection, the community of the Church and the utopian promise of the peaceable kingdom.

Finally, if we do take into account Marx's inversion of the relation between fetishism and idolatry, then it opens theology up to what might be called the sting in the tail of fetishism. Let me put it this way: the theological criticism of idolatry does so in the name of the one true God. All these other 'gods' are destructive idols because they draw our worship away from God. At this point, the deeper logic of the biblical depiction of idolatry comes to the fore,[65] for its premise is that idolatry is a deluded effort to attribute divine status to a material object made by human hands, or perhaps a human or animal figure. This polemic seeks to undermine the beliefs of the worshipper of that

---

[63] Marx 1988, pp. 457–8.
[64] Marx 1972.
[65] See especially Isaiah 44: 9–20, but also Isaiah 40: 19–20; 41: 6–7; 42: 17; 45: 16–17 and 46: 1–2, 5–7.

'idol': he or she does not believe that the object itself is a god; rather, it points towards the god (in much the same way that the Bible or the pope does so). Worship is, therefore, not directed at the object in question, but the believer offers worship to the god via the object. In response to this belief concerning the object, the polemic of idolatry wants to break the signifying chain between object and god; there is no god out there, it says, and so what you worship is no more than this piece of wood or stone.

Of course, this polemic raises an urgent question regarding one's own god. If all the other gods do not exist, and if these representations of the god point nowhere, then does that also apply to my own god? For this reason, we find in the second commandment not merely the ban on worshipping other gods, but also the famous ban on graven images. Once you get rid of the images, it is no longer possible to break the signifying link between that image and the deity. It is not for nothing that in the Hebrew Bible the word for God, *Yahweh*, is to be read as *Adonai*, 'my lord'.[66] Later Jewish tradition even avoided *Adonai*, so one came to read *Hashem*, 'the name'. This move has the potential to become an endless chain in a desperate effort to avoid the logic of idolatry. God cannot be represented; if you make an image of God yet set up the possibility that this signifying link too may be broken. Marx, like many others, did take the next step and argued that there is no God. What we are left is idols and nothing else. As he points out in an analogy with bourgeois economists, theologians like to establish two kinds of religion: 'Every religion which is not theirs is an invention of men, while their own is an emanation from God'.[67] The same applies to the liberation-theologians who deal with idolatry: the idols of capitalism are false, evil, and oppressive, but God is not.

The critique of idolatry/fetishism is perhaps one of the most fruitful engagements between Marxism and theology,[68] yet, through the paradox of the ontological reserve, the liberation-theologians fall short, failing to explore the full

---

[66] Hebrew was originally a consonantal text, with the vowels assumed. So, when the later scribes introduced vowels to aid in understanding (when Hebrew was no longer a spoken language), the vowels for *Yhwh* did not suggest *Yahweh* but another word entirely, *Adonai*, 'my lord'. The difference is known at *Qere* (what is read) and *Ketibh* (what is written). Gutiérrez 1999, p. 24, tries a similar move, arguing for a decentring of the subject, human and divine, in an effort to avoid the idolatry of the word 'God'.

[67] Marx 1996, p. 92, n. 1; Marx 1972b, p. 96, n. 33.

[68] See Scott 1994, pp. 75–109.

range of Marx's many-sided deployment of fetishism, neglecting the inversion of the relation between idolatry and fetishism and thereby subsuming fetishism within idolatry, treating fetishism as a description of our current sinful state for which theology provides the solutions and opening themselves up to the sting in the tail of the connection between idolatry and fetishism. For, as soon as theology invests too deeply in the idolatry/fetishism argument, it must face the sting: does the logic of fetishism, and thereby idolatry, apply to its god too?

One or many?

In *The War of Gods*, Löwy makes much of the new historical chapter opened up in Latin America with liberation-theology: it is a new social and historical movement with continuing consequences for that continent. Implicit in his argument is a claim to uniqueness for the movement. In this section, I want to explore whether it is in fact as new or indeed as unique as seems to be the case.[69] Let me begin with a common critique of liberation-theology, namely that it collapses all types of discrimination into the all-encompassing category of the 'poor'. Now, Löwy does note the difference with the Marxist category of the proletariat, but he quickly moves on after pointing out that there is a 'socio-ethical "kinship"' between the poor and the proletariat.[70] The catch with a category like the poor is that it is both inclusive and exclusive. Here, I am interested in what it excludes, a move that Gutierrez makes explicit:

> From the beginning...we spoke of subjugated peoples, exploited classes, despised races, and marginalised cultures. Then, there was expressed a concern for the discrimination against women....But what is clear is that these different aspects did not take on their most strident and demanding form until solidarity with the world of the poor became deeper in the last few years.[71]

It is an interesting list: subjugated peoples, classes, races, cultures, women – but all these are subsumed under the solidarity with the poor. Or are they

---

[69] In this section, I am indebted to the brilliant research of Ibrahim Abraham, a former research-assistant.

[70] Löwy 1996, p. 69.

[71] Gutiérrez 1999, p. 24.

subsumed? May it also be the case that they could be excluded by the category of the poor? This is where the backgrounds of the first liberation-theologians are telling, for, while they were not all of middle-class background (Gutiérrez, for instance, is a *mestizo* (mixed Hispanic and Quechuan descent) from a slum in Lima), they were theologians trained in European institutions through the Church, particularly the Roman-Catholic Church. It is worth noting that there were no well-known black Latin-American liberation-theologians, especially in a continent with a long history of vigorous slave-trading (more slaves were transported to Brazil than the USA) and with a population of over 70 million who are of African descent.[72] A similar observation applies to women, who were just as active in the early movement among the base-communities, but who had to overcome limits in education and the culture of machismo. That situation changed somewhat in the later years, especially when this failing became clear, but, even then, the number of women liberation-theologians remains woefully small.[73]

While we may be tempted to see the global spread of liberation-theology – into Korean Minjung theology and South-African contextual theology, or into feminist, black, Dalit (Indian), indigenous, gay and/or queer liberation-theologies – as fanning out from a point of origin in Latin America, that is not the case.[74] For example, the same global turmoil of the 1960s produced a work called *A Black Theology of Liberation*, written by James Cone. It appeared in 1970, but not in Latin America, for Cone is an African American living in the USA. What is important about this militant landmark text is that, in Cone's words, 'I was completely unaware of the beginnings of liberation-theology in the Third Word, especially in Latin America'.[75] The immediate context may be different – the confluence of a new consciousness of black theology in light of the civil-rights movements and black nationalism and black power – but the outcome was remarkably similar, for it was a theology from the perspective of marginalised people who had resisted oppression for all too long. Except for

---

[72] Cone 1984, p. 73.

[73] Tamez 1989, 1993, 1996, 1997; Aquino 1993; Fabella and Oduyoye 1993; Bingemer 1989; Bingemer 1997.

[74] An assumption that lies behind many of the essays in Rowland 1999, a collection that at the same time attempts a contradictory effort to widen liberation-theology to include black and feminist forms (but not queer), as well as other geographical locations such as South Africa and Asia.

[75] Cone 1990, p. xii. See also Cone 1975, 1984, 1986, 1999.

one point: this articulation of liberation-theology took place in terms of race rather than the 'poor' or indeed class. If anything, black liberation-theology was much more militant: 'If God is not for us, if God is not against White racists, then God is a murderer and we had better kill God'.[76]

As with black liberation-theologies, so also with feminist and queer liberation-theologies, for they too emerged from the 1960s and they too arose from the praxis of groups marginalised by dominant ideologies and economic practices. However, in these cases, we can trace a subsequent influence from Latin-American liberation-theology, but only after the initial statements of their respective positions. Before this influence, in 1968, Mary Daly published *The Church and the Second Sex*,[77] which arose from the struggles for women to gain the right to ordination in the Christian churches. A trenchant critique of the marginalisation of women within the Roman-Catholic tradition, the affinities between this feminist work and black and Latin-American liberation-theologies soon became apparent. And then, within this feminist liberation-movement, the privilege of white women in secure academic positions speaking on matters of oppression and 'sisterhood' led, in response, to the growth of womanist, Mujerista and lesbian-feminist versions of liberation-theology.[78]

And that brings me to gay and lesbian liberation-theology, or, as it became known, queer liberation-theology. By now, the story is familiar: for specific historical, cultural and economic reasons, a marginalised group – now in terms of sexuality and in response to deep-seated homophobia – finds theological expression through the experiences of the extraordinary period of the 1960s. In this case, the motivating event was the Stonewall Riots: on the night of 27 June 1969, police tried to eject gays and lesbians from the Stonewall Inn in New York. Four nights of riots ensued and gays and lesbians around the world watched a mixed bunch of 'butch lesbians, Puerto Rican drag queens, and effeminate gay men – marginal people even within their own marginalized population – lead charges against rows of uniformed police officers'.[79] It was the spark that led to the Gay Liberation Front a year later. It also led to the process of reflecting theologically on the gay and lesbian liberation-

---

[76] Cone 1990, p. 27.
[77] Daly 1968.
[78] See especially Fiorenza 1996.
[79] Comstock 1993, p. 123. See also Comstock 1991; Edwards 1984; Macourt 1977; Goss 1993.

movements. In this case, theologians drew upon the existing feminist and black-power movements, as well as Latin-American liberation-theology, for gay and lesbian theologians soon saw affinities between their own concerns and other liberation-movements. Here, too, the movement grew and changed, most notably with queer liberation-theology in the 1990s, which challenged the identity-politics of earlier styles of liberation-theology and included bisexuals, transsexuals, and practitioners of S/M and fetishism, to name but a few of the possibilities of marginal sexual activity.[80]

Instead of a singular origin – Latin America – from where liberation-theology spread to other parts of the world, each type of liberation-theology comes out of distinct but comparable experiences of marginalisation and oppression. Even more, Latin-American liberation-theology has felt the impact of black, feminist, womanist and queer liberation-theologies. For example, as the Cuban theologian, Miguel De La Torre puts it in relation to queer theology, 'if we say that Jesus is in solidarity with "the least of my people" and if gays find themselves victims of oppressive acts, then we must conclude ... Jesus is gay'.[81] The most influential of liberation-scholars to challenge the blind spots was Marcella Althaus-Reid, who stressed the need to consider issues of sexuality, bodies, queerness and postcolonialism in the name of an 'indecent theology'.[82] Althaus-Reid was refreshingly impolite, asking what the practices of fetishism, transvestitism and exhibitionism might contribute to traditional reflections on Christology and the Virgin Mary.

To be fair to Löwy, his purview is Latin America, so we can hardly expect him to include these avenues of liberation-theology. Yet they are important, not least because they relativise the claim to a unique and new historical chapter, and because they raise questions about who is included and excluded within the various marginalised groups. Of course, these questions are not restricted to theology, as anyone with a passing knowledge of the questions concerning identity-politics, or the politics of difference, with which the Left has had to deal in the last few decades will recognise.

By now, it should be clear that Latin-American liberation-theology, however important, is neither a unique nor original form of such theology.

---

[80] Stuart 1997, 2002.
[81] De La Torre 2002, p. 130.
[82] Althaus-Reid 2000; Althaus-Reid 2004.

Instead, its value comes from the way it has enlivened a much longer tradition of revolutionary theologies. Thus far, I have dealt with liberation-movements and their theological articulations after the period of massive unrest that followed in the wake of the decolonising impetus which followed World-War II and came to a head in the 1960s. This brief historical period is only one of the most recent in a much longer history, for there have been repeated revolutionary theological movements throughout the two millennia of Christianity.

In his published work, Löwy deals with two of those moments, one concerning the tendency of Jewish intellectuals in late nineteenth- and early twentieth-century Central Europe to take up various forms of romantic anticapitalism and the other concerning liberation-theology from the 1960s. Yet he is also fully aware of the earlier historical manifestations of Christian revolutionary efforts. In a brief and incisive survey in *The War of Gods,* he runs through a range of Marxists, from Marx to Mariátegui, who have been interested in religion for various reasons.[83] But I am most intrigued by Löwy's comments on Engels, Kautsky and Luxemburg, more for what he does not say. On Engels, Löwy is relatively effusive, tracing Engels's provocative argument that early Christianity was a revolutionary movement that shows many affinities with socialism; similar observations apply to the 'peasant-revolution' with Thomas Müntzer and even the puritans in England. Luxemburg's effort to build on Engels's observations concerning early Christianity receives a brief paragraph from Löwy without assessment, but, when Löwy gets to Kautsky, he is dismissive of what he feels is Kautsky's crass materialism.

However, Kautsky is the one who provided the most complete information on what he called 'the forerunners of socialism'.[84] Beginning with earliest Christianity, Kautsky identifies not only the communistic tendencies of the monastic orders, mystics and ascetics, but also traces a series of heretical movements: the Waldensians, who derive from the twelfth century and still exist today in Piedmont, holding to the model of Christian communism in Acts 2: 44–5 and 4: 32–5; the Apostolic Brothers around Gerardo Segarelli, who formed a similar community of poor women and men in the thirteenth

---

[83] Löwy 1996, pp. 8–18. A truncated version of this section appears in Löwy 2005b. See also Löwy 1998; Löwy 2008.

[84] Kautsky 2006; Kautsky 1947b; Kautsky 1947c; Kautsky and Lafargue 1977; see also Kautsky 1977. See my detailed treatments of Kautsky and Luxemburg in Boer 2009a. On Engels, see Boer forthcoming.

century, urged penitence and preached the imminent end of the world; the Beguines and Beghards of the Low Countries in the twelfth century who lived alone or in groups, were self-sustained, lived lives of simple piety and assisted others; the Lollards, followers of Wycliffe in the fourteenth century who stressed personal faith, divine election, and the Bible, who were deeply hostile to the Church, were involved in a series of uprisings in England, and who provided fertile ground for later dissent; the Bohemian Brethren from the fifteenth century, later known as the Moravian Brethren, who stressed personal piety, a focus on the world to come through their worship and communal life, and who settled under the protection of Count Zinzendorf at Herrnhut (60 km east of Dresden) in 1721; the Taborites, an extreme fifteenth-century party of the Hussites (who followed the pre-Reformation teachings of John Huss (1375–1415)) who championed asceticism, communal living and the establishment of the kingdom of God by force of arms. Kautsky reserves his greatest admiration for Thomas Müntzer (here, he follows Engels) and Thomas More.[85] The criteria for admission to Kautsky's long list was not only an effort to recover the radical elements of the Bible and early Christianity, but also the fact that these movements set themselves up against – sometimes by force of arms – the medieval ruling class, which very much included the church-hierarchy.

Whatever Kautsky's failings as a writer, or indeed the questions one might have concerning the communal and revolutionary credentials of some of these groups, Kautsky provided what is really the first socialist church-history from the perspective of the underdogs. It seems rather obvious, then, that liberation-theology, whether of Latin-American, feminist, black or queer versions, is a continuation of this long line of radical-theological movements. They were certainly not affairs of the head, limited to disputes among theologians secure in church teaching institutions; rather, they were the expressions and justifications of a distinct oppositional praxis, for they too saw 'the least of the earth' as their concern.

Despite this obvious connection between these earlier movements and liberation-theology from the 1960s, it is somewhat strange to find that Löwy does not make such a connection. It is implicit in the way he introduces

---

[85] Kautsky 1947c; Kautsky 1979.

The War of Gods with the briefest of surveys, but then he largely agrees with Marx and Engels that the protest element of Christianity ground to a halt late in the nineteenth century. A curious caesura, is it not? The rest of the book shows implicitly that Latin-American liberation-theology is hardly unique or all that new, but is rather a continuation of this tradition.

Conclusion

I end up with a mixed assessment of Löwy's efforts to see the links between theology – both Christian and Jewish – and Marxism. As a methodological tool, elective affinity shows promise, but is far too vague and leaves too many questions unanswered: are the two sides always equal and rational agents? Why exclude influence, especially in complex earlier histories of interaction? What of the role of political erotics or indeed dialectics? In regard to liberation-theology, Löwy offers a sympathetic assessment from one who does not share the religious commitments of the protagonists of liberation-theology. He is keen to urge the secular Left to reconsider the role of religion in political movements that give voice to those ground down through exploitation. I too share this sense that a politics of alliance between the religious and secular Lefts is both long overdue and highly desirable. However, Löwy misses some of the features of liberation-theology that keep Marxism at a distance – the tradition of Roman-Catholic social teaching and the ontological reserve – and he tends to buy into the assumption that liberation-theology is a singular and original expression of theology. A brief consideration of other autonomous liberation-theologies, especially black, feminist and queer, shows that liberation-theology is one particular manifestation of a wider phenomenon. Further, these liberation-theologies may be seen as the latest moments in a much longer tradition of theological radicalism.

There remains the unfinished business of the dialectic, which is implicit within Löwy's vague elective affinity but never quite brought to the fore. In my discussion of fetishism and idolatry – a quilting point between Marxism and liberation-theology – I argued we land in the midst of a dialectic: the ontological reserve as it manifests itself in the critique of idolatry ensures that liberation-theology keeps its distance from Marxism, yet that distance has the potential of bringing about one of the most fruitful linking of arms with Marxism, specifically on the question of fetishism. The form of that dialectic is, I would suggest, a more useful way to understand the links between liberation-theologies and Marxism.[86]

This dialectic is a much better way to understand the 'fusion' of Marxism and theology that Löwy seeks. He puts it in terms of elective affinity – a true marriage, a union that produces a new figure, a love-child if you will, or perhaps the elusive gold sought by the alchemists. Does gold emerge from the depths of the smoky pot into which Marxism and theology have been poured? Löwy feels he has found gold with an impressive list of examples: the Nicaraguan Revolution in 1979, the guerrilla uprisings in El Salvador and Guatemala, the Workers' Party and the Landless Peasants' Movement in Brazil and even in the indigenous people's movement in Chiapas. More recently he has suggested that the mass-movements in Ecuador, Bolivia, and Venezuela owe a good part of their impetus to liberation-theology, with the shift from a traditional Marxist focus on the working class to that of the poor: 'The idea that the poor have to liberate themselves, and organise to do so is not so far from Marx's idea that the workers must take on the task of liberating themselves'.[87] Then there is an impressive list of statements by councils, individual bishops, a high-profile martyr (Oscar Romero)[88] and a large number of individual priests, religious and believers who joined revolutionary movements, of whom Camillo Torres Restrepo is the most well-known example,[89] but there were a good number of others such as Néstor Paz in Bolivia and J. Guadalupe Carney in Honduras.[90] These two statements from these ordinary Christian revolutionaries sum up the feelings of many who joined the movements:

> Yahweh our God, the Christ of the Gospels has announced the 'good news of the liberation of man', for which he himself acted.... We believe in a 'New Man', made free by the blood and resurrection of Jesus. We believe

---

[86] In contrast to the approach of Turner 1999, who follows Kee 1990 in arguing that liberation-theology is not Marxist enough and that it should pursue the possibilities of apophatic or negative theology in order to deal with Marx's radical atheism. Apart from the problematic mysticism of apophatic theology, Turner's reading of Marx is somewhat superficial and lacking in proper engagement with Marx's texts.

[87] Quoted in Lister 2006. Although initially enthusiastic about the Brazilian Workers' Party (Löwy 2000), he has, however, expressed disappointment at the way President Lula has since his election merely implemented neoliberal economic policies. See Löwy 2006.

[88] Sobrino 2004c.

[89] Boer 2007b, pp. 120–5.

[90] See Paz 1975; Carney 1985.

in a New Earth, where love will be the fundamental law. This will come, however, only by breaking the old patterns based on selfishness.[91]

In the twentieth century there is no 'third way' between being a Christian and being a revolutionary. To be a Christian is to be a revolutionary. If you are not a revolutionary, you are not a Christian![92]

Instead of an alchemical fusion between Marxism and theology, I suggest that a dialectical approach makes better sense of these statements. Note that neither of these statements refers to Marx. We could go back through the statements of those movements I mentioned earlier and find very similar statements, for there is a strand in the Bible and in Christian theology that tends in this direction. It is a costly discipleship, but it does not depend on Marx, nor need it rely on Marx in order to attain that point. In order to justify joining insurrections in one Latin-American country after another, the Christian revolutionaries made it clear that it was their Christian commitment that led them to do so.

And that is precisely my point. It is neither a case of finding overlapping themes between Marxism and (liberation-)theologies, nor is it an effort at finding common ground through compromise and negotiation. Instead, there is an internal dynamic to both theology and Marxism (more strongly in the latter) that leads to a revolutionary position. At that moment do they make contact.

---

[91] Paz 1975, pp. 22 and 25.
[92] Carney 1985, p. 441.

Chapter Five

The Myths of Roland Barthes

> No denunciation without an appropriate method of detailed analysis, no semiology which cannot, in the last analysis, be acknowledged as *semioclasm*.[1]

Semiotics, structuralism, everyday life, popular culture, being gay at the Collège de France, occasional lover of Michel Foucault and avid student of the intricacies of literary theory, popular magazines and all things French – these are the things for which Barthes is known and still read (perhaps not so much in regard to Foucault). But I am interested in a less-travelled path through Barthes's work, namely the writings on religion by this man who was brought up a Protestant.[2] More specifically, his deliberation on myth in the long essay, 'Myth Today', is the focus of my intimate commentary.[3] Around this theoretical centrepiece cluster a large number of incisive pieces in which contemporary myth is dissected and

---

[1] Barthes 1993a, p. 9; Barthes 2002k, p. 673.
[2] Barthes 1985, p. 306; Barthes 2002ss, p. 549.
[3] I am less interested in the other group of Barthes's writings on religion – the semiotic interpretations of Genesis 32 and Acts 10–11 (Barthes 1994, pp. 217–60; Barthes 2002ee; Barthes 2002mm). This is partly due to the fact that the readings of Genesis 32 and Acts 11–12 have been mined extensively by some biblical scholars (for example, see Collective 1995, pp. 130–5; Jobling, et al. 1995, pp. 48–9, 59–77) and partly due to the way they seem quite dated now. However, I have gained much insight from the work of Aichele, who has used Barthes creatively in order to develop a semiotic approach to interpreting biblical texts. See Aichele 1996, 1997, 2001, as well as Koosed 2008.

analysed – from steak and chips to the Tour de France, from margarine to Billy Graham.[4] In this essay, Barthes offers a full-blooded theory of myth (his demurrer that it is all very preliminary notwithstanding).

In unfolding my intimate commentary on Barthes's texts concerning mythology, I have divided my discussion into two parts. The first is an exposition that highlights the crucial moves in Barthes's text, drawing out the basics of semiology,[5] focusing on a tension in Barthes's analysis between description and criticism and tracking his forlorn efforts at resistance to the baleful effects of myth. The second part seeks to apply to Barthes's argument his own approach. He has a propensity to focus on the fragmentary hints and suggestions, the moments in a text – an odd feature of a sentence, an image evoked or a trigger – that make one pause, look up and follow a train of thought. In the same way that theorising those experiences of reading led Barthes to write, so also I use this approach on his own texts. In this second section, then, I begin to follow a series of hints and passing phrases that suggest other possibilities for myth, especially in terms of the dialectic of opposition that emerges from within myth. So what we find is that, despite Barthes finding myth baleful, distorting and best opposed, an undercurrent emerges in his analysis that leaves more room for myth – a cunning, oppositional and utopian one.

However, before I immerse myself in Barthes's texts, a brief word is in order concerning the infatuations and phases that mark his work. The usual critical narrative is that Barthes passed progressively from Marxism and psychoanalysis, through a long structuralist phase, to the final emergence of poststructuralism (the signs of this later shift appear quite clearly in the

---

[4] The usual and disconcerting story applies here to translations from French: the texts have been pulled apart and reassembled in strange new formations. The original French of *Mythologies* (Barthes 2002k) may be found spread out in two translations called *Mythologies* and *The Eiffel Tower and Other Mythologies*. (Barthes 1993a and Barthes 1997). The latter text adds a few extra essays that were not in the original French of *Mythologies*: Barthes 2002z; Barthes 2002v; Barthes 2002u; Barthes 2002o; Barthes 2002p. Beyond even these extras, there are individual essays that expand the analysis of myth into a number of further areas of French life, but they have not been translated into English: Barthes 2002b; Barthes 2002d; Barthes 2002c; Barthes 2002e; Barthes 2002i; Barthes 2002g; Barthes 2002h; Barthes 2002l; Barthes 2002q; Barthes 2002m; Barthes 2002s; Barthes 2002n; Barthes 2002r; Barthes 2002t; Barthes 2002aa. Finally, there are a few scattered and brief later reflections on mythology: Barthes 2002f; Barthes 2002kk; Barthes 1977, pp. 165–9; Barthes 2002o. Only one of these has been translated into English.

[5] Those familiar with semiology may skip this section on basics. I prefer 'semiology' to the more common 'semiotics'.

way former references to Saussure and Pearce give way to Derrida, Foucault and Lacan).[6] In contrast to this narrative of phases – the early, middle and late Barthes – Barthes himself offers a somewhat different perspective on his work. In the late and very personal *Camera Lucida*, the last book published in his lifetime, he mentions a methodological discomfort that has continually plagued him: 'the uneasiness of being a subject torn between two languages, one expressive, the other critical'.[7] He goes to say that he has been attracted by the various critical discourses, such as sociology, semiology and psychoanalysis, but that, after a while, he grew weary of them one by one. Whenever they tended to harden and become reductive, he grew unhappy and quietly left them behind. I suspect that the tendency to what he calls reductive systems – organisation in terms of a 'scientific' method, full of classification, terminology and a distinctly paedagogic style[8] – was an effort to rein in his tendency to rely on quick insight. It may be seen as a mistrust of what happens when he is drawn to magazines, photographs and fashion. Yet those works that express his intuitive insight, the ability to see something from an unexpected and often profound angle, remain far more alluring. I would go further and suggest that with these intuitive reflections we can see a desire to break the constituent elements of Marxist analysis down into their most basic, materialist forms. Nearly always brief, they have the feel of being written first thing in the morning on whatever item has grabbed his attention and triggered some

---

[6] The suspicion that Barthes was never quite Marxist enough was voiced already in the mid-1950s after he had written a few short pieces on mythology. In response, he wrote: 'one is not a Marxist by immersion, initiation or declaration, as if one were a Baptist, Trobriand Islander or Muslim.... Marxism is not a religion, but a method of explanation and action' (Barthes 2002j, p. 596). See also Barthes 2002a in which he offers a polemical reply to the criticism that Marxism and especially the PCF (French Communist Party) resemble a church. He argues that the possibility of making such a comparison is dependent upon the historical method of analogy, which developed in the nineteenth century. Even so, the analogy is pathetic and lacks content. In this light, Thody's argument that Barthes was not a political writer at all is difficult to sustain. See Thody 1987, p. 9, as well as Thody 1984.

[7] Barthes 1993b, p. 9; Barthes 2002uu, p. 794.

[8] Of course, much more is going on here as well, such as the institutional need to provide a legitimate basis for his interests within French academe and the desire to provide what is really a version of cultural studies with methodological rigour. In his earlier semiological works, he is extremely keen to argue that semiology is a science (the noun and adjective sprinkle his texts), with the hope that it will elevate the criticism of literature and culture to a level equal with the other hard sciences. As he sees later on, the elevation of semiology beyond history into a universal method becomes highly problematic.

reflection. It is like a photographer whose eye is always on watch for a distinct shot, a unique angle or a quirky feature. Indeed, the expressive and passing insights characteristic or earlier work like *Mythologies* (although, here too, we find a touch of semiology and psychoanalysis) return with rich vigour in later texts such as *The Pleasure of the Text, A Lover's Discourse* and *Camera Lucida*.[9] They are a stark contrast to the formidable and dry semiological works like *Elements of Semiology* and *The Fashion System*.[10]

Between description and accusation

An intimate reading shows us a semiological technician at work, an accusation that myth is a thief of language and an effort to find some purchase to resist all-enveloping myth.

Basics

Barthes begins with a careful and dispassionate dismantling of myth. Here, we see the semiotic technician, so let us stand beside him and watch him at work. He makes two important distinctions, one between form and content and the other between primary and secondary sign-systems. Myth turns out to belong to form and the secondary sign-system.

Invoking the hoary distinction between form and content, he puts the latter aside and opts for the former: myth is *une parole*, a form of speech. Not a bad move, since he can sideline the conventional points that myth concerns the threefold theogony, cosmogony and anthropogony – the origins of the gods, universe and human beings. In other words, myth is not determined by the content of its message, but by the way the message is told. These mechanisms determine what counts as myth and what does not. This move ensures that Barthes is not caught in the traditional concerns of myth as something archaic and primitive, which we as reasonable and enlightened people may now calmly put aside.[11] By taking on form, he can argue that everything can

---

[9] Barthes 1975; Barthes 2002nn; Barthes 1978; Barthes 2002qq; Barthes 1993b; Barthes 2002uu.

[10] Barthes 1973; Barthes 2002bb; Barthes 1983; Barthes 2002dd.

[11] Or, at least, he does his best to do so. There are moments when he argues, much like Benjamin and Adorno, that the most modern of activities have an archaic and mythical barbarity about them. For example, along with the displaced sacredness

become a myth, that no meaning is safe from myth, which really means the features of contemporary popular culture that entice him so much.

But why say myth is a *parole*? Why not a specific genre, or perhaps a form of thinking, or even a distinct system of thought? Barthes wants to steer the definition of myth close enough to his growing interest in semiology so that the latter can snare myth in its ever-extending reach. Of course, this is tied up closely with what is now known as the linguistic turn, in which semiology was a central player. The freshness and crispness of semiology shows through his text in the way he needs to offer both an introduction and seek to persuade the reader of its viability. Since semiology's focus was signs and their interplay, it could leap from the analysis of written texts to all manner of other 'texts' – Barthes mentions photography, cinema, reporting, sport, shows and publicity – since these too are sign-systems. Or, as Barthes puts it, they are all just as much types of speech [*paroles*] as your garden variety written text.

Already, Barthes is careful to make a distinction. All these items are not mythical per se, but they support mythical speech; or even more intriguingly, 'mythical speech is made up of a material which has *already* been worked on'.[12] In other words, myth is parasitic and he tries to show how through a semiological analysis. Barthes is not a bad paedagogue, stating a point succinctly and then immediately offering a number of examples.[13] Myth is, he argues, a secondary semiological chain. We begin with the first, identifying signifier and signified and then their union in the sign. In what is his most famous example, he mentions a copy of *Paris Match* (handed to him, he says, at the barber's, but he seemed to read that magazine and others quite regularly).

---

of the 'jet-man' (Barthes 1993a, pp. 71–3; Barthes 2002k, pp. 742–4), wrestlers turn out – at least in the ring – to be gods embodying the struggle of Good, Evil and Justice (Barthes 1993a, p. 25; Barthes 2002k, p. 688). Or the writer's logorrhoea – like an involuntary secretion – becomes the signal of the writer's divine nature (Barthes 1993a, p. 30; Barthes 2002k, p. 694). And, again, the 'Blue Blood Cruise' restores the god-like status of the decadent royals through the incongruity of their appearing to be 'normal' (Barthes 1993a, pp. 32–3; Barthes 2002k, pp. 695–7). Once more, the great exhibition of 'man' digs deeply into anthropogonic myths of Adam and creation (Barthes 1993a, pp. 100–2; Barthes 2002k, pp. 806–8). Finally, the space race between the USSR and the USA takes on the nature of an ancient cosmic struggle (Barthes 1997, pp. 27–9; Barthes 2002k, pp. 702–4). The distinction between archaic and modern may take other forms, such as Flood's problematic distinction between premodern religious myth and modern political myth. See Flood 2002.

[12] Barthes 1993a, p. 110; Barthes 2002k, p. 824; emphasis in original.

[13] The key statement appears over a couple of succinct pages. See Barthes 1993a, pp. 114–16; Barthes 2002k, pp. 828–30.

On the cover is a black soldier, probably from the French colonies in North Africa, and he offers a salute with his eyes raised and looking at something outside the picture. The signifier here is the black soldier and the signified is the Frenchness of the salute, which is directed, Barthes surmises, to the tricolour; the result is not a separation of terms but their unity in the French black soldier – the sign. The signifier and sign seem to be the same, but they are not, for the black soldier does not have meaning as signifier, while, as sign, he is overloaded with meaning. I must confess to some difficulty in separating the two, but Barthes does point out later that the achievement of Saussurian semiology is precisely to help us avoid the tendency to confuse signifier and sign.[14] Barthes suggests that from experience we are accustomed to seeing the sign as a unified whole, but that analytically we can separate the sign into its two components of signifier and signified (black soldier and Frenchness). Diagrammatically we get the following:

Signifier

        } Sign

Signified

But this is only the beginning of myth, for myth takes the final step of this primary chain and makes that its starting point. Now, we get a secondary signifying system: the sign becomes the new signifier, it points to another signified, which, in turn, produces yet another sign at a higher level. As for the saluting black soldier, this very French black soldier is now the initial signifier. But what does it signify? 'That France is a great empire, that all her sons, without any colour discrimination, faithfully serve under her flag, and that there is no better answer to the detractors of an alleged colonialism than the zeal shown by this black man in serving his so-called oppressors'.[15] Or, if we put it in terms of a diagram (glossing Barthes), we now get:

Signifier

    } Sign =   Signifier[a]

Signified   } Sign[a]

            Signified[a]

---

[14] Barthes 1973, pp. 38–9; Barthes 2002bb, pp. 657–8.

[15] Barthes 1993a, p. 116; Barthes 2002k, p. 830. I have altered the translation of 'ce noir' to 'this black man' since 'Negro' in the translation by Annette Lavers is hardly justified.

Now, a problem appears, for Barthes does not offer a description of the new sign. Obviously, the signified functions as the mythical content of this new system, but what of the second-order sign? In order to sidestep the problem, Barthes offers a new set of terms for the semiological triad of myth. The intersection between the overlapping systems (sign=signifier[a]) becomes, as the first term in the mythic triad, 'form'; signified[a] becomes the 'concept'; and the crucial third item, the sign in the first system, becomes 'signification'. So we get the following:

Signifier
} Sign =   Form
Signified   } Signification
Concept

At last, we have tracked down myth itself, for it is nothing less than signification, the second-order sign. Yet, like the sign, this mythical signification is really a relation between the two terms, between form and concept, which now become the pillars of myth – mythical form and mythical concept.

Let us pause for a moment. I have provided a close exposition of this section of Barthes's argument without much comment, since it lays out the theoretical basis for the rest of his analysis of myth. In light of his later work, it is a little basic and it does not bristle with the theoretical armoury of planes, syntagms and complex patterns of opposition.[16] Indeed, those who are familiar with Barthes will immediately recognise the first moments of what he will soon call denotation and connotation/metalanguage – the primary and secondary signifying systems that become an analytic staple, reshaped and made more complex, throughout his later work. One way to mark the distinction between denotation and connotation is to point out that denotation is the realm of 'normal' or 'literal' meaning – what you find in dictionaries or the meaning of proper nouns; connotation/metalanguage is then the collection of more complex senses that attach to this primary meaning.

To be more specific, Barthes designates myth as metalanguage. While the first system is what he calls a 'language-object', because it is the language

---

[16] See Barthes 1973; Barthes 2002bb; Barthes 1983; Barthes 2002dd. However, Jameson 1972, pp. 146–56, traces the basic functionality of this analysis of myth throughout all of Barthes's work, although it mutates into different shapes – as style, content and method.

of which myth 'gets hold in order to build its own system', metalanguage is 'a second language, *in which* one speaks about the first'.[17] Having recently picked up semiology, Barthes's terms are not precise at this point. Soon afterwards, he distinguishes (borrowing from Hjemslev),[18] between connotation and metalanguage. It all depends on which direction the sign of the initial system is taken. If it is taken as the signifier of the secondary system, pointing to yet another content, then it is connotation; if it becomes the signified of the second system, we have metalanguage.[19] The difference now is that metalanguage is a coherent system, one where we find methods such as semiology, or elaborate languages like that of the fashion-system. By contrast, connotation is discontinuous, scattered and diffuse, embodying the fragments of ideology. Here we are in the realm of culture and naturalised assumptions. However, in *Mythologies*, Barthes does not make this distinction between connotation and metalanguage; indeed, it is clear that he mingles the two in what he describes as the secondary system of myth.[20]

Baleful deformations of language

However, this careful and technical effort to dismantle myth is only one dimension of Barthes's analysis, for he is actually caught between two conflicting directions: one is dispassionate, the other impassioned; one is universal, the other specific. So, as we have seen, he sets out carefully and without judgement to pull apart the working pieces of all myth, lay them out and

---

[17] Barthes 1993a, p. 115; Barthes 2002k, p. 829.

[18] Hjemslev 1959.

[19] See Barthes 1973, pp. 89–94; Barthes 2002bb, pp. 695–8. Now, the signifier becomes the plane of expression (E), the signified becomes the plane of content (C), and the sign is the relation (R). See also Barthes 1990, pp. 6–9; Barthes 2002ii, pp. 123–6; Barthes 1991, pp. 3–20; Barthes 2002y.

[20] At this point a track opens up to the side, which leads to a forest full of debate over semiology and then structural analyses of language, a crowd of theoreticians of whom the most notable are Ferdinand de Saussure, C.S. Peirce, Gottlob Frege, Louis Hjemslev, Roman Jakobson, Umberto Eco, Julia Kristeva and Vladimir Propp, and all manner of refinements and new directions, not least of which is the tendency to build more levels on top of the original two, as we see most extensively with *The Fashion System* (Barthes 1983, pp. 27–41; Barthes 2002dd, pp. 928–42; see also the earlier pieces leading up to this study: Barthes 2006, pp. 41–58; Barthes 2002w). And then there is the whole complex territory of structural analysis of narrative, as in Barthes 1994, pp. 95–135; Barthes 2002cc. Tempting as it might be, I do not wish to follow that path, for it takes me too far from the central issue of myth.

determine the function of each one. For this taking apart, he draws upon what was at the time the new method of semiology. But then the target of that analysis is the quite specific mythology of the bourgeoisie. On this matter, he is not so sanguine, for what he finds objectionable about bourgeois mythology is that it has a pretence to being 'natural'. So, he sets out to denaturalise that mythology, to reveal its artificiality and strangeness.

A useful way of dealing with this tension in Barthes's work between the dispassionate semiological technician and impassioned political critic of bourgeois myth is in terms of a well-known distinction in Marxist treatments of ideology. On the one side there is a 'critical' approach in which ideology is false consciousness (erroneous beliefs about the world that need to be corrected), while, on the other side, appears a 'descriptive' or functional approach in which ideology is a necessary and inescapable feature of human existence.[21] While Marx tended to favour the critical function of ideological analysis, there is sufficient material in his writings that may also be seen as descriptive of an inescapable and universal feature of human existence – a line picked up by a host of others such as Lenin, Althusser and Gramsci.

In his more semiological moments, Barthes draws near to the descriptive side of ideology, for he clearly offers a universal theory of myth which eschews value judgements. And, if it is a universal theory, then what he describes turns out to be universal as well. At the same time, Barthes also engages in a version of demystification, a classic Marxist inversion, or, rather, a standing on its feet of the topsy-turvy relation between myth and reality.[22] Myth's presentation of a simple truth – this is how it is – must be shown up as duplicity and distortion. At this level, Barthes is, in many respects, a Marxist mythologist, who deciphers myth, discovers a distortion and thereby demystifies it.[23] Does this mean that Barthes's analysis of myth is merely a refined form of Marxist *Ideologiekritik*?[24] At one level, the answer to this question must be affirmative, especially when Barthes argues that bourgeois myth is a distortion that must be resisted at all costs. However, he also seeks to move beyond mere

---

[21] For example, see Barrett 1991, pp. 18–34; Larrain 1983b; Larrain 1983a; Dupré 1983, pp. 238–44 and McLellan 1995, p. 16. Later, Barthes tends more to the descriptive side; see Barthes 1985, pp. 96–7; Barthes 2002gg, pp. 678–9.

[22] Barthes 1989, p. 65; Barthes 2002kk, p. 873.

[23] See Barthes 1993a, p. 128; Barthes 2002k, pp. 840–1.

[24] So Csapo 2005, p. 278, but he goes too far in arguing that Barthes's Marxist analysis has merged all myth into ideology.

ideology-critique by carving out a distinct form of myth-analysis. In my response to Barthes, especially where I explore the hints within Barthes's own texts that point to another approach to myth, I try to take this distinct type of myth-analysis further.

As far as this critical negative assessment is concerned, Barthes depicts myth as distortion/deformation and duplicity. So, despite his best efforts to provide a value-neutral – 'scientific' – description of the workings of myth, Barthes always threatens to slip into judgement. The judgements quickly pile up: 'myth hides nothing: its function is to distort [*déformer*], not to make disappear';[25] 'the relation which unites the concept of myth to its meaning is essentially a relation of *deformation* [*déformation*]';[26] 'the ubiquity of the signifier in myth exactly reproduces the physique of the *alibi*'.[27] It is duplicitous, ambiguous and frozen; in short, 'myth is always a language robbery [*un vol de langage*]'.[28] The terms Barthes repeatedly uses are quite evocative: empty [*une forme vide*], parasite [...*parasite*], impoverishment [*il s'appauvrit*], evaporation of history [*l'histoire s'évapore*], abnormal regression [*regression anormale*], penury [*pauvreté*], putting at a distance [*l'éloigner*], draining out [*s'écoule hors*], shallow [*court*], isolated [*isolé*], robbery [*vol*], corruption [*tout corrompre*] and on and on. His favoured image is that of myth as a parasite feeding off the rich and full meaning of the denotated sign; to this I would add the closely related image of a weed that appears in foreign soil and sucks up the nutrients to which it is not entitled. All of these and more make it perfectly clear that Barthes has little sympathy for myth.

At this point, where Barthes launches his comprehensive attack on myth, his analysis becomes very interesting indeed. He lays a number of charges at the feet of myth, charges he feels condemn it beyond doubt. His basic accusation against myth is that it takes a sign full of history and meaning and scrapes it out, discarding that fullness of meaning so that it may be ready for a new set of associations. Once again, let us see how this works with the saluting black man on the cover of *Paris Match*: as the sign of the initial system he is full of biographical history, culture, society and religion, but all of this must be put aside when this meaning-full sign becomes the formal signifier of

---

[25] Barthes 1993a, p. 121; Barthes 2002k, p. 834.
[26] Barthes 1993a, p. 122; Barthes 2002k, p. 835. Emphasis in original.
[27] Barthes 1993a, p. 123; Barthes 2002k, p. 836. Emphasis in original.
[28] Barthes 1993a, p. 131; Barthes 2002k, p. 843.

myth. What takes its place? French imperialism, which evokes French history, colonial ventures and present difficulties. All of this is drawn from the concept, the second-level signified, which now rushes in to fill the void opened up by the signifier-as-form. In short, the myth of French imperialism replaces the concrete sign of the black man saluting.

So, despite Barthes's effort to provide a dispassionate and universal definition of myth, he actually undertakes a systematic effort to uncover every single reprehensible dimension of French bourgeois myth:

> ...our press, our films, our theatre, our pulp literature, our rituals, our Justice, our diplomacy, our conversations, our remark about the weather, a murder trial, a touching wedding, the cooking we dream of, the garments we wear, everything, in everyday life, is dependent on the representation which the bourgeoisie *has and makes us have* of the relations between man and the world.[29]

Most of his analysis is in fact limited to a particular political and cultural entity as well as a specific class. This is the sustained agenda of the brief forays into everyday French life that constitute the bulk of *Mythologies* – photographs, exhibitions, films, shows, newspaper-articles and so on. We find, for example, that the 'natural' fringes and sweaty faces of Romans in films actually indicate the hybridity and duplicity of bourgeois art.[30] Or the assumptions of both psychology and language which were used in the murder conviction of the illiterate 80-year peasant, Dominici, are distinctly bourgeois ones.[31] Or women-writers may be celebrated, but only if the nuclear family stays intact, they recognise the importance of men and keep producing children.[32] On it goes, with the nationalistic roles of wine and beefsteak,[33] the bourgeois travel-guides in which nature becomes picturesque (that is, 'uneven'),[34] the representation of cooking in magazines which expresses the bourgeois desire for ornamentation,[35] or the assumed political neutrality and

---

[29] Barthes 1993a, p. 140; Barthes 2002k, p. 851.
[30] Barthes 1993a, p. 28; Barthes 2002k, p. 693.
[31] Barthes 1993a, pp. 43–6; Barthes 2002k, pp. 708–11.
[32] Barthes 1993a, pp. 50–2; Barthes 2002k, pp. 713–15.
[33] Barthes 1993a, pp. 58–64; Barthes 2002k, pp. 727–31.
[34] Barthes 1993a, pp. 74–7; Barthes 2002k, pp. 765–7.
[35] Barthes 1993a, pp. 78–80; Barthes 2002k, pp. 770–2.

the fatuous claim to universal values of culture and style in bourgeois literary criticism.[36]

The overwhelming effect is to pick apart the threads of this bourgeois myth as to what society should be like. Barthes is annoyed at the way all these things are taken as so 'natural' and wants to show how they are constructed as myth. He unpacks his negative assessment with a well-organised series of observations – myth distorts, deforms, demands, is duplicitous, fleeting and multiple, has unhealthy motivations and numerous alibis, it freezes and steals language.

As we have seen, for Barthes, myth is at heart a deformation. It takes the rich and meaning-full sign of the first signifying system, empties it out and then refills it with its own pernicious content. Or, rather, as he later clarifies, it does not discard its former meaning. Instead, myth chops that meaning up, throws away some parts, reorganises the others and then adds its own new content to the mix. It is a fundamentally alienating process that wreaks havoc with the proper historical, social and cultural meaning of the sign. Or, to use another metaphor, myth is a thief, one who steals the meaning of the primary sign, claims it as its own and twists it to a new usage. Once transformed in some dank hideout, it tries to hock the deformed product in the market of ideas.

Many of Barthes's other comments on myth fill out this basic observation. So, we find that myth is unstable, moving back and forth between the sign upon which it feeds and its mythical form, drawing from the former, distorting it, and then moving back to suck yet more meaning from the sign. This means that myth is difficult to pin down, since it functions like an alibi: it is never where you think it is, for as soon you think you have spotted it, it has slipped away. Or, to put it in other terms, myth is both fleeting and multiple. As for the latter, Barthes argues that a whole series of items may substitute for one another in the second-level signifier, but they all relate to the one concept. We may replace the saluting black man with (adding to Barthes's examples) the president stepping off a plane in Algiers, or perhaps a French ship sailing from Tahiti to New Caledonia, or even a map of Francophony (the countries in the world that speak varieties of French from Africa to Canada). All of

---

[36] Barthes 1993a, pp. 81–3; Barthes 2002k, pp. 783–5. See also Barthes 2006, pp. 59–64; Barthes 2002x.

these fragmentary items evoke the same concept of French imperialism. The new signifier may be qualitatively weak, but it makes up for that puniness by the multiplicity of items on which it can draw. Further, the concept (second-level signified) is itself fleeting, for it constantly shifts, changes shape and may disintegrate. French imperialism is never stable, passing all too quickly from a glorious reach of French influence to a drain on resources and source of endless trouble.

Now, I want to ask why myth is slippery, unstable and fleeting, for it seems to be avoiding something. Let us leave that for a moment and deal with the next observation: myth arrests us and in doing so freezes up. With obvious allusions to Althusser's famous narrative of interpellation, Barthes argues that myth calls out to us and stops us in our tracks. It says: notice this simple fact, this harmless truth to which you cannot but give assent. Of course, everyone supports the local football-team, or the beneficent property-developer who wishes only to make life better for all, or the peaceful empire which showers so many gifts on its loyal sons and daughters. In arresting me so, the myth makes me complicit, makes me part of it and thereby locks me in. In this respect, myth congeals and solidifies. Once I am caught, myth freezes up and offers what seems to be a perfectly natural truth. The overwhelming feature of this naturalisation is the way the bourgeoisie effaces itself as a distinct class and becomes what is 'normal' and 'natural' for the nation as a whole.[37]

At first sight, these two observations seem like a blatant contradiction: how can myth be unstable and frozen, slippery and solid? Barthes does have a knack of touching lightly upon other critics, drawn to an idea or a suggestion in much the same way that his eye and ear are drawn to quirky features of a photograph, a magazine or a popular saying, or indeed in the same way that he reads, noting a word that fires off its own line of thought. The result can be that he glides over difficulties, not always seeing the tensions between them. In this case, I would suggest that the creaking connection between these two features appears because Barthes tries to connect semiology and ideological analysis, Saussure and Althusser. The latter famously argued that one feature of ideology is what may be called interpellation. Like a police-officer on the street, ideology addresses me with a 'Hey, you there!' As soon as I turn, I indicate that I am indeed the one addressed. At that moment, ideology has me

---

[37] See also Barthes 1989, pp. 101–5; Barthes 2002ll.

in its grasp and I am caught.[38] But, here, we find a twofold solution to the tension. First, myth itself may be fleeting and unstable, but when it is addressed to us it functions like ideology, tying us up in its embrace. This is the moment when myth passes from semiology to ideology, as Barthes puts it, when it corresponds to the assumptions and expectations of a particular society at a specific point in history.[39] Second, in this situation, myth behaves like a denotative system, assuring us that it states a simple truth that cannot be gainsaid.[40] The French Empire is a fact, it says, and this man who salutes constitutes the very presence of what Barthes calls 'imperiality'.

One final point: myth is also motivated. Unlike the pure arbitrariness of signs (there is no obvious reason why the word 'bicycle' refers to the two-wheeled vehicle leaning against the bookshelf), myth makes an intentional connection. It is no accident that the black salute means the French Empire, for that is motivated. Here, Barthes lets himself go, contrasting a healthy arbitrariness with a 'disturbing', 'sickening' and 'nauseous' motivation in myth.[41] However, as far as motivation is concerned, what Barthes has done here yet again is slip in a value-judgement based on content. He despises the content of the examples he gives, whether a black salute, the assumptions of the judicial system, or the faux-freedom of women writers. Fair enough, but what he means by 'motivation' is not merely the fact that there is some deliberate connection between a myth and the particular sign on which it relies; what he opposes is the political motivation behind that connection – a bourgeois one, to be precise. But what if that political motivation is different? On this matter, Barthes ignores another dimension of myth, namely that one of its basic functions is to provide motivation for a group of people for whom the myth is important. This was Sorel's insight into myth over a century ago. Sorel argued that myth is collective, irrefutable and motivational, for it provides continued inspiration especially for those who face repeated failures. For Sorel, myth

---

[38] Althusser 1971, pp. 173–4; Althusser 1995, p. 305. It is often forgotten that Althusser's other great example towards the end of his essay is a religious one: ideology functions like the call from God to the believer. See Althusser 1971, pp. 177–83; Althusser 1995, pp. 307–12; Boer 2007a, pp. 137–41.

[39] Barthes 1993a, p. 128; Barthes 2002k, p. 841. As always, Barthes touches lightly on Althusser, drawing what he wishes and leaving the rest aside.

[40] See Barthes 1993a, p. 128; Barthes 2002k, p. 840.

[41] Barthes 1993a, p. 126, n. 7; Barthes 2002k, pp. 838–9, n. 1.

is 'the framing of a future, in some indeterminate time'.[42] He spoke directly to the Left as it faced defeat after heart-rending defeat at the opening of the twentieth century and he proposed that the general strike become the centre of a new political myth. What if myth – political myth – had such a motivation? Would Barthes approve? It seems not, for myth in its very form is baleful.

Desperate resistance

Thus far, I have followed Barthes's argument reasonably closely. To sum up, he argues that myth is a second-order signifying system that builds upon a prior one. As such, it is a deformation of language, one that draws upon the primary sign, steals it and then offers a very different product – myth. Barthes has managed to get myth to blurt out its dirty little secret; as such, it is a reprehensible feature of human existence. Yet, if that is all, then the implications for theology and the Bible are not the best. The crucial stories of the Bible are nothing more than the distortion of language and so we should dispense with them as quickly as is seemly possible. Many would, of course, concur. But is that all? Does Barthes offer a somewhat depressing account of the workings of myth and then call it a day? Not quite, for the second half of his 'Myth Today' essay offers a variety of possible modes of resistance. Let me be clear on this matter: Barthes wishes to find ways to oppose myth as a whole, but I am more interested in finding ways that myth itself offers resistance.

Barthes begins his quest by asking whether some types of language offer more resistance to myth than others. Fuzzy and unclear language has no hope, argues Barthes, since it is a sitting duck for the deformations of myth. But what happens if meaning is completely full and closed off? Myth simply seizes it wholesale and turns it to its purpose. Barthes offers the example of mathematics, which we might expect to provide the most resolute resistance. But, eventually, it too falls and the conquest is as complete as the original resistance. The last fortress but one to stand up to a marauding myth is poetry, for its disordering of signs and breakdown of language offers myth no chink. Yet, it too falls, even more spectacularly than mathematics – although that fall

---

[42] Sorel 1961, p. 124. See further Tager 1986.

does not stop Barthes hoping rather forlornly that poetry (the search for the inalienable meaning of things) may provide refuge for the alienated mythologist, which is really Barthes himself.[43] Finally, there is the logical extreme beyond poetry, the attempt to pursue its pre-semiological tendency all the way. This is a push to the anti-nature of language, dispensing with all syntax, punctuation and meaning. Perhaps Philippe Sollers is the best embodiment of this approach,[44] but Barthes warns that this task is well-nigh impossible, for there is always some small outcrop left for myth to gain a foothold.

Even here, we find little hope, so Barthes takes another tack. In brief, he argues that since myth is depoliticised speech and since any myth of the Left is poverty-stricken and halting in its step, the only possibility of opposing myth is with political speech, for politics and myth grimly stand their ground as two great opponents. He begins this argument by pointing out that myth is by definition depoliticised. At this point, Marx makes his most obvious appearance in Barthes's text. In particular, Barthes plunders the classical-Marxist argument against idealism, namely that it has the world upside down; any criticism needs to stand the world on its feet. In the same way that one might deal with religion, or with Hegel's thought, or even with economic theory, so also with myth: it simply has things topsy-turvy. Myth presents its message as perfectly natural, as a given, and in the process it denies history, contradiction and memory. So the criticism of myth needs to show that all this is subterfuge.

Here, mythological criticism for Barthes is really a version of ideological criticism. In order to oppose myth, political speech is required, and by 'politics' Barthes means 'the whole of human relations in their real, social structure, in their power of making the world'.[45] Any alternative myth simply will not do, he argues, for the Left has a woeful collection of myths. Because it is not the determining feature of our age and because the bourgeoisie has been able to become 'anonymous' and thereby synonymous with the very identity of nationhood, culture and what is 'normal', the Left can offer only a feeble response. Precisely because the Left and its culture are not central to everyday life – cooking, the home, theatre, law and so on – the myths it offers are

---

[43] Barthes 1993a, pp. 158–9; Barthes 2002k, p. 868.
[44] Barthes 1987; Barthes 2002tt.
[45] Barthes 1993a, p. 143; Barthes 2002k, p. 854.

marginal.[46] However, the problem runs deeper than that, for the very process of mythologising weakens the Left. As soon as it becomes 'the Left' it has become a mythological entity, trying to become 'natural'; even worse, it may become embodied in a myth like that of Stalin.[47]

So, the only answer to myth is a purely denotative speech; only this language can be fully political. It is the speech of the oppressed, the poor and the colonised, those who have little time for the metalanguage of myth. Barthes puts himself in the place of a wood-cutter in the very process of production. By saying that he has cut down the tree, the wood-cutter speaks directly of what he has done. There is no fuss, for he is involved in production. The immediacy of his involvement leaves language at its denotative level. Only when those who are not woodcutters – those not involved in the process of production but living off those who are – talk about the cut-down tree does the tree become an object of metalanguage, a concept that is open to mythical elaboration. As with the tree, so also with capitalist society: the revolutionary who seeks to cut down that society is the one who speaks in a political manner.

This is a highly problematic argument for reasons that will become clear in the next section. However, even at this point, the argument runs into a contradiction with his earlier comments. There, we found that all of the other efforts to achieve such a denotative level, even the radical work of writers who seek to remove any signs from language, fall short of their goal. Barthes signals that he is all too conscious of this problem, for, in the process of writing about the woodcutter, production and even revolution, he operates at the level of metalanguage. His last refuge is to point out that the critic of mythology is alienated from both myth-production and consumption – that is, the community as a whole – through his critical act.[48] To my mind, this is a tacit

---

[46] Here we can detect a lament of the 'Left's failure in respect to culture', a lament we also find in Barthes's comment that pleasure is usually regarded as a myth of the Right, while the Left is given over to sobriety and commitment. It should not be so, argues Barthes, especially in *The Pleasure of the Text*; Barthes 1975, pp. 22–3; Barthes 2002nn, pp. 231–2.

[47] Later, in 1977 and after the surge in the Left from 1968, Barthes notes the inevitable process of constructing new myths, but he remains suspicious. See Barthes 1985, pp. 270–1; Barthes 2002rr, p. 374.

[48] Barthes 1993a, pp. 156–7; Barthes 2002k, pp. 865–7. The passing comments on the petite bourgeoisie also have this self-critical dimension to them, for as an intellectual who had taught in Romania and Egypt and was then ensconced in the CNRS (Centre Nationale de Recherche Scientifique) he was a classic case of the intellectual as petit bourgeois.

recognition that Barthes too cannot escape the process of mythmaking. And so even with the woodcutter, as soon as you have some sign – the tree or wood-cutter – then myth finds fertile ground to take seed. Indeed, the little story of the woodcutter is as mythical as any other – it harks back to simpler time, somewhere in a forest, and the woodcutter is an honest worker who needs to find wood for the fire and food for the table. In short, Barthes engages in his own piece of mythmaking for the Left.

Dialectics of opposition

Barthes's search for a viable way to oppose myth is actually a forlorn admission of failure, but only if you hold that myth is inescapably baleful. Barthes is not alone in this respect, for he stands in a long line of those who are profoundly suspicious of myth. For instance, Theodor Adorno argued that myth was the first moment of social ordering and fixation, when gender, class and racial roles were fixed, while Walter Benjamin understood myth as a barbaric nightmare, embodied above all in the Nazi-myth of blood and soil, from which we desperately need to wake.[49] For Barthes, it is the preserve of the bourgeois ruling class, whose ideas are, after all, the ruling ideas of the age.

However, we may take another path through Barthes's texts, a path that produces a different argument. Rather than hold out for as long as possible against the inevitable victory of myth, I suggest that it may well be possible to appropriate myth for more progressive purposes – or, rather, that myth itself may embody patterns of opposition and resistance, not so much to myth itself but to reaction and oppression. Barthes – at least the dominant voice in his text – argues that such myths are not possible, or that they are poverty-stricken and clumsy in contrast to the myths of political Right. Yet hints and suggestions appear in his arguments that suggest far more. In what follows, I trace these hints, digging them out and organising them in a coherent whole. I distinguish between two directions: one follows the trail deep into reaction-

---

[49] With good reason, for, as Lincoln has shown, the recovery of myth as a category of analysis towards the eighteenth century – when it was seen as a way of express-ing a deeper truth – was closely tied in with theories of *Volk*, Aryanism and then its mutation as the Indo-European hypothesis. See Lincoln 2000.

ary myths to identify resistance from within; the other tries to outline what such alternative myths might look like.

Hiding something?

I begin my search for resistance with the tip-off that something lies concealed within myth. On this question, Barthes's comments that myth is duplicitous – always finding alibis, fleeting, multiple and constantly on the move – say more than he suspects. When he points out that myth is given to alibis – offering another account and saying, 'I was not there; I was somewhere else' – one begins to wonder why such an alibi is needed. Is myth trying to hide something? Further, the dizzying turnstile of meaning – in which the myth switches back and forth between original sign and the new myth – may be seen as an effort by myth to cover its tracks when dealing with the troublesome content of the original sign. Even more, the sheer multiplicity of myth and the constant shifting between items that say the same thing – wine, children's toys, soap-powders, margarine, a new car, a court-case all speak of the dominant bourgeois mythology – suggests a nervousness on the part of myth.

So, if an accused criminal offers an alibi, slips quickly from one hiding place to another, provides multiple identities and distorts the truth, then we will want to ask why? Is he or she trying to hide something? Is there a crime that needs concealing? Barthes may well stop me in my tracks at this line of questioning, for he is keen to point out that myth 'hides nothing [*le mythe ne cache rien*]'.[50] All it does is distort; other than that, everything is on display. My answer: yes, everything is indeed available for examination, except the process of distortion itself. Barthes himself provides the explanation, for, when myth does grab me and makes me complicit, it stands its ground, locks into place and 'makes itself look neutral and innocent'.[51] It behaves like an accused criminal, for once I turn around and look, it stands its ground and appears as innocent as can be. I speak the simple truth, it wants to say, is it not obvious? So there is something myth wishes to conceal: its pretence to naturalness and

---

[50] Barthes 1993a, p. 121; Barthes 2002k, p. 834.
[51] Barthes 1993a, p. 125; Barthes 2002k, p. 838.

innocence is a cover for having stolen language and having transformed it into something twisted and distorted.[52]

Producing and concealing opposition

The question then becomes, what language, indeed what truth does myth distort? It is none other than the historical, social, cultural, political, and, I would add, the racial and religious truth of the initial sign. What Barthes finds reprehensible is the fact that myth removes these specific and rooted elements of the original sign and replaces them with what is, in many respects, their opposite. The black salute once again: the man comes from the French territories in North Africa; he has his own long history, from Phoenician and Roman dominance, Arab invasions and the French colonial expansion; he has his own language and culture, with its assumptions concerning everyday life; his religious background too has a long history, from conversions to Christianity in the second century and the strength of the early Church (the Church's theological hit-man, Augustine, was of Berber origin), through Muslim conversion in the seventh and eighth centuries and the recurring patterns of African practices and beliefs that continued within each new religious conversion. All this has been twisted by myth into something new: the eternal glory of the French Empire.

Taking the analysis a step further, what this myth does through all its swift-footed moves is attempt to deal with the fact that the French Empire has overrun not merely another people, but a people with a distinct history of their own. In other words, it conceals an unwelcome truth, a trauma even, that it cannot face: the empire is a brutal and alien imposition on a population that can only wish it good riddance. Or the myth may indeed recognise a snippet of such truth, thereby inoculating itself against the larger truth it cannot

[52] Here, Barthes's continual Freudian comments are revealing. Again and again, they turn up: the threefold pattern of signifier, signified and sign is like the connection between manifest and latent content in the dream itself; or the latent content of the dream, parapraxis, or neurosis occupies the position of the signified; or the poverty of the mythic signified (the concept) is like the thinness of the Freudian parapraxis and yet this thinness is out of proportion to its importance. On only one occasion, Freud does not come to Barthes's aid: the point that myth hides nothing is presented as a counter to Freud; the concept is not latent, it is not a concealed unconscious that needs to be uncovered through a psychoanalytical reading of myth. And, yet, as I argue, for Barthes myth does indeed hide something.

admit.[53] So, at this level, the myth's distortions seek to conceal the fact that there is widespread opposition to that empire. But this is only the first level, for now a paradox emerges: the opposition to that empire has actually been created by the empire itself. Had it not invaded in the first place, the opposition would not be a reality. In other words, the empire has created its own problem. That is what the myth seeks to conceal – a basic trauma that it must deny, for if it did reveal the trauma, then the empire would lose its reason for existence. The empire has brought about the opposition and it is the task of myth to efface it; the only way myth can do so is take the very figure of that opposition and turn him into something very different – a thankful son of the empire.

Preserving rebellion

But what happens to this opposition? Does myth – or, rather, what we should now call reactionary myth – succeed in closing it down? Perhaps not. In order to see why, let me return to the black salute as the distorted vehicle of a unified empire: Barthes observes that the initial meaning-full sign is 'deprived of memory, not of existence'. Further, it is 'at once stubborn, silently rooted there [à la fois têtus, silencieusement enracinés], and garrulous, a speech wholly at the service of the concept'.[54] The sign speaks with two voices, one in support of the new myth (the glorious French Empire) and another in silent protest (colonised Africa).

Yet, myth cannot overcome the stubborn, silent resistance embodied in the initial sign. I would suggest that, in these comments on the stubborn presence of resistance in such a myth, Barthes has stumbled on a vital feature of myth: it is a means of dealing with problems and contradictions. All too often, myth embodies a conflict that must be resolved in one way or another. It may be the primal conflict that is the staple of theogonic and cosmogonic myths, or a myth in which a trickster (Prometheus) hoodwinks the gods and is then punished, or one in which women take initiative (such as Eve and the fruit) only to be cursed, or periodic rebellion (the murmuring of the Israelites in the

---

[53] Barthes 1993a, pp. 150–1; Barthes 2002k, p. 861. For examples of how army and church inoculate a larger truth, see Barthes 1993a, pp. 41–2; Barthes 2002k, pp. 704–5.

[54] Barthes 1993a, pp. 122–3; Barthes 2002k, p. 835.

222 • Chapter Five

wilderness against Moses) that is punished through plague, fire, snake-bite and the earth opening up. Or, in our own day, it may be the myth of the state in a just and good war against the forces of evil – a 'free' and 'Christian' West against the evil 'barbarism' of Islam.

What we find with such myths is that they explore these types of pro-tests and rebellions only to close them down in the end. Disruption is not an option, says the myth, and this is why. Yet, in doing so, myths time and again preserve the moment of rebellion. It may be coded negatively, condemned as pride, sin and contumacy, but, in the very act of doing so, rebellion survives and so may be retrieved. In other words, in the effort to close down opposi-tion, myth embodies a deep contradiction within. We can go a step further: only through these myths of reaction and oppression does the possibility of subversion arise.[55] However much they might dislike each other, the two ele-ments are inseparable within myth; like a mutually dependent couple who can be together only by squabbling, the oppressive and subversive elements of myth cannot escape one another. But this means that reactionary myths contain the seeds of rebellion within them, so much so that there is an implicit dynamic within myth that leads to resistance against domination.

The cunning of myth

At this point, what I would like to call the cunning of myth comes into play, for it seems to me that myth has a knack of twisting out of its oppres-sive blanket. Barthes hints as much with regard to one of his favourite top-ics – pleasure – which may well be a revolutionary and asocial breakout from the myths of the Right, which seek to claim pleasure for themselves.[56] But a more sustained example appears with our consistent black salute. The North-African man cannot be wholly subsumed within the myth of empire; for that reason, myth shuffles about, moving back and forth in order to draw what it can from the man. His salute is indeed a genuine salute, myth urges, and not an ironic one. He does look upward to the flag, to the glorious possibilities of what the empire can achieve for him and everyone, and not to the Senegalese, Moroccan, Algerian, or any other flag of independence

---

[55] See above all Bloch 1972; Bloch 1968. See my discussion of Bloch in Boer 2007a, pp. 1–56.
[56] Barthes 1975, pp. 22–3; Barthes 2002nn, pp. 231–2.

from French dominion in Africa, the Pacific or South-East Asia. Yet, the resistance to this act of appropriation is indeed there, for, as Barthes points out, the myth of empire is uncertain and fragile and must therefore be constantly reasserted. Indeed, this myth asserts as strenuously as it can that those possibilities – of independence, of other allegiances and the throwing off of the empire – are overcome by this soldier.

An alternative myth begins to twist out from under its oppressive cover. That myth looks rather different: there is the assertion of a distinct history, of a religious and cultural identity; indeed, it wants to say that this distinct narrative demands its own destiny away from the French Empire. It becomes a myth of anticolonialism and independence. The opposition that the myth of empire tried to close down and appropriate for itself has twisted out of the empire's grasp and become a very different, oppositional myth. It cannot be contained forever; the mute protest is always ready to gain its own voice.

Alternative myths

Thus far, I have followed a path in which I asked whether myth tries to hide something (distortion), suggesting that it both produces and conceals opposition, thereby preserving rebellion. And I have suggested that there is a cunning of myth in which myths of rebellion twist out from under their dominant control. However, there is another feature of Barthes's argument that strengthens my search for a dialectic of opposition. The initial hint of another path actually appears in *Mythologies*. Desperate to find a way to resist bourgeois myth, he wonders whether the best option is not to outsmart myth by mythifying myth itself. Or, as he puts it, in the same way that myth builds a second layer on top of language, so also it should be possible to construct a third layer that gives myth a dose of its own medicine. It is a case of robbing the robber and turning what is stolen against the original thief.

This passing comment gains a whole new angle in Barthes's later observations on denotation, the primary system of language upon which myth – at least in *Mythologies* – builds its own signifying system through distortion and theft. The problem with Barthes's analysis in *Mythologies* is that the structural representation of the two overlapping sign-systems gives prominence and power to the second – mythological – system at the expense of the first – linguistic – system. Barthes constantly points out that such a representation has its limits, that it can only approximate the relation between the two sign-systems, and yet he uses it to argue for the distorting dominance of the mythological system. That system wreaks havoc on the initial denotating system, which can stand there only in mute protest.

By contrast, in his later work, Barthes completely undermines this structural dominance of the second system. Denotation is, he suggests in *S/Z*, by no means the primary site of meaning upon which connotation (and thereby metalanguage) builds its own system. In fact, the two zones play a game with one another, referring back and forth in an illusory fashion.[57] Even more, we may invert the whole relation and see denotation as the last in a series of connotations, one that appears to give the last word of simple and primitive truth, and it does so by appearing to be first. By now, Barthes speaks of denotation as operating primarily as an archaic myth of the natural origin of language. Denotation is nothing other than the 'old deity, watchful, cunning, theatrical, foreordained to *represent* the collective innocence of language'.[58]

We may read these observations as a retreat from his earlier Marxist assertion of the raw primacy of production and revolution. Nothing is left to resist myth, for denotation is, if anything, even more mythical. But I take these comments in a different sense, namely that here we find another angle on the possibility for myths of rebellion. It certainly makes sense of the way his story of the rough-and-ready woodcutter is already a myth the moment Barthes invokes it. The key here is that the woodcutter – who is involved directly in production and thereby embodies the only resistance to bourgeois myth – operates at the apparently primary level of denotation. It is nothing less than a denotative myth.

Now two other examples of alternative myths make much more sense. One comes from an extraordinarily sympathetic treatment by Barthes of Charlie Chaplin, especially the film *Modern Times*. Chaplin's depiction of a man locked in a cell, happily reading a newspaper with his legs crossed and sitting under a portrait of Lincoln, embodies as nothing else can the alienation of the petite bourgeoisie. Yet Barthes's other observations draw my attention, for they concern the proletariat. For Barthes, Chaplin provides one of the most powerful contemporary representations of the proletariat and indeed 'represents in art

---

[57] He already hints at such a move in *Mythologies*, when he points out that myth presents itself as a simple, literal truth, without ambiguity – in other words, as a denotative system. See Barthes 1993a, p. 128; Barthes 2002k, p. 840.

[58] Barthes 1990, p. 9; Barthes 2002ii, p 126.

perhaps the most efficient form of revolution'.[59] The value of this depiction is that it is not a didactic political endorsement of the proletariat – for that reason, it is far more powerful. Chaplin's character is, in many respects, at a stage of pre-class-consciousness. He is desperately hungry, imagining massive sandwiches, rivers of milk and pieces of fruit one tosses aside having barely touched them – a land flowing with milk and honey! And yet a strike is a disaster since it only exacerbates his hunger. This moment before the revolution portrays, as no socialist art has been able, the humiliated condition of the working class.

This example from Chaplin is hardly a pale and poor myth of the Left of which Barthes speaks elsewhere. Instead, we find a vibrant and powerful myth that succeeds through its understatement – a denotative myth *par excellence*. And it comes not from within the bowels of 'actually existing socialism' but from the land of the most overdeveloped capitalism – the United States, where even Marx saw harbingers of the full form of capitalism and the secular nation-state. Here is a dialectic which Barthes has evoked despite himself.

Towards utopia

The second example picks up another comment on denotation, namely that denotation may well be utopian, for it presents the possibility of the world of language that is beyond our own capabilities.[60] When I read this comment I immediately thought of the extraordinary *Empire of Signs*,[61] in which Barthes attempts to produce a semi-imaginary 'Japan', where the articulation of signs is so delicate there is no longer any meaning, no reference to an ultimate signified. In all those domains where bourgeois myth has its stranglehold – language, food, games, cities, street-signs, railway-stations, faces, writing, the individual subject, theatre, poetry, bodies and space – Barthes imagines a world where there is no meaning. It is simply not present – no soul, no God, no ego, no metaphysics and so no myth. Nothing less than a utopian

---

[59] Barthes 1993a, p. 40; Barthes 2002k, p. 702; translation modified.

[60] Barthes 1983, p. 30; see also pp. 281–6; Barthes 2002dd, p. 931; see also pp. 1179–84. See further Barthes 1985, p. 83; Barthes 2002jj, p. 667; Barthes 1989, p. 77; Barthes 2002pp, p. 801.

[61] Barthes 1982; Barthes 2002ff. See also his comments on the utopian form of *musica practica* where nothing is left over – Barthes 1991, pp, 265–6; Barthes 2002hh, p. 450.

project,[62] the complete absence of signs, the application of semioclasm to the idea of the sign itself,[63] should be able to withstand myth, at least according to his argument in *Mythologies*. Not so, for what happens is that Barthes produces his own myth in what is perhaps his most enticing work. In fact, it goes beyond the myths of denotation, for it even refuses the initial connection between signifier and signified that produces the sign.

What we find in *Empire of Signs* is a utopian world that will have been – if I may use the future perfect in such a way.[64] Myth trades on this utopian, even eschatological dimension. Now, this is a distinctly formal point, for it makes little difference whether the utopian future is a reactive and oppressive one, or whether it is one of liberation from such oppression. Formally, they operate in a similar fashion. We can see how this works with the photograph of the black salute (for the last time). The mythical signification of this photograph is that of the French Empire, which effaces the concrete social history of the peoples it overruns and dominates. The image wants to say, argues Barthes, that all France's sons (and presumably) daughters share the ideals of the Empire; we are as one under the flag. Is that a reality or is it an ideal? I would suggest that the function of such a myth is to present a desired position in which the empire might be but is certainly not yet. In other words, there is a distinct eschatological ideal to which that myth points, a desired utopian image of a magnanimous empire at peace within itself and proud of its achievements.

Barthes is the last one to feel that this is a desirable ideal. Yet, if we focus on form rather than content, then we find a basic feature of myth, one that shows up again and again in Barthes's own text: the presentation of an ideal – or, at least, better – future that has not yet been achieved. This point actually applies to any myth, whether of the Right or the Left, or indeed any other political content they may take. We may find some content more appealing that others, but that does not diminish the formal point. Even the most retrograde myth – of Nazism, say, or slavery or sexual oppression or a theocracy as we find in the biblical text of Chronicles[65] – still presents an image of what the desired, ideal or better society might look like. At a formal level, this utopian dimen-

---

[62] Barthes 1985, p. 97; Barthes 2002gg, p. 678.
[63] Barthes 1985, p. 85; Barthes 2002hh, p. 669.
[64] See Badiou 2004, pp. 119–33; Badiou 2006a, pp. 391–435; Badiou 1988, pp. 429–75.
[65] See Boer 2006, pp. 136–68; Schweitzer 2007.

sion of myth applies to any political position of the Right or the Left, as we see in *Empire of Signs* or, indeed, Charlie Chaplin's film. These myths present the possibility an imaginary, enticing and desired world. Yet, once we have dealt with form, content begins to return, especially since the opposition is an artificial one that may work for analysis. But that is another task.

Conclusion

Throughout this chapter, I have done nothing more that read Barthes's texts in the way in which he himself deals with texts and other cultural artefacts. By focusing on the odd moments and fragmentary glimpses that open up other lines, I have been able to piece together a way of reading myth that does not see it only as a baleful and dismaying distortion against which resistance is almost futile. As a result, myth turns out to bear within itself a pattern of opposition and resistance. Rather than Barthes's futile effort to resist myth from outside, I have been able to trace another pattern: resistance takes place within myth through a dialectics of opposition. In other words, I have pushed Barthes's own analysis towards a more dialectical understanding of myth in which resistance to domination is both concealed and preserved, where moments of cunning appear and even the occasional alternative and utopian possibility.

One problem remains: how do myths of resistance and liberation avoid a comparable dialectical move? In the same way that myths of oppression contain within them the seeds of resistance, do not the mythical celebrations of liberation also bear within them the danger of regression to tyranny and barbarism? The biblical myth of Exodus for the Boers in South Africa turned into the justification for apartheid; for the Jews who founded the modern state of Israel, the same myth became a story of dispossession for the Palestinians; and, in the United States, it became a validation not only for decimating indigenous peoples, but also for the sense of being God's chosen agent in world-history. I would suggest that one reason for Barthes's deep suspicion of myth is due to examples such as these. He shared that suspicion with Adorno and Benjamin (but not Bloch), although the determining instances for them were the myths of blood, soil and Blond Beast of fascism on one side and, on the other, the new man and woman of Stalinism, along with a pernicious personality-cult.

228 • Chapter Five

How does any engagement with myth by the Left deal with this dialectical problem, namely the tendency for myths of liberation to bear within them the germ of validation for oppression? One option, pursued with some despair by Barthes, is to have done with all myth and seek to oppose it from outside. Another possibility, which we also find in his texts, is to rob the robber and turn myths of oppression against themselves. I prefer this second option, at least in response to those myths of repression and tyranny, as my earlier discussion has made clear. A minimal position, then, would be to argue that one focuses on those myths and identifies their moments of rebellion and cunning.

But many will want to go beyond this modest position, seeking more full-blooded myths for the Left. Rather than the dearth of such myths that Barthes bemoans, they are legion; not a famine but a rich feast.[66] For communism, it is the old myth of 'from each according to his abilities, to each according to his need';[67] for anarchists, it involves self-organisation by collectives and the absence of the state, captured in Bakunin's principle, 'absolute rejection of every authority including that which sacrifices freedom for the convenience of the state';[68] for pacifists, it is an entirely different social formation that is co-operative over against all hitherto forms of human society which have been built around conflict; for the many branches of feminism, the basic requirement is an end to the long and cruel history of the complex domination of one gender by another, although what the alternative looks like may be equality, separate social and economic systems or the myths of socialist feminism; and for the greens, perhaps the most imaginative and constructive of all, the premise is an economy and society that does not destroy the natural environment of which we are a part, although, among the greens, there is immense discussion, planning and debate concerning the shape of society, new forms of global government, uses of technology and science, the role of religion and the structure of the economy. There are many more possible myths, whether from the religious Left, or from overlaps such as eco-feminism, eco-socialism or primitivist anarchism. But I have provided a brief list to stress a multiplicity of myths rather than the singularity of a master-myth. Such multiplicity is one way to

---

[66] See further Boer 2009b, pp. 168–92.
[67] Marx 1989, p. 87.
[68] Bakunin 1980, p. 77.

check the dialectical tendency for myths (especially of the Left) to become unstuck. Add to that the need for constant debate, negotiation, experiment, failure and beginning again – in short, an openness and incompleteness – and we have the beginnings of a way not only of avoiding the penchant for running into the mud, but also of a way to get the wheels moving again.

Chapter Six

The Flights of Gilles Deleuze and Félix Guattari

> I think that Félix Guattari and I have remained
> Marxists, in our two different ways...[1]

With Deleuze, it is advisable to take Adorno's advice regarding Kierkegaard: one should not be mesmerised and seduced by Deleuze, for that is the most treacherous feature of his work.[2] I must admit to being not a great admirer of Deleuze, partly due to the almost endless number of disciples and commentators[3] and partly due, I suspect, to the absence of any erotics of knowledge. In short, Deleuze does not strike me as a sexy thinker, one who gets my juices flowing and fires up my passions. But perhaps that is a better way to approach someone like Deleuze, for then we are able to resist his many seductions. In fact, it is only when he becomes the double voice of Deleuze and Guattari that he, or rather they, become enticing.

---

[1] Deleuze 1995, p. 171.

[2] See Adorno 1989, p. 11; Adorno 2003b, p. 19.

[3] These commentators and critics often seek a lever to Deleuze's thought, a lever that can then shift that thought into a manageable position. So we find that rhizome, or deterritorialisation, or immanence, or becoming, or lines of flight, or creation, or the One, or beatitude becomes the beacon that can guide us through the mists. I find myself wanting to say that Deleuze cannot be captured by any one of these ideas, for all of them are true (this observation was made by the brilliant Lars Nøregård from Copenhagen).

My interest in Deleuze and Guattari is quite specific – the connection between Marx and theology in their work. In particular, what draws my attention is another angle on a recurring theme throughout this study: a tension between oppression and liberation, between reaction and revolution within religion, especially theology. In earlier chapters, I have explored an argument for a dialectical connection between an authentic, honest religion that resists in all its fibres the compromise of religion with the state (Horkheimer); a slow awareness that Christianity has within it the resources for revolutionary politics as much as for reaction (E.P. Thompson); a careful tracing of the way some of the New-Testament materials, especially in the mouth of Jesus of Nazareth, were comprehensively blocked and feverishly reinterpreted as Christianity became established (G.E.M. de Ste. Croix); and an argument for the elective affinity between certain types of Christianity and Marxism (Löwy). However, in each, there is a leaning towards binary oppositions, a coalescing of the various strands of oppression and liberation into two great blocks, or, in the case of Löwy, of two relatively equal but distinct entities of Marxism and Roman-Catholicism. Deleuze and Guattari take a very different line, spying multiple patterns of resistance to what they characterise as the despotic state.[4] To my mind, this is their greatest contribution to the theme of reaction and revolution within religion. I am, of course, not the first to encounter Deleuze and Guattari in terms of rethinking oppositional politics, especially for the Left, but what I set out to do is trace, critique and appropriate the way Deleuze and Guattari do so in interaction with the Bible and theology.

Yet, before we can get to that topic, I should mention what I do not set out to do, namely, deal with Deleuze's solo encounters with the more traditional topics of systematic theology or indeed search for some theological themes hidden in the folds of his coat. We find these encounters when Deleuze comes to grips with his 'Christ of philosophers', Spinoza.[5] I do not deal with this

---

[4] The drive to multiplicity is well-known: 'Let us return to the story of *multiplicity*, for the creation of this substantive marks a very important moment. It was created precisely in order to escape the abstract opposition between the multiple and the one, to escape dialectics, to succeed in conceiving the multiple in the pure state, to cease treating it as a numerical fragment of a lost Unity or Totality or as the organic element of a Unity or Totality yet to come, and instead distinguish between different types of multiplicity' (Deleuze and Guattari 1988, p. 32).

[5] Deleuze and Guattari 1994, p. 60. See Deleuze 1988; Deleuze 1990.

material for the reason that, when Deleuze speaks of theology in relation to Spinoza, he does so without Marx and without Guattari. Even more, Deleuze rarely passes judgement on the theological topics in Spinoza's thought.[6] By contrast, when Deleuze casts his eyes over the Bible, he does so in the company of both Guattari and Marx. I much prefer this Deleuze, peering over the Bible shoulder to shoulder with Marx and Guattari.[7]

The texts relevant for my discussion are two. I engage in close critical commentary on a few extraordinary pages in *A Thousand Plateaus* called 'On Several Régimes of Signs',[8] as well as the plateau on the war machine, 'Treatise on Nomadology',[9] which I propose to read as part of the chapter on régimes of signs. In these texts, we encounter tribes, warlike nomads, despotic states, scapegoats and 'flight', but we also run into Moses, his father-in-law Jethro, the Israelites, the ark of the covenant, even modes of production as well as passages such as Leviticus 16 and Exodus 18.

Through these two texts by Deleuze and Guattari, I highlight an overriding concern with the patterns of resistance against despotism. Their key

---

[6] This situation of the solitary Deleuze pondering theology has led to a number of studies that seek a key theological theme running through his work. So Alain Badiou has argued that Deleuze is really a quasi-theological thinker of the 'One' (Badiou 2000), Peter Hallward has followed up with the argument that Deleuze is a spiritual and other-worldly philosopher of creation (Hallward 2006), and Philip Goodchild has traced an atheistic metaphysics and what he calls the motif of beatitude (Goodchild 2007). See also the excellent study by Cullen and Hainge 2010, which traces the continued presence of the motif of double expressivity from Deleuze's study of Spinoza through to *A Thousand Plateaus*. Other studies include Teschke 2004, Smith 2001, Albert 2001 and Goodchild 2001, who deal with Deleuze's persistent effort to avoid the 'contamination' of philosophy by theology, his celebration of and desire to uphold the eighteenth-century revolution in which philosophy freed itself from theology; thereby they attempt to enfold him back within theology. Against this scholastic universalism, I prefer a Deleuze who is, in many respects, the other side of Calvin: in a way comparable to Calvin's argument against the contamination of theology by philosophy (which becomes equivalent to paganism), so also does Deleuze celebrate the freedom of philosophy from theology.

[7] For this reason, most of the essays in the excellent collection by Bryden (ed.) 2001 are not directly relevant for my chapter. Although the writers in this collection are interested in Deleuze and theology, Marx and, often, Guattari have been quietly ushered out of the room.

[8] Deleuze and Guattari 1988, pp. 111–30; Deleuze and Guattari 1980, pp. 140–64. See the patient study by Bogue 2001, who traces the influences (Lindon and Beaufret) behind the characterisation of the betrayal of God and prophecy in this section of *A Thousand Plateaus*.

[9] Deleuze and Guattari 1988, pp. 351–423. Also published separately in English as Deleuze and Guattari 1986.

contribution is to trace not one mode of opposition but multiple modes – what they call the pre-signifying, counter-signifying and post-signifying régimes of signs.[10] Each of them relates to and resists a fourth régime, the despotic signifying régime itself. These four may be appear in terms of the polyvocal and segmented tribe (pre-signifying), the numbered war-bands of the nomads (counter-signifying), the escapees who flee an oppressor and gain an identity (post-signifying) and the centralised despotic state (signifying). The biblical overlays with these four régimes are significant: Pharaoh, David and Solomon as despot-gods, Moses, who does double-duty as nomadic warlord and leader of the newly-freed Israelites from Egyptian oppression, and the scapegoat which is banished from the despotic régime. In some respects, I argue, Deleuze and Guattari make a significant contribution to the complexity of biblical patterns of resistance, especially by identifying multiple lines of such resistance. However, I also raise some questions about their own analysis, often via the biblical texts with they engage and occasionally via biblical scholarship concerning these texts and ancient Israel.

Let me put it this way: in a crucial passage on nomadology they write, 'there has always been a State, quite perfect, quite complete.... But of greater importance is the inverse hypothesis: that the State has always been in a relation with an outside and is inconceivable independent of that relationship'.[11] Three points are worth nothing in this text. First, the state in question is one if not the prime manifestation of the despotic régime of signs, although Deleuze

---

[10] The wholesale reshaping of semiotics that we find in this section of Deleuze and Guattari's work could not have taken place without the tradition that lies behind it, a tradition whose earlier stage is reflected in the spade work of someone like Barthes (see Chapter Five), let alone the usual suspects like Greimas, Peirce or Hjemslev. Yet Deleuze and Guattari also take up a much larger shovel, dig deep and thoroughly overturn the settled assumptions of semiology. Voicing comparable reservations to the later Barthes, they resist the ossification of semiology into an over-arching and all-explanatory system, a metalanguage that is universally valid and sufficient unto itself (far too close to the despotic state, as we shall see). So Deleuze and Guattari argue that semiology is not *the* system or method for understanding language and signs; it is merely one system and by no means the most important one. For this reason, they prefer 'régime of signs [*régime de signes*]'. Like semiology, the régime of signs deals with language, signs (obviously) and their constellations; unlike semiology, the idea of régimes stresses the diversity, mixture and fluidity of any system of signs. Above all, these régimes are impure, connecting and make 'assemblages' – *agencements*, or organisations, arrangements and even collections of technical equipment – with non-linguistic systems.

[11] Deleuze and Guattari 1988, p. 360; Deleuze and Guattari 1986, p. 15.

and Guattari work overtime to caution against such concrete fixations. Second, the state has always existed; indeed, they point out that the more archaeological work is done, the more empires turn up, ever earlier in human history. Third, there is a tension in the nature of the state's relation to opposition, which is also eternal. Deleuze and Guattari much prefer an outside, external opposition. It is the default position when they explore the various régimes which oppose the despotic state. Yet they also recognise that such opposition is absolutely necessary (the constitutive exception); the state is inconceivable without that relationship.

Now an anomaly appears: although Deleuze and Guattari prefer 'an outside', they continually admit, at times begrudgingly and at times more openly, that this constitutive tension is also an inside job. The brief and compact description of that anomaly, or rather series of anomalies, is as follows. The closer we look at Deleuze and Guattari's arguments, the clearer it becomes that this outside opposition turns out to be crucial to the internal workings of the despotic state – the focus for each form of opposition. So, we find that with the pre-signifying segmented tribes, the invocation of reverse causality – the pre-signifying régime operates to block that state that it wishes not to be and thereby brings it about – also applies in reverse – the despotic state is constituted by mechanisms to ward off the pluralities of the segmented tribes. Further, with the counter-signifying régime of the nomadic war-machine, what appears to be a thoroughly external threat, continually wiping out empires and razing states, is dramatically drawn into same arena since both nomads and the despotic state are actually part of the same world created by the mythical world of the biblical texts. In the régime of signs of the despotic state itself, the scapegoat may appear to be a foreign body which must be expelled, but that scapegoat is precisely what the despotic state needs in order to exist in the first place. And so, when we finally arrive at the post-signifying régime (the Israelites in the wilderness after fleeing Egypt), it turns out that this régime is an extension, now appropriated as a positive sign, of the scapegoat itself. So much for the brief description; in the rest of the chapter, I spin this argument out via close engagements with the biblical texts invoked by Deleuze and Guattari.

Going tribal, or, primitive pre-signifiers

Imagine for a moment a quasi-anthropological outfit – Deleuze, Guattari and I – on a trek to meet the various régimes of signs. Although they warn perpetually against concretions and temporalities of these régimes, the truth is, as they recognise, that we cannot avoid such concrete examples.[12] Our first encounter is with the pre-signifying régime, which turns out soon enough to be the segmented and rather cunning tribe. I, for one, am most interested in its potential for resistance, although Deleuze and Guattari prefer to see such resistance as external to what it opposes (the despotic régime). The pre-signifying régime resists reduction to a univocal and one-dimensional system, and thereby it resists the takeover of power by the signifier, which ends up (as we shall see) being the despot. Above all, a pre-signifying régime maintains the connection between 'expressive forms' and their content; each sign is extracted from a distinct concrete territory or segment. This régime is the closest Deleuze and Guattari wish to come to (the early) Barthes's denotative semiological system – the régime is, they point out, much closer to 'natural' codings which actually operate without signs. These signs have not, in other words, been swept up into a complex and over-arching system in which signs refer to other signs, in which there is a circularity of signs that is impervious to the specific location of those signs.

What are to do with this pre-signifying régime? I wish to sit down, note-book in hand, and inquire concerning three matters: the connections between the pre-signifying régime and the reconstructions of ancient societies in both Marxism and biblical studies; the challenges to those reconstructions; and then the question of reverse causality, which brings me to the issue of external and internal resistance.

As for Marxism, I want to suggest that this pre-signifying régime is a whole-sale reworking of that conventional category of primitive communism – the realm of hunting and gathering, agriculture and husbandry, with its tribal society and the horde. Deleuze and Guattari hint as much, with their references to the concrete locations or segments of signs in 'the camp, the bush, the moving of the camp', in the way expressive forms such as corporeality, gestures, rhythm, dance and rite exist alongside a vocality that cannot dominate,

---

[12] Deleuze and Guattari 1988, p. 135; Deleuze and Guattari 1980, p. 168.

in the reference to kinship-lineages, which are defined by their segmentary nature and are thereby plurilinear, and, of course, in the reference to cannibalism as a mode of both ending the name (it too is eaten) but also of resistance, for the one eaten is precisely one denied to the oppressive régime.[13]

Soon enough, we make the relatively small step into the reconstruction of ancient biblical societies – a tiny step, since the prime textual referent for Deleuze and Guattari is the Hebrew Bible and since the biblical scholars who interest me here are informed by Marxist approaches. In that strain of biblical criticism, there is a persistent, if somewhat shadowy, presence of primitive communism. I think not of the story of Paradise but of studies that continue to argue for a socio-economic formation that was relatively more egalitarian. Variously called the communitarian, household- or familial mode of production, it was first mooted in the monumental study by Norman Gottwald, *Tribes of Yahweh*.[14] Gottwald famously argued that early Israel was, in the years 1250–1050 BCE, an oppositional movement from within the Canaanite population. He did allow for the possibility of a small band of clerics from Egypt, but his great breakthrough, now assumed by nearly all biblical scholars, was that early Israel was an indigenous movement. However, Gottwald also applied Marxist analysis and argued that this group of people retreated into the hill-country, made use of new technologies such as iron for tools and weapons, lime-cisterns for water-storage and terracing for agriculture, and reshaped their economic and social system in terms of what he called a 'communitarian' mode of production. Characterised by kinship-arrangements, collective decision-making, the absence of a head of state or even chieftain, a greater sharing of labour between genders and, above all, a co-operative system of labour and economics, this new mode of production also produced a new religious system – Yahwism, with a god who was one of justice and a fair go for the oppressed.

I have argued elsewhere that this proposal is actually a combination of the conventional Marxist categories of primitive communism and neolithic agriculture.[15] Gottwald is keen to avoid the connections with primitive communism, so it slips into the background, still informing his depiction of early

---

[13] Deleuze and Guattari 1988, pp. 117–18; Deleuze and Guattari 1980, pp. 147–8.
[14] Gottwald 1999.
[15] Boer 2002a, pp. 108–12.

Israel, but hidden away like that embarrassing relative. I hardly need to point to the relevance of Gottwald's proposal for Deleuze and Guattari's pre-signifying régime of signs. Here, too, we find segmentary patterns (kinship), the plurivocal resistance to domination and control and the earthiness of signs. However, the reconstruction has a number of other components that need to be mentioned. To begin with, although the proposal for a communitarian mode of production has undergone some modifications, it is alive and well in criticism of the Hebrew Bible – now as the household- or familial mode of production. Adapted initially from Marshall Sahlins,[16] the familial mode of production postulates an economic system in which the household – understood loosely as an extended family – is the primary focus of economic and social activity in terms of the production of food, the reproduction of children, kinship-relations and modes of governance. But this familial or household-mode of production continues to carry the sense of a relatively more egalitarian system and the hidden baggage of primitive communism.

It needs to be pointed out that, since Gottwald's work (it first appeared in 1979), the possibility of reconstructing any history of ancient Israel during the period of time he proposes has become more difficult. A large question-mark hangs over the use of the Bible as the only available resource for anything before the seventh century BCE. Very little, if anything, reliable may be retrieved from the archaeological record before that time, which means that all those stories of early Israel in the books of Judges, the kingships of David and Solomon and even the divided monarchy (Israel and Judah) up until the seventh century BCE slip into the realm of legend and myth.[17] I will have more to say about myth below, but, at this point, it means that Gottwald's historical reconstruction and those that rely in some way upon him find themselves standing on shaky ground indeed.

And yet, despite these shifts in scholarship, Gottwald's reconstruction has taken on a life of its own. Read in prisons, used to make flip-charts by nuns in Third-World schools, a foundational text in the Church's struggle against apartheid in South Africa and a key element in the biblical exegesis of liber-

---

[16] Sahlins 1968; Sahlins 1972. Those who have taken up the idea in various ways in include Meyers 1988; Meyers 1997; Jobling 1991; Jobling 1998, pp. 144–50; Yee 2003; Simkins 1999b; Simkins 2004. See my detailed criticism of this work in Boer 2005b.

[17] See Lemche 1988; Lemche 1998b; Lemche 1998a; Davies 1995; Davies 2008; Thompson 1999; Thompson 2000.

ation-theology,[18] the story of an oppositional and alternative early Israel has become an inspiration for resistance by Christian groups in many different parts of the world. In other words, Gottwald's reconstruction has tapped into a consistent current of oppositional and revolutionary Christianity, one that was traced in his own way by Karl Kautsky and inspired Ernst Bloch so much.[19]

I have spent some time with this connection to debates in biblical criticism, since they etch out more clearly a crucial feature of Deleuze and Guattari's treatment of the pre-signifying régime, namely its fundamentally oppositional nature. For Gottwald and company, the proposed communitarian/ household/familial mode of production is set up in response to an oppressive tributary mode of production characteristic of the Canaanite city-states. Now, Gottwald calls this is a 'tributary' mode, since the prime mechanism for generating surplus was a blood-sucking tribute-system, but it is a really a variation on the controversial Asiatic mode of production.

At this moment, we pass on to a whole new continent – the signifying system of the despot and the face in Deleuze and Guattari, or ancient Near-Eastern economics in biblical scholarship. But one item bothers me, as it will no doubt trouble the careful reader of Deleuze and Guattari: my neat fit of Gottwald's version of primitive communism (the 'communitarian' mode of production) and the pre-signifying system of *A Thousand Plateaus*. For here we find a people, a language, a distinct period of time and even an economic and social system, or what is known as a social formation. So, let us move on to the second matter I mentioned earlier, namely the challenges Deleuze and Guattari pose to reconstructions of ancient societies in both Marxism and biblical criticism. I wish to pinpoint three of those challenges, one against conventional Marxist periodisation, another that seeks to shake up the assumptions concerning causation within Marxist criticism and yet another that wishes to avoid the congealing associated with identifying a régime of signs with any social formation.

On the matter of periodisation, Deleuze and Guattari are keen to collapse temporality entirely, stressing not only that in any one moment we may find

---

[18] On these examples, see Boer 2002b, pp. 166–7; Gottwald 2002, p. 181; Pixley 1987; Mosala 2002.
[19] Kautsky 2006; Kautsky 1947b; Kautsky 1947c; Kautsky 1977; Kautsky 2007; Bloch 1972; Bloch 1968. See Boer 2007a, pp. 1–56; Boer 2009a, pp. 91–120.

240 • Chapter Six

different régimes rubbing up against one another, but even that each régime may in fact be a combination of many régimes. Above all, they desperately want to avoid the mode of production narrative – the march from primitive communism, through neolithic agriculture, the Asiatic mode of production, the ancient or slave-based mode, feudalism, and then capitalism – for what they seek to do is juxtapose wildly different moments with one another in order to generate insights out of the unexpected friction.

Further, Deleuze and Guattari challenge the conventional Marxist notion of causation in which a distinct economic system – primitive communism, say, or the Asiatic mode of production – generates its own patterns of social relations and ideologies. Instead, they state that they are interested in 'assemblages' – *agencements*, or organisations, arrangements and modes of ordering. They seek to map these assemblages of régimes of signs, tracing how they come together, mingle and reform. All of this does not mean that they dispense with categories such as people, language or period of time; rather, these categories become secondary to the assemblages, which now become the determining features of any arrangement of people, language or time. As long as we retain as our basis this complete reshuffling of causal connections, we may still speak of people, periods, or languages, or even 'a given style, fashion, pathology, or miniscule event in a limited situation' and we may even go so far as determining 'the predominance of one semiotic or another'.[20]

Closely related to the previous point is the effort by Deleuze and Guattari to free their signifying systems from any coagulation into a specific location and time. They argue that no reason exists to attach a régime to a particular people or a historical moment: 'There is such mixture [*un tel mélange*] within the same period or the same people that we can say no more than that a given people, language, or period assures the relative dominance of a certain régime'.[21] Connections like these may happen, as they may to social formations, pathological delusions or historical events, but the régime in question is far too liquid to congeal into any one of them and thereby be identified with it.

The upshot for any notion of an oppositional social form that was either primitive communism or early Israel is quite profound, to say the least. At an initial glance, there seemed to be a reasonably good fit between Deleuze and

---

[20] Ibid.
[21] Deleuze and Guattari 1988, p. 119; Deleuze and Guattari 1980, p. 149.

Guattari's pre-signifying régime and the familial mode of production of early Israel in some Marxist-inspired biblical reconstructions.[22] But, if a régime cannot be locked into a particular people, language, religion, social structure and time, then the fit is not so snug after all. Deleuze and Guattari's argument militates against the periodisation of early Israel in terms a distinct group of people at a particular time, who may have responded to a more oppressive régime (or indeed fell back into such a pattern later), against the causal relation between social formation and related sign-system and against the tendency to coagulate the multitude of oppositional currents into any one location.

The last point is particularly important. As I have indicated elsewhere in this book (see especially the discussions of Horkheimer, Thompson, Ste. Croix and Löwy), and in *The Criticism of Heaven and Earth* series as a whole, there is a consistent and multifarious tradition which finds in the Bible inspiration for opposition and often political revolution, the latest phase of which is the spate of studies arguing that the New Testament especially is, in many respects, an anti-imperial document.[23] Yet, all of these efforts have a tendency to congeal that pattern of resistance in a distinct people, place and time. It may be early Israel (however fictional such an entity turns out to be), or Jesus of Nazareth, or the communism of the early Christians, but, in each case, there is an unexamined need to solidify that resistance into something we can grasp and identify with.

Deleuze and Guattari challenge the need to congeal such resistance. They agree that there is an oppositional current, but it is far more mingled and impure – in terms of régimes, peoples, languages, times or even modes of production. Resistance is symbiotically connected with what it opposes, such as oppression, state power and despotism. Any effort at concretising the pattern of opposition runs the risk of ignoring this mingling but also – more perniciously – concealing what is oppressive under the banner of resistance. For example, with the legendary early Israel of Gottwald and company, what are the patterns of despotism, state-power and dissolution embodied within the very structures of the proposed breakaway group dubbed 'early Israel'? Or, in the case of the New Testament: if we grant for a moment that it is in

---

[22] I leave aside the criticisms that may be directed at these reconstructions from within biblical criticism. See Boer 2005b.

[23] See especially the representative collection of Horsley 2008a, where many of the proponents of this position outline their arguments.

many respects anti-imperial (which I sincerely doubt),[24] then what imperial elements are caught up with such resistance? How does it both emulate and enable precisely the imperial tendencies it seeks to overcome? The later history of early Christianity and the ease with which it slipped into bed with imperial power would suggest a good deal of that opposition to empire was modelled on the empire itself.

So how does the pre-signifying régime offer resistance? On this matter, I move to the third topic I mentioned earlier – the dialectical trap of the argument for reverse causality. Deleuze and Guattari invoke all too briefly what may be called an argument of anticipatory resistance. This pre-signifying régime is 'animated by a keen presentiment [*lourd pressentiment*] of what is to come',[25] a mode of resistance built into the very system itself. So, through the régime's plural and segmentary nature, it effectively blocks all that would abolish it – despotism, priesthood, the state-apparatus, or, in the terms beloved by Deleuze and Guattari, the dominance of the signifier and a vicious circle of signs that have lost touch with their expressive contexts. In other words, the pre-signifying régime resists the despotic state by anticipating what that state might be. A couple of items are worth noting about this argument for anticipatory resistance: the pre-signifying régime is external to what it opposes for the simple reason that it blocks an intrusion from outside; the idea of anticipatory resistance is a form of the argument for reverse causality.

The catch with reverse causality is that it works both ways. Deleuze and Guattari invoke this argument in one direction only – from pre-signifying régime to an external threat (the despotic state). A word on reverse causality is in order before I uncover the catch in the argument. Reverse causality is an argument that has been put to use fruitfully in physics, biology and economics.[26] For reverse causality an event in the future can act on the present, or indeed the present may act on the past. More preferably, reverse causation challenges such a linear perception of causality, in which an act now – say, my lighting a cigarette – becomes the cause of an event to come – relaxation, concentration and then eventually lung-cancer or any of the other myriad results of smoking. Reverse causality questions such an assumption. For example,

---

[24] See Boer 2009c.
[25] Deleuze and Guattari 1988, p. 118; Deleuze and Guattari 1980, p. 148.
[26] See Surin 2009, whom I follow closely here.

the discovery of 'swine-flu' (or flu virus H1N1) in human beings in 2009 produced a series of frenetic responses: quarantining of cases, slaughter of pigs, warnings of a pandemic, the rush to a vaccine and daily reporting on the news media. Yet it turned out that swine-flu was no worse than many of the other severe influenza-viruses that appear and make the rounds. However, what happened with swine-flu was a relatively simple pattern of prevention that falls into the logic of reverse causality: an anticipated threat that has not materialised as yet produces a string of responses as though the threat had materialised. One could go a step further and argue that swine-flu brought about its own amelioration: by existing as a potential reality it brought about a number of actions that mitigated that reality. Even more, the example of swine-flu structured reality – quarantines, a spike in doctor's visits, the employment of medical specialists in the rush for a vaccine, suspicions over sniffles – in response to an anticipated pandemic in a way that made the pandemic real.

One more example, this time from the Bible, which is after all the text on which Deleuze and Guattari focus: in Genesis 2–3, the so-called narrative of the Fall, we have a comparable example of reverse causality, or at least the text may very well be read this way. The command from God not to eat from the tree of the knowledge of good and evil, indeed the very placing of such a tree in the garden, may be seen as an effort to prevent the dissolution of the moment in the garden itself (and 'garden' has here its myriad utopian associations). So the possibility of toil and sweat, of failing bodies and a painful death, of antagonism and hatred between the man and woman, of a constant war between man and beast – all these appear as a threat to be thwarted. The command not to eat from the tree then functions as the effort to forestall such a reality. Yet, by having the tree in the garden, the narrative makes that threat real. The flaw in the crystal becomes the reality it was supposed to prevent.[27]

The logic of these examples is the same as that invoked by Deleuze and Guattari. This primitive-communist pre-signifying régime operates in the fashion of reverse causality. All these multifarious and segmented systems are not due to barbaric or uncivilised ignorance; they are due to the effort to block what would undo them – the despotic régime of a powerful signifier.

---

[27] I leave aside many other possibilities of interpretation, such as the argument for the narrative necessity of disobedience (what a boring text the Bible would be without it), or that the story is one of coming to maturity, or that the serpent is the only one who speaks the truth.

But, now, the catch with the argument for reverse causality emerges. If we stay with the same logic, the very act of blocking such a possibility actually recognises its virtual existence in the here and now. The despot is coming; in a fashion comparable to the narrative of Genesis 2–3 with its trees, fruit and disobedience, the pre-signifying system gives birth to the signifying régime.

In other words, the despotic régime is far more internal to the pre-signifying régime of the segmented tribe than at first appeared to be the case. It already exists in the effort to block it. Here, we find one of the reasons why there is no narrative of the state's emergence in Deleuze and Guattari. The state has always existed, for it even affects those who appear to be stateless – the pre-signifying tribal régime – in their efforts to block the arrival of that state. Gone is the narrative of differentiation beloved of Marxists and so many others,[28] which moves from an undifferentiated to a differentiated condition. Triggered by unequal opportunity, whether in soil-quality, rainfall-patterns, the fortunes of war or illness, some in a community become stronger than the others. Differences exacerbate and, before we know it, we have the concentration of power in the hands of chieftains, kings and emperors; division of labour leads to class-conflict and, out of that tension, the state emerges. Not for Deleuze and Guattari, for the state has always existed – even for the pre-signifying régime where the threat of the state acts in a pattern of reverse causality to affect the structures of its segmentary and plurivocal system.

I have not yet exploited the full potential of the argument for reverse causality, especially in the way it folds back onto Deleuze and Guattari's own arguments regarding the pre-signifying régime. It is perfectly possible to apply reverse causality in reverse: the despotic régime too may be structured to prevent the disintegrating threat of the pre-signifying régime. Another example, now drawn from the threat of communist revolution or at least the dissolution of capitalism, illustrates my point rather well. In order to prevent such an event taking place, the various economic and state-arms of capitalism are in a position of perpetual mobilisation: global summits to deal with economic crises (as with the credit-crunch and stock-market collapse of 2008–9), global controlling bodies such at the IMF and the World Bank, the redefinition of 'terrorism' to include activists on the Left such as greens, anarchists and

---

[28] See my detailed discussion of this narrative of differentiation in Boer 2009a, pp. 91–120.

good old socialists, extensive surveillance of such groups by 'intelligence'-organisations and the perpetual ideological battle to discredit communism. An instance of this effort to ward off communism comes from the 1960s and 1970s in Australia, when the Liberal-Conservative government of Australia sought to counteract a communist revolution, even though the Communist Party of Australia had perhaps at most a few thousand members who posed no apparent threat. Yet the government of the day (under Prime Minister Robert Menzies) operated in an Australian version of the McCarthy-era in the United States. ASIO, the Australian Security Intelligence Organisation, kept massive files on all members of the Communist Party, the government of day railed against the communist threat and even attempted to have the massively threatening Communist Party banned (they failed). One could be forgiven for thinking that communism has been and still is a vibrant force, on the verge of taking over the world if it has not done so already. The point is by now obvious: an anticipated threat has a causal effect on the present in a way that makes that threat virtually present.[29]

What is good for the pre-signifying régime is good for the signifying despotic régime. The segmented tribe may well be structured to ward off the despotic state, thereby bringing about and recognising its existence; so, also, the despotic state may be organised to block the threat of the fissiparous tribe and so ensure its arrival. All of which means that the threat is not so much external but internal, a structural feature without which either could not exist. I would suggest the same logic applies to patterns of resistance in the biblical narratives that interest Deleuze and Guattari so much.

Numbers and nomads, or, the counter-signifying régime

Our tribal pre-signifiers, with their segmented structures and expressive signs, are by no means the only form of external opposition as far as Deleuze and Guattari are concerned. At a fortuitous meeting, we take the opportunity

---

[29] To these examples could be added the work of Henri Poincaré and his recurrence-theorem, in which any system that exists in isolation and has an unchanged total of energy will return in time (a very long time) to its initial set of molecular positions; or the argument that environmental degradation and poverty operate in a mutually causal relation – degradation induces poverty, but poverty brings one to act in a way that degrades the environment. See Surin 2009, pp. 554–5. For a treatment of causality in Deleuze see DeLanda 2002, pp. 117–22.

to pass from the hunter-nomads of the pre-signifying tribe to a different group – the warlike, animal-raising nomads, or the counter-signifying régime. We meet a mobile war-party, carefully numbered into units, innovators with weapons, led by none other than Moses, who is advised by Jethro, his father-in-law and priest of Midian. But we also meet a significant problem with Deleuze and Guattari's argument, especially in connection with the Bible: the effort to depict the nomadic war-machine as another form of external resistance to the despotic state will turn out to be internal to the complex world constructed by the biblical foundation-myth.

I will return to this problem soon enough, but first let us examine these new, warlike nomads, at least as Deleuze and Guattari characterise them. Their nature may be summarised with five terms – externality, espionage, number, prophecy and weaponry. These nomads are another form of external resistance to the state (which usually has the epithet 'despotic'). They exist outside the state, a counter to it, attacking and sacking fortress, temple and palace. Here, they draw near to the pre-signifying tribal groups, for these nomads also ward off the congealing tendency of the state, but now through perpetual warfare.[30] For this reason, the nomads may be described as counter-signifying. Further, number and arithmetic is the defining semiotic feature of these nomads, specifically in terms of numbering the war-bands in tens, fifties, hundreds and thousands. In their perpetual state of war against the state, the nomads operate via espionage and secrecy; one sends spies, infiltrates the city and undermines it from within. The prophet, too, is part of the nomadic band, manifesting the process by which religion, especially monotheistic religion, passes from its natural affinity with the state and the priest to that of war, especially holy war.[31] Finally, the nomadic war-machine is where the innovations in weaponry take place. Hyksos in Africa, Scythians in Europe and then India and Persia, Mongols on the steppes, Hebrews in the Sinai – all of them were the source of new 'miniature atomic bombs'[32] such as the man-animal-weapon, man-horse-bow, socketted bronze battle-axe, iron-sword and cast-steel sabre.

---

[30] Deleuze and Guattari 1988, p. 357; Deleuze and Guattari 1986, pp. 10–11.
[31] Deleuze and Guattari 1988, pp. 383–4; Deleuze and Guattari 1986, p. 56.
[32] Deleuze and Guattari 1988, p. 404; Deleuze and Guattari 1986, p. 90.

We do not need to look far for the biblical connection: a major exemplar for the nomadic war-machine is Moses, the prophet and warmonger. Deleuze and Guattari cite again and again the story of Moses and his father-in-law Jethro, who suggested that Moses organise the wilderness Israelites, recently escaped from the despotic state of Egypt, in terms of numerical units.[33] Once Moses had the idea, there was no stopping him – order of the desert-march, military organisation and judicial procedures all became numbered. However, rather than taking Deleuze and Guattari's word for it, let us look at the biblical material more closely.

To begin with, in that crucial passage of Exodus 18, Jethro, Moses's father-in-law, joins the Israelites at Mount Horeb/Sinai in the wilderness. Out of Egypt, the Israelites are external to the despotic state. The occasion of the visit is twofold: to return Zipporah, Moses's wife and Jethro's daughter, along with their two sons, Gershom and Eliezer, after Moses had sent them home to avoid the rough and tumble of the escape from Egypt; and to see how Moses was faring in the nomadic life of the wilderness. After the pleasantries of the first encounter – bowing, formal greetings, a long recounting of the escape from Egypt and the obligatory sacrifices (as one does) – we come across the crucial event. Jethro notices that Moses sits all day judging matters great and small while the people stand about for hours waiting on his word. Jethro shakes his head and asks Moses what in the world he thinks he is doing. Moses's explanation – that he must adjudicate in all disputes – does not impress Jethro. So Jethro gives his crucial advice: tell the people what the laws are and then:

> Choose able men from all the people, such as fear God, men who are trustworthy and who hate a bribe; and place such men over the people *as rulers of thousands, of hundreds, of fifties, and of tens*. And let them judge the people at all times; every great matter they shall bring to you, but any small matter they shall decide themselves; so it will be easier for you, and they will bear the burden with you.[34]

Moses heeds the advice and organises the people accordingly. The issue here is not the 'ruler' – the *sar*, a commander, person of note and later a prince.

---

[33] Deleuze and Guattari 1988, p. 118; Deleuze and Guattari 1980, p. 149; Deleuze and Guattari 1988, pp. 383, 388, 390, 392–4, 417; Deleuze and Guattari 1986, pp. 55, 63, 67, 70–4, 112.

[34] Exodus 18: 21–2.

Rather, the important point, as Deleuze and Guattari astutely note, is the numbering of the units themselves. And the purpose of such numbering is initially for judicial reasons, as well as the touching concern for Moses's health, but it becomes the organising principle of the people, so much so that it recurs throughout later texts.[35] To this material we could add the so-called census of Numbers 26, which is really an elaborate organisation of the people in the wilderness.

But is this numbering a defining feature of nomadic people as Deleuze and Guattari claim? They point out that the distinctive feature of numerical distinctions between tens, fifties, hundreds and thousands – a notably metric mode of organisation to be found among warlike nomads – is that it is intrinsic, not generated by a need from outside; the numbered bands are not for the purpose of administration, taxes, totals and control; instead, numbering is intrinsic to mobility, relations and arrangements. However, in Exodus 18, the purpose is judicial (and to relieve the burden on Moses). Only later in the narrative does the numbering attach itself to the war-bands. Another problem is that many of the references in the Hebrew Bible refer to the organisation of the army under a despotic state – that of Saul and David.[36] Deleuze and Guattari slip out of this problem quite easily: although, they argue, such a pattern of organisation may be found in the armies of the state, the state may appropriate this system and adapt it to its own use (witness the way armies so often form a distinct entity with wills of their own within the state, occasionally staging coups). We end up with a mixed semiotic. So also, it would seem, with the inter-relation between this numbered semiotic and the segmentary one of tribal organisation. The census-statistics of Numbers 26 – a reference cited by Deleuze and Guattari – do not operate purely in terms of thousands, hundreds, fifties and tens.[37] In fact, the text lists the Israelites in terms of tribes and then their numbers in a series of disparate subtotals that eventually rounds the number out to tens, producing that fabled total of 610,730. Here, we have a mixed semiotic indeed, enhanced by the tribal lists of Numbers 1–3, where the

---

[35] See Numbers 31: 14, 48, 52, 54; 1 Samuel 8: 12; 22: 7; 29: 2.
[36] 2 Samuel 18:1, 4; 21: 7; 2 Kings 11: 9; 1 Chronicles 13: 1; 26: 26; 27: 1; 28: 1; 29: 6; 2 Chronicles 1: 2; 23: 20; 25: 5.
[37] Although they give careful attention to the creation of the Levites from the firstborn of all the tribes, Deleuze and Guattari skip by this problem of disparate numbering with the census (Deleuze and Guattari 1988, pp. 392–3; Deleuze and Guattari 1986, pp. 70–1).

numbering is subordinated to the segmented tribal lineages (artificial though they may be). Pure numbering it is not, but then such a mixing should perhaps be expected, given that the pre-signifying tribe and the counter-signifying nomads overlap in their external opposition to the state.

What of the Midianites from whom Jethro comes – even though Deleuze and Guattari insist he is a Kenite – and to whom Moses is connected through marriage? Here, we are on good exegetical ground, for it seems they were, as far the biblical material is concerned, a pastoral nomadic group.[38] In later narratives, the peaceful connection with Jethro seems to have been lost, for we come across Midianite marauders, most notably with camels (as the man-animal-weapon assemblage) continually threatening the Israelites with their warlike bands.[39] One nomadic war-machine meets another, without resolution.

Three features from Deleuze and Guattari's list remain – spying, prophecy and weaponry. Espionage, of course, appears in the ill-fated narrative of Numbers 13–14, in which Moses sends out spies, one from each tribe, into the land of Canaan, only for the spies to return with the dismal report that the land is indeed fertile, flowing with milk and honey, but that the people are strong, the cities large and well-fortified and that the descendants of the giants (the Anakim) live there. Forlornly, the spies opine that they themselves seemed like grasshoppers before these warriors. The story is well-known: the people rebel, plan to return to Egypt, are threatened with annihilation by God, are spared and then condemned to spend another forty years in the wilderness until the current generation dies off. Only much later, under Joshua, do two spies complete the job (including spending a night with the prostitute Rahab in Jericho). In these narratives, we do find the nomadic war-machine coming face to face with the despotic state in all its apparent strength, even if the peo-

---

[38] Jethro appears on a number of occasions before the crucial advice to Moses in Exodus 18 – as the priest of Midian (called Reuel in Exodus 2: 18), an owner of flocks, probably of sheep and goats, and father of seven daughters, whom Moses impresses with a show of strength and forthwith finds himself married to one of them, Zipporah. And it is Jethro's flock that Moses is tending when he comes across the burning bush, the command to take off his sandals and encounters 'I am that I am' (Exodus 3), who sends Moses off on his little errand to rescue the enslaved Israelites from the Egyptians.

[39] See Numbers 31; Judges 6–8; Psalm 83: 9; Isaiah 9: 4, 10: 26.

ple are condemned for not trusting in the power of their own war-machine and, of course, the deity.

As far as the prophecy is concerned, Moses too becomes a prophet in the desert. As Deuteronomy 34: 10 puts it, 'there has not arisen a prophet since in Israel like Moses, whom the Lord knew face to face'. For some strange reason, Deleuze and Guattari make little of Moses the prophet, preferring to cite Mohammed as the prophet *par excellence*. In his hands, monotheism is transformed into a religion of perpetual war, the holy war against the state. Even if the initial impulse for religion comes from the state (a dubious claim), religion undergoes a radical deterritorialisation when it is wedded to the war-machine. To illustrate the point, Deleuze and Guattari refer to the Crusades, for which the conquest of the Holy Land became, especially after the first Crusade, a pretext for astonishing changes of direction and purpose.[40] The Crusades may have set out from the despotic states of Europe, but once on the road they began to exhibit all the signs of nomadic war-bands.

The prophet leads us into our last theme, weaponry and metalworking, although by an extraordinarily convoluted (nomadic?) path. Thus far, I have been reasonably content to stitch Deleuze and Guattari's proposed nomadic war-machine onto the biblical texts of the Pentateuch. So far, they seem to be on reasonably solid exegetical ground, for we can identify the various features of our nomads in the first books of the Hebrew Bible. But, now, the threads that connected them with the Bible begin to come apart, although in an unexpected direction. In order to see how this un-stitching happens we need to follow a torturous and fanciful line of biblical analysis.

Let me begin by noting that the last identifying item of the counter-signifying nomads is noticeably missing from our biblical narrative, namely, the smiths and makers of weapons. For Deleuze and Guattari, the nomadic war-machine is the inventor, manufacturer and deployer of a devastating superiority in weaponry.[41] Yet we search in vain for a reference to the Israelite arsenal, apart from the force of the deity in battle. On this matter, the Kenites come to our aid, or seem to do so. Again and again, Deleuze and Guattari mention that Jethro is a Kenite, not a Midianite. Yet that connection is based on but one verse. In Judges 1: 16, we find that the Kenites are listed

[40] Deleuze and Guattari 1988, pp. 383–4; Deleuze and Guattari 1986, pp. 56–7.
[41] Deleuze and Guattari 1988, pp. 394–415; Deleuze and Guattari 1986, pp. 75–109.

as the descendants of Moses's father-in-law (Jethro is not named directly). In other texts, the Kenites join the Israelites in the desert, appear largely as tent-dwellers and are thanked for assisting the Israelites in their passage from Egypt.[42] But let us go back to that curious reference to Moses's father-in-law in Judges 1: 16. On the basis of this slender text much hangs, not only for biblical scholars but also for Deleuze and Guattari. It reads, 'And the sons of the Kenite, Moses' father-in-law, went up with the people of Judah from the city of palms and into the wilderness of Judah'. As I mentioned above, Jethro is not named and yet scholars assume that he is the one in question. On the basis of this slimmest of 'evidence', an older generation of biblical scholars argued that the Kenites were a sub-group of the Midianites, since Jethro is described as a Midianite in other texts. They go further, suggesting that the specialty of the Kenites was metalworking, especially in bronze and iron. The 'evidence': a tenuous argument based purely on etymology, for Kenite, or *Qeni*, may be read via etymological connections as 'smith'. Then again, it may also derive from words that mean dirge, reed, nest, buy or create – the meaning is by no means certain. Once scholars have spun such fantasies, the etymological link to Cain [*Qayin*] is a small imaginative leap: this wanderer was also the forefather of Tubal-Cain, the 'forger of all instruments of bronze and iron'. The Kenites, if not the Midianites, end up being a tribe of smiths – a point Deleuze and Guattari unfortunately replicate in their own analysis.[43] To cap off this extraordinary piece of exegesis, we also find the suggestion that the Yahweh of Mosaic monotheism was nothing less than a Kenite/Midianite wilderness-god, appropriated and developed by Moses into the warlike and jealous Yahweh.[44] I am afraid that the Kenites will have the last laugh here, for with them

---

[42] Judges 4: 11, 17; 5: 24; 1 Samuel 15: 6.

[43] Deleuze and Guattari 1988, pp. 414–15; Deleuze and Guattari 1986, p. 107; Deleuze and Guattari 1988, p. 529, n. 14; Deleuze and Guattari 1980, p. 154, n. 14.

[44] Genesis 4: 22. As a small sample of biblical scholars who make these fantastical connections, see Albright 1953, pp. 98–9; Boling 1975, p. 57; Hastings 1903, p. 834; Bright 1980, p. 127. Deleuze and Guattari prefer to cite their own biblical scholars on this matter, namely Dhorme 1937 and Mayani 1956. See Deleuze and Guattari 1988, p. 529, n. 14; Deleuze and Guattari 1980, p. 154, n. 14. The problem with Dhorme and Mayani is that they worked at a time when the methodological paradigm of biblical scholarship was assumed – one explored the oral and written origins and history of the texts with a view to establishing the history behind the text, a history to which the text and scattered archaeological artefacts gave witness. Since the 1970s, that paradigm has been slowly unravelling, albeit not without a few efforts to draw the wagons in a circle and resist the wave upon wave of newer approaches.

matters begin to unravel. As we have seen, the argument that they are metal-workers is based purely on the speculative pastimes of some biblical scholars from a time when such pursuits were deemed to be 'scientific'. Their argument is tenuous at best, although I prefer to describe it as fantasy. The catch is that such scholars unwittingly replicate the text itself, for the material on the Midianites and Kenites is part of a much larger stretch of biblical material that can only be described as myth. Liberation-myth, foundation-myth, inauguration-myth – the epithets may vary, but the underlying point is the same: the textual collection from creation to conquest, from Genesis to Joshua, is a complex political myth.[45] We are, then, in the territory of myth, a very powerful myth that has been exploited in all manner of ways since to justify ideas of sovereignty, the state, exile, exodus and the conquest of promised lands. But it also means that the nomadic war-machine, with its numbering, espionage, weaponry and its external threat to the despotic state belongs to the realm of myth.[46] I have argued elsewhere that this complex biblical myth may best be understood as a political myth which is characterised by the construction of a labyrinthine world split by patterns of reaction and insurrection, repression and great cunning.[47] Despite the most excessive efforts within these mythical narratives to close down the opposition that keeps appearing, an opposition that is constructed by the myth in the first place, these stories have a cunning knack of twisting out of such a stranglehold.

Where does that leave our numbered war-machine roving in the desert? It too is a piece of this complex myth. Deleuze and Guattari have in effect identified a second pattern of opposition – warlike, numbered, given to spying and even weaponry, it is also theocratic, brutal and opposed to the despotic state in terms of its own despotism. Yet, the nomadic war-bands are no longer

---

[45] For example, Althalya Brenner speaks of the whole stretch of text from creation to conquest of Canaan as 'inauguration myth' or a 'liberation-cum-inauguration myth' (Brenner 1994, p. 11), while for Niels Peter Lemche it is a 'foundation myth' (Lemche 1998a, pp. 86–132; see also Thompson 1999). Even the grumpy reactionary, William Dever, can write, 'No scholar, revisionist or otherwise, thinks these materials anything other than "myth"' (Dever 2001, p. 98, n. 1).

[46] Into this myth falls one of the two dates that appear in the title of the chapter 'On Several Regimes of Signs'. 587 BCE has for too long been regarded as a fixed date of biblical scholarship, the moment when the temple in Jerusalem and the city itself was destroyed by the Babylonians. The problem is that the Solomonic temple and its destruction belong to material that is the product of the imagination rather than any verifiable historical event.

[47] Boer 2009b.

external to that state in any historical sense. They are part of a mythical world that includes both state and nomads, enemies locked in perpetual combat. They do so only within the internal world of that political myth. An external mode of resistance has become internal once again.

In bed with the despot, or, the signifying régime

Our time with the mythical nomad band has run out, so let us continue our trek, passing from the segmentary tribe and the numbered nomads in order to see what exactly they oppose in their different ways. Despite many warnings from our kinfolk and warrior-band, we enter the gates of the imperial city, pass by the temple with the priests engaged in debate over the interpretation of an interpretation and step into the palace of the despot, with whom we wish to come face to face. We are in the midst of the signifying régime and I am on the lookout for modes of resistance.

The scapegoat's arse

Immediately, I stand between the 'goat's arse and the face of the god [*le cul du bouc et le visage du dieu*]'[48] – the constitutive feature of the signifying system. Here is the tension between the state and its rebels, reaction and revolution, oppression and resistance and between the centralising religion of the state and its negation. Deleuze and Guattari would like to argue that the 'goat' embodies all that the state is not, the negative register that must be expelled, that it is really an 'outside' to the state, but that argument is difficult to sustain, as we shall see soon enough.

The goat is, of course, the scapegoat: 'a first expiatory goat is sacrificed, but a second goat is driven away, sent out into the arid desert'.[49] The reference is the immortalised (so to speak) scapegoat of texts such as Leviticus 16: 21–2:

> And Aaron shall lay both his hands upon the head of the live goat, and
> confess over him all the iniquities of the people of Israel, and all their
> transgressions, and all their sins; and he shall put them upon the head of

---

[48] Deleuze and Guattari 1988, p. 116; Deleuze and Guattari 1980, p. 146; translation modified.

[49] Ibid. Translation mine.

the goat, and send him away into the wilderness by the hand of a man who
is in readiness. The goat shall bear all their iniquities upon him to a solitary
land; and he shall let the goat go in the wilderness.

Some exegesis: the goat is known in Hebrew as *Azazel*, traditionally translated
as 'scapegoat', or 'the goat that goes', but the word may also mean – depending on the lines of derivation and etymology – a name for the demon of the
wilderness to whom the goat is sent, a jagged rock or a precipice to which
the goat is expelled, or the wrath of God that the goat is to appease.[50] Rather
than restricting the sense to one item in this semantic cluster (Deleuze and
Guattari stay with the initial etymology, translating it as *le bouc émissaire*),
I prefer to assume that *Azazel* has all these senses: the goat is the one that
goes out into the wilderness, to the rocky precipice where the demon lives
so as to appease the wrath of God. The word itself is a narrative, but it also
appears in an elaborate ritual of atonement.

Too often, the scapegoat is isolated from the wider ritual pattern in which
the high priest is crucial. Full of priestly vestments, ablutions, incense to cloud
the mercy-seat (of the Ark of the Covenant), bulls, rams and goats, the ritual
atones for the sins of the people. The slightly confused description of Leviticus 16 (a ram or two appear but play no role) depicts an abattoir: the bull is
slaughtered, sacrificed, its blood sprinkled on the mercy-seat and the remains
burnt outside the camp; lots are cast over the goats, one ending up with the
same fate as the bull, but the other becomes the scapegoat, upon whom is laid
the sins of the people before it is led out into the wilderness by a man designated for the task. When that man reaches the zone outside the camp, he lets
the goat go to meet the demon of the jagged precipice, turns and washes his
clothes and himself before re-entering the camp.

At least three observations among many others may be made about this
paradigmatic text. One is quite obvious: the focus is the community and its
survival, which is ensured by trying to banish all that is perceived to threaten
that survival. Note the obsession over sin – three times synonyms are used in
the Hebrew, for which translators scramble to find comparable terms in the
target language – as well as the careful attention to ensuring that the goat does
not run free within the camp, for a man designated for the task must lead the

---

[50] Clines 2007, p. 326.

goat outside the camp before it is to be released. Further, the scapegoat-ritual has more than a passing connection to the story of the garden in Genesis 2–3. The garden becomes the camp, which also has a flaw within which must be banished so that the camp itself does not implode. The difference is that in the story of the garden we follow the scapegoat (the man)[51] out of the garden, never to hear about goings-on within that boring idyll, whereas, in Leviticus 16, we stay in the camp and imagine all manner of terrors for the goat.

All of this is obvious from a careful reading of the text, yet there are a couple of features less obvious but vitally important. The ritual takes place not in the city of the despot but in the wilderness. This text is part of the longer stretch that concerns the desert wandering of the Israelites. The text has not a temple but a tabernacle, not a city but a camp, not a citizen-body but a mobile nomadic band (or perhaps a post-signifying group of escapees, as we will see below). In other words, Deleuze and Guattari have taken a text that concerns the nomadic wanderings of the Israelites in the desert and made it a central reference for the despotic state with its city and temple. The result is quite spectacular, for the nomads have come into the city; they are no longer outside but inside. Another feature of this text is that it too comes from that complex political myth of Genesis to Joshua. As I pointed out earlier, there is no reputable biblical scholar willing to stake his or her reputation on the claim that this material is anything but mythical, which means that the ritual is suspended, an imaginary construction of what the ritual of atonement might have looked like had the Israelites both been an ethnic identity and wandered in the wilderness in the first place.

With these observations in mind, I would suggest that Deleuze and Guattari's depiction of the signifying régime is a rather good if somewhat paranoid interpretation of Leviticus 16:

> The complete system, then, consists of the paranoid face or body of the despot-god in the signifying center of the temple; the interpreting priests who continually recharge the signified in the temple, transforming it into signifier; the hysterical crowd of people outside, clumped in tight circles, who jump from one circle to another; the faceless, depressive scapegoat

---

[51] In Genesis 3: 23–24, only the man is banished from the garden; the woman is not mentioned at all.

emanating from the center, chosen, treated, and adorned by the priests, cutting across the circles in its headlong flight into the desert.[52]

Given that the word-picture of the ritual of atonement in Leviticus is mythological, then this depiction by Deleuze and Guattari is not a bad representation of that scene: the people are in the wilderness; the tent of worship has been set up in the midst of the camp; the despot, Moses with the glowing face (see Exodus 34: 29–35), meets with his god inside the mobile temple (tabernacle); his brother, Aaron the high priest, undertakes a series of rituals hidden to all but him; the people stand outside, fearful of what is going on inside the tabernacle and terrified by what the despot-god might do; the scapegoat, who appears at the door of the tabernacle, is led by a man through the crowd and out of the camp and then released with much relief into the desert. It is perhaps a slightly more paranoid depiction of ancient Israel than that to which we have become accustomed, but any public ritual can feel the same way.

From outside to inside

But what do Deleuze and Guattari do with the scapegoat? It marks the famous 'line of flight' which has become a leitmotiv of a Deleuzian politics of resistance.[53] Cutting across the signifying circles and centralised signifier of the despotic régime, the goat flees headlong into the desert where it belongs. It embodies all that the despotic signifying system is not, all that is a threat and foreign to it. An initial reading of Deleuze and Guattari's interpretation gives the impression that they overload the biblical text with far more than it can bear, but then a closer look reveals a more detailed exegesis. In the same way that the sins, transgressions and iniquities bear down upon the goat with the weight of repetition, so also do Deleuze and Guattari spin out the implications of the 'sins' laid upon the goat:

> In the signifying régime, the scapegoat [*le bouc émissaire*] represents a new form of increasing entropy in the system of signs: it is charged with everything that was 'bad' in a given period, that is, everything that resisted

---

[52] Deleuze and Guattari 1988, p. 116; Deleuze and Guattari 1980, p. 146.
[53] See, for example, Surin 2009, who develops this Deleuzian line for an economics of delinking by peripheral economies.

signifying signs, everything that eluded [*échappé*] the referral from sign to
sign through the different circles; it also assumes everything that was unable
to recharge the signifier at its center and carries off everything that spills
beyond [*ce qui déborde*] the outermost circle.[54]

Entropy, resistance, elusion, unable to recharge, spills beyond – the three
terms for transgression in the biblical text have multiplied. If we look beyond
the semiotic rush of their interpretation, a significant point emerges: what
is so often presented as sin or transgression in the Hebrew Bible, especially
against Yahweh and the despotic ruler (Moses, Joshua, David, Solomon and
so on), is actually rebellion. Such insurrection must be banished or crushed,
for it perpetually threatens to overthrow the system itself.

So the scapegoat represents everything foreign to and outside the signifying system: absolute deterritorialisation versus the limited version of infinite
referentiality of sign to sign; cutting through to the wilderness versus the multiple circularity of signs; anus versus face, or defacement versus faciality; sor-
cerer versus priest, or curse versus blessing, or the inability to interpret versus
endless interpretation; in sum, flight versus the despotic régime. It is all too
easy to become mesmerised and then snared within the trap of Deleuze and
Guattari's language, so, in a moment, I will attempt to translate these terms
into concerns within biblical studies and those of the ancient Near East.

Note first, however, a vital shift in the argument, one that moves from
outside to inside. In order to locate this shift, we need to read backwards:
towards the close of their far too brief outline of the despotic régime, Deleuze
and Guattari push the line that the scapegoat is a foreign threat that must be
cursed and expelled:

> it incarnates that line of flight the signifying system cannot tolerate, in
> other words, an absolute deterritorialization; the régime must block a line
> of this kind or define it in an entirely negative fashion precisely because
> it exceeds the degree of deterritoralization of the signifying sign, however
> high it may be.... Anything that threatens to put the system to flight will
> be killed or put to flight itself.[55]

---

[54] Deleuze and Guattari 1988, p. 116; Deleuze and Guattari 1980, p. 146.
[55] Ibid.

Nothing too earth-shattering in this interpretation, for biblical scholars have been reading Leviticus in this way for centuries, although not in precisely such terms.

But, then, a little earlier, Deleuze and Guattari reveal how dubious the foreignness of the scapegoat really is: the terrible truth for the despotic régime is that it is one of us. The scapegoat is an inescapable part of the signifying régime; indeed, it is the constitutive exception that enables that régime in the first place. As Deleuze and Guattari put it, before the expulsion of the scapegoat appears the process of humiliation and torture of one who is the counter-body [*contre-corps*] of the despot.[56] The two – king and the one tortured, body and counter-body – are inseparably connected, for the king himself undergoes rituals of humiliation (here, they allude to the ritual descriptions from ancient Near-Eastern texts).[57] Unfortunately, Deleuze and Guattari are too keen to push past this point to the scapegoat's flight. If they had paused a little with that earlier moment in the narrative, they would have realised that the two goats, one blessed and sacrificed and the other cursed and cast out, signal this bond between despot and scapegoat, the body and counter-body that are constitutive of the system itself.

The outcome: resistance, revolution, line of flight are part and parcel of the despotic régime of signs. We need to push this point as far we can, for the fleeing scapegoat is not merely produced by the system and thereby expelled since it constitutes a fundamental threat; no, the system is unimaginable without this challenge. Three different angles reinforce such an argument: first, as I argued earlier, reverse causality ensures the despotic régime is constructed in response to a perceived threat of dissolution; second, the scapegoat is the constitutive exception, excluded and thereby vital for the very possibility

---

[56] Deleuze and Guattari 1988, pp. 115–16; Deleuze and Guattari 1980, p. 145.

[57] This humiliation took place during the so-called *Akitu* festival, which was celebrated in the main Mesopotamian cities such as Uruk, Nippur and Babylon, and which dates back at least to the middle of the third millennium BCE. In Babylon, the festival lasted for the first eleven days of the first month, Nisan. On the fifth day, the king was taken into the temple, stripped of his royal insignia and recited the formula to say he had not neglected the gods. Satisfied with the king's contrition, the priest would retrieve the various symbols of kingly office from the keeping of Bel/Marduk and return them to the king. On the following day, the king would take the statues of the gods out of the temple and bring them in solemn procession to a special house, the *Akitu*, outside the city. After a massive banquet and sacred marriage-ritual, the procession would return to the city on the last day of the festival. See the translation of the key ritual text in Pritchard 1955, pp. 331–4.

of the system itself; third, a dialectical argument (one that is both foreign to and yet inescapable for Deleuze and Guattari) in which the despotic régime can function only in terms of a contradiction between despot and scapegoat, a contradiction that régime both seeks to overcome but will also lead to its breaking apart.

Oriental despots

So we have a régime riven at its heart by a constitutive contradiction. But how does this signifying régime connect with both Marxism and the Bible? In answering that question, I would like to change tack from a critique of Deleuze and Guattari and look for a usable contribution, albeit in light of my recasting of their thought. That contribution runs in two directions, one towards the ongoing discussions concerning mode of production in ancient Israel and another towards Marxism itself and the Asiatic mode production. The following discussion operates in terms of a triangulation: the signifying régime of Deleuze and Guattari locks in with the Asiatic mode of production and then both of those with what is known as the tributary mode of production in ancient Israel.

I suggest that the relation between the three points of our triangle may be understood as follows: Deleuze and Guattari, at least in the way I have read them, offer a correction to a deep flaw within the traditional Asiatic mode of production, namely the absence of a systemic and constitutive contradiction; they also suggest a way through a roadblock in biblical economic history, namely the tendency to see contradictions between different modes of production rather than within each one. In other words, the shift in Deleuze and Guattari from an external opposition to an internal one is a shift I also seek in biblical discussions.

I am not the first to point out that Deleuze and Guattari's signifying régime is, in part, a reinterpretation of the much-debated Marxist category of oriental despotism, or, more preferably, the Asiatic mode of production (AMP).[58] Marx's own description is as well known as it is controversial. Written on the fly, often in the rush of preparing a newspaper-article in between his

---

[58] Even if they make the mistake of citing Karl Wittfogel's wayward hydraulic hypothesis for the despotic state – Deleuze and Guattari 1988, p. 363; Deleuze and Guattari 1986, p. 21; Wittfogel 1963.

sustained economic studies, Marx's ideas on the Asiatic mode of production are spread out over some three decades of disparate pieces – newspaper-articles, letters, critiques of political economy and ethnological research.[59] The main features may be listed quite easily: common property in land held by the village-commune; a self-sufficient and decentralised economic world of villages with their resilient combination of agriculture and handicrafts over against the imperial state; personification of the state in the figure of the god-ruler; centralised control of public works by the government (irrigation, building, roads and so on); the social division of labour in terms of usefulness; the appropriation of surplus through tribute/tax/corvée. Marx saw this system at work in the ancient Near East, in the ancient empires of South America and in China and India of his own day. Although Marx does write at times of the complexity of this social formation, exploring matters of exchange, surplus, rent (in labour and in kind) and tax operating within the village-community, between communities, between communities and the state and then between the state and the limited long-distance trade generated by manufacturers, he infamously says that the AMP was a stagnant economic form that changed little over millennia. Charges of orientalism aside, the flaw with this observation concerning stagnation and the unchanging nature of the AMP is that it negates the need for a basic economic contradiction at the heart of the AMP. We may point to the implicit conflict between village-commune and imperial centre, often mediated via vassal ruling classes and manifested in tribute, or we may enhance the tension between the centre and periphery, in which the smaller states were both subject to the imperial centre and yet sought to break away from it, but there is little in the way of an economic contradiction in Marx's own scattered descriptions.[60]

---

[59] An early sustained attempt comes in *The German Ideology* (Marx and Engels 1976, pp. 32–5; Marx and Engels 1973, pp. 21–5), but the most complete discussions are from *Grundrisse* (Marx 1986, pp. 399–439; Marx 2005, pp. 383–422) and the preface to *A Critique of Political Economy* (Marx 1987, pp. 261–5; Marx 1974c, pp. 7–11). A number of distillations of Marx's various statements exist, such as Bailey and Llobera 1981, Krader 1975, especially pp. 286–96, Lichtheim 1990 and Shiozawa 1990. See also Pryor 1990 for a survey of the Western literature up until 1980. The problem is that these summaries tend to lose sense of Marx's dialectical dynamic in dealing with precapitalist modes of production.

[60] I have written enough elsewhere of the chequered and often disjunctive histories of the concept in both Western and Soviet studies (Boer 2007c; Boer 2008c), so I see little point in repeating those stories here.

Yet contradiction or tension is precisely what Deleuze and Guattari introduce through the signifying régime. A brief description immediately highlights how extensive that reconstruction is: the *infinity* of signs, in which each sign refers to another without ceasing and is therefore deterritorialised; this infinitude produces a *circularity* of signs, or, rather, multiple circles that are self-enclosed and inescapable – all one can do is leap from circle to the other; the role of the *interpreting priest* (and, of course, the psychoanalyst if not the scholar) whose task it is to interpret not so much texts or signs but other interpretations in yet another manifestation of the circularity of signs; *faciality*, which is the centre of the vortex of circularity and interpretation and which functions as both supreme signifier and the redundancy of the signifier; this face is that of the paranoid *despot-god*, upon which the whole system hinges and where it becomes reterritorialised; *deception* at all levels, in the careful control of the circles of signs, the interpretations by the priests and in the public face of the despot; the *scapegoat*, which embodies all that threatens the despotic régime and yet is constitutive of that régime. Infinity, circularity, interpretation, face, despot, deception and scapegoat – these terms provide the sum of features of the signifying régime.

Now for the connections: the state lurches onto centre-stage with Deleuze and Guattari, dominating the scene with its despot and his face, the point of reterritorilisation and location of the signifier on which every thing must touch. This is the imperial centre, the home of the oriental despot who is either a god himself (Egypt), the son of the gods (Mesopotamia) or the god's special appointment on earth (Israel). The village-communes have become the multiple circles of signs, kept in chain by the despot. People may jump from one to another self-sufficient circle but never out of them entirely. Tribute and the centralised control of 'public' works have become the myriad and infinite range of signs focused on the despot and his face – he is everywhere; nothing is hidden. The great addition by Deleuze and Guattari is the role of the priest and interpreter, or, I would suggest, the propaganda-machine.[61]

---

[61] We can spy Nietzsche's hidden figure in the priest, especially the debilitating effect of the all-pervasive priestly role; for Nietzsche, the priests are masters of *ressentiment*, haters of the body, clever men whose task is to control the sickly people, the sick leading the sick. See Nietzsche 1994, pp. 17, 97–101, 113, 127–8; Nietzsche 1974, pp. 256–7.

The gain of this reconstruction is obvious, for it inserts the necessary element of resistance to and indeed contradiction within the despotic régime. Marx's own description strangely fails on that ground, for there is relatively little in terms of external or internal resistance. Subsequent efforts to plaster up the gaps have only made the cracks more visible. On my reading of Deleuze and Guattari, we need to locate the necessary contradiction much closer to the core, specifically through the scapegoat which is both banished and yet needed, a constitutive exception without which the régime would collapse.

On another count, it seems to me that Deleuze and Guattari seek to overcome the false problem of the inflexibility of modes of production. This sense of inflexibility is largely a result of dreary debates and assumptions, in which we come across the standard narrative with minor variations running from primitive communism to capitalism. The fixedness of this narrative and the tendency to lock in key features and then argue that they could not be found in any other mode of production (slaves, for example, or private property), led on the one hand to the modes-of-production controversy in the 1970s[62] and, on the other, to problems within biblical criticism, as we shall see. In response, Deleuze and Guattari smash this inflexibility by arguing that the signifying régime may apply to any subjected and hierarchical group – political parties, literary movements, psychoanalytical associations, families, although I am tempted to add churches or any religious movement, academic meetings and sporting events. It may seem they have gone too far, desperate to avoid locking the despotic régime in any one historical period or among any one people. Yet should not mode of production be a high flexible category? Any mode of production entails conflicting layers, traces and anticipations of other modes of production. Indeed, the shifting arrangements [*agencements*]

---

[62] The modes-of-production controversy arose out of the problem of relations between 'developed' and 'undeveloped' societies: did developed economies – i.e., indigenous capitalist ones – rely on undeveloped or Third-World economies within which capitalism was a foreign body? The response was to develop a series of articulations between capitalist and non-capitalist modes of production – protocolonial, colonial, postcolonial, peasant, patriarchal-subsistence, subsistence, simple-commodity mode and so on. Once the fever spread, others began multiplying modes of production in the ancient world as well. For example, Georges Dhoquois proposed, among others, Asiatic, sub-Asiatic, para-Asiatic and Asiatic feudal modes of production, along with slavery and European feudal modes of production. See Dhoquois 1971; Feiner 1986; Foster-Carter 1978.

of items within may well appear in other modes of production in very different arrangements. For example, the Romans may have invented private property and used money, just as capitalism does, but the way those features were arranged and interacted with one another made the Roman, or rather slave-based, economic system quite distinct from capitalism.

The gain of Deleuze and Guattari's renovation also comes with a significant loss, for they volatilise economics. Gone is any sustained sense of an economic system per se, a pattern of surplus, tribute, division of labour or exploitation. Or, rather, they have all been volatilised into signs, their infinitude, circularity and centralisation on the despot. The insertion of a constitutive conflict has come at a high price with their version of a left Nietzscheanism, for this entrancing description of the signifying régime misses economic reasons for the processes of resistance. Deleuze and Guattari may have offered a brittle and brilliant account of such despotic centralisation and its constitutive opposition in terms of régimes of signs, but I seek something more in the arena of economics.

Before I explore that possibility, let me pick up the other point of our triangulation. A lively tradition exists within biblical social sciences that has appropriated and transformed the Asiatic mode of production, but, for that, we need to return to Norman Gottwald.[63] Over against the communitarian mode of production, which I traced out earlier, Gottwald proposed what he called the tributary mode of production. Characteristic of the Canaanite city-states against which early Israel rebelled, the tributary mode of production was hierarchical and systemically oppressive. Gottwald was keen to find some grip for central Marxist categories such as division of labour, class-conflict and the way surplus was extracted. The solution lay along the differences between the agricultural villages and the state-structures: the small local court with its chieftain or king, priests, scribes, tax-collectors and sundry hangers-on made up the ruling class, while the vast majority of peasants became the exploited class. The extraction of surplus took the shape of tribute, mostly in kind and in labour (the corvée), a process that was punishing and impoverishing for the peasants. Add to that the exorbitant cuts taken by the tax-collectors, the process of latifundism as a result of the inability of peasants to pay their debts, the extra tribute required by an imperial overlord beyond the small

[63] Gottwald 1999.

local government, and you had a punishing system that drove peasants to desperation. Against this tributary mode, argues Gottwald, the early Israelites formed their communitarian social formation in the highlands of Judea.

Apart from the occasional objection[64] and apart from being broken up into native-tributary and foreign-tributary modes (one's exploiter is either the local king and/or the more distant emperor),[65] this model has become a staple of social-scientific criticism of the Bible. It takes little imagination to see that it is a slightly modified version of the Asiatic mode of production, albeit decked out in a new wardrobe. However, one feature of this tributary mode of production stands out: the inability to account for any simultaneously productive and limiting pattern of resistance from within. Instead, like Deleuze and Guattari's preferred approach, resistance must come from outside, although now taking the form of the construction of a new mode of production, the communitarian (or household or familial). As with my reading of Deleuze and Guattari, I find this argument passing strange. If there is a distinct pattern of economic contradiction (between exploited peasants and a ruling élite), and if this exploitation leads to periodic problems within the system driven by debt-bondage and excruciating conditions for peasants, then why does resistance not appear in the midst of the tributary mode of production? Why does it need to take the form of an external and new mode outside the structures of the tributary mode?

As with the AMP, a translation of terms – features of the tributary mode of production (assuming its validity for a moment) and the terms of the signifying régime of Deleuze and Guattari – is needed in order to highlight these internal patterns of contradiction. I would suggest that despot and scapegoat are not merely signs within a régime of signs, but also markers of economic and social patterns of domination and resistance. Indeed, they function as the ideological traces of an effort to deal with such a contradiction. Further,

---

[64] Simkins 1999b; Simkins 1999a; Simkins 2004. Simkins bases his objections on the work of Hindess and Hirst 1975, pp. 178–220. Hindess and Hirst argued that the Asiatic mode of production is unworkable theoretically due to three factors: no mode of production can be developed from the tax-rent couple, the so-called stasis of community-based production is a feature of other modes of production such as the feudal, as is tax and/or tribute. A further objection is that the state is never a class, but, as I have argued elsewhere, the argument that the state is restricted to the ruler's court suffers from the simple flaw of excluding the vast majority of people from the state, namely the peasants. See Boer 2007c.
[65] For example, see Yee 2003; Jobling 1998.

as with the Asiatic mode of production, the infinity of signs and their circularity inscribe the self-sufficient worlds of the village-communes with their local deities and rituals, while the all-controlling and centralising despot is the tribute-gathering chieftain, monarch or emperor, who ensures the flows of tribute through the web of tribute-gatherers and soldiers. However, with the tributary mode of production, we can also find a place for the interpreting and deceptive priests as producers of the texts we have in the Hebrew Bible (as a collection of mythology, legend, law and ritual).

But what of the scapegoat, which presents its arse to the despot? Is there a face-arse opposition within the tributary mode? That contrast may be what has been described as the centripetal-centrifugal pressures of the tributary mode of production. In this case, the imperial centre (Asshur, Babylon, Uruk, or Nineveh) draws its vassals into its orbit, constantly seeking to expand its influence through conquest and plunder. But the smaller states under its control perpetually seek to break free, seizing on weaknesses and the absence of imperial armies to assert their independence. The catch with this centripetal-centrifugal model is that the states which break free then attempt to become empires themselves – like a palace-intrigue, with one ruling group seeking to oust another. A far better location for the tension is between the ruling centre and the peasant village-commune. Now the despot-scapegoat contrast gains some traction, for the despot is, of course, located in the palace, hard by the temple in the major town (Jerusalem in our case), but the goat comes from the village-commune. Let us return to the interpretation of Leviticus 16 which is central to Deleuze and Guattari's proposal. As Leviticus 16: 5 says, 'And he [the high priest] shall take from the congregation of the people of Israel two male goats for a sin offering'. Who is this fearful congregation gathered outside the tabernacle? They are the peasants from the village-communes. And from whom do the goats come? A peasant for whom goats are valuable indeed; take it, you bastard-priest, and I will starve. As always, the peasants of the village-commune must provide from their valuable flocks the animals for sacrifice, including the goat which is to be slaughtered and the goat to be cursed and banished. The goat is the people; the despot-priest the oppressive élite. And the peasants are simultaneously slaughtered under the burden of tribute *and* expelled into the wilderness as a threat to the system. Yet the system cannot exist without them, for without the tribute in kind and in labour the tributary/signifying régime would collapse.

In other words – to use the terms of Gottwald's construction – the communitarian mode exists within the tributary. There is no need to postulate an external alternative, for it is constitutive of the tributary itself. Or, to put it in terms of subsequent biblical critics, the household- or familial mode of production does not exist as an entity on its own; it is part and parcel of the tributary or Asiatic mode. This communitarian or familial mode is both absolutely necessary for the tributary/Asiatic system to function and yet a profound threat to its very existence – the constitutive contradiction of any worthwhile Marxist historiography.

Thus far, I have sought to bring Deleuze and Guattari's signifying régime into a gentle embrace with both the problematic Asiatic mode of production of Marxist theory and the tributary mode of production of biblical scholarship. While the signifying régime answers a distinct problem within the Asiatic mode of production, it abandons much of the economic clout of that mode. When it touches the tributary mode of production from biblical scholarship, the signifying régime alerts the stiff and inflexible tributary mode that it lacks a constitutive contradiction even though such a contradiction is there for everyone to see.

On the tail of the scapegoat, or, the post-signifying régime

Deleuze, Guattari and I have trekked from the segmented tribe to the despotic state via the nomadic war-band. And, on each occasion, I have not quite believed what they were telling me – that the multiple resistances to that signifying despotic régime were external. With the segmented and plurivocal tribe, the logic of reverse causality turned back on itself and we found it applied just as much to the state and what it wishes to ward off as to the tribe. So also with the nomadic war-machine, but now I found that what appeared to be a constant external counter to the despotic state was dramatically overturned. They are both part of the mythological construction of a world or multiple worlds in which they are intimate companions. When we finally staggered into the fortified city of the despot only to find a goat's derriere, I managed to extract a grudging admission that the scapegoat was very much part of the internal structure of the state, a constitutive exception without which the signifying régime could not exist. Here, too, we found that a paradigmatic text, Leviticus 16, concerning the function of the paranoid despotic state, actually brought the nomadic war-bands close to home, for this text is drawn from that mythological narrative of nomadic existence, not the state.

As I have stated on a number of occasions, one of the great values of Deleuze and Guattari's proposal is that there is more than one type of resistance. So far, we have come across three – segmented tribe, nomadic war-machine and banished scapegoat. The first two have their respective place in the constellation of régimes of signs, one pre-signifying and the other counter-signifying, but the third remains nameless. Or not quite, for the final régime follows the scapegoat and becomes the counter-signifying régime, to which Deleuze and Guattari devote most of that fascinating chapter in *A Thousand Plateaus*. So now we climb on the back of that poor scapegoat as it staggers out of the city (or rather camp) and towards to wilderness where Azazel dwells by the jagged precipice.

Who should we meet but Moses once again, this time in charge of 'a sign or packet of signs' which has detached 'from the irradiating circular network'.[66] The portable packet of signs turns out to be the Ark of the Covenant and Moses has fled with the people from the despotic face of Pharaoh. From here, Deleuze and Guattari pile on one example after another, running the gamut of biblical narratives – temples, kings, prophets, Cain, Jonah, Jesus and even the Tower of Babel – and out into Jewish and Christian history, with the Reformation, Luther and the devil, Descartes and even Althusser's theological interpellation, until we spill into myriad lines of flight beyond any religious register. Indeed, the multiple references evince in form the basic motif of the lines of flight themselves.

Let me grab hold of Deleuze and Guattari before they run around madly in their effort to escape and ask them a few questions. To begin with, what has happened to the scapegoat? It certainly has not run off just yet, for it has undergone a transformation. Whereas, within the despotic régime, it had a purely negative value, expelled with all that would threaten that state, now it gains a positive value. Why? The scapegoat becomes the sign of a people with a new subjectivity, although Deleuze and Guattari are careful to point out that such a coalescing around a people is an effect of historical circumstances and by no means necessary. It is, of course, the Jewish people, who

---

[66] Deleuze and Guattari 1988, p. 121; Deleuze and Guattari 1980, p. 152.

now gain an identity by appropriating the scapegoat as their own: misfortune, grievance, exile, all with the fragile and mobile temple (either as tabernacle or as destroyed – hence the dates, 587 BCE and 70 CE). The implications for the logic of the scapegoat are profound: there can be no new scapegoat, for they are the scapegoat; the god hides his face; punishment becomes indefinitely postponed; and betrayal becomes a leitmotiv. This appropriation of suffering and punishment, albeit postponed, defines this new subjectivity as passional.

What about Moses? Is he not the quintessential nomad and prophet? Does he not command the war-machine which emerges once they hit the desert? Yes, of course, but Deleuze and Guattari are quick to point out that this post-signifying régime is intimately related to the counter-signifying régime of the nomad war-machine. The two régimes intermingle, elements of the war-machine are present, so much so that the nomadic side has a profound influence on the new line of flight. In the same way, there is a constant tendency to revert to despotism, either as a longing for Egypt or as a desire to establish their own state with its king and priesthood. It is a narrow road indeed, between a jagged cliff-face on one side and a plunging precipice on the other.

This last point brings me to my next question: is this post-signifying régime, this line of flight, really external, really an escape from the despotic régime? Deleuze and Guattari would like to think that it is, that it offers a troubled way out, but it has become difficult to maintain that line. Obviously, clinging to the back of the scapegoat ensures that we can draw a line not merely out of the constitutive contradiction in the despotic régime but all the way back again. And it is not so much a tendency to fall back on the régime from which they have escaped as a recognition that they cannot escape it at all. For instance, in the biblical narratives, Egypt is not necessarily that evil realm of oppression, but it too is a land flowing with milk and honey, a land of leeks, lentils, cucumbers and flesh-pots, a promised land in its own way.[67] Deleuze and Guattari admit as much, pointing out that there is no pure régime, that the régimes constantly combine in ever new formations, or are able to be translated into one another.

However, the most significant admission comes in the opening discussion of the post-signifying régime where they change tack and deal with psychi-

---

[67] See the detailed discussion of all the biblical references in Boer 2008d.

atry (on the argument that any régime has multiple manifestations). Here, Deleuze and Guattari trace the development in psychiatry of two types of madness. In the first group, people seem entirely mad but are not (Schreber was able to keep his life and wealth together, able to distinguish the different circles of his life), while, in the second, they seem perfectly normal but are not (manifested in outbursts of quarrels, arsons, assassinations and seeking of redress). So the psychiatrist is caught, arguing on the one hand for leniency, understanding and open asylums, and on the other for security, surveillance and high-security asylums. Of course, these two types are our 'paranoid, signifying, despotic régime of signs and a passional or subjective, postsignifying, authoritarian régime'[68] – Pharaoh and Moses!

This detour through psychiatry brings them around to what I have been arguing throughout this chapter. This opposition 'lies at the heart of the constitution of the psychiatrist', so much that 'psychiatry was not at all constituted in relation to the concept of madness, or even as a modification of that concept, but rather by *its split in these two opposite directions* [*avec sa dissolution dans ces deux directions opposées*]'.[69] Just to make sure we have not missed the point, they note, 'And is that not our own double image, all of ours: seeming mad without being it, then being it without seeming it?'.[70] So also with the signifying and post-signifying régimes, with Pharaoh and Moses, despot and scapegoat, but then so also with segmented tribe, nomadic war-band and the despotic régime.

Conclusion

The signifying régime and its multiple oppositions are, then, not merely opposed to each in terms of inside versus outside. This much Deleuze and Guattari admit, even if I have had to coerce them a little to make them blurt out the truth. I see no need either to reiterate my criticisms of Deleuze and Guattari here, or indeed to repeat the potential contributions to Marxist and biblical debates over ancient societies. Instead, I would like to mention briefly the implications for understanding political tensions within religion

---

[68] Deleuze and Guattari 1988, p. 121; Deleuze and Guattari 1980, p. 152.
[69] Deleuze and Guattari 1988, p. 120; Deleuze and Guattari 1980, p. 151.
[70] Deleuze and Guattari 1988, pp. 120–1; Deleuze and Guattari 1980, p. 151.

as such, although I will return and deal with those tensions more fully in the conclusion to this book. In line with the arguments in this chapter, the political tensions in religions should be seen as internal as well as external, multiple and fluid. Religions like Christianity do not have a default-setting for cosy and corrupt deals with power and the state, even though it often seems to be the case. Instead, there is an internal dynamic that constantly tempts religion to make such trysts as well as oppose them. This much we have already seen with Horkheimer, Thompson, Ste. Croix and even Löwy. Deleuze and Guattari go further on two counts. Instead of a binary contrast so beloved by the others with whom I have dealt in this book, Deleuze and Guattari suggest that modes of opposition are multiple, overlapping and frequently mixed. Further, against the penchant for congealing resistance into identifiable groups – people, language, place, class, political party, faction or what have you – the modes of opposition are far more fluid, constantly reforming into new assemblages.

Chapter Seven

The Radical Homiletics of Antonio Negri

> What a sublime and, at the same time, sordid
> vocation this theological discipline has.[1]

I close this book with Antonio Negri since he is one
of the few that deeply and thoroughly engages me,
drawing me back, time and again, to read one more
time. It is not just the energetic joy and enthusiasm
that suffuses his texts (even the most dense and
involved), nor the effort to reconstruct Marxism for
our times, but that he has not, like so many, become
fixed and opinionated. Instead, he links rigour with
a refreshing openness of mind that is always prepared to consider a new position, explore a blockage
and enthuse over a discovery. And he has been a
militant as few of us will ever be.

In this chapter, my major concern is Negri's
recently translated *The Labor of Job*,[2] a detailed philosophical exegesis of the 'marvellous' biblical book
of Job.[3] Five features of Negri's analysis stand out,
at least for one trained in that arcane discipline of
biblical criticism: radical homiletics, philosophical

---

[1] Negri 2009, p. 29.

[2] Negri 2009. This chapter is a much expanded version of the afterword I wrote for
the publication of *The Labor of Job*.

[3] Negri and Defourmantelle 2004, p. 157. In offering a careful reading of a biblical
book, Negri enacts an older form of freedom – free access to the Bible that was once
considered so dangerous by the authorities. The analogous form of freedom in the
present is access to knowledge and language, especially by the poor. See Negri and
Defourmantelle 2004, p. 63.

commentary, the opposition of *kairós* and *ákairos*, one between measure and immeasure and then the politics of cosmogony. Let me say a little more about each one, as I follow the ropes that moor Negri's *The Labor of Job* to the Bible and biblical criticism.

At the heart of the book is what I would like to call a radical homiletics. A discipline much neglected these days, homiletics is really the art of connecting a text like the Bible with the realities of everyday-life, moving from the intricacies of textual analysis to the application to life. Negri's homiletics is radical for two reasons, one political, resting on Marx, and the other textual, reading Job as a pre-eminent document for our time. Job both describes our time and offers a way through the impasse of left action. Further, this book is a philosophical commentary. Caught in the rough ground between two camps – radical philosophy and biblical criticism – it is not conventional biblical criticism, if such a thing actually exists. Negri does not come to the text with all of those unquestioned assumptions, methods and skills that characterise all too many of your garden-variety biblical critics. Is he then a lone philosopher making a foray into biblical analysis? Without a sense of what may be called the 'megatext' of biblical criticism, is he bound to trip up? Not quite, for there is another patchwork-tradition of what may be called philosophical exegesis or commentary. Some texts of the Bible – Genesis 1–11, the letters of Paul, Job – continue to call forth commentary from philosophers and sundry critics of other persuasions. Negri's text falls in with this group.

Third, Negri broaches the theme of *kairós* and time, Job being a challenge to mechanical, dead and chronological time. At this point, I turn to some other works, especially *Kairós, Alma Venus, Multitudo*,[4] where Negri develops his argument for *kairós* in much greater detail. However, I find Negri wanting on *kairós*, mainly for missing the subversive side of *ákairos*. And the reason I do so is that the base-senses of *kairós* and *ákairos* connect with the fourth major theme, namely measure and immeasure, arguably the major organising axis on the commentary on Job. After exploring the permutations of this opposition, moving as it does from negative measure and immeasure to a positive and creative immeasure and measure (in that order), I seek to reshape that tension as one between chaos and order, opting for the former rather than the latter. Political cosmogony, or, more specifically, the political dimensions

---

[4] Negri 2003, pp. 139–261.

of chaos, then enables a creative linking of the akairological and immeasurable, what is out of place and untimely. In some respects, my reading seeks out undercurrents and hidden connections in his thought, only to find them embodied in his interpretation of a crucial final text in Job. But more of that as this commentary unfolds.

Radical homiletics

> The problem of salvation is all the more important for those who have been Marxists.[5]

The basic question for homiletics is: how does this ancient grab-bag of various types of texts from very different places and times connect with our lives as we live them now? In other words, how does the text 'speak' to us? I do not have in mind some theological agenda – the text becomes God's medium of addressing us – except in the way such an agenda highlights the issues of relevance and application. We might equally argue that Homer's *Odyssey* seems extraordinarily contemporary, as does *The Epic of Gilgamesh*, but one will be hard pressed to argue that it is God who addresses us through these texts (I am sure there are one or two who would do so, but we may conveniently ignore them). Yet homiletics is, above all, a matter of technique: it brings together the skill in languages, the minute task of textual exegesis, the craft of writing for an audience and the skill of an orator. It is the art of the sermon, except that 'sermon' bears the sense of haranguing and hectoring. For that reason, I have opted for the slightly archaic term, homiletics.

In Negri's hands, such homiletics is radical on two counts. The more obvious sense is directly connected with his politics, radically recasting Marx in a form that he feels will work in our vastly changed situation. But there is another sense that relates to his practice of exegesis: Negri reads Job as a document for our time. The various arguments, positions and issues may be read off as descriptors of what is happening now, to us. Above all, it offers a way through the dilemmas we now face in the politics of overcoming capitalism.

As an example of what I mean, let me begin with the radical homiletics of another Italian, Pier Paolo Pasolini, who wished to make a film about Paul set

---

[5] Negri 2009, p. 9.

274 • Chapter Seven

in our current world. As Badiou reports, on the basis of the full script of a film that was never made,[6] Pasolini's idea was to situate Paul in the modern world but keep all of his statements unaltered. Thus, while Rome becomes New York, Jerusalem becomes Paris, Damascus becomes Barcelona and the early Christians become the resistance, Paul's condemnations, attacks, pain, calls for repentance and statements of love and acceptance all speak directly to our own situation. As Badiou puts it, 'The most surprising thing in all this is the way in which Paul's texts are transplanted unaltered, and with an almost unfathomable naturalness, into the situations in which Pasolini deploys them: war, fascism, American capitalism, the petty debates of the Italian intelligentsia...'.[7] Another Italian radical with another biblical text attempts very much the same thing. Like Pasolini on Paul, Negri on Job offers a radical homiletics.

Sprinkled throughout the book, we find statements that bring Job into very intimate contact with today. On theodicy, he writes: 'It was, of course, a very different route from that travelled by classical theodicy, and by Job in particular, but in the end *it was all the same*'.[8] Above all, Job speaks directly to the question of a 'theodicy of capital'. With neither bourgeois theory nor proletarian practice able to provide such a theodicy, everything becomes far more brutal:

> Capital is truly Behemoth and Leviathan, Hiroshima and Auschwitz. And here we are on the other side, where the proletariat is able to directly construct value thanks to the accretion of pain that it has experienced.[9]

Job and the proletariat mesh here, while capital goes the way of Leviathan and Behemoth. Or, on the question of retribution, the theological position of Job's three friends, we find that all the great systems have been fundamentally retributive:

> The great historical time of the Occident has been dominated by empty retributive conceptions – from Aristotle, through Christianity's reactionary accounts of it, and through to the more advanced capitalist ones. Socialism

---

[6] Badiou 2003, pp. 36–9; Badiou 1997, pp. 38–41.
[7] Badiou 2003, p. 39; Badiou 1997, p. 41.
[8] Negri 2009, p. xix; emphasis mine.
[9] Negri 2009, p. 75–6. For a different reading of Behemoth and Leviathan as monsters outside the order of being and therefore a location of resistance, see Negri and Casarino 2008, p. 195.

is the apologia for a retributive theory of justice, of human action, and of social rewards.[10]

Before Job's withering sarcasm all of them are found desperately wanting. There are many more examples, such as the Church's appropriation of Bildad's 'divine over-determination' (it is all due to God's grace and power),[11] or Job's very modern-seeming 'cosmogonic materialism' that resists positions like those of Bildad,[12] or the critique of unexpected and overwhelming love, pushed by the last interlocutor Elihu, rubbished by Job and targeted at the purveyors of 'Christian love'.[13] At the end of the last chapter of the book, Negri goes into overdrive. Job is nothing less than the 'parabola of modernity':

> The *Book of Job* is *the parabola of modernity*, of the forever unfinished dialectic
> of world and innovation, being and relation, which characterises it. And the
> problem of the *Book of Job* is that of modernity – of the alternative between
> the totalisation of the domination of science and technology over the world,
> and the liberation of new subjectivity.[14]

The problem of the book of Job is that of modernity – radical homiletics indeed. But Negri goes on to sweep into Job's modern agenda all of the subjects of the book: ethics, pain, labour, value, power, subjects, collectives, in short, ontology and metaphysics. Indeed, we can organise the very sense of modern time in terms of the great narrative pattern of Job: 'We can see no better way to periodise the time within which we live than through the analogy with the suffering and resurrection of Job'.[15] Or, rather, this is the source of communist hope, which must pass through Behemoth and Leviathan in order to see the flowers that grow on the thorns.

Both the figure of Job and story that bears his name (Negri often elides the two) become the exemplum for Negri's own practice. Job functions as the fulcrum between Italian revolutionary practice and French thought (Negri escaped from one to the other while writing the book). More than one reader may begin to ask the question he himself poses: why Job? The obvious answers

---

[10] Negri 2009, p. 36.
[11] Negri 2009, p. 39.
[12] Negri 2009, p. 48.
[13] Negri 2009, pp. 63–78.
[14] Negri 2009, p. 103.
[15] Negri 2009, p. 104.

may be gleaned from the text: the text of Job helped him process the abysmal defeat of the radical movements of the 60s and 70s. With its challenge to Power and God, with the massive question of 'Why?', the book of Job is, in one respect, a natural refuge. But then Negri could have chosen any other great text or thinker to explore the same problems. Or, in terms of biblical interpretation, it is the old problem of exegesis versus eisegesis, reading (literally 'leading') out of a text over against reading 'into' a text. Does not Negri engage in a heavy bout of eisegesis here? Is all this really in Job? Yet biblical interpretation is neither one nor the other: eisegesis and exegesis are inseparable: the heuristic framework with which one begins reading invariably wobbles and changes shape in the face of the text's own words and sentences. More simply, what we bring in is altered, often drastically, by what comes out.

Philosophical commentary

> In general, the biblical texts have always been extremely important for me.[16]

The royal road to homiletics is the careful task of textual interpretation, or what is usually called exegesis (somewhat misleadingly as my earlier comments indicate). My argument is that Negri takes up what can be called a philosophical exegesis or commentary. In this respect, he offers a commentary on Job in a way that is comparable with his reading of other philosophers such as Spinoza, Marx or even Descartes.[17] Indeed, Job joins the ranks of these philosophers and so may be read in a way that raises profound philosophical questions. That may seem obvious to anyone who reads this short book, but there is a thicket of issues that comes with such a commentary. They all turn on the point that Negri's philosophical exegesis is a way of resolving a series of tensions in interpretation. Those tensions range over style and structure and over the struggle between historical-critical and literary readings of the Bible. In each case, the desire for philosophical exegesis is an effort at resolution and a way forward.

I begin with style. As one who has become somewhat accustomed to the careful, even plodding philosophical texts of Negri, where he deals with a

---

[16] Negri and Casarino 2008, p. 168.
[17] Negri 1991b; Negri 2004; Negri 2006; Negri 1991a.

string of knotty problems, this pamphlet on Job breathes a different life. Here, we find very careful sections (especially when he is drawing on biblical critics and interpreting the text directly) interspersed with flowing rhetorical fire. Poet meets scientist, careful philosopher meets lyrical ecstatic. It is as though the careful textual work of *The Savage Anomaly* and *Marx Beyond Marx* meets the brio and political passion of the essays in *Subversive Spinoza* or the speeches collected in *Empire and Beyond*.[18]

This bifurcation of style is but the first step, the first sign of deeper tensions, for we also find them in the structure of the book. What jumps out is the way Negri uses a conventional chapter-structure (with a neat pattern of three subheadings in each chapter) and then a series of 'Notes' irregularly added to the tails of the chapters. What we find is that the notes carry on an intermittent conversation with a motley collection of philosophers while the remaining text largely concerns itself with the biblical text. So, we find an exploration of the likenesses and differences between Spinoza and Job in Note A, a short and sharp engagement with René Girard's mistaken reading of Job as scapegoat in Note B, a fascinating intense burst on laughter in Note C, the sublime in Note D, negative theology in Note H, pain, community and communication in Wittgenstein in Note I, and then Habermas's mistakes concerning modernity in Note J.[19]

(Let me add a note of my own. Everybody, it seems, loves negative theology – often the meeting ground between theology, literature and philosophy. So it is refreshing to find Negri taking such theology to task. Using Eckhart as his model, Negri stresses the distance between Job and the *via negativa*: 'The ontological consistency of power, which the entire Book of Job illustrates, serves to exclude any relationship with "negative theology"'.[20] Not only do I applaud Negri's suspicion of apophatic theology, but the fact that much of the Bible is not theology at all needs to be stated loudly, clearly and often.)

I have listed the topics of most of these 'Notes', since I want to stress that, in his main text, Negri by and large keeps away from the cloud of philosophical witnesses to Job. Occasionally, philosophers do turn up, such as Spinoza and then Hegel early on in the text, and then Plato and Aquinas a little later on the

---

[18] Negri 1991b; Negri 1991a; Negri 2004; Negri 2008b.

[19] Note E deals with the resurrection of the flesh, Note F with Marx and Note G with negative theology.

[20] Negri 2009, p. 91. See also Negri and Defourmantelle 2004, p. 101.

matter of love being beyond measure since it is the measure of all else. Apart from these slips, Negri maintains the discipline, carefully exegeting the text of Job in his own main text and then allowing his philosophical desires to have a controlled run in the notes tacked onto the end of the chapters.

What is going on here? Negri could have taken a line like that of Agamben's *The Time That Remains*,[21] a book on Paul where we find precious little engagement with biblical critics and a cloud of philosophical witnesses and issues. Although there are one or two stunning insights, such as the unstable nature of the remnant or the implicit relativising of theology, the danger with Agamben's effort is that it runs the risk of leaning too far towards using Paul as a convenient sounding board. By contrast, Negri is careful to ensure that the philosophical interlocutors have their place, out in the backroom, where one might go for a smoke and a chat. Pride of place is reserved for the text of Job and a small number of biblical commentators. Quite simply, Negri wants this to be a close engagement with the book of Job, the text on which he wishes to work out some crucial issues. They may be philosophical matters (hence my descriptor as 'philosophical commentary'), but he wants to work those matters through an engagement with the text. The focus is the text and then its application – i.e. homiletics – and not the thoughts of other philosophers.[22]

As if to reinforce his point, Negri structures his study to show just how much he wants this to be a reading of Job. Often, we find that there are large slabs of text quoted from Job (in translation, of course) interspersed with running commentary and linking passages. What we have here is not the use of a biblical text as an example of a point Negri has made but the meshing of Job's text with Negri's argument. That is, the words from the biblical book and Negri's own adhesive comment meld into one another as he develops his argument. This structure proclaims loudly and clearly that this is a biblical reading. So also does the charming appeal to read your 'family Bible', and

---

[21] Agamben 2005; Agamben 2000. See also Boer 2009a, pp. 181–204.

[22] In this way, Negri avoids the problem that bedevils many of the current efforts to engage philosophers and biblical critics on the letters of Paul. Biblical scholars, locked into their own history and set of assumed questions, tend all too quickly to dismiss the engagements of the likes of Badiou, Agamben, Žižek or even Kristeva. On their side, these philosophers find the questions that interest biblical scholars – authorship, textual provenance, context in the Jewish milieu and Roman Empire – do not connect with their own interest in Paul as a political thinker. What we really have is a dislocation of two traditions of commentary with their different histories, rhythms and mega-texts. See further Boer 2008a; Boer 2009, pp. 121–54.

the comment that, if you do not have one, you should go and buy one. Apart from the term 'family Bible', which evokes an unread and dusty tome with a family-tree in the front-cover, I find such a comment refreshing. Most works on the Bible assumes that its readers know the text. Even more, these works throw up a barrage of textual references to back up their arguments in a way that implicitly invokes the hidden authority of the text for those arguments. Negri has no such assumption. He does not wish to rely on the text's sacred or literary authority. Instead, he enters into a contract with the reader: just as you will be reading your Bible, I will read mine with you.

However, this desire for Job's text leads Negri quite nicely into a problem that lies at the heart of biblical criticism. It is another tension with which he must grapple, namely between what is called historical criticism and literary approaches to the Bible. The former may be more homogenous and the latter quite scattered, but, in Negri's discussion, they take the shape of two options: either the text is a fragmented collection gathered over time, or it has a literary integrity that gives unity to a disparate piece. (Very roughly, and for those not up to speed on biblical criticism, historical criticism arose in the heady mix of religion and politics of Germany in the early to mid-nineteenth century and became the hegemonic method for a century or so; over against historical criticism's search for the history of the literature of the Bible and the history behind that literature, the so-called literary approaches represent a breakout from historical-critical orthodoxy from the 1970s onwards, asking a whole range of different questions about the nature, ideology and function of literature.)

Even with the limited resources that were at his disposal when writing *The Labor of Job*, Negri is very careful to read both text and biblical commentators.[23] In the process, he replicates this tension between historical criticism and literary approaches within his discussion. So, we find a careful representation of the historical-critical assumptions concerning the structure and history of the text now known as Job. The prose prologue and epilogue (Chapters 1–2; 42: 7–17) become the most ancient layer of the text, after which we find the poem of Job's complaint, the engagement with the three lawyers Eliphaz,

---

[23] After a comment on the translations of Job that he used, Negri is careful to list the biblical materials first before adding the philosophical works with which he is more at home. Yet these works do not swamp the list.

Zophar and Bildad, the subsequent additions of the mythical cosmogony and the monsters Leviathan and Behemoth, all of which we find in the famous voice from the whirlwind in Chapters 38–41, then the insertion of Elihu's speeches, and finally the last added layer, the 'Hymn to Wisdom' (Job 28). Negri even provides the obligatory 'dates' that stretch from an unspeakably ancient and un-datable basis through to the third or second century BCE.[24]

Now, one would expect that such an approach to the book would produce an inevitable fragmentation, especially if it is coupled with an assumption (still far too strong in biblical criticism) that what is earliest is the most authentic and genuine. Indeed, fragmentation is one of the well-known outcomes of historical-critical analysis. All we are left with is a text broken in little pieces. Another outcome is the interminable and irresolvable debates about precisely how to break up the text. Or, rather, how many layers do we have and how do they relate to each other? For example, I was taught that the prose-prologue and epilogue were actually later accretions to the poetic text. And, in a typical twist, the folktale may be old (but then who really knows?) but it was added at a later date. Necessary as such engagements may be, they are also highly hypothetical. With nothing more than the text in hand (there is simply no external evidence as to how Job might have come together or when it was written), historical critics have notoriously claimed a 'scientific' status for their work. Even now, when it is on the defensive, I still hear, all too often, the claim that such an approach is 'real' biblical criticism. Negri neatly sidesteps the quagmire of such minute arguments, a quagmire that has swallowed up more than one promising mind.

For all his obligatory nods to historical-critical positions concerning Job, to the point of listing in his bibliography some of the main commentators on Job, Negri is by no means beholden to them. In fact, when I first read his text, I thought he was opting for a poetic-literary coherence characteristic of some of the newer literary readings. Influenced in part by the 'new criticism', as well as a half-concealed reverence for the text that was proclaimed in terms of literary artistry and the compositional skill of the supposed authors, one branch of the newer approaches argues strenuously for a deeper coherence and integrity of the biblical texts that had been torn to pieces by historical

---

[24] For all of this see Negri 2009, pp. 2–3.

criticism.[25] This seemed to be Negri's path. Add to it the names of some of the commentators whom he invokes and the picture looks complete. We find Norman Habel's commentary,[26] a curious work that attempts to use narrative theory in order to interpret a poetic text, but a work that does argue for the composite integrity of Job. More regular than Habel is Samuel Terrien's sensitive commentary.[27] Terrien is no hack, having written some very fine work, but he also a theologian. He has written variously an atlas of the Bible for children, works on music and worship and two well-known books on biblical theology.[28] From this background, Terrien is keen to find texts from the Bible that are – to put it bluntly – good for you if you read them. For all my enjoyment of Terrien in the 1980s, when his work was quite popular, he always struck me as a bit of SNAG (sensitive new-age guy).

Despite the number of times Negri defers to Terrien's judgement, he sidesteps those more 'snaggy' bits. Indeed, although Negri initially seemed to me to be opting for a poetic-literary position of integrity and coherence, or even a theological assumption concerning the text's deeper role for good, he does neither of these things. Instead, what we find is an argument for *philosophical* coherence. Let me give a few examples. When he broaches the supposedly final and late-layer addition of the 'Hymn to Wisdom' in Job 28, he writes:

> It is almost certainly a passage inserted very late into the book of Job – perhaps the very last of the additions to the text. But, like the other additions, *a logical and fitting one* – this, and only this, interests us.[29]

The issue with which the wisdom-hymn must deal is: who is God if he is not a just judge? Negri makes a similar move for philosophical integrity

[25] See especially Alter 1981; Alter 1985; Polzin 1980; Polzin 1989; Polzin 1993.
[26] Habel 1975.
[27] Terrien 1963; Terrien 2004a. Terrien also provides Negri with useful surveys of positions and a rather full bibliography (for the time at least). Negri also relies heavily on Italian materials, especially when working with the text since he does not have Hebrew. For example, in a note on p. 41 he refers to Gianfranco Ravasi, *Giobbe, Commenti biblici*, Rome: Borla, 1984, pp. 527ff., and the summary of 'the best of the research' he finds there. In a subsequent communication with me, Negri points out that, while in Paris writing his book on Job, he made use of the Dominican Le Sauchoir Library, which assisted him in overcoming, in some respects, his sense of working in a field outside his own. I would actually argue that this situation is to Negri's benefit, since he is not tied to the expectations and limits of biblical criticism, especially those critics with some religious commitment to the Bible as sacred text.
[28] Terrien 1972; Terrien 1986; Terrien 1994; Terrien 2004b; Terrien 1978.
[29] Negri 2009, p. 45; emphasis added.

when he engages with the wonderful figures of Leviathan and Behemoth and related cosmogonic content (the supposed third layer): 'There should be little doubt about where I place myself on the question of the interpretations of these passages: where we are led necessarily by philology we are also led by *strictly poetic and philosophical considerations*'.[30] Then again, in relation to Elihu's speeches (fourth layer of the text):

> In whatever manner things stand, I am interested in studying these discourses for what is said in them, for the further, strong variant that they insert in the *philosophical architecture* of the book of Job. These discourses are in fact far from being simply an internal articulation of the text; *they represent rather a new critical position*.[31]

So, we have a collection of observations – a logical and fitting addition, philosophical considerations, a new critical position within the philosophical architecture – that really point toward an argument for philosophical integrity. Each new insertion or each new layer on the historical-critical reconstruction of the text actually becomes an effort to deal with the problems that have arisen from the previous insertion or layer. In short, what Negri has done is absorb the historical fragmentation and layering of the text, bounce off the literary and the theological arguments for coherence and then make his own argument for philosophical integrity. Not a bad way to move, if you ask me.

To sum up, Negri's philosophical commentary is the outcome of various efforts to deal with tensions in his reading of Job. His initial step is to focus on the biblical text and keep the philosophers in the background (the 'Notes'). But this then leads him into an ongoing tension over method within biblical studies: either the fragmented layering and insertions of historical-critical readings or the poetic coherence of literary and, indeed, theological readings. Here, he takes on board the first, listens closely to the second and then argues for his own brand of philosophical integrity. What we end up with is a philosophical commentary that faces the text and mediates the critical positions it generates. Implicitly, this position is also a challenge to the age-old assumption of the origins of theology: the Bible might have supplied the stories but the philosophy

---

[30] Negri 2009, p. 52; emphasis added.
[31] Negri 2009, p. 63; emphasis added.

comes from the Greeks. The blending of the two in the first centuries of the common era produced that unique discipline known as theology. By contrast, for Negri, a text like Job is a fully fledged philosophical text.

Kairós *and* ákairos

> Religion is a big rip-off in itself, but it can also be a great instrument of liberation.[32]

What does this philosophical commentary find in Job? I focus on two key features which will turn out to be closely connected to one another: the opposition between measure [*misura*] and immeasure [*dismisura*] and the question of *kairós*. Briefly put, for Negri, (im)measure is the thread – much like a necklace – that strings together value, labour, pain, ontology, time, power, evil, theodicy, creation and cosmogony. It is a complex opposition that has both positive and negative registers for each term, with Negri searching for a way beyond the negative senses of measure and immeasure – as oppressive order and unending evil – to find more positive senses. As for *kairós*, it falls into a rather conventional sense of the opportune time and thereby, via the New Testament, the time of crisis, the end-times with their trials and hopes. Or, in Negri's words, *kairós* is a time of rupture, an 'exemplary temporal point'.[33] Immediately, we face a problem, for even though I seek to connect (im)measure and *kairós*, Negri does not do so himself. So, I have some work to do, tracing how these terms are involved in an intimate embrace. In what follows, I begin with *kairós*, exploring what Negri both does and does not say about the term, before offering a rereading of *kairós* that will bring it into the arms of (im)measure.

For Negri's most compelling statement concerning *kairós*, we need to turn for a moment to another study, the extraordinary *Kairós, Alma Venus, Multitudo*. Here, two comments capture his effort to reshape time as *kairós*: it is the 'moment when the arrow of Being is shot' and it is 'the immeasurability of production between the eternal and the *to-come*'.[34] The first picks up

---

[32] Negri and Scelsi 2008, p. 205.
[33] See Negri and Defourmantelle 2004, pp. 104–6; Negri 2003, p. 152.
[34] Negri 2003, pp. 154, 180, and Negri and Defourmantelle 2004, p. 104. See also Negri 2008a, p. 97; Hardt and Negri 2004, p. 357.

the sense of the 'exemplary temporal point'. *Kairós* is an opening up in time that is eminently creative; it is the edge of time when Being is created. Two brief comments in Negri's conversations with Anne Defourmantelle reveal the obvious theological connection: we are always at the point of creativity; it is the moment each day when, 'one creates God': everything one does is a creation of God, since 'to create new Being is to create something that, unlike us, will never die'.[35] Further, this process of creativity is marked by naming, especially the common name. In *Kairós, Alma Venus, Multitudo* Negri observes without comment, 'Whatever thing I name exists'.[36] In case we missed the gloss on Genesis 1, when God names the items of creation, and Genesis 2, when Adam names the animals, Negri makes it explicit in his discussion with Anne Defourmantelle: 'Naming is at once the Bible and what makes epistemology possible'.[37]

The second comment I quoted above – 'between the eternal and the *to-come*' – constitutes Negri's challenge to the measurable piling up of time as past, present and future, in which our present is a moving point between the fixed detritus of the past (to be collated, measured and studied by historiography, to be celebrated in triumph or mourned as disaster) and the future (as a repeat performance of the past). Instead, he proposes that the 'before' should be understood as the sign of eternity – time rests in the eternal – and that the 'after' must be recast as the 'to-come'. Once again, it is not difficult to pick up a theological undertone: *kairós* operates not merely *sub specie aeternatis*, for it is part of eternity; from that context *kairós*, as a perpetual moment of creativity, looks towards an eschatological 'to-come'. In its passage, *kairós* gathers more and more features: it is immeasurably productive, the home of living labour, restlessly in motion, multiple, common, the source of joy, corporeal and material, and thereby resists domination and oppression.

Despite all this compelling energy, Negri still rests with a very temporal *kairós*, opposing it to chronological time and then attempting to reshape it in terms of revolutionary creativity and desire. Indeed, his book on Job shows how regular Negri's approach to *kairós* really is.[38] For Negri, Job provides an energetic counter to the idea that time is empty, static and measured. This

---

[35] Negri and Defourmantelle 2004, pp. 146–7.
[36] Negri 2003, p. 147.
[37] Negri and Defourmantelle 2004, p. 119.
[38] Negri 2009, pp. 83–6.

sense of time came into its own only with neo-Platonic thought, when time became abstract, a form of being, transcendent and dominating – precisely when Christianity became the dominant ideological force of empire. What does Negri find in Job? Here, time is concrete, lived, painful, common, immanent and even filled with theophany; it is a stark contrast with abstract and dominating time. In particular, the time of Job is characterised by rhythm, movement and event (what Negri calls time-movement). In short, it is ontological time. Is this notion of time really in Job? It is when you take pain and death – and, here, Negri is able to deal with death in a way that few materialists are able to do – as the basis for understanding time as the common reality of our existence and as the source of the desire and power to eliminate such suffering. More specifically, Negri argues that, in Job, time is both a being towards death (he quotes Job 7: 4, 6–8 and 9: 25–6) and a fullness and state of happiness (now it is 29: 2–6). As content and part of existence, this time in Job is the point of contact between lived, concrete time and the linear movement of divine epiphany – here, earth and heaven touch. This is, of course, *kairós*, which now becomes the point of contact between Job's lived time of pain and divine epiphany, the creative labour of suffering opening out to liberation. This ontology of time is nothing less than the 'immeasurable opening of *kairós*'.

These arguments are variations on a persistent motif, *kairós* as the time of crisis and as a period of what can only be described as opportune, revolutionary time. With some modifications, we find comparable arguments in Walter Benjamin (blast and flash), Giorgio Agamben (time that remains), Alain Badiou (event and laicised grace), Ernst Bloch (*Novum* and *Ultimum*), apocalypse and rupture (Fredric Jameson). However, on this score, the New Testament bears heavy responsibility.[39] In that collection of texts, *kairós* may mean the period when fruit becomes ripe, a season (spring, autumn and so on), the time of birth or death, the present, a designated period that is more often signalled by the plural, *kairoí*. But the term also identifies a specific moment, often in the dative 'at the right time', which may be opportune or favourable, or it may be dire and risky. However, increasingly, the word takes the definite article, 'the time [*ho kairós*]', and, in this form, its sense is the time of crisis or the last times. So it becomes one of the New Testament's major eschatological

---

[39] See Kittel, et al. 1985, pp. 389–90; Barr 1969.

terms, specifying the longed-for, albeit troubled, time of final conflict, the end of history, the reign of the Evil One and Christ's return to vindicate the faithful. These senses dominate, for good or ill, our sense of *kairós*, holding up and restricting *kairós* as a term devoted to time and gathering the semantic field around that point.

However, in order to undermine the surreptitious dominance of the New Testament on our perceptions of *kairós*, I would like to move back to classical Greece. And, there, a few surprises await us. To begin with, *kairós* is not only a term of time but also of *place*. The temporal sense is largely the same as the one I have explored above – the right, critical and proper time or season. For a largely agricultural economy, *kairós* indicates the right season for planting or reaping, with a particular emphasis on the time the fruit is ripe, so much so that *kairós* also bears the sense of fruitfulness and advantage. But, in its spatial sense, *kairós* designates what is in or at the right place, particularly in terms of the body. *Kairós* and especially its adjective, *kaírios*, designate a vital part of the body. For example, in Homer's *Iliad*, the adjective is used to mark the right place on the body for an arrow to find its mark. And, in the works of Pindar, Aeschylus and Euripides, the word means a target, especially on the body in battle: it is the point where a weapon can inflict the most damage.[40]

What are we to make of this extended sense of *kairós*, one that goes well beyond time? To begin with, both temporal and spatial senses of the term find their basis in the meaning of measure, proportion or fitness. As time, *kairós* is, then, a distinct measure or the appropriateness of time – the exact, critical and opportune time. As place, it becomes measured space, as well as the way space is proportioned, preferably 'correctly' when one refers to the body where everything is in its right place. It takes little imagination to see that such a kairological, that is, properly-proportioned, body would be a male body, athletic, warlike and virile. There is a distinct sense that *kairós* actually refers to what is in its right place and time, duly measured, appropriate and opportune. Indeed, although *kairós* takes on a range of meanings – convenience, decorum, due measure, fitness, fruit, occasion, profit, proportion, propriety, symmetry, tact, wise moderation, as well as opportunity, balance, harmony, right and/or proper time, opening, timeliness – the semantic cluster coalesces around the idea of what is duly measured and proportional, in

---

[40] See Onians 1973, pp. 343–7; Rickert 2007, p. 72.

short, the right time and right place. As Hesiod puts it in *Works and Days*: 'Observe due measure, and proportion [*kairós*] is best in all things'.[41]

Not quite the sense of *kairós* to which we have become accustomed – due measure and proportion. Yet, given this fuller meaning of *kairós*, a question lurks in the shadows of this classical *kairós*: what is its opposite? Not *kronos*, and thereby chronological time – the standard line in most philosophies of time (including Negri's) that seek to oppose *kairós* and *kronos* – for *kronos* became a byword for an old fool or dotard, especially in the comedies of Aristophanes. As a proper name, Kronos is, as is well known, the father of Zeus; but he also designates that period before our era, the distant past which may be either a golden age or the dark ages, depending on one's perspective.

Instead of *kronos*, the opposite of *kairós* is determined by a series of prepositions: *apó kairoû*, away or far from *kairós*; *parà kairón*, to the side of or contrary to *kairós*; *pró kairoû*, before *kairós* or prematurely; *kairoû péra*, beyond measure, out of proportion and unfit. These senses all bear the weight of what is outside the zone of *kairós*, untimely and out of place. But these various senses of what is opposed to *kairós* gather together under the term *ákairos*. If *kairós* designates the well-timed, opportune and well-placed, then *ákairos* means the ill-timed, inopportune and displaced. I cannot emphasise enough how important this opposite of *kairós* is: over against measure we have beyond measure; timely versus untimely; in the right place versus the wrong place. One who is *ákairos* is in the wrong place at the wrong time. This opposition will become vitally important soon enough when I return to Negri.

Before I do, one or two further points demand attention. Too often, commentators neglect the unavoidable economic dimensions of *kairós*, especially with its agricultural flavour. In this case, as the quote above from that agricultural text par excellence, Hesiod's *Works and Days*, indicates, *kairós* means the right season of the year for planting, cultivating and harvesting crops and fruit. But it also indicates the right place, due to soil, landform and amount of moisture, for planting a particular crop or orchard. But now, the economic sense explodes well beyond these agricultural references. I would suggest it beats a path to a collection of terms in Greek that have simultaneous moral, class- and economic dimensions. *Kairós* and *ákairos* join words such as *agathos* and

---

[41] Hesiod 1973, p. 81. Translation by Rickert 2007, p. 72. On *kairós*, see further Rickert 2007; Carter 1988; Untersteiner 1954; Kinneavy 1983; Sipiora and Baumlin 2002.

kakos, good and bad, as well as a host of related terms, in which moral and class-status, as well as physical appearance are closely interwoven – good vs. bad, wealthy vs. poor, noble vs. ignoble, brave vs. cowardly, well-born vs. ill-born, blessed vs. cursed, lucky vs. unlucky, upright vs. lowly, élite vs. masses, pillars of society vs. dregs, beautiful vs. ugly.[42] It soon becomes apparent how the spatial sense of *kairós*, with a focus on the human body as one that is appropriately proportioned with every item in its 'proper' place, also has a class-sense. The (male) body out of proportion, one that is 'ugly' and ill-formed, is also the body of the poor, exploited majority of Greek society – what, following Negri, we might call the monstrous.[43] From here, *kairós* may also, in connection with this cluster of other terms, apply to social measure and order. A kairological social order has everything in its proper place – aristocratic élites, exploited peasants, driven slaves, women and so on. It goes without saying that such a proportioned and fit society, one characterised by *'eugenia'*, ensures the ruling élite remain precisely where they are. Disorder and immeasure, what is contrary to *kairós* and thereby *ákairos*, designate an unfit society, one in turmoil and on the rocks, when time is out of joint and events take place outside their proper time and season.

Is not the wildcat-strike an excellent example of *ákairos*? For Negri and his comrades, of course, the industrial involvement of the 1960s and 1970s, with its ongoing battles and wildcat-strikes, was a key component in the development of workerism, or *operaismo*. And, for the ferociously independent Georges Sorel, the strike was as much a potent political weapon as it was a myth.[44] This great admirer of action over against contemplation saw in the general strike the most forceful weapon in the war of socialism against capitalism. And both Negri and Sorel still have a point, given the way business and the owners of capital seek to curtail the possibility of the strike. While we still see the use of scab-labour to replace striking workers, in our own time the big end of town prefers to pressure governments to enact more and more

[42] See Ste. Croix 2006, pp. 338–9, who provides a host of related terms: *hoi tas ousias echontes, plousioi, pacheis, eudaimones, gnōrimoi, eugeneis, dunatoi, dunatōtatoi, kaloi kagathoi, chrēstoi, esthloi, aristoi, beltistoi, dexiōtatoi, charientes, epieikeis* – all for the 'good' propertied classes; for the 'bad' unpropertied classes we have *hoi penētes, aporoi, ptōchoi, hoi polloi, to plēthos, ho ochlos, ho dēmos, hoi dēmotikoi, mochthēroi, ponēroi, deiloi, to kakiston*. See also Ste. Croix 1972, pp. 371–6.
[43] Negri and Casarino 2008, pp. 193–218.
[44] Sorel 1961. For Sorel, the myth of the general strike, with its collective, motivational and irrefutable nature, was as necessary and as powerful as the act itself.

legislation in order to restrict the strike to an appropriate time. They say: you may strike only at this point [*kairós*] in the process of negotiating a new award; before or after is illegal and you will be charged. The untimely, *ákairos*-strike must be brought to order, allotted its place and time.

Kairós has turned out to be far more multifaceted than we might have expected. Not content to be restricted to a temporal register, it has now spilled out to include agricultural and bodily spaces, the sense of measure and then blurted out its sinister class-allegiances. In this light, any alignment with or appropriation of *kairós* is a risky move to make. For the invocation of *kairós* runs the danger of siding unwittingly with the well-proportioned over against ill-fashioned bodies, ruling élites rather than downtrodden peasants and slaves; in short, with the interweaving of moral, economic and biological factors, *kairós* sides with the good, beautiful, well-born, wealthy and educated aristocrats. In this wider context, my own political options are clear: I would rather join the bad boys and girls, ugly bodies, poor peasants, cowardly slaves, ill-born labourers, cursed, unlucky and lowly masses, in short, the dregs of society. And this means that I side with what is contrary to and beyond *kairós*, with *akairós*, with what is untimely and out of place.

Now that we thrown in our lot with *ákairos*, what are the implications for Negri's use of *kairós*? Should we dispense with them as weighed down too heavily with a theological heritage of opportune or exemplary time, at the edge of creation? Or should we rough it up – shirt torn, pants filthy, black-market cigarette scrounged from a passer-by – and cross to the wrong side of the tracks, taking *kairós* into the zones of *ákairos*? I prefer the latter, but, in order to do so, I draw upon the opposition between measure [*misura*] and immeasure [*dismisura*] that is central to his exegesis of the book of Job. I am intrigued: measure-immeasure immediately connects with my earlier discussion of the base sense of *kairós-ákairos*; yet Negri makes nothing of the link (I can only assume he is not aware of it). So let us see what happens when we bring the two together.

Measure and immeasure

However, before I make the connection, I need ask what Negri does with measure and immeasure. This opposition may be regarded as a substantial realignment of some old philosophical distinctions, especially those between eternity and contingency, universal and particular and, on a theological or mythical register, of chaos and order – a basic motif of myths of creation and one that both is central to the book of Job and has significant political ramifications. In the commentary on the book of Job, measure-immeasure also becomes the means of reorganising an impressive string of topics: value, labour, pain, ontology, time, power, evil, theodicy, creation and cosmogony.[45] I would like to focus on three items in relation to measure and immeasure: their changing values in Negri's interpretation; their intersection with the themes of chaos and creative order; and their overlap (unbeknownst to Negri) with *kairós*.

To begin with, Negri (through Job) dismisses all forms of measure and comes out as a champion of immeasure. However, this is only the beginning; although Negri wants to dispense with a negative, retributive measure in favour of a creative immeasure, that chaotic moment is only a transition to a new, positive form of measure. That is to say, by the time Negri draws near to the end of his commentary on Job the valuation of measure and immeasure shifts: at first, measure is negative and immeasure positive, but when we encounter a negative immeasure, a new, creative measure begins to appear.

As for measure, it affects the crucial categories of value, labour, time, ethics, justice, good and evil. And it does so through the filter of retribution, which turns up in the mouths of Job's erstwhile legal friends, Eliphaz and Zophar. The logic of retribution goes as follows: if I perform an evil act, I will be punished for it; so also with a good act. Balance is the key: evil at one moment will find an equal measure (now as retribution) at another moment; so also will good eventually produce a balance of good in the moment of reward. Ergo, if Job is suffering, he must have done something evil to deserve it, even if he does not know what that evil act is. In other words, one can measure evil and good in neat quantities.[46] So also with justice, which becomes a simple formula that matches the correct measure of reward or punishment for the act in question. Or ethics, which becomes a calculation of the balance of good and evil and which, along with justice, provides us with vital advice as to how we should live our lives. In our own day, we can add labour and time: our economic

---

[45] In *The Porcelain Workshop*, he designates the immeasurable, or measurelessness [*démesure*], as excess. See Negri 2008a, p. 39.

[46] Although Elihu, the fourth interlocutor, is not part of the original circle of three, his argument for transcendent providence and Job's pride is for Negri the last possible moment of rationalisation (Negri 2009, pp. 63–9).

system relies on the ability to calculate how much labour is spent on a job, how overtime is to be calculated, what the right wage is for the labour-time sold, with heavy emphasis at the moment on the measurement of immaterial labour, and so on. It is all so simple – even the eternal conundrum of theodicy ceases to be a problem, for it is merely a question of calculated and quantifiable measure. The operation of retributive measure seems so common sense, working its way into the smallest mundane acts: the cost of a loaf of bread, whether I should reciprocate that invitation from people I cannot stand, the grades a child receives at school – the *lex talionis* of everyday life.

Job's response is simply to dismiss any form of measure in these situations. In reply, Bildad, the third 'friend', tries to compensate for the loss of measure. Bildad advocates an over-charged and extra-transcendent God (Negri calls this over-determined approach the 'mystical deception') who comes in as an enticement to and guarantee for worthiness. All one can do before such a God is surrender and offer devotion and adoration. Or, as Negri points out, it is a craven apologia for dictatorial power. Job's perpetual refusal to acknowledge either a system of retribution or an over-charged deity who commands devotion simply does not compute for his friends: 'When Job decisively rejects the transcendent motif as well, his lawyers – who are on the brink of becoming his ideological enemies – accuse him of titanic *hybris*'.[47]

One term from my original list of items which are strung together under the theme of measure-immeasure is left: value. Superficially, Negri is after another theory of value, especially since he is scathing about the Marxist labour-theory of value. One can no longer measure labour-power (x hours in the working day), surplus-value (x+ hours and greater efficiency within those hours, i.e. absolute and relative surplus-value), or, indeed, exchange- and use-values. They are all so much scrap-iron. One of Negri's tasks is to find a completely new theory of value and Job is one of those enlisted to help him do it. Quite straightforward, it would seem: a recovery of value without measure. The catch is that this is not the only sense of value operating in Negri's text. Alongside the economic one, there is also an ethical one: the labour-theory of value slips into an ethical code of value and back again.

On this ethical calculus, what is the value of labour? It is evil, argues Negri. And it is evil precisely because labour is subject to immeasurable exploitation.

---

[47] Negri 2009, p. 38.

Now, we need to pay very close attention, for the argument has some sharp turns and we need to choose our path with care. Negri wishes to recover value, to rescue it from its subservience to measure, control or limit. He proposes to do so via the theological narrative 'of an immensely powerful, creative ontology that emerges from chaos'.[48] This slow process involves Job gaining power in his stand against God, which requires, as it were, a return to the chaos that precedes creation and a re-creation of the world from the ground up. A tall order, perhaps, but Negri sees it in Job and wants it for his own time.

However, in the process of making this argument, the opposition between measure and immeasure begins to shift. It happens first with immeasure. One's initial impression is that Negri attaches a positive value to immeasure and a negative one to measure. Chaos, in other words, is good and order not so much. But, when Negri mentions that exploitation itself is immeasurable, this all-too-convenient opposition starts to break down. Add to this the immeasurable nature of evil,[49] which, in itself, questions the realms of reason and measure, and we have a different ball-game entirely.

The more conventional track from this point is to attribute this immeasurable exploitation and evil to the unsettling realm of chaos and then seek out order in response as some way of controlling such evil. Social sanctions, the law, police and army all play this role, attempting to keep a lid on the riotous riff-raff on the streets. But Negri is not interested in that path – he has suffered too much at the hands of the forces of order. Instead, he fixes on the immeasurable nature of pain and suffering – the central topic of Job – and argues that the only way to overcome the immensity of evil is through the immeasurability of pain. Only when we have descended into the depths of immeasurable, undeserved and guiltless pain are we able to get anywhere at all. From the midst of this undeserved suffering, power first emerges, a power that is creative. In short, one immeasurable force responds to and is greater than another; endless suffering and pain overcomes immeasurable evil and exploitation.

Even more, pain leads to the creative power of labour. So, the opposition shifts again: the immeasurableness of evil now finds itself face to face with

---

[48] Negri 2009, p. 73.
[49] Negri 2009, pp. 8–9.

the immeasurable creative power of labour. The stakes are high, for, on the one side, we find God. In a move reminiscent of Ernst Bloch, God becomes the name for all that is oppressive. So, even though the book is set up as a struggle between God and man, it is a very unequal struggle. God, it would seem, is far too powerful, or, as Negri puts it, immeasurable, imbalanced, dispro-portionate.[50] Since God's plays the role of both judge and an adversary who laughs sarcastically at an increasingly rebellious Job, God actually takes the side of oppression: 'God is the seal of the clearest, fiercest, deepest of social injus-tices (Chapter 24 screams forth human anger and desperation in this regard – from within the darkness, the misery and the most terrible unhappiness)'.[51] In other words, in contrast to the measured God of the scholastic theologians for whom God was an ordered being with fixed characteristics,[52] this God of Job is the site of immeasurable evil. A quick survey of Christian or indeed Jewish or Islamic history (the three religions that claim Job as a sacred text) leads to quick agreement with such an observation: persecutions, Inquisitions, Cru-sades, jihads, genocides, wars on terror and dispossessions in the name of God only begin the list.

In response to the firepower of evil, Negri piles up as many desirable terms as he can on the side of immeasurable pain: power, creation, love, labour, democracy (pain is democratic over against fear which is dictatorial), com-munity, time (as a concrete, lived and common reality which can lead to a time for liberation), value and, later than the book on Job, the common.[53] In a sentence: the value of labour may be found in democratic pain and suffering which produces the power of creative labour. This lived experience is quite literally *ontology*. So it not merely immeasure that has value over against mea-sure, but, rather, two types of immeasure, the one evil, oppressive and divine and the other chaotic, creative, powerful, and … good. Soon enough, I will stitch this sense of immeasure in with what I have called *akairós*, but note what has happened: measure has been revalued. Not restricted to the dread-ful patterns of payback, in which reward and punishment are appropriate to the initial act, measure has been dismantled and reshaped for a new task. This

[50] Negri 2009, pp. 28–9.
[51] Negri 2009, p. 43.
[52] Negri and Defourmantelle 2004, p. 80.
[53] The common, as an 'antagonistic and/or multitudinous construction' is 'the reconstruction of different measure' (Negri 2008a, p. 75).

294 • Chapter Seven

powerful and creative ontology that emerges from chaos is comparable to the chaotic immeasure that precedes creation so that the world may be re-created from the beginning. In other words, through the two types of immeasure, one evil and oppressive and the other creative and powerful, a new measure emerges, the creation of a very different and just order.

Let me summarise the moves as follows: negative measure $\Rightarrow$ negative immeasure $\Rightarrow$ positive immeasure $\Rightarrow$ positive measure. If we think that a retributive system of carefully measured patterns of labour, time and value is bad enough, then we are in for a shock; immeasurable labour and exploitation are far worse. Yet, in the midst of this untold pain and suffering, a new creative power emerges, one that will lead to a thoroughly new measure, a new order that has nothing to do with the old.

The politics of cosmogony

> Even the old God of Genesis, not at all inclined to benevolence, was satisfied
> with his work.[54]

That is all very well, but is not the far more interesting moment that of immeasure? I must confess to being drawn to immeasurability rather than some search for a new measure, particularly because Negri's terminology overlaps significantly with that old mythological (and biblical) pattern of chaos and created order. Indeed, a politics of myth and of cosmology surges beneath Negri's text.

As far as myth is concerned, Negri's interpretation of Job in terms of measure and immeasure, pain and release, evokes the mythical pattern of descent and return. It has many variations, but it comes back to the same rhythm. It may be pain that leads to power, suffering to creation, sacrifice to liberation, abjection to exultation, torture to salvation, or death to resurrection. This is the fundamental pattern of Negri's argument: immeasurable evil is overcome by the creative power of labour. Indeed, at the close of the book, he invokes precisely this pattern, but now in a theological key:

> We can see no better way to periodise the time within which we live than
> through the analogy with the suffering and resurrection of Job. And it

---

[54] Negri and Casarino 2008, p. 216.

appears beautiful to us to conceive of redemption as the growth of our passion. Of course, it is paid for by an even higher possibility of suffering. But who, through historical avarice, would refuse us this happiness on the basis that its flower is full of thorns? Or refuse communism because the path that leads to it passes through Behemoth and Leviathan?[55]

This pattern is not new, by any means, nor is it exclusively Christological. You will find it in the earliest myths and in the latest propaganda put forward by one politician after another – pain now for a glorious future. The Jewish myth of oppression and exodus, exile and restoration, or, indeed, the Christ-myth of passion, death and resurrection are by no means the sources of this theme; they are variations on a deeper and more pervasive rhythm.[56] This mythical pattern does not need to be new in order to be effective. From oppression comes liberation; from death resurrection. The question is: does Negri or the Left in general really want to re-appropriate this mythical rhythm for its own agenda?

Even more, I wonder whether Negri wants to bring about another created order that overcomes chaos. Now, the thread of the measure-immeasure contrast starts to show its deeper layers. I am interested here in the way Negri sinks himself into the matter of cosmogony and how the opposition of immeasure and measure becomes one between chaos and order. There are more than enough suggestions in Negri's text for the connection between immeasure and chaos. For instance, the primeval beasts of chaos, Leviathan and Behemoth, appear without measure. Indeed, at this point, his ambiguous reference to 'a great chaos, a great immeasurableness'[57] puts us squarely in the realm of the myths of creation. The basic narrative sequence of the story of creation is deceptively simple and perhaps too well known: out of chaos comes the

<hr/>

[55] Negri 2009, p. 104.
[56] It is unfortunate that Negri makes a great deal out of resurrection in his commentary on Job, especially the redemptive pattern of death-resurrection and the importance of the resurrection of the flesh. Now, I actually agree that the doctrine of the resurrection of the flesh is an important materialist affirmation (see also Negri and Defourmantelle 2004, p. 180), but it comes from Paul's letters in the New Testament, not from Job, for this text speaks of death and resurrection neither for the individual nor for a collective at the end of the age. Despite the attention Negri devotes to the idea (a whole section of Chapter 5), it does not belong in a commentary on Job. Like hell and the sufferings in that abode, the belief in resurrection emerges a few centuries later.
[57] Negri 2009, p. 52.

careful ordering of creation in which every thing finds its place. We might fill
out this bare structure with all manner of detail – chaos may be the destructive
force of older, cranky gods, as in the Mesopotamian creation-myth, *Enuma
Elish*, or it may be the formless and void state of the 'deep', the *tehom*, in the
account of Genesis 1, or it may be the pure absence of apparent form and
clear demarcation, the proverbial primeval swamp. In response to such chaos,
creation involves victory over chaos (variously, a monster, the sea, a serpent,
an older opponent from an earlier generation of the gods), the demarcation
of heaven and earth, planets in their paths, seasons at the right time, and the
careful ordering of created life, usually in some form of hierarchy that places
humans at the top or, as is more often the case, subordinates human beings to
the gods. Or, we might turn to the flood-narrative of Genesis 6–9 for another
version of the same story: the initial creation (measure) has turned out to be
flawed, characterised by extraordinary evil and exploitation. In order to begin
again, God makes use of a beneficial chaos (the flood) to wipe out the old
and begin again with a new, created order. Or, in Negri's own take on this
narrative, when 'measure fades into the disorder of the universe and evil is
reflected in chaos, in the immeasurable',[58] we need 'the collective creation of a
new world' that 'is able to reconstitute a world of values'.[59]

The effect of these mythological connections is to highlight the way cosmogonic myths are inherently political. The crucial questions are: is it chaos
that is revolutionary or is it (re-)creation? Translated into Negri's terms: is
immeasure the truly revolutionary moment, or is that moment found in
another form of measure? Negri wants a new creation that emerges out of
immeasurable chaos, and he wants to claim it for radical politics. But I am
more interested in cosmological chaos, since there is a feature of that chaos
which too often slips by without notice, camouflaged behind the screen of
natural chaos: it is also, if not primarily, a political chaos.

Once again, Negri unwittingly brings the connection to the fore,[60] although
now in his opposition between eugenics and the monster, the one a favoured
theme from the Greeks onwards (meaning to be well-born, good and
beautiful – note the connections with *kairós*) and the other a marker of what

---

[58] Negri 2009, p. 49. This comment relates to Job 28: 23–7.
[59] Negri 2009, p. 14.
[60] Negri and Casarino 2008, pp. 193–218.

resists. In the creation-myths, the monster is, of course, the one that must be overcome through the creation of order. These stories of creation are usually depicted as cosmogonic (creation of the natural world), theogonic (creation of the gods) and anthropogonic (human beings come into the picture). Nice and neat, but far too limited, for they are also what I would like to call poligonic.[61] They deal with the origins of, and thereby provide ideological justification for, the current political and social order. For instance, the Mesopotamian myth *Enuma Elish* is keen to point out that the Babylonian king is a direct descendent of Marduk, the warrior- and creator-god, and the myth spends a good deal of time with the ordering of society, the construction of Babylon and the establishment of the state. Similarly, the creation-story in the Bible does not end with the seven days of Genesis 1 or indeed the alternative story of Genesis 2 with its more earthy narrative of the garden. It runs all the way through the stories of the patriarchs and matriarchs (Abraham and Sarah, Isaac and Rebekah, Jacob and Leah and Rachel, and then the twelve sons and one daughter, Dinah), the migration to Egypt, Moses and the Exodus, wilderness wandering and formation of a state in waiting, and then ends with the conquest of the Promised Land. In other words, it is primarily a political myth of creation. So, if created order means political order, then the chaos against which that order continually struggles is as much political as it is natural. Primeval abyss and catastrophic flood are inseparable from disobedience regarding the tree of good and evil in the garden, from murmuring and insurrection in the wilderness, from the perpetual challenges to the divinely-given power of Moses and so on.

Now, at last, I can come back to the matter of *kairós*, which begins to look rather different from my initial foray into Negri's treatment of that theme. Two lines intersect at this point: the extraordinary way measure slots into *kairós*, immeasure into *ákairos*; and the way in which chaos and order have an inescapably political dimension. As for the first line, recall that the base sense of *kairós* is indeed measure, and that the temporal and spatial senses of the term are modifications on this basic sense. *Kairós* is both the properly proportioned body (physical, political and social) and the right or opportune time. It takes little imagination to see that the myths of creation – especially in their poligonic dimension – express this double sense of *kairós*: they provide

---

298 • Chapter Seven

narratives as to how everything finds its spatial (from the heavenly bodies through the creation of human beings to seat of power in the city) and its temporal (days, months, seasons and their proper relations) order.

What, then, is contrary to *kairós*, is outside it or far away from it, or indeed beyond *kairós*? Immeasure, obviously, or as I have called it earlier, *ákairos* – the ill-timed, unseasonable and out of place. Negri, of course, wants to find a retooled measure and indeed *kairós*, but he tarries long with immeasure, with the monstrous and thereby with *ákairos*. Here, the very political nature of chaos comes into play, for, if chaos marks the constitutive resistance to oppressive power, then we need to dwell in the midst of that chaos. Among others in the innovative *operaismo*-movement in Italy, Negri should be the one to identify most closely with such resistance; as he has argued repeatedly, state- and economic power are not givens to which people resist; no, that resistance is primary and to it oppressive political and economic power must constantly respond and adapt.[62] So it is with the narratives of chaos, which have already been joined by our comrades, immeasure and *ákairos* – the fathomless, ill-timed and displaced. We see it again and again in those creation-myths where chaos – disobedience, murmuring, insurrection, challenges to divinely appointed leaders and simple refusal – is the constitutive force that must be countered in ever new ways. But we also see it in our own day with the running riots in Paris in 2005, even in the hooligans who burn cars and smash shop-fronts, the brazen disregard for police by gangs of youths, the massed protests in Seattle, Genoa and countless other moments of anticapitalist protest. All of these are dubbed as chaotic and monstrous, threats to social order and the state, the work of thugs and criminals. They are, I would suggest, manifestations of *ákairos*.

It is time to review my argument concerning *kairós* and (im)measure. In exploring Negri's radical homiletics and philosophical commentary, we began with what turned out to be a rather conventional and biblical understanding of *kairós* – as the right season and opportune moment – only to raise questions about its moral and class-allegiances in classical Greek thought. After siding with *ákairos*, we turned to investigate the organising role of (im)imeasure in Negri's commentary on Job. But, as we did so, the close interweaving with *kairós* and *ákairos* began to emerge, so much so that we sought the political con-

---

[62] See, for example, Negri 2008a, pp. 156–7.

nections between immeasure and *ákairos*. It has been a creative engagement with Negri's commentary on Job, an effort to take a productive argument a few steps further – all by means of a book of the Bible. Here, the various lines came together, especially in the immense possibilities of immeasure, which is not only cognate with *ákairos* but also intersects with the theme of chaos as a distinctly political motif. In short, I have sided quite clearly with those who are untimely, not in the right place, chaotic and beyond measure.

Negri's *aporia*

I have drawn my major argument – the connection between *ákairos* and immeasure – out of Negri despite his own argument, seeking connections implicit within his text, a search that has also led me to read against his own take on *kairós* and even (im)measure. But does this possibility of my reading appear more obviously in Negri's text? It does and it occurs in a small but crucial moment when Negri offers what is a brilliant and original reading of the infamous 'Voice from the Whirlwind' in Job 38–41. 'Then Yahweh answered Job out of the whirlwind',[63] it begins, and from there we get a grand tour of the created universe, as well as the question thrown to Job: what is your suffering compared to all *this*?

In contrast to many opinions on this text – a useful reminder of our puny status before such powers and wonders; or the need for thanks and awe; or a useless effort at divine boasting – Negri offers a unique reading: the very fact that God actually appears is the sign of Job's victory.[64] Up until this point, God had remained conspicuously silent, not even bothering to answer Job's increasingly bitter challenges. In God's place, we found the various arguments, such as retribution (Eliphaz and Zophar), mystical overdetermination (Bildad) and transcendent providence (Elihu), each of which Job rejects. Finally, Job stings God enough to make an appearance and actually respond to the accusation. At this moment, Job triumphs. The key verse is Job 42:5: 'I had heard of thee by the hearing of the ear, but now my eye sees thee'. Job has seen God, an event that normally leads to instantaneous death. Even Moses

---

[63] Job 38: 1.

[64] 'Job is really the theory of the vision of the inside of desire – a desire that contains its object: my God, I have seen you, therefore I possess you' (Negri and Defourmantelle 2004, p. 157).

was allowed only a glimpse of the divine derriere. Job has seen God, *and* he is not bowed. As Negri puts it:

> I have seen God, thus God *is* torn from the absolute transcendence that constitutes the idea of Him. God justifies himself, thus God is dead. I have seen God, hence Job can speak of Him, and he – Job – can in turn participate in divinity, in the function of redemption that man constructs within life – the instrument of the death of God that is human constitution and the creation of the world. The materialist reading of the vision of God has, thus, the capacity to capture the creative moment of this ontological immersion of man – whether it be Adam or Job – in the relationship with the divine; and, thus, of linking ontologically – not morally, not merely intellectually – the human powers [*potenze*] to those divine, i.e., the singular in the universal.[65]

Somewhat ecstatic, is it not? In fact, the last pages of the book breathe a prophetic fire of ecstasy. Yet the point is clear: Job reaches up to God and sees him, he calls God to account and forces him to justify himself. Or, as Negri puts it elsewhere, it is the moment when 'transcendence is bent into immanence'.[66] No matter how much God tries to belittle Job, God is forced to answer Job.

Excursus on the Messiah

In a moment, I will explore a profound uncertainly in Negri's reading, but before doing so, let us explore a little what it means for Job to be the hero of the book, for he is the one who calls God to account and forces him to answer. The key-term here is messianism. Negri makes much of the messiah, claiming that the 'sense of the Messiah is present throughout the *Book of Job*',[67] a sense he tries to track in detail so that he can declare: 'In 16, 19–21 the *idea of a divine conciliator* finally appears fully-formed'.[68] Further, in Note F, we come across a short burst on the proletarian Adam and the Marxist mes-

---

[65] Negri 2009, pp. 96–7. See also Negri and Defourmantelle 2004, pp. 146–7, where Negri identifies this reaching up and bringing God down to the Spinozist re-creation of God each day through what one does.

[66] Negri and Fadini 2008, p. 667.

[67] Negri 2009, p. 69.

[68] Ibid.

siah. And this messiah certainly achieves a lot: labour can become value without measure, that is, as creative labour. How does the messiah achieve this revaluing of labour? He does so through the resurrection of the flesh, which is really, within communism, 'the sign of the resurrection of labor'.[69] Or, rather, the messiah is this sign. Finally, the messiah is the pivot on which time moves from the time of exploitation to the time of liberation, that is, from death to resurrection.

I must admit to having an innate suspicion of messiahs, especially since the Left, on occasion, succumbs to the personality-cult and expresses a deep wish to find a messiah or two.[70] It might be Eagleton's recovery from his early days in the Catholic Left of a very earthly, political Jesus of Nazareth in his latest works. Or it may be Walter Benjamin's enigmatic search for a weak messianic time, a softly-softly messiah who has always left the room the moment one arrives. Or it may be Giorgio Agamben's effort, inspired in part by Benjamin, to uncover the logic of messianic time in Paul's letters in the New Testament. As I have argued elsewhere, these messiahs fall under the strictures of Adorno's ban on idolatry and the logic of the personality.[71] At times, I wonder whether we should, as with love,[72] ban all talk of messiahs or the messianic for at least half a century.

In regard to the book of Job, Negri seems to get himself into trouble by relying too heavily on the biblical commentators, whose theological agendas betray them into finding messiahs with a distinctly Christian hue. To be

---

[69] Negri 2009, p. 72.
[70] But see Negri's warning against false prophets in Negri and Defourmantelle 2004, p. 186.
[71] Boer 2007, pp. 391–445; Boer 2009, pp. 181–204.
[72] I leave aside the comments by Negri on love, especially in the closing few pages of *Multitude* which have occasioned more critical response than the brief and unoriginal appearance warranted, since I have argued elsewhere against the political cul-de-sac of love and suggested that there should be a ban on the use and discussion of the word love for at least half a century. See Hardt and Negri 2004, pp. 351–2, 356, 358. See further Negri 2009, pp. 74–5, 98, Negri 2008a, pp. 167–8; Hardt and Negri 2000, pp. 78, 186; Negri and Defourmantelle 2004, pp. 146–7; Boer 2007a, pp. 364–71. Note that it is precisely Elihu, the fourth of Job's 'friends', who invokes love as a proposed answer. Because Job suffers from the sin of pride he can no longer experience the transcendent love of God. Indeed, only 'love could suddenly, unexpectedly, grant this prize – undeserved by Job's foolishness' (Negro 2009, p. 67). In Elihu's hands, love becomes another form of oppression and servile submission. The problem and the source of Job's sarcasm is that he is clearly *unloved* by both God and his 'friends'. God's love means nothing in a theodicy that fails to account for the unloved.

fair, these commentators actually want to correct Christian mis-readings by arguing that Christ is not at issue here; what we have is the development of a Hebrew messiah. All very well, but, after some two millennia, the search for messiahs cannot escape the Christian taint.

However, just when Negri seems to have succumbed to conventional and problematic notions of the messiah, he gives the whole idea an extraordinary twist. Although he never says so directly, Negri pushes towards the suggestion that the messianic figure is none other than Job. He is a strange messiah indeed, for rather than being some agent of God who inaugurates redemption and a new age, Job actually takes on God. The key verse is Job 19: 25: 'For I know that my redeemer [go'el] lives, and that at the last he will stand upon the earth'. As any commentary will tell you, go'el (participle of g'l) is originally someone who pays the cost to 'redeem' a dispossessed relative or property of a relative.[73] It refers to a financial transaction to meet someone's unpaid debt, usually a clan-member to keep them from debt-slavery. Of course, the term later becomes one of the metaphors used to speak of Christ's redemption on the cross – he pays the price for you and me – but in the text of Job it is someone who will come to Job's aid, someone who will stand up to God, challenge him and exonerate Job. The catch is that this redeemer is neither God nor an agent of God. Job himself comes to his own assistance, stands up to the suffering inflicted by God and challenges God to give account.

Back to the whirlwind

As brilliant as Negri's reading – in the midst of the whirlwind – of the last sections of Job might be, it faces at least two problems. Firstly, this argument for the creative sun of human beings is not so new. Marx himself became quite ecstatic when, in the first flush of Feuerbach's 'discovery' that the gods and all that they entailed were projections by human beings, he proclaimed that 'for man the root is man himself'. In contrast to the illusory sun of religion, man needs to 'revolve round himself and therefore round his true sun'.[74] And Ernst Bloch argued that, in the Bible itself, we find the 'exodus out of Yahweh', the seeds of a protest-atheism that would eventually

---

[73] For example, see Van Wolde 1997, p. 78.
[74] Marx 1975a, pp. 182 and 176; Marx 1974b, pp. 385 and 379.

depose God and allow the *homo absconditus* to emerge and stand on his or her own feet for the first time. The creative and powerful man without God would face the universe with confidence.[75] What we have in Negri's hands is a well-worn Marxist story, although he cranks it up to the mythical level of cosmogonic creativity.

The problem is that I am not sure it is the best sort of political myth Marxists would want to latch onto. The reason is that it over estimates the ability of human beings to engage in such grand creative tasks. My misgivings do not concern *hybris* (their efforts may indeed be seen as an effort to stare *hybris* in the face and say that it's a worthwhile goal) so much as a need for some modesty and awareness of limits. Far too many projects of reconstruction by the Right or the Left have ended in brutal failure for one to get too carried away by the re-creative potential of human beings.

The problem I have just outlined feeds into the second trip-wire with this argument of the re-creative power of human beings. Let us recall my earlier point about anarchism and socialism, especially the difference between revolutionary chaos and revolutionary order, or, in Negri's terms, between immeasure and measure. I have shown in some detail how Negri keeps re-valorising these terms, but, in the end, he wants a very different, re-created measure, where we find reconstituted labour, value, time and so on. In refusing the vertiginous appeal of the abyss of chaos and immeasure, Negri is, in the end, a Marxist. And the hard-nosed realists will agree: a chaotic, anarchistic agenda may be very appealing (it is for me, to some extent), but no society can function without some type of sanctions, without some order. But there is a catch. Let me put it this way: the schema of Negri's overall argument may be represented as follows: bad order ⇒ bad chaos ⇒ good chaos ⇒ good order (substitute 'measure' for 'order and 'immeasure' for 'chaos', if you so wish). What is to prevent the next step from occurring (again): good order ⇒ bad order. It is the old revolutionary problem: how do you prevent the revolution from running into the mud?

For these reasons, I prefer the undercurrent of uncertainty in Negri's text, one that draws nigh to an akairological and immeasurable reading.[76] He

---

[75] Bloch 1972; Bloch 1968.

[76] I prefer this incompleteness to his effort to claim that Job has been misinterpreted. In each case – Job is patient, his *hybris* becomes *pietas*, the text is misogynist (Mrs Job wants him to suffer) – Negri argues that there is a misrepresentation or

cannot actually close out his reading as he would like, stumbling over the famous Verse 6 in Chapter 42 of Job: 'therefore I despise myself and repent in dust and ashes'.[77] As the last line of poetry before the prose-epilogue,[78] it is supposed to sum up the vast personal-cosmic struggle of the preceding two score chapters. As might be expected, commentators have been drawn to it like bees to a honey-pot. Traditionally, the idea that Job actually 'repents' is enough of a sign that he has reconciled himself with his suffering and God and seeks forgiveness for his blasphemous challenges. Yet others have pointed out that the Hebrew is highly ambiguous and may well mean: 'therefore I reject and repent of dust and ashes', or even 'regret' or 'avenge myself on dust and ashes'. The key Hebrew words are *m's*, the meanings of which include reject and despise, and *nhm*, which covers senses such as regret, repent, have compassion, comfort oneself and avenge.[79] With these possible senses of the two key-words, a range of opposed meaning are possible: Job either despises himself and repents of dust and ashes (he gives in), or he rejects and avenges himself on dust and ashes (he does not give in). And, so, commentators line themselves up on either side: does Job actually give in and repent or does he stand up for himself and not give in? However, it seems to me that the ambiguity between repentance and resistance is crucial to this verse. It is unclear what Job the character does in response to God's rant from the whirlwind. Does he crawl to God in abject submission and repent of his rebellion? Or does he turn his back on dust and ashes and stand up to the God he has called to account?

To his credit, Negri reflects this uncertainty. It shows up first in his puzzle-ment over why Elihu in Chapters 32–7 seems to say largely the same as God himself in Chapters 39–41. Why, asks Negri, does Job reject what Elihu says but accept what God says? I would add to this something Negri, without the benefit of knowledge of Hebrew, does not pick up: the confusion in the tex-

---

even amnesia in the tradition (see Chapter 6). However, apart from the problematic separation between original text and misinterpretation, the text of Job is not quite so clearly in Negri's favour.

[77] Job 42: 6.

[78] An epilogue Negri describes brilliantly: 'The return of the folkloric discourse at the end of this enormous, cosmic, theological, human adventure is like a shower, a bath, a rest after having traversed great mountains' (Negri 2009, p. 98).

[79] Hebrew is originally a consonantal text, so convention is to cite the consonants alone, especially when referring to verbal roots.

tual status of Job. It has a very high number of *hapax legomena*, words whose meanings can only be ascertained through educated and not always reliable etymological arguments. Also, the further we delve into the book the more confused the speakers become. This is particularly true of the Elihu chapters (32–7), where Job is apparently attributed with Elihu's words and vice versa. Translations and commentators do the same as the editors of the *Marx and Engels Collected Works* – they correct these 'slips' without comment. The text, then, is not so clear and full of inconsistencies and ambivalences – Job, Yahweh and Elihu meld into one another.

Finally, Negri's discussion of the crux in Job 42: 6 – on whether Job repents of or rejects dust and ashes – shifts around a great deal. To begin with, the real problem is that Job seems to acquiesce to Yahweh, so Negri must come to terms with this outcome without the Hebrew. Then he falls back on a long quotation from Samuel Terrien's commentary, who argues that Job does not repent. After all, Negri suggests, repentance is not needed for redemption or liberation. Not altogether happy with this, he then suggests that the answer is not to be found in the words but in the vision-prophecy. Once again, Negri is not entirely satisfied, so he quotes Paul quoting Job in Galatians 1: 17–25, and then, finally, reverts to talking about the messiah. This formal uncertainty on Negri's part manifests the biblical text's own ambiguity. It is as though Negri has picked the ambiguity up at a subliminal level and then replicated in the form of his own text.

Job 42: 6 is an immeasurable verse, one that refuses to be roped into a concise, measured and kairological interpretation. Unruly and akairological, the verse leaves Negri unresolved, open, with a little more chaos than he perhaps expected. That is how it should be, it seems to me.

Conclusion

I close with a slightly different question, one that emerges from the preceding engagement: why on earth is Negri, the avowed atheist and frequent critic of the brutality sanctioned by religion, reading the Bible? One reason is that it provides him with a way to think through the brutal defeat of the Left in Italy in the 1970s – the police-roundup, court-cases, prison-terms and exile. Another is that, for this atheist, Job enables him to make some sense of Judaism and Christianity, if not his brief time with Catholic Action in the

1950s where theology and politics came into contact with one another and where the central problem of the common – community, giving a hand, love of others – first arose.[80] As he points out, he has nothing against religion, admits to an omnipresence of a pagan 'religiosity of doing' in his work, finds the ascetic tradition immensely appealing, calls for a thorough rethinking of communism comparable to the way the church-fathers reshaped Christianity in the first few centuries, admits somewhat tongue-in-cheek to having offered the smallest of prayers to his mother when in prison awaiting word on his petition for parole, and goes so far as to say that the only definition of God he is prepared to admit is one of 'overabundance, excess, and joy' – these are the 'only forms through which God can be defined'.[81] These are some of the reasons why Job draws him in, for Job is, in fact, a figure of the new militant (like Francis of Assisi),[82] one who brings transcendence to account through a sheer act of desire.

Yet two far deeper reasons inform Negri's reading of the Bible. The first concerns a long tradition of revolutionary readings of the Bible, which we have already encountered earlier in this book. The hint that Negri is aware of this tradition comes with his salute to liberation-theology's intersection with historical materialism. As I have discussed liberation-theology at length in the chapter on Michael Löwy, I see no need to repeat those points here, save to note Negri's salute:

> It is very important that we underline the convergence, through the revolutionary process, of materialist and religious thought in this reinvention of value. The Marxist thinkers of the 1930s, in the hell of fascism, the Christian authors of the 1970s, in the hell of underdevelopment, have rediscovered the same themes: it is no coincidence that Ernst Bloch has the same rhythms of the Job of the Theology of Liberation.[83]

What themes? They are the convergence of salvation and liberation and a pattern that moves from misery to liberation.[84] The allusion in this quotation

[80] Negri and Casarino 2008, pp. 41, 44.
[81] Negri and Defourmantelle 2004, p. 101. For the other observations noted in this sentence, see Negri and Defourmantelle 2004, pp. 106–7, 134; Negri and Casarino 2008, pp. 106–7, 179, 181; Negri and Scelsi 2008, pp. 26–7.
[82] Hardt and Negri 2000, p. 413.
[83] Negri 2009, p. 75.
[84] See also Negri and Scelsi 2008, pp. 158–9.

is to Ernst Bloch's *Atheism in Christianity*, especially the section on Job where Bloch argues that Job stands up to God and challenges the arrogant deity who refuses to answer and then finally tries to dismiss Job. The hero of this story is one of the bearers of the seed of atheistic rebellion, a standing on one's feet against an oppressive God of the rulers.[85] Negri ends up disagreeing with this position on Job in some respects (the dismissive deity of Chapters 38–41 is in fact one who has been called to account and squirms as a result), but he implicitly acknowledges Bloch's influence.[86] As for the phrase, 'the Job of the Theology of Liberation', I cannot avoid thinking of Gutiérrez's book, *On Job: God-Talk and the Suffering of the Innocent*,[87] even though Negri never once mentions it directly. For Gutiérrez, the issue is undeserved suffering, both that of Job and of the poor in Latin America. The answer lies in prophecy when Job moves beyond his own suffering (admittedly a consistent focus) and contemplation in response to God's own appearance in the whirlwind of Chapters 38–41.

All this discussion of liberation-theology lands us squarely in the revolutionary tradition of the religions that claim the Bible as their sacred text. This is an old theme of which we can find a hint in Marx with his comment that religious suffering is 'a *protest* against real suffering' and that religion 'is the sigh of the oppressed creature'.[88] But it was Engels who would take this idea and run with it, to the point where he sits at odds with Marx. We find the theme of revolutionary Christianity scattered throughout Engels's writings, but it culminates in one of the last texts published before he died, *On the History of Early Christianity*. Engels argues that Christianity was originally a revolutionary movement among the poor and oppressed, one that eventually won over the Roman Empire, although it lost some of its revolutionary fervour on the way and tended to offer an other-worldly solution to this world's problems.[89] Given the imprimatur of one of the founders, a series of Marxists have pursued such a theme, especially Rosa Luxemburg, Karl Kautsky, Ernst Bloch, Max Horkheimer, E.P. Thompson and, most recently, Michael Löwy.

---

[85] Bloch 1972; Bloch 1968.
[86] See Moylan 1997.
[87] Gutiérrez 1987.
[88] Marx 1975a, p. 175; Marx 1974b, p. 378.
[89] Engels 1990b; Engels 1972. See the detailed discussion of this consistent theme in Engels's writings in Boer forthcoming.

Negri, I would suggest, reads Job in a comparable fashion: this is a revolutionary text, one that seeks nothing less than a re-creation of the world. Or, rather, this is one side of his reading, for he is fully aware that the Bible, and indeed theology as a whole, also contain plenty of material that may be described as reactionary.[90] All too often, we come across the call for obedience to an oppressive ruler or God, for the subservience of slaves, the grovelling of repentance for the 'sin' of rebellion, beginning with none other than Eve and Adam in the Garden. Even in the New Testament, we find a profound tension between Paul's doctrine of grace as an undeserved and unexpected eruption and the call to obey one's rulers since they have been placed where they are by God. For these reasons, Negri has always been careful about 'continuously winking on the sly at superstition',[91] a superstition that is regressive and reactionary. Yet he also wishes that he might have been able to write a history of what he calls 'the other European civilisation',[92] a monstrous civilisation with its alternative stories, characters, needs and exigencies. At this point, Negri draws nigh unto Ernst Bloch,[93] who was keen to establish an alternative tradition, a thread of resistance, heretical, sectarian, taking myriad forms in its opposition to the dominant forms of Power and running through from the Bible into Marxism. In the same way that Bloch sought an 'exodus' out of an all-powerful and repressive Yahweh of the Bible, so also does Negri seek an exodus from and refusal of the repressive patterns of capitalism. And, like Bloch, within Negri's 'other civilisation' are Machiavelli, Spinoza (of course), Francis of Assisi, sectarian elements of Protestantism like Thomas Müntzer and heretical strains of theology that sought to bend transcendence into revolutionary immanence.[94] Job, too, joins this heretical tradition.

Another, deeper reason informs Negri's reading of the Bible; or, rather, this reason enables him to read the Bible and indeed deal with theology without succumbing to secularised theology or being trapped by the absolute truth

---

[90] 'At times there is a certain type of theology that intersects with revolutionary events. It is necessary, however, to clearly designate exactly what kind of theology we are speaking about. We must be clear here because it is equally certain that not all theologies cross revolutionary phenomena but, on the contrary, there are some theologies that cross the opposite of revolution: namely, pure ideological reproduction of Empire' (Negri and Fadini 2008, p. 666).

[91] Negri and Scelsi 2008, p. 45; see also p. 134.

[92] Negri and Casarino 2008, p. 81.

[93] See especially Negri and Fadini 2008.

[94] Negri and Fadini 2008, pp. 666–8; Negri 2008a, p. 129.

claims of theology. The key is that Negri enacts what I have called the rela-tivising of theology,[95] which negates theology's claims to both absolute truth and to the origins of much (if not all) contemporary thought. In a crucial foot-note to the essay 'Reliqua Desiderantur' in *Subversive Spinoza*,[96] Negri deals with the arguments for the continuity of theological concerns in Spinoza's secularisation of political concepts. It may be the unfolding of a theological nucleus, the internal logic of secularisation within theology, or the argument that Spinozian democracy was a result of a specific form of religious alliance and civic association. In reply, Negri initially questions whether one can guar-antee continuity across the treacherous bridge of secularisation; he suspects not. But then he takes a much stronger position, arguing that Spinoza, like Marx and Machiavelli, brings about a profound rupture with any process of secularisation or laicisation, offering a materialist and atheistic break with any theological continuity.[97] Elsewhere, he identifies this break in terms of the refusal to rely on the transcendence that bedevils Western political thought, for which transcendence is manifested in hierarchy and legitimacy. He calls this refusal of obnoxious transcendence as an 'operational materialism' and 'wholehearted atheism'.[98]

However, I suggest that Negri is pushing towards a relativisation of theol-ogy. By questioning the continuity of theology in secularisation, and especially by arguing for the profound rupture of a materialist approach, he effectively negates the claims made on behalf of theology to be the *fons et origo* of all (political) thought. And, by arguing for the brand new beginnings of Spinoza, Machiavelli[99] and Marx, he puts theology in its place as one possible mode of thinking politics, or indeed culture, economics, society and so on. Or, rather, this is how I read what he is doing, even if he pushes the argument for a profound rupture a little too hard at times. This process of relativising theol-ogy shows up time and again in his detailed engagements with Spinoza, the

[95] See Negri 2004, pp. 203–41, 49–50.
[96] Negri 2004, p. 54, n. 4. See also Negri 1991b, pp. 92–3.
[97] So also, implicitly, with the interpretation of the Bible. See Negri 2004, pp. 98–101.
[98] Negri 2004, p. 24. See also Negri and Defourmantelle 2004, p. 158.
[99] For Machiavelli, religious allegiance is subservient to the political pact. See Negri 2004, p. 54, n. 15.

comrade of Job.[100] Thus, in both *The Savage Anomaly* (itself a brilliant materialist reading of the Dutch and Spinozian anomalies) and *Subversive Spinoza*, Negri constantly interprets Spinoza's engagements with theology – the proofs of God's existence, prophecy, miracles, pietas, love, salvation and the Bible – in terms of other substantive issues – Power and power,[101] imagination, liberation, freedom, democracy, collectivity, the body, hermeneutics and so on. In other words, Negri enacts the relativisation of theology by reading Spinoza in a materialist register, or, as he puts it, Spinoza's ostensibly theological concerns, such as theism and pantheism, are 'dissolved' in his materialism.[102] But that also means that theology does not need to be cast out into the outer darkness, there to gnash its teeth in the company of other superstitions; it becomes part of a much wider intellectual and political programme, as Negri finds with Spinoza's *Ethics*. Spinoza does so with his radical synthesis of reason and religion, materialism and religiosity [*pietas*], but only when he has made his own exodus from the strictures of religion (for Spinoza it was his Jewish heritage) and created his own new philosophical universe.[103] Thus, theology and materialism become two possible codes, two ways to approach the same problems, often at loggerheads but, at times, crossing paths. So too with Negri's commentary on the book of Job.

---

[100] See 'Note A' in *The Labor of Job* (Negri 2009, pp. 16–17) and Negri 2004, p. 51: 'If there is a biblical spirit here, it is certainly not that of the secularized version of the TTP [*Tractatus Logico-Politicus*] but instead of the extremely profound materialist *pietas* of the Book of Job'.

[101] Following Michael Hardt's decision in translating *The Savage Anomaly*, the Latin *potestas* becomes Power and *potentia* power – the key issue in Negri's reading of Spinoza.

[102] Negri 2004, p. 95.

[103] Negri 1991b, pp. 10–15.

Conclusion

As with the previous two volumes in this series –
Criticism of Heaven and *Criticism of Religion* – I do
not propose to dwell on the problems and shortfalls
of the seven with whom I have dealt in this book. I
much prefer to focus on what may be salvaged and
reshaped for a constructive approach to Marxism
and theology. So, let me briefly summarise the criticisms before passing on to those retrievable items.

Even though Max Horkheimer's argument for
an authentic and resisting Christianity which was
then betrayed provides a distinctive approach to
Christianity from a Marxist, I found the argument
problematic, largely because he has a tendency to
let his dialectical rigour slip from time to time. With
E.P. Thompson, the difficulties were strongest in
his characterisation of methodism as psychic terror.
Thompson's agenda in his dealings with methodism
I can actually applaud, namely the need to debunk
the legend that methodism lay at the roots of trade-
unionism and working-class radicalism in England.
Yet, he pushes the argument too far and tries to
argue away the consistent evidence for a deep political ambivalence within methodism. Later, of course,
Thompson comes around to see that certain aspects
of Christian theology, especially the antinomianism
of various religious sects in England with which
William Blake had contact, have distinctly revolutionary resonances. As for G.E.M. de Ste. Croix, he
too follows a narrative of betrayal comparable to

that of Horkheimer: the words of Jesus of Nazareth may well have attacked the assumptions and self-serving justifications of the 'propertied class', but the early Church worked overtime to blunt those attacks through ingenious interpretations. I found that this historical narrative misses some of the complexity of the early Church, a complexity that shows up within Ste. Croix's own evidence, especially in terms of the anomalies in the early Church in which some leaders and theologians recognised the radical nature of Jesus's sayings and acts. On the economic front, I took Ste. Croix to task for failing to deal with matters of property (particularly when a key term for his analysis is 'propertied classes') and mode of production. In regard to Michael Löwy, I found that, while the idea of 'elective affinity' shows some promise, it was far too vague and left too many methodological issues unresolved. All the same, his engagement and indeed advocacy for Latin-American liberation-theology is an important moment for Marxist reassessments of religion, even if his analysis is limited in some respects.

In the case of Roland Barthes, I found that his take on myth via a nascent semiology was not only too negative, but that too many cracks appeared in his argument. So, I read him against himself, seeking to make the fibres of his argument open up and reveal other patterns whereby myth may also be of use to the Left. As for Deleuze and Guattari, my wariness of the pair actually enabled me to identify a good deal that was worth embracing and developing further – especially the multiple forms of resistance. However, I did find problematic their assumption that resistance was external to the despotic state instead of being part of the very possibility of that state. Finally, with the engaging Antonio Negri, I exegeted closely *The Labor of Job*, trying to unfold the many layers of his usage of measure and immeasure, re-reading it in terms of a conjunction with *kairós* and *ákairos*, as well as the deep pattern of chaos and order/creation in Job. And so, I wondered whether Negri wanted, in the end, a refashioned order, a beneficial and thoroughly new 'measure' that overcame the destructive possibilities of unfathomable 'immeasure'. Why not stay with an akairological immeasure a little longer? Why not allow revolutionary uncertainty and chaos to run on?

So much for the criticisms; now, let me move on to the much more enjoyable task of collecting the odd bits and pieces from these seven (at times wayward) Marxists and see what I can construct. I like to imagine a process which I undertake on a regular basis in my spare time. Scouring piles of old building materials, demolition-sites and stacks of hard rubbish, I am constantly on the watch for quality-timber that may have been thrown out – a piece of cedar on an old chest here, some Oregon pine on a bench there, a plank of ironbark elsewhere. Then, I ponder what may be constructed out this disparate collection of raw, painted and chipped wood, drawing up plans in my head, how these odd pieces might be transformed into a larger whole. Sawing, paint-stripping, pulling out rusty nails, sanding, hammering and dowelling, I eventually come up with something – a bookshelf perhaps, or a desk, or a chest, or a small table. In what follows, I undertake the preliminary task of collecting quality items that will be reshaped and reworked for the last book in the series.

For convenience, I list the main points first,[1] before undertaking the task of reshaping:

1. The major theme that has emerged in my study is *the pattern of accommodation and resistance* within theology. This theme took almost as many forms as critics who dealt with it: resistance and accommodation as two grand protagonists who cannot see eye to eye (Ste. Croix) but are, in fact, dialectically connected (Horkheimer); an authentic resistance that ends up betraying itself (Ste. Croix and Horkheimer again); implacable denunciation of reactionary Christianity to an awareness of more radical possibilities (E.P. Thompson); an 'elective affinity' between some radical strains of Christianity and Marxism (Löwy); a proposal for multiple forms of internal resistance rather than one (Deleuze and Guattari); and a rereading of the complex patterns of measure and immeasure in terms of *kairós* and *ákairos* (Negri).

2. The question of *myth* appeared most obviously in the chapter on Roland Barthes, but also in the way Deleuze and Guattari deal with biblical texts, so I wish to say something further on myth.

3. *Economics*, especially in the ancient Near East, ancient Greece and thereby biblical societies came to occupy my attention in the treatments of Ste. Croix and Deleuze and Guattari.

---

[1] Two other valuable topics also turned up in my reading, namely fetishism and utopia. However, I have dealt with them at some length in the conclusions to *Criticism of Heaven* (Ernst Bloch), *Criticism of Religion* (Fredric Jameson) and *Criticism of Earth* (Marx and Engels) – Boer 2007a; Boer 2009a; Boer forthcoming.

4. The combination of myth and economics raises the persistent matter of the tension between *idealism and materialism*, specifically in relation to religion. This issue rose to the surface in my engagements with Löwy and Ste. Croix, but it has lurked below the surface for much of the way.

Since the first topic – the patterns of resistance and accommodation in religion – is by far the most important one, I shall leave it to last. I begin, then, with the second topic, myth, which, somewhat minimally, I have defined elsewhere as an important story. The mention of myth usually invokes the specific concerns of anthropologists, historians of religion and perhaps the occasional biblical scholar. To my mind, this is a mistaken approach to myth, for, as I have argued in my *Political Myth*,[2] it is vitally important for any engagement with politics and thereby for Marxism. The great value of Barthes's very political analysis of myth is that it reminds us, more than fifty years after it was published, how crucial such analysis remains. Indeed, one of the reasons for engaging with Barthes on myth was to bring him into touch with other thinkers on the Left who have argued for the importance of myth, especially Georges Sorel and Ernst Bloch.[3] Barthes's approach may be one-sided, denouncing all myth as distortion and theft of language, universalising the nature of myth from the particular examples drawn from the dominant culture of the French bourgeoisie. But, in this respect, he shares a profound suspicion of myth with Theodore Adorno and Walter Benjamin, to name but a few. However, I argued in the chapter on Barthes that his treatment betrays a more complex function of myth, which I will not hesitate in calling dialectical. Barthes argues that myth is a vehicle of deception and oppression, the worst form of propaganda because it remains unnoticed and natural. Yet, in his effort to characterise myth in this way I spied a few strands that suggested within Barthes's own analysis a somewhat different way of reading myth. It is as though he has told one side of the story and that the other side lies poorly concealed within his own dominant narrative, a side that indicates cunning,

---

[2] Boer 2009b. See also my brief discussion of myth in *Criticism of Religion*, especially the chapters on Rosa Luxemburg and Karl Kautsky (Boer 2009a, pp. 80–8, 113–18), where I argue that the myth of early Christian communism has remained an empowering utopian story.

[3] Sorel 1961; Bloch 1972; Bloch 1968. See my discussion of Sorel in Boer 2009b and of Bloch in Boer 2007a, pp. 1–56.

the inability of myths of domination to control the agenda, the constant presence of an alternative position that resists the prevailing story. Myth turns
out to be, in Barthes's own analysis, politically volatile. Oppressive myths can
be so only by negating, demonising, punishing and concealing the voices of
resistance within them. It is surprising how often a myth involves an act that
is condemned – as sinful, disrespectful, rebellious and so on. Think of the
story of the Garden of Eden, or the murmurings against Moses and Yahweh
by the Israelites in the wilderness, or the evil Canaanites whom the Israelites
must dispossess in order to conquer and colonise the 'Promised Land', or
indeed the myth of the saluting black man (in my re-reading) that is one
of Barthes's most well-known examples. The catch is that in the very act of
condemning rebellion, oppressive myths preserve that voice of resistance;
once preserved, resistance risks breaking out once again.

At this point, Deleuze and Guattari come into the picture, since I argued
that some of the key biblical texts on which they focus – Exodus 18 (on Jethro's
advice to Moses) and Leviticus 16 (concerning the scapegoat ritual on the Day
of Atonement) – are drawn from mythical material. The Exodus text comes
from the early stage of the wilderness wandering of the Israelites, soon after
they left Egypt and awaited the Ten Commandments and a host of other
instructions, such as the interior design of the tabernacle, while the Leviticus
text comes from a later stage of the same wanderings. As I pointed out in that
chapter, no reputable biblical scholar would argue that these texts are anything but myth, a foundation-myth to be precise. Indeed, the whole stretch
from creation to the founding of the state in Canaan is a complex political
myth, comparable to others from the ancient Near East such as the Babylonian
Enuma Elish, which give divine sanction for the current ruling order by constructing a narrative that begins with creation of the world. I would suggest
recasting Deleuze and Guattari's signifying system of the despotic state as the
dominant voice of this biblical political myth. However, they also show that
such a despotic state also faces multiple forms of resistance, especially from
within. Moses, for one, signals the internal nature of that resistance, being
both the despot himself in Leviticus 16 and the oppositional nomadic chief
(the counter-signifying régime) who numbers his forces in Exodus 18. The
doubling soon becomes a tripling, for the Israelites in the wilderness are also
the positive appropriation of the scapegoat, the post-signifying régime that
is constitutive of the despotic régime itself. They are despotic state, nomadic

war-band and scapegoat-community all rolled into one, internally opposed and fractured. Add to this the pre-signifying régime of anticipatory resistance and the multiple patterns of resistance from within this larger political myth are difficult to avoid.

With the reconstructions of the economies of ancient Greece, the ancient Near East and Israel, I move to what seems to be different ground. In the chapters on Ste. Croix and Deleuze and Guattari, economics soon came to the fore, although at different levels. For Ste. Croix the concern was class as the motor of Greek history, while Deleuze and Guattari raised implicitly that perennial Marxist problem of the Asiatic mode of production – really two different levels of the embracing concerns of Marxist economic analysis. So let me make a few comments about each level. As far as Ste. Croix is concerned, he offers an extraordinarily detailed defence of class as the key to history in his 'Greek world'. He also provides welcome comments on the limits of trade as the generator of surplus, comments that still need to be heeded today. And I found most persuasive his account of the fall of the Roman Empire in terms of class – the disaffection of the peasants who had been driven into the status of serfs or *coloni* and who simply could not care less about Rome. However, since this later period begins to fall outside my brief, I prefer to focus on what is the most promising (and curiously under-developed) element of Ste. Croix's proposal, namely the spatial analysis in terms of *chora* and *polis*, with particular reference to Palestine and other places conquered and colonised by the Romans. In these cases, the *polis* became the locus of Roman imperial control, Hellenistic culture and the basis for widespread exploitation and enslavement of the people. The *chora* was, by contrast, the zone outside the *polis*, the countryside with its farms, flocks and villages, where Aramaic and not Greek was spoken. This distinction is vitally important for understanding why the texts of the New Testament exhibit such political tensions, which were then bequeathed to Christianity in terms of the opposition between accommodation and resistance to the powers that be. I will return to this matter below.

On one matter, I did find Ste. Croix wanting and that was the studied avoidance of mode of production. That aversion actually hobbles his analysis of the changes in class-structure from slavery to serfdom as the way in which surplus was produced for the ruling classes. He argues that they were two types of unfree labour and that the Romans viewed the serfs in the same terms as slaves. However, Ste. Croix neglects a basic point: change in class-structures is one of the signals of shifts in modes of production. On this matter, let us turn to that very unconventional engagement with mode of production by Deleuze and Guattari. In their case, I sought to connect the various régimes of signs with the diverse modes of production – an issue Ste. Croix studiously avoids – that have been proposed for the ancient Near East. In doing so, I was trying to encourage both Marx and the Bible to come out of the shadows of Deleuze and Guattari's text. So I suggested that the despotic signifying régime of signs is, at one level, a retooled Asiatic mode of production, or, in terms used by Marxist biblical critics, the tributary mode of production.[4] Further, I sought links between the pre-signifying, segmented tribe and what has been described in Marxist biblical criticism as the familial or household-mode of production, which was opposed to the tributary mode. Yet, Deleuze and Guattari also go well beyond these two possibilities with the numbered nomadic war-band and the scapegoat-community of the wandering Israelites. Each type of resistance to the despotic state I read in terms of internal patterns of constitutive exemptions, or the internal contradictions of any mode of production. But, here, I need to point out that the proposed tributary mode of production within Marxist biblical criticism faces a basic problem: tribute or tax, which may be understood as forms of plunder, needs something to be plundered. In other words, the production of surplus from tribute is secondary. The primary mode of producing surplus, or at least the material subject to tribute (which was often not even 'surplus'), was agricultural. So, any reconstruction of the economy of the ancient Near East must begin at this point. Further, Deleuze and Guattari, or, rather, my rereading of them offers a distinct angle on the opposition between tributary and familial modes of production which is popular in biblical criticism. Why, I wonder, must this opposition be cast as an external one? Why must they constitute distinct modes of production? Surely the opposition between a tribute-gathering and plundering ruling class and a 'familial' – that is, village-based and agricultural – productive class is one that is internal to the system. The mistake, in this case, is to confuse external modes of production with an internal class-dynamic. Of course, some biblical critics are keen to find a model for communal and less exploitative living within the

---

[4] At one level, because Deleuze and Guattari, of course, argued that the signifying régime, or indeed any régime of signs, cannot be located in any one social formation, people, language or place. Yet, many of their examples keep coming from the ancient Near East. See further Reed 2003.

Bible, and early Israel as a familial mode of production provides that model. But it simply does not work as a mode of production on its own. This all-too-brief discussion of ancient economics is another way of saying that the matter remains wide open for a creative, Marxist-inspired reconstruction of the economies of the ancient Near East and biblical societies.

Thus far, I have concerned myself with myth and ancient economics, two topics that may seem to have little to do with each other. However, they embrace one another, albeit stiffly, when it comes to the hoary contrast between idealism and materialism. Is not myth, and indeed religion as such, an idealistic category, belonging more properly to the superstructure and there joining the likes of philosophy, culture and politics? This question will become important when I turn to discuss the various mutations on the tension within Christianity between reaction and revolution. Here, Löwy does have something to contribute: in his *The War of Gods* he deftly shifts his focus from liberation-theology to liberationist Christianity. The reason: liberation-theology belongs to the realm of ideas, but liberationist Christianity is a matter of action, life lived and institutional structures. And that liberationist Christianity opposes the very concrete realities of economic exploitation. Yet, I would suggest that this move is not completely necessary, for an ideological system like theology does not operate in a vacuum. It entails various apparatuses (to gloss Althusser) such as ecclesial structures, or for those not inside the Church, institutional structures like a university or other support-networks. Those institutions have their economic concerns – pay for staff, buildings, facilities, production of written work and so on – which are meshed in with wider economic realities. This much is obvious, although it unfortunately needs to be restated since too often one gets the impression that theology floats free in the minds of theologians. A Marxist response would be to point to the difference in starting points; is theology itself, as a more or less coherent system of ideas, the ultimately determining instance, or is it those wider institutional and economic formations? While the answer is obvious for any historical-materialist analysis, I would like to take it a step further and argue that such an analysis should deal as much with the idealist side as the materialist side; an inclusive analysis, characteristic of full-scale Marxist approaches, is the key rather than one's starting point. In many respects, this is the approach I have taken in this and the other volumes in the series.

From these observations on idealism and materialism, it is a small step to what became, more by accident than design, the key theme of this book – the tension between reaction and revolution within Christianity. One may exchange the terms of the opposition – oppression and resistance, domination and insurrection – but it comes down to a tension at the heart of Christianity. That tension has turned up again and again in nearly all the figures studied in this book. For Horkheimer, it is one between resistance to this world and betrayal. Authentic Judaism and Christianity owe their allegiance to a totally other and for that reason will not, or rather, should not be conformed to this world, especially in terms of the state. Horkheimer offers a materialist version of the ontological reserve characteristic of liberation-theology. If these religions do compromise, then they have betrayed themselves and made a deal with the devil. While Horkheimer eventually provides a more dialectical understanding of this tension, especially where betrayal is necessary for survival of the impulse to resistance, the same cannot be said of Ste. Croix. Jesus may have resolutely opposed the economics and values of Hellenistic society, but his followers soon betrayed that position and made their dirty deals with the state in unseemly haste. For E.P. Thompson, the tension became one between the psychic terror of methodism and the antinomianism of William Blake and other fringe religious sects, although I also found enough hints within his texts for a tension within methodism itself. In Löwy's case, the devil, at least within liberation-theology, became vicious capitalist exploitation in Latin America, which is characterised as an omnivorous idol (or fetish), and against which liberation-theology took its stand. With Barthes, bourgeois myth turned out to be the distorting, all-powerful force against which resistance was well-nigh impossible, except perhaps through a utopian myth in which signs were effaced. Deleuze and Guattari offered a more complex proposal in which the tension is not binary but multiple; the despotic signifying régime faces multiple forms of resistance from within and without. Finally, Negri showed that he is fully aware of the reactionary or revolutionary 'crossings' of Christianity, identifying in Blochean fashion an alternative tradition he wishes he could have explored in more detail, one that includes Machiavelli, Spinoza, Francis of Assisi, sectarian Protestantism, Thomas Müntzer and heretical theological traditions. His early book on Job joins that tradition.

In nearly every case, I argued for a complex, often dialectical approach to the various permutations of this opposition between reaction and revolution. In some cases, our critics provided a distinct angle on such a dialectic (Horkheimer, Löwy, Deleuze and Guattari, and Negri), but, in other cases, I worked closely with their texts to uncover some dialectical complexities (Thompson, Ste. Croix and Barthes). But a question remains: what should I do with all these permutations on the patterns of resistance and oppression within Christianity? The answer to that question has two terms: multiplicity and economics. The first of these terms obviously comes from Deleuze and Guattari, but, in filling it out, I simply list the various types of resistance: against the state (Horkheimer and Deleuze and Guattari); against the law (Thompson); against property (Ste. Croix); against economic exploitation (Löwy); against oppressive myth (Barthes); and against a god who is enmeshed with state and cruel Church and who is brought to account (Negri). In other words, these types of resistance are political, legal, propertied, economic, mythical and even theological – multiple, indeed, and all from within a religion like Christianity!

The final word belongs to economics. Here, I would like to draw down from earlier my comments on idealism and materialism, for now I widen my analysis to offer a distinctly materialist analysis. I am not the first to observe that Christianity has this inherent tendency to both revolt and reaction. In earlier volumes, I explored in some detail the way Ernst Bloch had made a similar argument, as did Rosa Luxemburg, Karl Kautsky, and Slavoj Žižek. However, none of these analyses offer a plausible materialist reason why Christianity has this tendency. It is not enough to point to some of the words of Jesus, say they are radical and leave it at that. Nor will it do to suggest that Paul offers resistance to empire through his doctrines of grace or his observations on love and not ask why they can have this radical sense. Even more, it does not work to argue that an original voice or two – Jesus, Paul, the early Christian communities – were radically anti-empire, anti-property, antinomian and communistic, but that these ideals were later betrayed, the rough edges smoothed over as Christianity slipped into a seat among the powerful.

The reason for the constant play of reaction and revolution lies, I would suggest, with two different economic situations. For the Hebrew Bible, these tensions are the literary manifestations of irresolvable tensions with an economic system I prefer to call the sacred economy. However, for the New Testament and early Christianity, we find a clash between two modes of production, one a slave-economy brutally imposed by Rome and the other made up of remnants of the sacred economy. I will not go into the reasons here for using the term 'sacred economy', suffice to point out that it is a thorough reworking of what has variously been called the Asiatic mode of production or the tributary mode of production characteristic of the ancient Near East. What is relevant for my purposes here is that the system operated with a basic tension between the agricultural village-commune and the mechanisms of exploitation focused in a small ruling class made up of the monarch with his entourage of clerics, scribes, courtiers and body-guards. As I pointed out earlier, among Marxist biblical scholars, these two are usually separated in terms of familial and tributary modes of production. I cannot think of one good reason why they should be separated in this fashion, for they are really two elements of the same economic system. However, this conflict at an economic level makes sense of the diverse and apparently contradictory political positions that appear in the texts of the Hebrew Bible. I do not mean a simplistic lining up of all radical and insurrectionist texts on the side of the village-communes and all texts of domination on the side of the exploiting class. Rather, I suggest that the economic tensions manifest themselves in all manner of ways in the literature produced. Those manifestations may be formal, they may concern content and they may shape the very structure of the myriad myths of the Hebrew Bible that concern rebellion, sin and its punishment. And they show up in the multiple patterns of resistance and reaction in the Hebrew Bible.

A very similar argument applies to the New Testament, except that the conflict is now an external one between a slave-economy and an older sacred economy, or rather its remnants. As the Romans gradually but brutally imposed a slave-economy in the province of Judaea in the period of the New Testament and the early Church, the members of the ruling class of the older sacred economy either made their deal with the new order and adapted or they were simply eliminated. At this point, Ste. Croix's distinction between *chora* and *polis* has some traction, for the *polis* marks the increasing presence of a new form of exploitation in the slave-economy while the *chora* is the location of the older village-communes and countryside. However, unlike Ste. Croix, I do not argue that Jesus took a dangerous stand against the propertied classes only to have that stand betrayed by later interpreters of the Church. Instead, I suggest that the tension between resistance and reaction is generated out of this clash between economic systems. Once again, everything radical does not belong to the *chora* and everything bad to the *polis*; rather, the tension itself generates all manner of efforts to overcome it at a literary level, efforts that in turn lead to the multiplicity of conflicting political positions. For example, the fact that the Apostle Paul can be read either as a solid conservative, concerned for order, the subordination of women and one who did nothing to alleviate slavery, or as a progressive who saw the explosive possibilities of a doctrine of grace that overcomes the law, is due precisely to the economic conflicts I have sketched all too briefly. Indeed, the manifold binaries within his texts – between grace and law, death and life, flesh and spirit, man and woman, Jew and Greek and so on – are manifestations at the level of thought of these deep tensions in the social formation in which he lived. The question is not whether one Paul or another is the 'real' Paul – both are equally real.[5]

Since this is the close of the third volume in *The Criticism of Heaven and Earth* series, let me say a few words about how these various items I have discussed in the conclusion fit within the series as a whole. Here, I have gathered a number of items: myth, economics, idealism versus materialism and the patterns of resistance and reaction. I have drawn them out from the eight Marxists studied in this volume, but, soon enough, they will join the choice pieces I have gathered from the preceding two volumes – *Criticism of Heaven* and *Criticism of Religion*. Along with a large collection from my study of Marx and Engels, *Criticism of Earth*, I will set out to cut, resize and reshape the whole lot in the final book of the series.

However, the last word at this stage of the series belongs to Antonio Negri, whose radical homiletics not merely of the Bible but also of a range of philosophers, social theorists and activists, is a good model to follow. Homiletics is, of course, steeped in the theological tradition of identifying an urgent message from these ancient texts for today. In Negri's hands, it becomes a call to comprehensive rethinking and radical action, for, as Marx would have it, the point is not merely to interpret the world, but to change it.

---

[5] See further Boer 2009c.

References

Adorno, Theodor W. 1973 [1964], *The Jargon of Authenticity*, translated by Knut Tar-nowski, and Frederic Will, Evanston: Northwestern University Press.
—— 1989 [1962], *Kierkegaard: Construction of the Aesthetic*, translated by Robert Hullot-Kentor, Volume 61, *Theory and History of Literature*, Minneapolis: University of Min-nesota Press.
—— 2003a [1964], *Jargon der Eigentlich: Zur deutschen Ideologie*, in *Gesammelte Schriften*, Volume 6, Frankfurt am Main: Suhrkamp.
—— 2003b [1962], *Kierkegaard: Konstruktion des Ästhetischen*, in *Gesammelte Schriften*, Volume 2, Frankfurt am Main: Suhrkamp.
——, Emil Blum, Emil Brunner, Martin Dibelius, Heinrich Frick, Max Horkheimer, Karl Mannheim, Carl Mennicke, Friedrich Pollock, Kurt Rietzler, Hermann Schafft, Hans Freiherr von Soden, Paul Tillich and Lilli Zarncke 1987 [1931], *Diskussion über die Aufgabe des Protestantismus in der säkularen Zivilisation*, in *Gesammelte Schriften*, Volume 11, Frankfurt am Main: Fischer Taschenbuch.
Agamben, Giorgio 2000, *Il tempo che resta. Un commento alla Lettera ai Romani*, Turin: Bollati Boringhieri.
—— 2005, *The Time That Remains: A Commentary on the Letter to the Romans*, translated by Patricia Dailey, Stanford: Stanford University Press.
Aichele, George 1996, *Jesus Framed*, London: Routledge.
—— 1997, *Sign, Text, Scripture: Semiotics and the Bible*, Sheffield: Sheffield Academic.
—— 2001, *The Control of Biblical Meaning: Canon as a Semiotic Mechanism*, Lewisburg: Trinity Press International.
Albert, Éliot 2001, 'Deleuze's Impersonal, Hylozoic Cosmology: The Expulsion of The-ology', in Bryden (ed.) 2001.
Albright, William Foxwell 1953, *Archaeology and the Religion of Israel*, Baltimore: Johns Hopkins University Press.
Alter, Robert 1981, *The Art of Biblical Narrative*, New York: Basic Books.
—— 1985, *The Art of Biblical Poetry*, New York: Basic Books.
Althaus-Reid, Marcella 2000, *Indecent Theology: Theological Perversions in Sex, Gender and Politics*, London: Routledge.
—— 2004, *From Feminist Theology to Indecent Theology: Readings on Poverty, Sexual Iden-tity and God*, London: SCM.
Althusser, Louis 1971 [1970], *Lenin and Philosophy and Other Essays*, translated by Ben Brewster, New York: Monthly Review Press.
—— 1995, *Sur la Reproduction*, Paris: Presses Universitaires de France.
—— and Étienne Balibar 1979 [1968], *Reading 'Capital'*, translated by Ben Brewster, London: Verso.
——, Étienne Balibar, Roger Establet, Pierre Macherey and Jacques Rancière 1996 [1968], *Lire 'Le Capital'*, Paris: Presses Universitaires de France.
Anderson, Perry 1974a, *Lineages of the Absolutist State*, London: New Left Books.
—— 1974b, *Passages from Antiquity to Feudalism*, London: New Left Books.
—— 1992, *A Zone of Engagement*, London: Verso.
Aquino, María Pilar 1993, *Our Cry for Life: Feminist Theology from Latin America* trans-lated by Dinah Livingstone, Maryknoll: Orbis.

Arthur, Marylin B. and David Konstan 1984, 'Marxism and the Study of Classical Antiquity', in *The Left Academy: Marxist Scholarship on American Campuses*, edited by Bertell Ollman and Edward Vernoff, New York: Praeger.

Badiou, Alain 1988, *L'être et l'événement*, Paris: Éditions du Seuil.

—— 1997, *Saint-Paul: la fondation de l'universalisme* Paris: Presses Universitaires de France.

—— 2000 [1997], *Deleuze: The Clamor of Being*, translated by Louise Burchill, Minneapolis: University of Minnesota Press. [Original edition, Hachette Littératures, 1997.]

—— 2003 [1997], *Saint Paul: The Foundation of Universalism*, translated by Ray Brassier, Stanford: Stanford University Press.

—— 2004, *Theoretical Writings*, edited by Ray Brassier and Alberto Toscano, London: Continuum.

—— 2006a [1988], *Being and Event*, translated by Oliver Feltham, London: Continuum Press.

—— 2006b [2003–5], *Polemics*, translated by Steve Corcoran, London: Verso.

Bailey, Anne M and Josep R. Llobera 1981, 'The AMP: Sources of Information and the Concept', in *The Asiatic Mode of Production: Science and Politics*, edited by Anne M. Bailey and Josep R. Llobera, London: Routledge & Kegan Paul.

Bakunin, Mikhail 1980, *Bakunin on Anarchism*, Montreal: Black Rose Books.

Barr, James 1969, *Biblical Words for Time*, 2 ed, London: SCM.

—— 1977, *Fundamentalism*, London: SCM.

—— 1984, *Escaping Fundamentalism*, London: SCM.

Barrett, Michèle 1991, *The Politics of Truth: From Marx to Foucault*, Stanford: Stanford University Press.

Barthes, Roland 1973 [1965], *Elements of Semiology*, translated by Annette Lavers, New York: Hill and Wang.

—— 1975 [1973], *The Pleasure of the Text*, translated by Richard Miller, New York: Hill and Wang.

—— 1977, *Image – Music – Text*, translated by Stephen Heath, New York: Hill and Wang.

—— 1978 [1977], *A Lover's Discourse*, translated by Richard Howard, New York: Farrar, Straus and Giroux.

—— 1982 [1970], *Empire of Signs*, translated by Richard Howard, New York: Hill and Wang.

—— 1983 [1967], *The Fashion System*, translated by Matthew Ward and Richard Howard, Berkeley: University of California Press.

—— 1985 [1981], *The Grain of the Voice: Interviews 1962–1980*, translated by Linda Coverdale, Berkeley: University of California Press.

—— 1987 [1979], *Writer Sollers*, translated by Philip Thody, Minneapolis: University of Minnesota Press.

—— 1989 [1984], *The Rustle of Language*, translated by Richard Howard, Berkeley: University of California Press.

—— 1990 [1970], *S/Z*, translated by Richard Miller, Oxford: Blackwell.

—— 1991 [1982], *The Responsibility of Forms*, translated by Richard Howard, Berkeley: University of California Press.

—— 1993a [1957], *Mythologies*, translated by Annette Lavers, London: Vintage.

—— 1993b [1980], *Camera Lucida*, translated by Richard Howard, New York: Vintage.

—— 1994 [1985], *The Semiotic Challenge*, translated by Richard Howard, Berkeley: University of California Press.

—— 1997 [1957], *The Eiffel Tower and Other Mythologies*, translated by Richard Howard, Berkeley: University of California Press.

—— 2002a [1951], 'A propos d'une métaphore (Le marxisme est-il une « Eglise »?)', in *Œuvres complètes*, Volume I: 1942–1961, Paris: Seuil.

—— 2002b [1953], 'Folies-Bergère', in *Œuvres complètes*, Volume I: 1942–1961, Paris: Seuil.

—— 2002c [1953], 'Littéature inhumaine', in *Œuvres complètes*, Volume I: 1942–1961, Paris: Seuil.

—— 2002d [1953], 'Visages et figures', in *Œuvres complètes*, Volume I: 1942–1961, Paris: Seuil.

—— 2002e [1954], 'Le Grand Robert', in *Œuvres complètes*, Volume I: 1942–1961, Paris: Seuil.

—— 2002f [1954], 'Petite mythologie du mois', in *Œuvres complètes*, Volume V: 1977–1980, Paris: Seuil.

—— 2002g [1955], 'La vaccine de l'avant-garde', in *Œuvres complètes*, Volume I: 1942–1961.

—— 2002h [1955], 'Le group-captain Townsend', in *Œuvres complètes*, Volume I: 1942–1961.

—— 2002i [1955], 'Pour une histoire de l'enfance', in *Œuvres complètes*, Volume I: 1942–1961.

—— 2002j [1955], 'Suis-je marxiste?', in *Œuvres complètes*, Volume I: 1942–1961.

—— 2002k [1957], *Mythologies, suivi de Le Mythe, aujourdhui*, in *Œuvres complètes*, Volume I: 1942–1961.

—— 2002l [1958], 'Le mythe de l'acteur possédé', in *Œuvres complètes*, Volume I: 1942–1961.

—— 2002m [1959], 'Cinéma droite et gauche', in *Œuvres complètes*, Volume I: 1942–1961.

—— 2002n [1959], 'Le choix d'un métier', in *Œuvres complètes*, Volume I: 1942–1961.

—— 2002o [1959], 'Les deux salons', in *Œuvres complètes*, Volume I: 1942–1961.

—— 2002p [1959], 'New York, Buffet et la hauteur', in *Œuvres complètes*, Volume I: 1942–1961.

—— 2002q [1959], 'Qu'est-ce qu'un scandale?', in *Œuvres complètes*, Volume I: 1942–1961.

—— 2002r [1959], 'Sur en emploi du verbe « être »', in *Œuvres complètes*, Volume I: 1942–1961.

—— 2002s [1959], 'Tables ronde', in *Œuvres complètes*, Volume I: 1942–1961.

—— 2002t [1959], 'Tragédie et hauteur', in *Œuvres complètes*, Volume I: 1942–1961.

—— 2002u [1959], 'Tricots à domicile', in *Œuvres complètes*, Volume I: 1942–1961.

—— 2002v [1959], 'Wagon-Restaurant', in *Œuvres complètes*, Volume I: 1942–1961.

—— 2002w [1960], '« Le bleu est à la mode cette année »', in *Œuvres complètes*, Volume I: 1942–1961.

—— 2002x [1961], 'Des joyaux aux bijoux', in *Œuvres complètes*, Volume I: 1942–1961.

—— 2002y [1961], 'Le message photographique', in *Œuvres complètes*, Volume I: 1942–1961.

—— 2002z [1964], 'La Tour Eiffel', in *Œuvres complètes*, Volume II: 1962–1967.

—— 2002aa [1964], 'Mythologie de l'automobile', in *Œuvres complètes*, Volume II: 1962–1967.

—— 2002bb [1965], *Eléments de Sémiologie*, in *Œuvres complètes*, Volume II: 1962–1967.

—— 2002cc [1966], *Introduction à l'Analyse structurale des Récits*, in *Œuvres complètes*, Volume II: 1962–1967.

—— 2002dd [1967], *Système de la mode*, in *Œuvres complètes*, Volume II: 1962–1967.

—— 2002ee [1970], 'L'Analyse structurale du récit. A propos d'« Actes » 10–11', in *Œuvres complètes*, Volume III: 1968–1971.

—— 2002ff [1970], *L'Empire des signes*, in *Œuvres complètes*, Volume III: 1968–1971.

—— 2002gg [1970], '« L'Express » va plus loin avec… Roland Barthes', in *Œuvres complètes*, Volume III: 1968–1971.

—— 2002hh [1970], 'Musica Practica', in *Œuvres complètes*, Volume III: 1968–1971.

—— 2002ii [1970], *S/Z*, in *Œuvres complètes*, Volume III: 1968–1971.

—— 2002jj [1970], 'Sur « S/Z » et « L'Empire des signes » (avec R. Bellour)', in *Œuvres complètes*, Volume III: 1968–1971.

—— 2002kk [1971], 'La mythologie aujourd'hui', in *Œuvres complètes*, Volume III: 1968–1971.

—— 2002ll [1971], 'La paix culturelle', in *Œuvres complètes*, Volume III: 1968–1971.

—— 2002mm [1972], 'La lutte avec l'ange: Analyse textuelle de « Genèse » 32.23–33', in *Œuvres complètes*, Volume IV: 1972–1976.

—— 2002nn [1973], *Le plaisir du texte*, in *Œuvres complètes*, Volume IV: 1972–1976.

—— 2002oo [1974], 'Mythologie', in *Œuvres complètes*, Volume IV: 1972–1976.

—— 2002pp [1975], *Le bruissement de la langue*, in *Œuvres complètes*, Volume IV: 1972–1976.

—— 2002qq [1977], *Fragments d'un discours amoureux*, in *Œuvres complètes*, Volume V: 1977–1980.

—— 2002rr [1977], 'A quoi sert un intellectuel? (avec B.-H. Lévy)', in *Œuvres complètes*, Volume V: 1977–1980.

—— 2002ss [1978], 'Propos sur la violence (avec J. Sers)', in *Œuvres complètes*, Volume V: 1977–1980.

—— 2002tt [1979], 'Sollers écrivain', in *Œuvres complètes*, Volume V: 1977–1980.

—— 2002uu [1980], *La chambre claire: Note sur la photographie*, in *Œuvres complètes*, Volume V: 1977–1980.

—— 2006, *The Language of Fashion*, translated by Andy Stafford, Oxford: Berg.

Bauer, Bruno 1838, *Kritik der Geschichte der Offenbarung: Die Religion des alten Testaments in der geschichtlichen Entwicklung ihrer Prinzipien dargestellt*, Berlin: Ferdinand Dümmler.

—— 1839, *Herr Dr. Hengstenberg: Ein Beitrag zur Kritik der religiösen Bewußtseins. Kritische Briefe über den Gegensatz des Gesetzes und des Evangeliums*, Berlin: Ferdinand Dümmler.

—— 1840, *Kritik der evangelischen Geschichte des Johannes*, Bremen: Karl Schünemann.

—— 1841, *Kritik der evangelischen Geschichte der Synoptiker*, 2 vols, Leipzig: Otto Wigand.

—— 1842a, *Die Gute Sache der Freiheit und meine eigene Ungelegenheit*, Zürich and Winterthur: Verlag des literarischen Comptoirs.

—— 1842b, *Kritik der evangelischen Geschichte der Synoptiker und des Johannes, Dritter und letzter Band*, Braunschweig: Fr. Otto.

—— 1843a, *Das entdeckte Christenthum. Eine Erinnerung an das 18. Jahrhundert und ein Beitrag zur Krisis des 19. Jahrhundert*, Zürich and Winterthur: Verlag des literarischen Comptoirs.

—— 1843b, *Die Fähigkeit der heutigen Juden und Christen, frei zu werden* in *Einundzwanzig bogen aus der Schweiz*, edited by Georg Herwegh, Zürich and Winterthur: Zürich Verlag des Literarischen Comptoirs.

—— 1843c, *Die Judenfrage*, Braunschweig: Otto Wigand.

—— 1850–1, *Kritik der Evangelien und Geschichte ihres Ursprungs*, 3 vols, Berlin: Gustav Hempel.

—— 1852, *Die theologische Erklärung der Evangelien*, Berlin: Gustav Hempel.

—— 1978 [1843], 'The Capacity of Present-Day Jews and Christians to Become Free', *Philosophical Forum*, 2–4: 135–49.

—— 1983 [1841], *Die Posaune des jüngsten Gerichts über Hegel den Atheisten und Antichristen: Ein Ultimatum*, Aalen: Scientia Verlag. [Original edition, Leipzig: Otto Wigand.]

Belo, Fernando 1975, *Lecture matérialiste de l'évangile de Marx: Récit-Pratique-Idéologie*, revised ed, Paris: Les Éditions du Cerf.

—— 1981 [1975], *A Materialist Reading of the Gospel of Mark*, translated by M.J. O'Connell, Maryknoll: Orbis.

Bentley, G.E. Jr. 2001, *The Stranger from Paradise: A Biography of William Blake*, New Haven: Yale University Press.

Berdyaev, Nikolai 1937, *The Origin of Russian Communism*, translated by R.M. French, London: G. Bles.

Berman, Harold Joseph 1983, *Law and Revolution: The Formation of the Western Legal Tradition*, Cambridge, MA.: Harvard University Press.

—— 2006, *Law and Revolution, II: The Impact of the Protestant Reformations on the Western Legal Tradition*, Cambridge, MA.: Harvard University Press.

Bess, Michael D. 1993, 'E.P. Thompson: The Historian as Activist', *American Historical Review*, 98, 1: 18–38.

Bidney, Martin 2004–5, 'Neo-Blakean Vision in the Verse of E.P. Thompson: The "Abstraction" of Labor and Cultural Capital', *Science & Society*, 68, 4: 396–420.

Bingemer, Maria Clara 1997, 'A Post-Christian and Postmodern Christianism', in *Liberation Theologies, Postmodernity, and the Americas*, edited by David Batstone, Eduardo Mendieta, Lois Ann Lorentzen and Dwight N. Hopkins, London: Routledge.

—— 1989, 'Women in the Future of the Theology of Liberation', in *The Future of Liberation Theology: Essays in Honor of Gustavo Gutierrez*, edited by Marc H. Ellis and Otto Maduro, Maryknoll: Orbis.

Blackledge, Paul 2006, *Reflections on the Marxist Theory of History*, Manchester: Manchester University Press.

Blake, William 1997, *The Complete Poetry and Prose of William Blake*, New York: Random House.

Bloch, Ernst 1968, *Atheismus im Christentum: Zur Religion des Exodus und des Reichs*, Volume 14, *Werkausgabe*, Frankfurt am Main: Suhrkamp.

—— 1972, *Atheism in Christianity: The Religion of the Exodus and the Kingdom*, translated by J.T. Swann, New York: Herder and Herder.

Boer, Roland 2002a, 'Marx, Method and Gottwald', in *Tracking The Tribes of Yahweh: On the Trail of a Classic*, edited by Roland Boer, London: Continuum.

—— 2002b, 'Political Activism and Biblical Scholarship: An Interview with Norman Gottwald', in *Tracking The Tribes of Yahweh: On the Trail of a Classic*, edited by Roland Boer, London: Continuum.

—— 2003, *Marxist Criticism of the Bible*, London: Continuum.

—— 2005a, 'Terry Eagleton and the Vicissitudes of Christology', *Cultural Logic*, 8. Available at: <http://eserver.org/clogic/2005/boer.html>.

—— 2005b, 'Women First? On the Legacy of Primitive Communism', *Journal for the Study of the Old Testament*, 30, 1: 3–28.

—— 2005–6, 'Phases of the Gonic: Re-Reading Genesis to Joshua as Myth', *Literary Newspaper (Bulgaria)*, 13, 21 December–January 2006: 18.

—— 2006, *Novel Histories: The Fiction of Biblical Criticism*, Atlanta: SBL.

—— 2007a, *Criticism of Heaven: On Marxism and Theology*, Historical Materialism Book Series, Leiden: Brill.

—— 2007b, *Rescuing the Bible*, Oxford: Blackwell.

—— 2007c, 'The Sacred Economy of Ancient "Israel"', *The Scandinavian Journal of the Old Testament*, 21, 1: 29–48.

—— 2007d, 'Twenty Five Years of Marxist Biblical Criticism', *Currents in Biblical Research*, 5, 3: 1–25.

—— 2008a, 'Julia Kristeva, Marx and the Singularity of Paul', in *Marxist Feminist Criticism of the Bible*, edited by Roland Boer and Jorunn Økland, Sheffield: Sheffield Phoenix.

—— 2008b, *Last Stop Before Antarctica: The Bible and Postcolonialism in Australia*, Revised ed., Atlanta: SBL.

—— 2008c, 'A Titanic Phenomenon: Marxism, History and Biblical Society', *Historical Materialism*, 16, 4: 141–66.

—— 2008d, 'Leeks, Lentils and Fleshpots: Egypt as a Symbolic Space' [in Chinese], in *Hermeneutics and the Reading of the Bible*, edited by Ken-Pa Chin and Samuel Pin-Cheong Chia, Taipei: CCLM Publishing.

—— 2009a, *Criticism of Religion: On Marxism and Theology II*, Historical Materialism Book Series, Leiden: Brill.

—— 2009b, *Political Myth: On the Use and Abuse of Biblical Themes*, Durham, NC.: Duke University Press.

—— 2009c, 'Resistance Versus Accommodation: What to Do With Romans 13?', in *Postcolonial Interventions: Essays in Honor of R.S. Sugirtharajah*, edited by Tat-siong Benny Liew, Sheffield: Sheffield Phoenix.

—— forthcoming, *Criticism of Earth: On Marx, Engels and Theology*, Historical Materialism Book Series, Leiden: Brill.

Bogue, Ronald 2001, 'The Betrayal of God', in Bryden (ed.) 2001.

Boling, Robert G. 1975, *Judges*, Anchor Bible, Garden City: Doubleday.

Boyarin, Daniel and Jonathan Boyarin 1995, 'Diaspora: Generation and the Ground of Jewish Identity', in *Identities*, edited by K.A. Appiah and H.L. Gates, Chicago: University of Chicago Press.

Bracht, Heinrich, Peter Brückner, Max Horkheimer, Alexander Mitscherlich and Hans Götz Oxenius 1989 [1963], 'Das Ende einer Illusion? Religionskritik heute [Eine Diskussion über Horkeheimers ›Theismus-Atheismus‹', in *Gesammelte Schriften* Volume 13, Frankfurt am Main: Fischer Taschenbuch.

Brenner, Athalya 1994, 'Introduction', in *A Feminist Companion to Exodus to Deuteronomy*, edited by Athalya Brenner, Volume 6, Sheffield: Sheffield Academic Press.

Bright, John 1980, *A History of Israel*, 3 ed, London: SCM.

Brittain, Christopher Craig 2005, 'Social Theory and the Premise of all Criticism: Max Horkheimer on Religion', *Critical Sociology*, 31, 1–2: 153–68.

Bronowski, Jacon 1943, *William Blake 1757–1827: A Man Without a Mask*, London: Secker and Warburg.

Brosses, Charles de 1760, *Du culte des dieux fétiches ou Parallèle de l'ancienne religion de l'Égypte*, Paris: n. p.

Bryan, Christopher 2005, *Render to Caesar: Jesus, the Early Church, and the Roman Superpower*, Oxford: Oxford University Press.

Bryden, Mary (ed.) 2001, *Deleuze and Religion*, London: Routledge.

Butler, Marylin 1995, 'Thompson's Second Front', *History Workshop Journal*, 35, 1: 71–8.

Carney, J. Guadalupe 1985, *To Be A Revolutionary: An Autobiography*, San Francisco: Harper & Row.

Carter, Michael 1988, '*Stasis* and *Kairos*: Principles of Social Construction in Classical Rhetoric', *Rhetoric Review*, 7, 1: 97–112.

Carter, Warren 2001, *Matthew and Empire: Initial Explorations*, Harrisburg: Trinity Press International.

—— 2006, *The Roman Empire and the New Testament: An Essential Guide*, Nashville: Abingdon.

Castelli, Elizabeth 2004, *Martyrdom and Memory: Early Christian Culture Making*, New York: Columbia University Press.

Clévenot, Michel 1976, *Approches matérialistes de la Bible*, Paris: Les Éditions du Cerf.

—— 1985 [1976], *Materialist Approaches to the Bible*, translated by William J. Nottingham, Maryknoll: Orbis.

Clines, David A. (ed.) 2007, *The Dictionary of Classical Hebrew*, Volume 6, Sheffield: Sheffield Phoenix.

Collective, Bible and Culture 1995, *The Postmodern Bible*, New Haven: Yale University Press.

Comstock, Gary David 1991, *Violence Against Lesbians and Gay Men*, New York: Columbia University Press.

—— 1993, *Gay Theology Without Apology*, Cleveland: Pilgrim Press.

Cone, James H. 1975, *God of the Oppressed*, New York: Seabury.

—— 1984, *For My People: Black Theology and the Black Church*, Maryknoll: Orbis.

—— 1986, *My Soul Looks Back*, Maryknoll: Orbis.

—— 1990, *A Black Theology of Liberation (20th Anniversary Edition)*, Maryknoll: Orbis.

—— 1999, *Risks of Faith: The Emergence of a Black Theology of Liberation, 1968–1998*, Boston: Beacon.

Copjec, Joan (ed.) 1996, *Radical Evil*, London: Verso.

Crossan, John Dominic 1993, *The Historical Jesus: The Life of a Mediterranean Peasant*, San Francisco: Harper.

—— 1995, *Jesus: A Revolutionary Biography*, San Francisco: Harper.

Csapo, Eric 2005, *Theories of Mythology*, Oxford: Blackwell.

Cullen, Jason and Greg Hainge 2010, 'Formulating God: The Ongoing Place of Theology in the Philosophy of Gilles Deleuze', in *Traces of the Hidden Other: Theological Remnants in 20th Century French Philosophy*, edited by Wayne Cristaudo and Phillip Tolliday, Adelaide: ATF Press.

Currie, R. and R.M. Hartwell 1965, 'The Making of the English Working Class?', *The Economic History Review*, New Series, 18, 3: 633–43.

D'iakonoff, Igor M. 1969, 'The Rise of the Despotic State in Ancient Mesopotamia', in D'iakonoff (ed.) 1969.

—— 1974, 'The Commune in the Ancient East as Treated in the Works of Soviet Researchers', in *Introduction to Soviet Ethnography*, edited by Stephen P. Dunn and E. Dunn, Berkeley: Copy Centers of Berkeley.

—— 1987, 'Slave-Labour vs. Non-Slave Labour: The Problem of Definition', in *Labor in the Ancient Near East*, edited by Marvin A. Powell, New Haven: American Oriental Society.

—— 1999, *The Paths of History* Cambridge: Cambridge University Press.

—— (ed.) 1969, *Ancient Mesopotamia: Socio-Economic History. A Collection of Studies by Soviet Scholars*, Moscow: "Nauka" Publishing House.

—— (ed.) 1991, *Early Antiquity*, Chicago: Chicago University Press.

Daly, Mary 1968, *The Church and the Second Sex*, New York: Harper & Row.

Dandamaev, Muhammad 1984, *Slavery in Babylonia: From Nabopolassar to Alexander the Great (626–331 BC)*, DeKalb: North Illinois University Press.

Dandamaev, Muhammad, I. Gershevitch, Horst Klengel, G. Komoroczy, M.T. Larsen and J.N. Postgate (eds.) 1982, *Societies and Languages of the Ancient Near East: Studies in Honour of I.M. Diakonoff*, Warminster: Aris and Phillips.

Davies, Philip 1995, *In Search of Ancient Israel*, Sheffield: Sheffield Academic Press.

—— 2008, *Memories of Ancient Israel: An Introduction to Biblical History – Ancient and Modern*, Louisville: Westminster John Knox.

Dawkins, Richard 2006, *The God Delusion*, Boston: Houghton Mifflin.

De La Torre, Miguel 2002, *Reading the Bible from the Margins*, Maryknoll: New York.

Deissman, Adolf 1929, *The New Testament in the Light of Modern Research*, Garden City: Doubleday, Doran and Company.

—— 1978 [1908], *Light From the Ancient East*, Grand Rapids: Baker Book House.

DeLanda, Manuel 2002, *Intensive Science and Virtual Philosophy*, London: Continuum.

Deleuze, Gilles 1988 [1970], *Spinoza, Practical Philosophy*, translated by Robert Hurley, San Francisco: City Lights Books.

Deleuze, Gilles 1990 [1968], *Expressionism in Philosophy: Spinoza*, translated by Martin Joughin, New York: Zone Books.

—— 1995 [1990], *Negotiations: 1972–90*, translated by Martin Joughin, New York: Columbia University Press.

Deleuze, Gilles and Félix Guattari 1986 [1980], *Nomadology: The War-Machine*, translated by Brian Massumi, New York: Semiotext(e).

—— 1994 [1990], *What Is Philosophy?*, translated by Hugh Tomlinson and Graham Burchell, New York: Columbia University Press.

—— 1980, *Mille Plateaux: Capitalisme et schizophrénie*, Paris: Les Éditions de Minuit.

—— 1988 [1980], *A Thousand Plateaus: Capitalism and Schizophrenia*, translated by Brian Massumi, London: Athlone Press.

Dennett, Daniel C. 2007, *Breaking the Spell: Religion as a Natural Phenomenon*, Harmondsworth: Penguin.

Dever, William G. 2001, *What Did the Biblical Writers Know and When Did They Know It? What Archaeology Can Tell Us about the Reality of Ancient Israel*, Grand Rapids: Eerdmans.

Dhoquois, Georges 1971, *Pour l'histoire: Essai d'histoire matérialiste comparative*, Paris: Anthropos.

Dhorme, Eduard 1937, *La religion des Hébreux nomades*, Brussels: Nouvelle Société d'Éditions.

Docker, John 2001, *1492: The Poetics of Diaspora*, London: Continuum.

Dreyer, Frederick 1986, 'A "Religious Society under Heaven": John Wesley and the Identity of Methodism', *The Journal of British Studies*, 25, 1: 62–83.

—— *The Genesis of Methodism*, Bethlehem, PA.: Lehigh University Press.

Dunn, Stephen P. 1981, *The Fall and Rise of the Asiatic Mode of Production*, London: Routledge & Kegan Paul.

Dupré, Louis 1983, *Marx's Social Critique of Culture*, New Haven: Yale University Press.

Dworkin, Dennis 1997, *Cultural Marxism in Postwar Britain: History, the New Left and the Origins of Cultural Studies*, Durham, NC.: Duke University Press.

Eagleton, Terry 2001, *The Gatekeeper: A Memoir*, London: Penguin.

—— 2003a, *After Theory*, New York: Basic Books.

—— 2003b, *Figures of Dissent: Critical Essays on Fish, Spivak, Žižek and Others*, London: Verso.

—— 2003c, *Sweet Violence: The Idea of the Tragic*, Oxford: Blackwell.

—— 2007, *Jesus Christ: The Gospels (Revolutions)*, London: Verso.

—— 2009, *Reason, Faith, and Revolution: Reflections on the God Debate*, New Haven: Yale University Press.

Edwards, George 1984, *Gay/Lesbian Liberation: A Biblical Perspective*, Cleveland: Pilgrim.

Elliott, Neil 1994, *Liberating Paul: The Justice of God and the Politics of the Apostle*, Maryknoll: Orbis.

—— 2000, 'Paul and the Politics of Empire: Problems and Prospects', in *Paul and Politics: Ekklesia, Israel, Imperium, Interpretation. Essays in Honor of Krister Stendahl*, edited by Richard A. Horsley, Harrisburg: Trinity Press International.

—— 2008, *The Arrogance of Nations: Reading Romans in the Shadow of Empire*, Minneapolis: Fortress.

Engels, Friedrich 1972 [1894–5], *Zur Geschichte des Urchristentums*, in *Marx Engels Werke* Volume 22, Berlin: Dietz.

—— 1973a [1850], *Der deutsche Bauernkrieg*, in *Marx Engels Werke*, Volume 7, Berlin: Dietz.

—— 1973b [1882], 'Bruno Bauer und das Urchristentum', in *Marx Engels Werke*, Volume 19, Berlin: Dietz.

—— 1973c [1913], 'Engels an Marx 19.November 1844', in *Marx Engels Werke*, Volume 27, Berlin: Dietz.

—— 1973d [1925], 'Engels an Eduard Bernstein Juli 1884', in *Marx Engels Werke*, Volume 36, Berlin: Dietz.

—— 1974 [1846], *Die Lage der arbeitenden Klasse in England. Nach eigner Anschauung und authentischen Quellen*, in *Marx Engels Werke*, Volume 2, Berlin: Dietz.

—— 1975a [1840], 'Requiem for the German Adelszeitung', in *Marx and Engels Collected Works*, Volume 2, Moscow: Progress Publishers.

—— 1975b [1842], *The Insolently Threatened Yet Miraculously Rescued Bible or: The Triumph of Faith, To Wit, the Terrible, Yet True and Salutary History of the Erstwhile Licentiate Bruno Bauer; How the Same, Seduced by the Devil, Fallen from the True Faith, Became Chief Devil, and Was Well and Truly Ousted in the End: A Christian Epic in Four Cantos*, in *Marx and Engels Collected Works*, Volume 2, Moscow: Progress Publishers.

—— 1975c [1842], *Schelling and Revelation: Critique of the Latest Attempt of Reaction Against the Free Philosophy*, in *Marx and Engels Collected Works*, Volume 2, Moscow: Progress Publishers.

—— 1975d [1843], 'Letters from London', in *Marx and Engels Collected Works*, Volume 3, Moscow: Progress Publishers.

—— 1975e [1843], 'Progress of Social Reform on the Continent', in *Marx and Engels Collected Works*, Volume 3, Moscow: Progress Publishers.

—— 1975f [1846], *The Condition of the Working-Class in England*, in *Marx and Engels Collected Works*, Volume 4, Moscow: Progress Publishers.

—— 1975g [1913], 'To Friedrich Graeber, February 22, 1841', in *Marx and Engels Collected Works*, Volume 2, Moscow: Progress Publishers.

—— 1975h [1913], 'To Wilhelm Graeber in Barmen, Bremen, November 20, 1840', in *Marx and Engels Collected Works*, Volume 2, Moscow: Progress Publishers.

—— 1975i [1920], 'To Friedrich Graeber, Bremen, February 19, 1839', in *Marx and Engels Collected Works*, Volume 2, Moscow: Progress Publishers.

—— 1975j [1920], 'To Friedrich Graeber in Berlin, Bremen, about April 23–May 1, 1839', in *Marx and Engels Collected Works*, Volume 2, Moscow: Progress Publishers.

—— 1976 [1842], 'Exzerpte aus Bruno Bauer: Kritik der evangelischen Geschichte der Synoptiker', in *Marx Engels Gesamtausgabe*, Volume IV:1, Berlin: Dietz.

—— 1978 [1850], *The Peasant War in Germany*, in *Marx and Engels Collected Works*, Volume 10, Moscow: Progress Publishers.

—— 1982 [1913], 'Engels to Marx in Paris, Barmen, 19 November 1844', in *Marx and Engels Collected Works*, Volume 38, Moscow: Progress Publishers.

—— 1985a [1840], 'Requiem für die deutsche Adelzeitung', in *Marx Engels Gesamtausgabe*, Volume 1:3, Berlin: Dietz.

—— 1985b [1842], *Die frech bedräute, jedoch wunderbar befreite Bibel. Oder: Der Triumph des Glaubens. Unter Mitwirkung von Edgar Bauer*, in *Marx Engels Gesamtausgabe*, Volume 1:3, Berlin: Dietz.

—— 1985c [1842], *Schelling und die Offenbarung. Kritik des neuesten Reaktionsversuchs gegen die freie Philosophie*, in *Marx Engels Gesamtausgabe*, Volume 1:3, Berlin: Dietz.

—— 1985d [1843], 'Briefe aus London', in *Marx Engels Gesamtausgabe*, Volume 1:3, Berlin: Dietz.

—— 1989 [1882], 'Bruno Bauer and Early Christianity', in *Marx and Engels Collected Works*, Volume 24, Moscow: Progress Publishers.

—— 1990a [1883], 'The Book of Revelation', in *Marx and Engels Collected Works*, Volume 26, Moscow: Progress Publishers.

—— 1990b [1894–5], *On the History of Early Christianity*, in *Marx and Engels Collected Works*, Volume 27, Moscow: Progress Publishers.

—— 1995 [1925], 'Engels to Eduard Bernstein in Zurich, London, July 1884', in *Marx and Engels Collected Works*, Volume 47, Moscow: Progress Publishers.

—— 2008a [1913], 'An Wilhelm Graeber, 20. November 1840', in *Marx Engels Werke* Volume 41, Berlin: Dietz.

—— 2008b [1913], 'An Friedrich Graeber, 22. Februar 1841', in *Marx Engels Werke*, Volume 41, Berlin: Dietz.

—— 2008c [1920], 'An Friedrich Graeber, 19. Februar 1839', in *Marx Engels Werke*, Volume 41, Berlin: Dietz.

—— 2008d [1920], 'An Friedrich Graeber, um den 23. April–1. Mai 1839', in *Marx Engels Werke*, Volume 41, Berlin: Dietz.

Erdman, David 1977, *Blake: Prophet Against Empire*, Fourth ed., Princeton: Princeton University Press.

Evans, C. Stephen 1984, 'Redeemed Man: The Vision Which Gave Rise to Marxism', *Christian Scholar's Review*, 13, 2: 141–50.

Fabella, Virginia and Mercy Amba Oduyoye (eds.) 1993, *With Passion and Compassion: Third World Women Doing Theology*, Maryknoll: Orbis.

Feiner, Susan 1986, 'Property Relations and Class Relations in Genovese and the Modes of Production Controversy', *Cambridge Journal of Economics*, 10, 1: 61–75.

Feuerbach, Ludwig 1924 [1841], *Das Wesen des Christentums*, Leipzig: Friedrichs & Bley.

—— 1989 [1841], *The Essence of Christianity*, translated by George Eliot, Amherst: Prometheus Books.

Fine, Robert 1994, 'The Rule of Law and Muggletonian Marxism: The Perplexities of Edward Thompson', *Journal of Law and Society*, 21, 2: 193–213.

Finley, Moses I. 1999, *The Ancient Economy*, updated ed., Volume 43, *Sather Classical Lectures*, Berkeley: University of California Press.

Fiorenza, Elisabeth Schüssler (ed.) 1996, *The Power of Naming*, Maryknoll: Orbis.

Fitzmyer, Joseph A. 2008, *First Corinthians, Anchor Yale Bible Commentaries*, New Haven: Yale University Press.

Flood, Christopher G. 2002, *Political Myth: A Theoretical Introduction*, New York: Routledge.

Foster-Carter, Aidan 1978, 'The Modes of Production Controversy', *New Left Review*, I, 107: 47–77.

Freire, Paolo 1970, *Pedagogy of the Oppressed*, New York: Continuum.

Fromm, Eric 2001, *The Fear of Freedom*, London: Routledge.

Gianaris, Nicholas V. 1996, *Modern Capitalism: Privatization, Employee Ownership, and Industrial Democracy*, Westport: Greenwood Publishing.

Gilbert, Alan D. 1979, 'Methodism, Dissent and Political Stability in Early Industrial England', *Journal of Religious History*, 10, 4: 381–99.

Goldmann, Lucien 1959, *Le Dieu caché: Études sur la vision tragiques dans les Pensées de Pascal et dans le théâtre de Racine*, Paris: Éditions Gallimard.

—— 1964, *The Hidden God: A Study of the Tragic Vision in the Penséés of Pascal and the Tragedies of Racine*, translated by Philip Thody, New York: The Humanities Press.

—— 1980, *Essays on Method in the Sociology of Literature*, translated by William Q. Boelhower, St. Louis: Telos Press.

Goodchild, Philip 2001, 'Why Is Philosophy So Compromised with God?', in Bryden (ed.) 2001.

—— 2007, 'Deleuze and Philosophy of Religion', Nottingham. Available at: <http://www.theologyphilosophycentre.co.uk/papers.php>.

Goss, Robert 1993, *Jesus Acted Up: A Gay and Lesbian Manifesto*, San Francisco: HarperSanFrancisco.

Gottwald, Norman K. 1999, *The Tribes of Yahweh: A Sociology of Liberated Israel 1250–1050 BC*, Reprint with new Preface, Sheffield: Sheffield Academic Press.

—— 2002, 'Response to Contributors', in *Tracking The Tribes of Yahweh: On the Trail of a Classic*, edited by Roland Boer, London: Continuum.

Griswold, Wendy 1987, 'A Methodological Framework for the Sociology of Culture', *Sociological Methodology*, 17: 1–35.

Gur-Ze'ev, Ilan 1998, 'Walter Benjamin and Max Horkheimer: From Utopia to Redemption', *The Journal of Jewish Thought and Philosophy*, 8: 119–55.

Gutiérrez, Gustavo 1983, *The Power of the Poor in History*, Maryknoll: Orbis.

—— 1987, *On Job: God-Talk and the Suffering of the Innocent*, Maryknoll: Orbis.

—— 1997, 'Renewing the Option for the Poor', in *Liberation Theologies, Postmodernity, and the Americas*, edited by David Batstone, Eduardo Mendieta, Lois Ann Lorentzen and Dwight N. Hopkins, London: Routledge.

—— 1999, 'The Task and Content of Liberation Theology', in *The Cambridge Companion to Liberation Theology*, edited by Christopher Rowland, Cambridge: Cambridge University Press.

—— 2001 [1969], *A Theology of Liberation*, translated by Caridad Inda and John Eagleson, London: SCM.

—— 2005 [1983], *We Drink from Our Own Wells: The Spiritual Journey of a People*, translated by Matthew J. O'Connell, London: SCM.

Habel, Norman 1975, *The Book of Job*, Cambridge: Cambridge University Press.

Habermas, Jürgen 1981, *Theorie des kommunikativen Handels*, Frankfurt am Main: Suhrkamp.

—— 1987, *The Theory of Communicative Action*, translated by Thomas McCarthy, Boston: Beacon.

Hallward, Peter 2006, *Out of This World: Deleuze and the Philosophy of Creation*, London: Verso.

Hamilton, Scott 2008, 'Between Zhdanov and Bloomsbury: the Poetry and Poetics of E.P. Thompson', *Thesis Eleven*, 95, 1: 95–112.

Hansen, Karen V. and Ilene J. Philipson (eds.) 1990, *Women, Class, and the Feminist Imagination: A Socialist-Feminist Reader*, Philadelphia: Temple University Press.

Hardt, Michael and Antonio Negri 2000, *Empire*, Cambridge, MA.: Harvard University Press.

—— 2004, *Multitude: War and Democracy in the Age of Empire*, New York: Penguin.

Harrill, Albert J. 2006, *Slaves in the New Testament: Literary, Social and Moral Dimensions*, Minneapolis: Fortress.

Harris, Sam 2005, *The End of Faith: Religion, Terror and the Future of Reason*, New York: W.W. Norton.

—— 2006, *Letter to a Christian Nation*, New York: Knopf.

Harvey, David 1999, *The Limits to Capital*, 2nd ed., London: Verso.

—— 2000a, 'Geoffrey de Ste Croix: Historian Who Unravelled the Mysteries of the Class Struggle in the Ancient World and the Decline of the Roman Empire', in *The Guardian*, (Manchester, 10 February): 43.

—— 2000b, *Spaces of Hope*, Berkeley: University of California Press.

Hastings, James 1903, *A Dictionary of the Bible*, Volume 2, Edinburgh: T. & T. Clark.

Heathorn, Stephen 1998, 'E.P. Thompson, Methodism, and the "Culturalist" Approach to the Historical Study of Religion', *Method & Theory in the Study of Religion*, 10, 2: 210–26.

Hempton, David 1984, *Methodism and Politics in British Society: 1750–1850*, Stanford: Stanford University Press.

—— 2006, *Methodism: Empire of the Spirit*, New Haven: Yale University Press.

Hempton, David and John Walsh 2002, 'E.P. Thompson and Methodism', in *God and Mammon: Protestants, Money, and the Market, 1790–1860*, edited by Mark A. Noll, Oxford: Oxford University Press.

Hesiod 1973, *Hesiod and Theognis*, translated by Dorothea Wender, Harmondsworth: Penguin.

Hess, Moses 1837, *Die Heilige Geschichte der Menschheit* Stuttgart: n. p.

—— 1961 [1841], *Die Europäische Trierarchie* in *Philosophische und sozialistische schriften, 1837-1850*, edited by Auguste Cornu and Wolfgang Müncke, Berlin: Akademie Verlag.

—— 2004 [1837], *The Holy History of Mankind and Other Writings*, edited by Shlomo Avineri, Cambridge: Cambridge University Press.

Heyman, George 2007, *The Power of Sacrifice: Roman and Christian Discourses in Conflict*, Washington, DC.: The Catholic University of America Press.

Hill, Bridget and Christopher Hill 1994, 'E.P. Thompson's Blake', *Literature and History*, 3, 1: 83–8.

Hill, Christopher 1972, *The World Turned Upside Down: Radical Ideas During the English Revolution*, Harmondsworth: Penguin.

Hindess, Barry and Paul Q. Hirst 1975, *Precapitalist Modes of Production*, London: Routledge and Kegan Paul.

Hinkelammert, Franz J. 1986, *The Ideological Weapons of Death: A Theological Critique of Capitalism*, translated by Phillip Berryman, Maryknoll: Orbis.

Hitchens, Christopher 2007, *God Is Not Great: How Religion Poisons Everything*, New York: Twelve Books.

Hjemslev, Louis 1959, *Essais Linguistiques*, Copenhagen: Nordisk Sprog- og Kulturforlag.

Hochschild, Ralph 1999, *Sozialgeschichtliche Exegese: Entwicklung, Geschichte und Methodik einer neutestamentlichen Forschungsrichtung*, Göttingen: Vandenhoeck & Ruprecht.

Horkheimer, Max 1973, 'Foreword', in *The Dialectical Imagination: A History of the Frankfurt School and the Institute of Social Research, 1923–1950*, edited by Martin Jay, Berkeley: University of California Press.

—— 1978, *Dawn and Decline: Notes 1926–1931 and 1950–1969*, translated by Michael Shaw, New York: Seabury.

—— 1982 [1972], *Critical Theory: Selected Essays*, translated by Matthew J. O'Connell et al., New York: Continuum.

—— 1985a [1939–1942], *Aufzeichnungen und Entwürfe zur Dialektik der Aufklärung 1939–1942*, in *Gesammelte Schriften*, Volume 12, Frankfurt am Main: Fischer Taschenbuch.

—— 1985b [1943], 'Plan des Forschungsprojekts über Antisemitismus', in *Gesammelte Schriften*, Volume 12, Frankfurt am Main: Fischer Taschenbuch.

—— 1985c [1943], 'Zur Psychologie des Antisemitismus', in *Gesammelte Schriften*, Volume 12, Frankfurt am Main: Fischer Taschenbuch.

—— 1985d [1945], 'New Yorker Notizen 1945', in *Gesammelte Schriften*, Volume 12, Frankfurt am Main: Fischer Taschenbuch.

—— 1985e [1957], 'Zum Begriff des Menchen', in *Gesammelte Schriften*, Volume 7, Frankfurt am Main: Fischer Taschenbuch.

—— 1985f [1960/1967], 'Zue Ergreifung Eichmanns', in *Gesammelte Schriften*, Volume 8, Frankfurt am Main: Fischer Taschenbuch.

—— x 1985g [1961], 'Über die deutschen Juden', in *Gesammelte Schriften*, Volume 8, Frankfurt am Main: Fischer Taschenbuch.

—— 1985h [1963], 'Theismus – Atheismus', in *Gesammelte Schriften*, Volume 7, Frankfurt am Main: Fischer Taschenbuch.

—— 1985i [1965], 'Bedrohungen der Freiheit', in *Gesammelte Schriften*, Volume 8, Frankfurt am Main: Fischer Taschenbuch.

—— 1985j [1966], 'Letzte Spur von Theologie – Paul Tillichs Vermächtnis', in *Gesammelte Schriften*, Volume 7, Frankfurt am Main: Fischer Taschenbuch.

—— 1985k [1967], 'De Anima', in *Gesammelte Schriften*, Volume 7, Frankfurt am Main: Fischer Taschenbuch.

—— 1985l [1967], 'Erinnerung an Paul Tillich [Gespräch mit Gerhard Rein]', in *Gesammelte Schriften*, Volume 7, Frankfurt am Main: Fischer Taschenbuch.

—— 1985m [1967], 'Religion und Philosophie', in *Gesammelte Schriften*, Volume 7, Frankfurt am Main: Fischer Taschenbuch.

—— 1985n [1968], 'Christentum, Marxismus und studentische Protestbewegung. Gespräch mit Dagobert Lindlau', in *Gesammelte Schriften*, Volume 7, Frankfurt am Main: Fischer Taschenbuch.

—— 1985o [1968], 'Psalm 91', in *Gesammelte Schriften*, Volume 7, Frankfurt am Main: Fischer Taschenbuch.

—— 1985p [1969], 'Die Funktion der Theologie in der Gesellschaft. Gespräch mit Paul Neuenzeit', in *Gesammelte Schriften*, Volume 7, Frankfurt am Main: Fischer Taschenbuch.

—— 1985q [1970], 'Die Sehnsucht nach dem ganz Anderen [Gespräch mit Helmut Gumnior]', in *Gesammelte Schriften*, Volume 7, Frankfurt am Main: Fischer Taschenbuch.

—— 1985r [1971], 'Bemerkungen zue Liberalisierung der Religion', in *Gesammelte Schriften*, Volume 7, Frankfurt am Main: Fischer Taschenbuch.

—— 1985s [1971], 'Zur Zukunft der Kritische Theorie [Gespräche mit Claus Grossner]', in *Gesammelte Schriften*, Volume 7, Frankfurt am Main: Fischer Taschenbuch.

—— 1987a [1926–31], 'Notizen zue Dämmerung', in *Gesammelte Schriften*, Volume 11, Frankfurt am Main: Fischer Taschenbuch.

—— 1987b [1930], 'Anfänge der bürgerlichen Geschichtsphilosophie', in *Gesammelte Schriften*, Volume 2, Frankfurt am Main: Fischer Taschenbuch.

—— 1987c [1934], *Dämmerung: Notizen in Deutschland*, in *Gesammelte Schriften*, Volume 2, Frankfurt am Main: Fischer Taschenbuch.

—— 1987d [1944/1946], 'Antisemitismus: Der soziologische Hintergrund des psychoanalystischen Forschungsansatzes', in *Gesammelte Schriften*, Volume 5, Frankfurt am Main: Fischer Taschenbuch.

—— 1987e [1945], 'Zur Klassification jüdischer Einwanderer', in *Gesammelte Schriften*, Volume 5, Frankfurt am Main: Fischer Taschenbuch.

—— 1988a [1934], 'Zum Rationalismusstreit in der gegenwärtigen Philosophie', in *Gesammelte Schriften*, Volume 3, Frankfurt am Main: Fischer Taschenbuch.

—— 1988b [1935], 'Gedanke zur Religion', in *Gesammelte Schriften*, Volume 3, Frankfurt am Main: Fischer Taschenbuch.

—— 1988c [1935], 'Zum Problem der Wahrheit', in *Gesammelte Schriften*, Volume 3, Frankfurt am Main: Fischer Taschenbuch.

—— 1988d [1936], 'Autorität und Familie', in *Gesammelte Schriften*, Volume 3, Frankfurt am Main: Fischer Taschenbuch.

—— 1988e [1936], 'Egoismus und Freiheitsbewegung', in *Gesammelte Schriften*, Volume 4, Frankfurt am Main: Fischer Taschenbuch.

—— 1988f [1936], 'Zu Theodor Haecker's Der Christ und der Geschichte', in *Gesammelte Schriften*, Volume 4, Frankfurt am Main: Fischer Taschenbuch.

—— 1988g [1938], 'Montaigne und die Funktion der Skepsis', in *Gesammelte Schriften*, Volume 4, Frankfurt am Main: Fischer Taschenbuch.

—— 1988h [1939], 'Die Juden und Europa', in *Gesammelte Schriften*, Volume 4, Frankfurt am Main: Fischer Taschenbuch.

—— 1988i [1940], 'Die gesellschaftliche Funktion der Philosophie', in *Gesammelte Schriften*, Volume 4, Frankfurt am Main: Fischer Taschenbuch.

—— 1988j [1941], 'Neue Kunst und Massenkultur', in *Gesammelte Schriften*, Volume 4, Frankfurt am Main: Fischer Taschenbuch.

—— 1988k [1949–69], *Nachgelassene Schriften*, in *Gesammelte Schriften*, Volume 14, Frankfurt am Main: Fischer Taschenbuch.

—— 1988l [1950–70], *Späne. Notizen über Gespräche mit Max Horkheimer, in unverbindlicher Formulierung aufgeschrieben von Friedrich Pollock*, in *Gesammelte Schriften*, Volume 14, Frankfurt am Main: Fischer Taschenbuch.

—— 1989a [1961], 'Paul Tillich [Zum 75. Geburtstag]', in *Gesammelte Schriften*, Volume 13, Frankfurt am Main: Fischer Taschenbuch.

—— 1989b [1963], 'Skepsis und Glaube [Ein Brief an Götz Harbsmeier]', in *Gesammelte Schriften*, Volume 13, Frankfurt am Main: Fischer Taschenbuch.

—— 1991a, *Notizen, 1949–1969*, in *Gesammelte Schriften*, Volume 6, Frankfurt am Main: Fischer Taschenbuch.

—— 1991b [1967], *Zur Kritik der instrumentellen Vernunft*, in *Gesammelte Schriften*, Volume 6, Frankfurt am Main: Fischer Taschenbuch.

—— 1993, *Between Philosophy and Social Science: Selected Early Writings*, translated by G. Frederick Hunter, Matthew S. Kramer and John Torpey, Cambridge, MA.: MIT.

—— 1995 [1934], 'Max Horkheimer an Paul Tillich, Chilwark, Mass., 21.8.34', in *Gesammelte Schriften*, Volume 15, Frankfurt am Main: Fischer Taschenbuch.

—— 1996, *Critique of Instrumental Reason*, translated by Matthew J. O'Connell and et al., New York: Continuum.

—— 1996a [1941], 'Max Horkheimer an Paul and Hannah Tillich, Gatlinburg, Tenn., Den 19. Juli 1941', in *Gesammelte Schriften*, Volume 17, Frankfurt am Main: Fischer Taschenbuch.

—— 1996b [1942], 'Max Horkheimer an Paul Tillich, Bar Harbor, Maine, 12. August 1942', in *Gesammelte Schriften*, Volume 17, Frankfurt am Main: Fischer Taschenbuch.

—— 1996c [1942], 'Max Horkheimer an Paul Tillich, New York, February 11, 1942', in *Gesammelte Schriften*, Volume 17, Frankfurt am Main: Fischer Taschenbuch.

—— 1996d [1947], 'Max Horkheimer an Paul Tillich, East Hampton, Long Island, New York, August 29, 1947', in *Gesammelte Schriften*, Volume 17, Frankfurt am Main: Fischer Taschenbuch.

—— 1996e [1950], 'Max Horkheimer an Hannah Tillich, New York, 18. Mai 1950', in *Gesammelte Schriften*, Volume 18, Frankfurt am Main: Fischer Taschenbuch.

—— 1996f [1961], 'Max Horkheimer an Paul Tillich, Hamburg, den 17.6.61', in *Gesammelte Schriften*, Volume 18, Frankfurt am Main: Fischer Taschenbuch.

—— 1996g [1965], 'Max Horkheimer an Hannah Tillich, Chicago, 28. Oktober 1965', in *Gesammelte Schriften*, Volume 18, Frankfurt am Main: Fischer Taschenbuch.

—— 1996h [1965], 'Max Horkheimer an Hannah und Paul Tillich, Santa Barbara, Calif., 5.Januar 1965', in *Gesammelte Schriften*, Volume 18, Frankfurt am Main: Fischer Taschenbuch.

—— 2004 [1947], *Eclipse of Reason*, London: Continuum.

—— 2006 [1968], 'Psalm 91', in *Marx, Critical Theory, and Religion: A Critique of Rational Choice*, Leiden: Brill.

Horkheimer, Max and Theodor W. Adorno 1985 [1943], 'Diskussion zu den ›Elementen des Antisemitismus‹ der *Dialektik der Aufklärung*' in *Gesammelte Schriften*, Volume 12, Frankfurt am Main: Fischer Taschenbuch.

—— 1987 [1947], *Dialektik der Aufklärung: Philosophische Fragmente*, in *Gesammelte Schriften*, Volume 3, Frankfurt am Main: Fischer Taschenbuch.

—— 2002, *Dialectic of Enlightenment: Philosophical Fragments*, translated by Edmund Jephcott, Stanford: Stanford University Press.

Horrell, David G. 2007, 'The Label...: 1 Peter 4:16 and the Formation of Christian Identity', *Journal of Biblical Literature*, 126, 2: 361–81.

Horsley, Richard 1989, *Sociology and the Jesus Movement*, New York: Crossroad Publishing Company.

—— 1992, *Jesus and the Spiral of Violence: Popular Jewish Resistance in Roman Palestine*, Philadelphia: Augsburg Fortress.

—— 1995, *Galilee: History, Politics, People*, Philadelphia: Trinity Press International.

—— 1996, *Archaeology, History and Society in Galilee*, Philadelphia: Trinity Press International.

—— 2002, *Jesus and Empire: The Kingdom of God and the New World Order*, Minneapolis: Augsburg Fortress.

—— 2007, *Scribes, Visionaries, and the Politics of Second Temple Judea*, Louisville: Westminster John Knox.

—— (ed.) 2008a, *In the Shadow of Empire: Reclaiming the Bible as a History of Faithful Resistance*, Louisville: Westminster John Knox.

—— 2008b, 'Jesus and Empire', in *In the Shadow of Empire: Reclaiming the Bible as a History of Faithful Resistance*, edited by Richard Horsley, Louisville: Westminster John Knox.

Hudson, Michael and Baruch A. Levine (eds.) 1996, *Privatization in the Ancient Near East and Classical World, Peabody Museum Bulletin 5*, Cambridge, MA.: Peabody Museum of Archaeology and Ethnology, Harvard University.

—— (eds.) 1999, *Urbanization and Land Ownership in the Ancient Near East*, Cambridge, MA: Peabody Museum of Archaeology and Ethnology, Harvard University.

Hudson, Michael and Marc van de Mieroop (eds.) 2002, *Debt and Economic Renewal in the Ancient Near East*, Bethesda: CDL.

Hudson, Michael and Cornelia Wunsch (eds.) 2004, *Creating Economic Order: Record-Keeping, Standardization, and the Development of Accounting in the Ancient Near East, International Scholars Conference on Ancient Near Eastern Economies 4*, Bethesda: CDL Press.

Hughes, John 2003, 'Unspeakable Utopia: Art and the Return to the Theological in the Marxism of Adorno and Horkheimer', *Cross Currents*, 53, 4: 475–92.

Jaffe, J.A. 1989, 'The "Chiliasm of Despair" Reconsidered: Revivalism and Working-Class Agitation in County Durham', *The Journal of British Studies*, 28, 1: 23–42.

Jameson, Fredric 1972, *The Prison-House of Language: A Critical Account of Structuralism and Russian Formalism*, Princeton: Princeton University Press.

Jobling, David 1991, 'Feminism and "Mode of Production" in Ancient Israel: Search for a Method', in *The Bible and the Politics of Exegesis: Essays in Honor of Norman K. Gottwald on His Sixty-Fifth Birthday*, edited by David Jobling, Peggy L. Day and Gerald T. Sheppard, Cleveland: Pilgrim Press.

—— 1998, 1 *Samuel*, Collegeville: Liturgical Press.

Jobling, David, Tina Pippin and Ronald Schleifer 1995, *The Postmodern Bible Reader*, Oxford: Blackwell.

Jolowicz, H.F. 1952, *Historical Introduction to the Study of Roman Law*, Cambridge: Cambridge University Press.

Kautsky, Karl 1947a [1888], *Thomas More und seine Utopie: mit einer historischen Einleitung*, 3rd ed, Berlin: Dietz.

—— 1947b [1895–7], *Vorläufer des neueren Sozialismus I: Kommunistische Bewegung im Mittelalter*, Berlin: Dietz.

—— 1947c [1895–7]-b, *Vorläufer des neueren Sozialismus II: Der Kommunismus in der deutschen Reformation*, Berlin: J. H.W. Dietz.

—— 1977 [1908], *Der Ursprung des Christentums: eine historische Untersuchung*, Stuttgart: Dietz.

—— 1979 [1888], *Thomas More and His Utopia*, translated by Henry James Stenning, London: Lawrence and Wishart.

—— 2006 [1897], *Communism in Central Europe in the Time of the Reformation*, translated by J.L. and E.G. Mulliken, Whitefish: Kessinger.

—— 2007 [1908], *Foundations of Christianity*, translated by H.F. Mins, London: Socialist Resistance.

Kautsky, Karl and Paul Lafargue 1977 [1922], *Vorläufer des neueren Sozialismus*, Stuttgart: J.H.W. Dietz.

Kaye, Harvey J. 1984, *The British Marxist Historians*, Oxford: Polity.

Kee, Alistair 1990, *Marx and the Failure of Liberation Theology*, London: SCM.

Keener, Craig S. 2005, *1–2 Corinthians, New Cambridge Bible Commentary*, Cambridge: Cambridge University Press.

Kelley, Nicole 2006, 'Philosophy as Training for Death: Reading the Ancient Christian Martyr Acts as Spiritual Exercises', *Church History*, 75, 4: 723–47.

Kenny, Michael 2000, 'Socialism and the Romantic "Self": The Case of Edward Thompson', *Journal of Political Ideologies*, 5, 1: 105–27.

Kent, John 2002, *Wesley and the Wesleyans: Religion in Eighteenth-Century Britain*, Cambridge: Cambridge University Press.

Kim, Andrew E. 1996, 'Critical Theory and the Sociology of Religion: A Reassessment', *Social Compass*, 43, 2: 267–83.

Kinneavy, James 1983, 'Kairos: a Neglected Concept in Classical Rhetoric', in *Rhetoric and Praxis: The Contribution of Classical Rhetoric to Practical Reasoning*, edited by Jean Dietz Moss, Washington, DC.: Catholic University of America Press.

Kittel, Gerhard, Gerhard Friedrich and Geoffrey William Bromiley (eds.) 1985, *Theological Dictionary of the New Testament*, Grand Rapids: Eerdmans.

Kolakowski, Leszek 1981, *Main Currents of Marxism*, translated by P.S. Falla, Volume 1, Oxford: Oxford University Press.

Koosed, Jennifer L. 2008, 'Nine Reflections on the Book: Poststructuralism and the Hebrew Bible', *Religion Compass*, 2, 4: 499–512.

Kowalinski, P. 1972, 'The Genesis of Christianity in the Views of Contemporary Marxist Specialists in Religion', *Antonianum*, 47: 541–75.

Krader, Lawrence 1975, *The Asiatic Mode of Production: Sources, Development and Critique in the Writings of Karl Marx*, Assen: Van Gorcum.

Kyrtatas, Dimitris J. 1987, *The Social Structure of Early Christian Communities*, London: Verso.

Lamont, William 2006, *Last Witnesses: Muggletonian History, 1652–1979*, Aldershot: Ashgate.

Larrain, Jorge 1983a, 'Ideology', in *A Dictionary of Marxist Thought*, edited by Tom Bottomore, Oxford: Blackwell.

—— 1983b, *Marxism and Ideology*, London: Macmillan.

Leaving Certificate from Berlin University 1975 [1926], in *Marx and Engels Collected Works*, Volume 1, Moscow: Progress Publishers.

Lefebvre, Henri 1991 [1984], *The Production of Space*, translated by Donald Nicholson-Smith, Oxford: Blackwell.

Lemche, Niels Peter 1988 [1984], *Ancient Israel: A New History of Israelite Society*, translated by Fred Cryor, Sheffield: Sheffield Academic Press.

—— 1998a, *The Israelites in History and Tradition*, London: SPCK.

—— 1998b, [1996] *Prelude to Israel's Past: Background and Beginnings of Israelite History and Identity*, translated by E.F. Maniscalco, Peabody: Hendrickson.

Leo XIII 1891, *Rerum Novarum: On Capital and Labour*, Rome: Libreria Editrice Vaticana.

Lichtheim, George 1990, 'Marx and the "Asiatic Mode of Production"', in *Marxian Economics, Volume I*, edited by J. E. King, Aldershot: Elgar.

Lincoln, Bruce 2000, *Theorizing Myth: Narrative, Ideology, and Scholarship*, Chicago: University of Chicago Press.

Linklater, Andrew 2000, *International Relations: Critical Concepts in Political Science*, New York: Routledge.

Lischer, Richard 1973, 'The Lutheran Shape of Marxian Evil', *Religion in Life*, 42, 4: 549–58.

Lister, John 2006, 'Latin America: A Continent in Revolt', in *Socialist Resistance*. Available at: <http://www.isg-fi.org.uk/spip.php?article226>.

Longenecker, Richard N. 1990, *Galatians, Word Biblical Commentary*, Volume 41, Waco: Word Books.

Löwith, Karl 1949, *Meaning in History: The Theological Implications of the Philosophy of History*, Chicago: University of Chicago Press.

Löwy, Michael 1980, 'Jewish Messianism and Libertarian Utopia in Central Europe (1900–1933)', *New German Critique*, 20, 2: 105–15.

—— 1985, 'Revolution Against "Progress": Walter Benjamin's Romantic Anarchism', *New Left Review*, I, 152: 42–59.

—— 1988a, *Marxisme et théologie de la libération*, Cahiers d'étude et de recherche, Amsterdam: IIRE.

—— 1988b, *Redemption and Utopia: Jewish Libertarian Thought in Central Europe*, translated by Hope Heaney, Stanford: Stanford University Press.

—— 1989a, 'Religion, Utopia and Counter-Modernity: The Allegory of the Angel of History in Walter Benjamin', *Social Compass*, 36, 1: 95–104.

—— 1989b, 'Weber Against Marx? The Polemic Against Historical Materialism', *Science & Society*, 53, 1: 71–83.

—— 1993, 'Marxism and Christianity in Latin America', *Latin American Perspectives*, 20, 4: 28–42.

—— 1996, *The War of Gods: Religion and Politics in Latin America*, London: Verso.

—— 1997, 'Lucien Goldmann or the Communitarian Wager', *Socialism and Democracy*, 11, 1: 25–35.

—— 1998, 'Friedrich Engels on Religion and Class Struggle', *Science & Society*, 62, 1: 79–87.

—— 2000, 'A "Red" Government in the South of Brazil', *Monthly Review*, 52, 6. Available at: <http://www.monthlyreview.org/1100lowy.htm>.

—— 2004, 'Le concept d'affinitié élective chez Max Weber', *Archives de Sciences Sociales des Religions*, 127: 93–103.

—— 2005a, *Fire Alarm: Reading Walter Benjamin's 'On the Concept of History'*, translated by Chris Turner, London: Verso.

—— 2005b, 'Opiate of the People? Marxism and Religion', *International Viewpoint*. Available at: <http://www.internationalviewpoint.org/article.php3?id_article=807>.

—— 2005c, *The Theory of Revolution in the Young Marx*, Chicago: Haymarket Books.

—— 2006, 'Heloisa Helena, a Socialist Woman for the Brazilian Presidential Elections', *ZNet: The Spirit of Resistance*. Available at: <http://www.zmag.org/znet/viewArticle/3360>.

—— 2008, 'Communism and Religion: José Carlos Mariátegui's Revolutionary Mysticism', *Latin American Perspectives*, 35, 2: 71–9.

—— 2009, 'Capitalism as Religion: Walter Benjamin and Max Weber', *Historical Materialism*, 17, 1: 60–73.

Luxemburg, Rosa 1970 [1905], *Socialism and the Churches*, in *Rosa Luxemburg Speaks*, edited by Mary-Alice Waters, New York: Pathfinder Press.

—— 1982 [1905], *Kirche und Sozialismus*, Frankfurt am Main: Stimme-Verlag.

Lynd, Staughton 1997, *Living Inside Our Hope: A Steadfast Radical's Thoughts on Rebuilding the Movement*, Ithaca: Cornell University Press.

Mack, Burton 2008, *Myth and the Christian Nation: A Social Theory of Religion*, London: Equinox.

Macourt, Malcolm (ed.) 1977, *Towards a Theology of Gay Liberation*, London: SCM.

Makdisi, Saree 2003, *William Blake and the Impossible History of the 1790s*, Chicago: University of Chicago Press.

Martin, Dale, B. 1999, *The Corinthian Body*, New Haven: Yale University Press.

Martyn, J. Louis 2004, *Galatians*, Anchor Yale Bible Commentaries, New Haven: Yale University Press.

Marx, Karl 1972, *The Ethnological Notebooks of Karl Marx*, edited by Lawrence Krader, Assen: Van Gorcum.

—— 1972a [1847], 'Der Kommunismus des "Rheinischen Beobachters"', in *Marx Engels Werke*, Volume 4, Berlin: Dietz.

—— 1972b [1867], *Das Kapital. Kritik der politischen Ökonomie. Erster Band Buch I: Der Produktionsprozeß des Kapitals*, in *Marx Engels Werke*, Volume 23, Berlin: Dietz.

—— 1973 [1924], 'Thesen über Feuerbach', in *Marx Engels Werke*, Volume 3, Berlin: Dietz.

—— 1974a [1844], *Zur Judenfrage*, in *Marx Engels Werke*, Volume 1, Berlin: Dietz.

—— 1974b [1844], 'Zur Kritik der Hegelschen Rechtsphilosophie. Einleitung', in *Marx Engels Werke*, Volume 1, Berlin: Dietz.

—— 1974c [1859], *Zur Kritik der Politischen Ökonomie*, in *Marx Engels Werke*, Volume 13, Berlin: Dietz.

—— 1975a [1844], 'Contribution to the Critique of Hegel's Philosophy of Law: Introduction', in *Marx and Engels Collected Works*, Volume 3, Moscow: Progress Publishers.

—— 1975b [1844], *On the Jewish Question*, in *Marx and Engels Collected Works*, Volume 3, Moscow: Progress Publishers.

—— 1976a [1842], 'Exzerpte aus Charles de Brosses: Ueber den Dienst der Fetischengötter', in *Marx Engels Gesamtausgabe*, Volume 4:1, Berlin: Dietz.

—— 1976b [1847], 'The Communism of the Rheinische Beobachter', in *Marx and Engels Collected Works*, Volume 6, Moscow: Progress Publishers.

—— 1976c [1924], 'Theses on Feuerbach (Original version)', in *Marx and Engels Collected Works*, Volume 4, Moscow: Progress Publishers.

—— 1986 [1939–41], *Economic Manuscripts of 1857–58 (First Version of Capital) [Grundrisse]*, in *Marx and Engels Collected Works*, Volume 28, Moscow: Progress Publishers.

—— 1987 [1859], *A Contribution to the Critique of Political Economy*, in *Marx and Engels Collected Works*, Volume 29, Moscow: Progress Publishers.

—— 1988 [1976–82], *Economic Manuscript of 1861–63: A Contribution to the Critique of Political Economy*, in *Marx and Engels Collected Works*, Volume 30, Moscow: Progress Publishers.

—— 1989 [1891], 'Critique of the Gotha Programme', in *Marx and Engels Collected Works*, Volume 24, Moscow: Progress Publishers.

—— 1996 [1867], *Capital: A Critique of Political Economy, Volume I*, in *Marx and Engels Collected Works*, Volume 35, Moscow: Progress Publishers.

—— 2005 [1939–41], *Ökonomische Manuskripte 1857/1858 [Grundrisse]*, in *Marx Engels Werke*, Volume 42, Berlin: Dietz.

Marx, Karl and Friedrich Engels 1975 [1845], *The Holy Family, or Critique of Critical Criticism*, in *Marx and Engels Collected Works*, Volume 4, Moscow: Progress Publishers.

—— 1976 [1932], *The German Ideology: Critique of Modern German Philosophy According to Its Representatives Feuerbach, B. Bauer and Stirner, and of German Socialism According to Its Various Prophets*, in *Marx and Engels Collected Works*, Volume 5, Moscow: Progress Publishers.

—— 1972 [1845], *Die heilige Familie oder Kritik der kritischen Kritik*, in *Marx Engels Werke*, Volume 2, Berlin: Dietz.

—— 1973 [1932], *Die deutsche Ideologie. Kritik der neuesten deutschen Philosophie in ihren Repräsentanten Feuerbach, B. Bauer und Stirner und des deutschen Sozialismus in seinen verschiedenen Propheten*, in *Marx Engels Werke*, Volume 3, Berlin: Dietz.

Matera, Frank J. 2007, *Galatians, Sacra Pagina*, Collegeville: Liturgical Press.

Mayani, Zecharia 1956, *Les Hyksos et le monde de la Bible*, Paris: Payot.

McLellan, David 1995, *Ideology*, Minneapolis: University of Minnesota Press.

McLennan, Gregor 1981, *Marxism and the Methodologies of History*, London: Verso.

McNutt, Paula M. 1999, *Reconstructing the Society of Ancient Israel*, London: SPCK.

Mee, John 1992, *Dangerous Enthusiasm: William Blake and the Culture of Radicalism in the 1790s*, Oxford: Oxford University Press.

Meyers, Carol 1988, *Discovering Eve: Ancient Israelite Women in Context*, Oxford: Oxford University Press.

—— 1997, 'The Family in Early Israel', in *Families in Ancient Israel*, edited by Leo S. Purdue et al., Louisville: Westminster John Knox.

Miéville, China 1998, *King Rat*, London: Macmillan.

—— 2000, *Perdido Street Station*, London: Macmillan.

—— 2002, *The Scar*, London: Pan Macmillan.

—— 2004a, *Between Equal Rights: A Marxist Theory of International Law*, Historical Materialism Book Series, Leiden: Brill.

—— 2004b, *Iron Council*, London: Pan Macmillan.

—— 2005, *Looking for Jake and Other Stories*, London: Pan Macmillan.

—— 2006, *Between Equal Rights: A Marxist Theory of International Law*, London: Pluto Press. Original edition, Miéville 2004a.

Miranda, José P. 1974, *Marx and the Bible: A Critique of the Philosophy of Oppression*, translated by John Eagleson, Maryknoll: Orbis.

—— 1982, *Communism in the Bible*, translated by Robert R. Barr, Maryknoll: Orbis.

Moore, Stephen 2006, *Empire and Apocalypse: Postcolonialism and the New Testament*, Sheffield: Sheffield Phoenix.

Mosala, Itumeleng 2002, 'The Politics of Debt and the Liberation of Scriptures', in *Tracking The Tribes of Yahweh: On the Trail of a Classic*, edited by Roland Boer, London: Continuum.

Moxnes, Halvor 1997, *Constructing Early Christian Families; Family as Social Reality and Metaphor*, Louisville: Westminster John Knox.

—— 2003, *Putting Jesus in His Place: A Radical Vision of Household and Kingdom*, Louisville: Westminster John Knox.

Moylan, Tom 1997, 'Bloch Against Bloch: The Theological Reception of *Das Prinzip Hoffnung* and the Liberation of the Utopian Function', in *Not Yet: Reconsidering Ernst Bloch*, edited by Jamie Owen Daniel and Tom Moylan, London: Verso.

Myers, Ched 1989, *Binding the Strong Man: A Political Reading of Mark's Story of Jesus*, Maryknoll: Orbis.

Negri, Antonio 1991a [1979], *Marx Beyond Marx: Lessons on the Grundrisse*, translated by Harry Cleaver, Michael Ryan and Maurizio Viano, Brooklyn: Autonomedia.

—— 1991b [1981], *The Savage Anomaly: The Power of Spinoza's Metaphysics and Politics*, translated by Michael Hardt, Minneapolis: University of Minnesota Press.

—— 2003 [1997 and 2000], *Time for Revolution*, translated by Matteo Mandarini, London: Continuum.

—— 2004 [1985–98], *Subversive Spinoza: (Un)contemporary Variations*, translated by Timothy S. Murphy, Michael Hardt, Ted Stolze and Charles T. Wolfe, Manchester: Manchester University Press.

—— 2006 [1970], *The Political Descartes: Reason, Ideology and the Bourgeois Project*, translated by Matteo Mandarini and Alberto Toscano, London: Verso.

—— 2008a [2003], *The Porcelain Workshop: For a New Grammar of Politics*, Los Angeles: Semiotext(e).

—— 2008b [2006], *Empire and Beyond*, translated by Ed Emery, Cambridge: Polity Press.

—— 2009 [2002], *The Labor of Job*, translated by Matteo Mandarini, Durham, NC. Duke University Press.

Negri, Antonio and Cesare Casarino 2008, *In Praise of the Common: A Conversation on Philosophy and Politics*, Minneapolis: University of Minnesota Press.

Negri, Antonio and Anne Defourmantelle 2004 [2002], *Negri on Negri*, translated by M.B. DeBevoise, New York: Routledge.

Negri, Antonio and Gabriele Fadini 2008, 'Materialism and Theology: A Conversation', *Rethinking Marxism*, 20, 4: 665–72.

Negri, Antonio and Raf Valvola Scelsi 2008 [2006], *Goodbye Mr. Socialism*, translated by Peter Thomas, New York: Seven Stories Press.

Nietzsche, Friedrich 1974 [1889/1895], *The Gay Science, with a Prelude in Rhymes and an Appendix of Songs*, translated by Walter Kaufman, New York: Vintage.

—— 1994 [1889/1895], *On the Genealogy of Morality*, translated by Carol Diethe, Cambridge: Cambrdige University Press.

Noerr, Gunzelin Schmid 2002, 'Editor's Afterword: The Position of "Dialectic of Enlightenment" in the Development of Critical Theory', in *Dialectic of Enlightenment: Philosophical Fragments*, edited by Max Horkheimer and Theodor W. Adorno, Stanford: Stanford University Press.

Núñez C., Emilio Antonio and William David Taylor 1996, *Crisis and Hope in Latin America: An Evangelical Perspective*, Pasadena: William Carey Library.

Økland, Jorunn 2005, *Women in Their Place: Paul and the Corinthian Discourse of Gender and Sanctuary Space*, London: T. & T. Clark.
—— 2008, 'Paulsimone', in *Marxist Feminist Criticism of the Bible*, edited by Roland Boer and Jorunn Økland, Sheffield: Sheffield Phoenix.
Onians, Richard Broxton 1973, *The Origins of European Thought*, New York: Arno Press.
Ott, Michael R. 2001, *Max Horkheimer's Critical Theory of Religion: The Meaning of Religion in the Struggle for Human Emancipation*, Lanham: University Press of America.
—— 2006, 'The Notion of the Totally "Other" and its Consequences in the Critical Theory of Religion and the Rational Choice Theory of Religion', in *Marx, Critical Theory, and Religion: A Critique of Rational Choice*, edited by Warren S. Goldstein, Leiden: Brill.
—— 2007, 'Max Horkheimer's Negative Theology of the Totally Other', in *The Future of Religion: Toward a Reconciled Society*, edited by Michael R. Ott, Leiden: Brill.
Palmer, Bryan D. 1994, *E.P. Thompson: Objections and Oppositions*, London: Verso.
Paz, Néstor 1975, *My Life for My Friends: The Guerilla Journal of Néstor Paz, Christian*, translated by Ed Garcia and John Eagleson, Maryknoll: Orbis.
Pietz, William 1985, 'The Problem of the Fetish, I', *Res: Anthopology and Aesthetics*, 9: 5–17.
Pius XI 1931, *Quadragesimo Anno: On Reconstruction of the Social Order*, Rome: Libreria Editrice Vaticana.
Pixley, Jorge 1987, *On Exodus: A Liberation Perspective*, translated by Robert R. Barr, Maryknoll: Orbis.
Polanyi, Karl 1968, *Primitive, Archaic and Modern Economies*, Garden City: Anchor Books.
Polzin, Robert 1980, *Moses and the Deuteronomist*, Bloomington: Indiana University Press.
—— 1989, *Samuel and the Deuteronomist*, Bloomington: Indiana University Press.
—— 1993, *David and the Deuteronomist*, Bloomington: Indiana University Press.
Pritchard, James B. (ed.) 1955, *Ancient Near Eastern Texts Relating to the Old Testament*, Princeton: Princeton University Press.
Pryor, Frederic L. 1990, 'The Asian Mode of Production as an Economic System', in *Marxian Economics*, Volume 1, edited by J.E. King, Aldershot: Elgar.
Reed, Evelyn 1970, 'Women: Caste, Class or Oppressed Sex', *International Socialist Review*, 31, 3: 15–17, 40–1.
Reed, Jason 2003, 'A Universal History of Contingency: Deleuze and Guattari on the History of Capitalism', *Borderlands*, 2, 3. Available at: <www.borderlands.net.au/vol2no3_2003/read_contingency.htm>.
Rickert, Thomas 2007, 'Invention in the Wild: Locating Kairos in Space-Time', in *The Locations of Composition*, edited by Christopher J. Keller and Christian R. Weisser, Albany: State University Press of New York.
Rieger, Joerg 2007, *Christ and Empire: From Paul to Postcolonial Times*, Minneapolis: Fortress.
Rix, Robert 2007, *William Blake and the Cultures of Radical Christianity*, Aldershot: Ashgate.
Robinson, John A.T. 1963, *Honest to God*, London: SCM.
Rose, Peter W. 1992, *Sons of the Gods, Children of Earth: Ideology and Literary Form in Ancient Greece*, Ithaca: Cornell University Press.
Rowland, Christopher (ed.) 1999, *The Cambridge Companion to Liberation Theology*, Cambridge: Cambridge University Press.
Runciman, W.G. 2004, 'The Diffusion of Christianity in the Third Century AD as a Case-Study in the Theory of Cultural Selection', *European Journal of Sociology*, 45, 1: 3–21.
Runions, Erin 2004a, 'Biblical Promise and Threat in U.S. Imperialist Rhetoric, Before and After 9.11', *The Scholar and Feminist Online*, 2, 2. Available at: <http://www.barnard.edu/sfonline/reverb/runions1.htm>.

—— 2004b, 'Desiring War: Apocalypse, Commodity Fetish and the End of History', *The Bible and Critical Theory*, 1, 1: 1–16. Available at: <http://publications.epress .monash.edu/doi/pdf/10.2104/bc040004>.

Sahlins, Marshall 1968, *Tribesmen*, Englewood Cliffs: Prentice-Hall.

—— 1972, *Stone Age Economics*, New York: Aldine de Gruyter.

Sand, Shlomo 2009, *The Invention of the Jewish People*, London: Verso.

Schweitzer, Steven 2007, *Reading Utopia in Chronicles*, London: T. & T. Clark.

Scott, Peter 1994, *Theology, Ideology and Liberation*, Cambridge: Cambridge University Press.

Segundo, Juan Luis 1976, *The Liberation of Theology*, translated by John Drury, Maryknoll: Orbis.

—— 1985, *The Historical Jesus of the Synoptics*, translated by John Drury, Maryknoll: Orbis.

Shaw, Brian J. 1985, 'Reason, Nostalgia, and Eschatology in the Critical Theory of Max Horkheimer', *The Journal of Politics*, 47, 1: 160–81.

Shiozawa, Kimio 1990, 'Marx's View of Asian Society and His "Asiatic Mode of Production"', in *Marxian Economics*, Volume 1, edited by J.E. King, Aldershot: Elgar.

Simkins, Ronald 1999a, 'Class and Gender in Early Israel', in *Concepts of Class in Ancient Israel*, edited by Mark Sneed, Atlanta: Scholars Press.

—— 1999b, 'Patronage and the Political Economy of Ancient Israel', *Semeia*, 87: 123–44.

—— 2004, 'Family in the Political Economy of Ancient Israel', *The Bible and Critical Theory*, 1, 1: 1–16. Available at <www.epress.monash.edu.au>.

Sipiora, Phillip and James S. Baumlin (eds.) 2002, *Rhetoric and Kairos: Essays in History, Theory, and Praxis*, Albany: State University Press of New York.

Smith, Daniel W. 2001, 'The Doctrine of Univocity: Deleuze's Ontology of Immanence', in Bryden (ed.) 2001.

Smith, Nigel 1994, 'Antinomian', *Essays in Criticism*, 44, 2: 147–55.

Sobrino, Jon 1978 [1976], *Christology at the Crossroads: A Latin American Approach*, translated by John Drury, Maryknoll: Orbis.

—— 2004a [1982], *Jesus in Latin America*, Eugene: Wipf and Stock.

—— 2004b [1985], *The True Church and the Poor*, translated by Matthew O'Connell, Eugene: Wipf and Stock.

—— 2004c [1990], *Archbishop Romero: Memories and Reflections*, translated by Robert R. Barr, Eugene: Wipf and Stock.

Sorel, Georges 1961, *Reflections on Violence*, translated by T. Hulme and J. Roth, New York: Collier.

Southern, R.W. 1970, *Western Society and the Church in the Middle Ages*, Harmondsworth: Penguin.

Stanton, Elizabeth Cady 1993 [1895], *The Woman's Bible*, Boston: Northeastern University Press.

Ste. Croix, G.E.M. de 1972, *The Origins of the Peloponnesian War*, London: Duckworth.

—— 1981, *The Class Struggle in the Ancient Greek World from the Archaic Age to the Arab Conquests*, Ithaca: Cornell University Press.

—— 2004, *Athenian Democratic Origins and Other Essays*, edited by David Harvey, Robert Parker and Peter Thonemann, Oxford: Oxford University Press.

—— 2006, *Christian Persecution, Martyrdom, and Orthodoxy*, edited by Michael Whitby and Joseph Streeter, Oxford: Oxford University Press.

Strauss, David Friedrich 1835, *Das Leben Jesu, kritisch bearbeitet*, Tübingen: C.F. Osiander.

—— 1836, *Das Leben Jesu, kritisch bearbeitet*, 2nd ed, Tübingen: C.F. Osiander.

—— 1839, *Das Leben Jesu, kritisch bearbeitet*, 3rd ed, Tübingen: C.F. Osiander.

—— 1840a, *Das Leben Jesu, kritisch bearbeitet*, 4th ed, Tübingen: C.F. Osiander.

—— 1840b, *Die christliche Glaubenslehre in ihrer geschichtlichen Entwicklung und im Kampfe mit der modernen Wissenschaft*, Tübingen: Osiander.

—— 1864, *Das Leben Jesu für das deutsche Volk*, Leipzig: Brockhaus.

—— 1902 [1840], *The Life of Jesus: Critically Examined*, translated by George Eliot, London: Swan Sonnenschein.

—— 1983, *In Defence of My Life of Jesus Against the Hegelians*, translated by Marilyn Chapin Massey, Hamden: Archon Books.

—— 1997, *The Old Faith and the New*, Amherst: Prometheus Books.

—— 2000 [1865], *Der Christus des Glaubens und der Jesus der Geschichte: eine Kritik des Schleiermacher'schen Lebens Jesu*, Waltrop: Spenner.

Streeter, Joseph 2006, 'Introduction: de Ste. Croix on Persecution', in Ste Croix 2006.

Stuart, Elizabeth 1997, *Religion Is a Queer Thing*, London: Cassell.

—— 2002, *Gay and Lesbian Theologies: Repetitions with Critical Difference*, Aldershot: Ashgate.

Suda, Max Josef 1978, 'The Critique of Religion in Karl Marx's *Capital*', *Journal of Ecumenical Studies*, 15, 1: 15–28.

Sugirtharajah, R.S. 2005, *The Bible and Empire: Postcolonial Explorations*, Cambridge: Cambridge University Press.

Sung, Jung Mo 2007, *Desire, Market, and Religion*, London: SCM.

Surin, Kenneth 2009, *Freedom Not Yet: Liberation and the Next World Order*, Durham, NC.: Duke University Press.

Tager, Michael 1986, 'Myth and Politics in the Works of Sorel and Barthes', *Journal of the History of Ideas*, 47, 4: 625–39.

Tamez, Elsa 1989, *Through Her Eyes: Women's Theology from Latin America*, Maryknoll: Orbis.

—— 1993, *Bible of the Oppressed*, Maryknoll: Orbis.

—— 1996, 'The Hermeneutical Leap of Today', *Semeia*, 75: 199–205.

—— 1997, 'When the Horizons Close Upon Themselves: A Reflection the Utopian Reason of Qohélet', in *Liberation Theologies, Postmodernity, and the Americas*, edited by David Batstone, Eduardo Mendieta, Lois Ann Lorentzen and Dwight N. Hopkins, London: Routledge.

Tawney, R.H. 1962 [1926], *Religion and the Rise of Capitalism: A Historical Study*, Gloucester, MA.: Peter Smith.

Taylor, Barbara 1995, 'Religion, Radicalism, and Fantasy', *History Workshop Journal*, 39: 102–12.

Taylor, Simon J. 2001, 'Christmas and the Cold War in the Poetry of E.P. Thompson', *The Expository Times*, 113, 3: 79–83.

Terrien, Samuel 1963, *Job, Commentaire de l'Ancien Testament*, Neuchâtel: Delachaux & Niestlé.

—— 1972, *The Golden Bible Atlas with Relief Maps in Full Color*, New York: Golden Press.

—— 1978, *The Elusive Presence: Toward a New Biblical Theology*, New York: Harper and Row.

—— 1986, *Holy Week (Proclamation 3: AIDS for Interpreting the Lessons of the Church)*, Minneapolis: Augsburg.

—— 1994, *The Magnificat: Musicians as Biblical Interpreters*, Mahwah: Paulist.

—— 2004a, *Job, Poet of Existence*, Eugene: Wipf & Stock.

—— 2004b, *Till the Heart Sings: A Biblical Theology of Manhood and Womanhood*, Grand Rapids: Eerdmans.

Teschke, Henning 2004, 'What is Difference? Deleuze and Saint Thomas', *Verbum*, 6, 2: 413–22.

Theissen, Gerd 1978, *Sociology of Early Palestinian Christianity*, translated by John Bowden, Philadelphia: Fortress.

—— 1987, *The Shadow of the Galilean: The Quest of the Historical Jesus in Narrative Form*, translated by John Bowden, Philadelphia: Augsburg Fortress.

—— 1999, *The Religion of the Earliest Churches: Creating a Symbolic World*, translated by John Bowden, Philadelphia: Augsburg Fortress.

Thiemann, Ronald F. 1985, 'Praxis: The Practical Atheism of Karl Marx', *Journal of Ecumenical Studies*, 22, 3: 544–9.

Thistleton, Anthony C. 2000, *The First Epistle to the Corinthians, New International Greek Testament Commentary*, Grand Rapids: Eerdmans.

Thody, Philip 1984, *Roland Barthes: A Conservative Estimate*, Chicago: University of Chicago Press.
—— 1987, 'Introduction', in Barthes 1987.
Thompson, Edward P. 1966, *The Making of the English Working Class*, 2nd ed, New York: Vintage.
—— 1976a, *William Morris: Romantic to Revolutionary*, 2nd ed., London: Merlin.
—— 1976b, 'On History, Sociology and Historical Relevance', *The British Journal of Sociology*, 27, 3: 387–402.
—— 1978, *The Poverty of Theory and Other Essays*, London: Merlin.
—— 1982a, *Beyond the Cold War: A New Approach to the Arms Race and Nuclear Annihilation*, New York: Pantheon Books.
—— 1982b, *Exterminism and Cold War*, London: New Left Books.
—— 1982c, *Zero Option*, London: Merlin.
—— 1983, *Infant and Emperor: Poems for Christmas*, London: Merlin.
—— 1985, *The Heavy Dancers*, London: Merlin.
—— 1988, *The Sykaos Papers: Being an Account of the Voyages of the Poet Oi Paz to the System of Strim in the Seventeenth Galaxy... selected and edited by Q; transmitted by timewarp to E.P. Thompson*, London: Bloomsbury.
—— 1993a, *Customs in Common: Studies in Traditional Popular Culture*, New York: The New Press.
—— 1993b, *Witness Against the Beast: William Blake and the Moral Law*, Cambridge: Cambridge University Press.
—— 1997, *The Romantics: England in a Revolutionary Age*, New York: The New Press.
Thompson, Edward P. and Dan Smith (eds.) 1980, *Protest and Survive*, Harmondsworth: Penguin.
—— 1987, *Prospectus for a Habitable Planet*, Harmondsworth: Penguin.
Thompson, Edward P. and Dan Thompson 1985, *Star Wars: Self-Destruct Incorporated*, London: Merlin.
Thompson, Thomas L. 1999, *The Mythic Past: Biblical Archaeology and the Myth of Israel*, New York: Basic Books.
—— 2000, *Early History of the Israelite People from the Written and Archaeological Sources*, Leiden: Brill.
Thorsen, Don 2005, *The Wesleyan Quadrilateral: Scripture, Tradition, Reason, & Experience as a Model of Evangelical Theology*, Lexington: Emeth Press.
Tillich, Paul 1951–63, *Systematic Theology*, 3 vols., Chicago: University of Chicago Press.
—— 1952, *The Courage to Be*, New Haven: Yale University Press.
—— 1996a [1947], 'Paul Tillich an Max Horkheimer, Pacific Palisades, Anfang September 1947', in Max Horkheimer, *Gesammelte Schriften*, Volume 17, Frankfurt am Main: Fischer Taschenbuch.
—— 1996b [1947], 'Paul Tillich an Max Horkheimer, Pacific Palisades, Aug. 14th 1947', in Max Horkheimer, *Gesammelte Schriften*, Volume 17, Frankfurt am Main: Fischer Taschenbuch.
Tillich, Paul and Hannah Tillich 1996 [1941], 'Paul and Hannah Tillich an Max Horkheimer, Pacific Palisades, Anfang Juli 1941', in Max Horkheimer, *Gesammelte Schriften*, Volume 17, Frankfurt am Main: Fischer Taschenbuch.
Tocqueville, Alexis de 2003, *Democracy in America*, translated by Gerald Bevan, Harmondsworth: Penguin.
Tomkins, Stephen 2003, *John Wesley: A Biography*, Grand Rapids: Eerdmans.
Troeltsch, Ernst 1992 [1911], *The Social Teaching of the Christian Churches*, 2 vols, Louisville: Westminster/John Knox.
Turner, Denys 1999, 'Marxism, Liberation Theology and the Way of Negation', in *The Cambridge Companion to Liberation Theology*, edited by Christopher Rowland, Cambridge: Cambridge University Press.
Untersteiner, Mario 1954, *The Sophists*, translated by Kathleen Freeman, Oxford: Basil Blackwell.

Van Wolde, Ellen 1997 [1991], *Mr and Mrs Job*, translated by John Bowden, London: SCM.

Warburton, D.A. 2003, *Macroeconomics from the Beginning*, Winona Lake, Indiana: Eisenbrauns.

Weber, Max 1923, *Wirtschaftsethik*, Tübingen: J.C.B. Mohr.

—— 1992 [1904–5], *The Protestant Ethic and the Spirit of Capitalism*, translated by Talcott Parsons, London: Routledge.

Wesley, John 1979, *The Works of John Wesley*, 14 vols, Grand Rapids: Baker Book House.

West, Gerald 1995, *Biblical Hermeneutics of Liberation: Modes of Reading the Bible in the Context of South Africa*, 2nd ed, Pietermaritzburg and Maryknoll, New York: Cluster and Orbis.

Whitby, Michael 2006, 'Introduction', in Ste Croix 2006.

Wickham, Chris 1994, *Land and Power: Studies in Italian and European Social History, 400–1200*, London: British School at Rome.

Wilson, Mona 1927, *The Life of William Blake*, London: Nonesuch Press.

Wittfogel, Karl 1963, *Oriental Despotism*, New Haven: Yale University Press.

Wood, A. Skevington 2007, *The Burning Heart: John Wesley, Evangelist*, Lexington: Emeth Press.

Wood, Ellen Meiksins 1997, *Peasant-Citizen & Slave: The Foundations of Athenian Democracy*, London: Verso.

Wood, Ellen Meiksins and Neil Wood 1978, *Class, Ideology and Ancient Political Theory*, Oxford: Oxford University Press.

Yee, Gale A. 2003, *Poor Banished Children of Eve: Woman as Evil in the Hebrew Bible*, Minneapolis: Fortress.

Yeo, Eileen 1981, 'Christianity in Chartist Struggle 1838–1842', *Past and Present*, 91: 109–39.

Index